THE ORDER OF MINIMS
IN SEVENTEENTH-CENTURY FRANCE

ARCHIVES INTERNATIONALES D'HISTOIRE DES IDEES

INTERNATIONAL ARCHIVES OF THE HISTORY OF IDEAS

20

P. J. S. WHITMORE

THE ORDER OF MINIMS
IN SEVENTEENTH-CENTURY FRANCE

P. J. S. WHITMORE

THE ORDER OF MINIMS
IN SEVENTEENTH-CENTURY FRANCE

MARTINUS NIJHOFF – THE HAGUE – 1967

PRINTED IN THE NETHERLANDS

ACKNOWLEDGEMENTS

I am grateful to the following for their help: Dr. W. H. Barber of Birkbeck College, University of London, for assistance over many years, for his advice and encouragement; Professor Dr. Paul Dibon for the interest that he has taken in the work, for much advice and many kindnesses; my wife and mother for unstinted help.

It is also a privilege to record help given by the authorities of many libraries and dépôts of archives, notably the British Museum, the Bibliothèque Nationale and the Archives Nationales. I am indebted to the Central Research Fund of the University of London for assistance in the purchase of microfilms.

I must also acknowledge my profound gratitude to the Prime Warden and Wardens of the Goldsmiths' Company and to the Schools' Committee of the City of London for the grant made to me and for leave during one term.

I trust that I have not omitted to make due acknowledgement in footnotes to specific instances of help and inspiration.

Highgate, London, 1966.   P. J. S. WHITMORE

TABLE OF CONTENTS

INTRODUCTION

The Order of Minims was one of the last religious orders to be founded before the Council of Trent. Mediaeval in its rules and in its ideals, it grew up in a Europe of rapidly changing opinions. The two most important foundations at the time of the Council of Trent, the Jesuits and the Oratorians, appear at once "modern" in their aims and in their organisation – the break with the older monastic tradition is distinct and decisive. The Minims, whose period of most rapid expansion was at precisely the same time as the rise of the French Oratory and of the great increase in Jesuit influence, were deeply rooted in traditions that were, or were becoming, archaic. The origins of the Order are to be found in the remote and almost desert country of Calabria where, in 1453, a hermit gathered round him a few kindred spirits and led with them a life of the utmost rigour and self-denial. The founder, later to be canonized as Saint François de Paule, was thirty-seven years of age at this time and had acquired some reputation in and around Paula, his birthplace, as a thaumaturge and as a man of conspicuous charity and humility; he was fifty-five before any official recognition was afforded to his brethren. Recognition was first made by a *costituzione*, "Decet nos ex officio," of 30 November, 1471, in which reference is made to the "Fratelli eremiti di Fratello Francesco di Paula." This was confirmed by a Papal brief (Sixtus IV, 18 June, 1472) in the following year. The idea of an "order" comes largely from Franciscan inspiration, the parents of this other Saint Francis having dedicated their child to the Saint of Assisi. The name "Minim" is also attributed to Franciscan inspiration: as the Order spread it acquired a different name in each country – "Fratelli Eremiti di Fratello Francesco di Paula" was retained in Calabria and in Italy; they were called "Bons Hommes" in France, "Paulani" in Germany (the Empire) and "Patres Victoriæ" in Spain. The Founder, however, used to sign himself "il minimo dei minimi," probably thinking of the text from the *Dies Irae* (S. Matthew, XXV, 40). It is also probable that this other Saint Francis, partly out of admiration for his illustrious compatriot of Assisi and partly from a compelling urge to be superlative in all things, chose the title in opposition to the Franciscans, the Fratres Minori,[1] who had previously adopted this style taken from Saint Matthew, XXIII, 8. The title "Minim" was confirmed in these words "... eosque Eremitos Ordinis Minimorum Fratrum Eremitarum F. Francesci de Paula in posterum nuncupari," taken from the Papal Bull, *Meritis religiosae vitae*, of 26 February, 1493.

The earliest reference to the Order in France is in a fragment preserved in the Bibliothèque de l'Arsenal called, *La règle et vie de Frère François, pauvre et humble hermite de Paule, laquelle donne à tous ses frères voulant entrer et vivre en son ordre.*[2] The dating of this manuscript should be accepted with considerable reserve; it bears a clearly legible "1474," although it seems most unlikely that any reference to an *Order* occurred before the Bull of 1493 or that any *Rule* appeared in French before the Founder's visit to Louis XI in 1483.[3] The fame of Francis and his reputation as a "guérisseur" had reached the French court where Louis XI was sick and dying; the King summoned him to the château of Le Plessis-lès-Tours, but it required the intervention of the Pope to make the hermit undertake the journey. His action on arrival was blunt; instead of any pretence at healing, he told Louis that he could do nothing for him and admonished him to set his house in order and prepare to die. In spite of this, he found favour at Court and, after Louis's death, continued to live on in France as a friend and protégé of the Royal Family. Political considerations may also have had their part in his continued residence in France: François de Paule had been slighted, if not actually ill-treated, by the King of Naples; when, therefore, Louis XI's son, Charles VIII, wrested the crown of Naples from the House of Aragon in 1495, François de Paule looked upon the act as an instance of divine retribution.[4] Even at this early stage in the development of the Order, its close association with the

---

[1] Confusion between "Minimes" and "Mineurs" is a frequent source of error in bibliographies and in some historical surveys. Grove, for example, refers to Mersenne as a Minorite in his *Dictionary of Music* thus perpetuating an error in Walther, *Musikalisches Lexikon*, Kassel, 1732, p. 399.

[2] Arsenal, MSS, No. 2272.

[3] 1482 is the date usually given; I am following le Chanoine Fiot who has shown that the date 1482 is arrived at by a confusion between "Old style" and "New style" – see his article *Jean Bourdichon et Saint François de Paule* in *Mémoires de la Société Archéologique de Touraine*, Tours, 1961.

[4] This is the opinion of P. Du Val, Minim, *Vie et Miracles de Saint François de Paule*, Rouen, 1640.

French crown is apparent; the French Minims became the protégés of the Royal Family and received important privileges at their hand. Members of the nobility, following the example of Royalty, joined the Tiers-Ordre des Minimes and were instrumental in founding "couvents" throughout France.[1] The Founder continued to live in France where he was joined by some of his relations whose descendants became prominent members of the Order in the seventeenth century; during the period under review these members, Olivier Chaillou (1568–1643), Hilarion de Coste, friend and biographer of Mersenne, (1595–1648), and François Victon (1596–1632), form an important link with the Founder and the early tradition of the Order.[2] François de Paule died in 1507 leaving behind him an Order whose 30 "couvents" (13 French) were divided amongst 6 provinces (3 French – Touraine; France, i.e. Paris; Aquitaine). It is from these modest beginnings that the Order grew in the XVIth century to take its place beside the older, mediaeval monastic foundations.

It was generally considered as the most austere of the orders, a reputation it enjoyed at least until the foundation of la Trappe in the XVIIth century; as well as the traditional vows, a Minim had to take a vow of living in perpetual Lent, eating no meat nor any carnal produce – milk, cheese, eggs: –

Singuli Fratres huius ordinis a cibis carnalibus omnino abstineant ... quod ipsi carnes ac omnia semenitanam originem a carnibus ipsis trahentia penitus vitent. Carnes igitur et pinguerdo ova butirum, caseus et quaevis lacticinia ex eisdem congesta et producta ...[3]

During the whole of the sixteenth century members of the Order were active preachers and proselytizers, and nowhere more so than in France, where the confronting Protestant and Catholic factions called forth their champions to enter the lists of public dispute and

---

[1] The term "couvent" has been used throughout in preference to "monastery" which implies a more extensive and more formal set of buildings than those inhabited by the Order in numerous instances; "house" would be more appropriate, but is often ambiguous when questions of ownership of property arise.

[2] Descent was claimed through the Founder's sister and the family of d'Alesso which settled in France in the Loire valley in the early XVIth century, see *Dossiers Bleus* in the Bibliothèque Nationale, under *d'Alesso*. The descendants of the Founder's sister successfully petitioned the Prévôt de Paris on 29 Dec. 1622 to constrain the Minim Claude du Vivier to alter a passage in his *Vie ... de S. François de Paule*, Paris, 1609, in which he declared that the Saint had no sister; La Garde de la Prévôté de Paris issued a writ on 11 Jan. 1623, and Gilles Camart (Provincial of Touraine) and the Corrector of le Plessis-lès-Tours issued certificates declaring the "non-existence" of the texts in du Vivier.

[3] From a MS commentary on the *Rule* of the Order by N. Lesguiller, Corrector of the Minimes de la Place Royale; dated 1639; MSS Arsenal, No. 1074, p. 307.

where, in the most brutal and senseless of civil wars, many on both sides fell as martyrs to the bigotry and intransigeance which exacerbated the national strife. Cardinal Bellarmine saw in the advent of the Order an important counterbalance to the heresy of Luther:

> Postremo hoc nostro saeculo, illo fere tempore, quo Martinus Lutherus sua zizania seminare coepit floruit in Italia alius quidam Franciscus, auctor et parens hominum illorum religiosorum, qui in Gallia Boni-homines, in Italia Minimi dicuntur.[1]

By the end of the XVIth century, therefore, the Order was closely associated with the counter-reformation and, together with the new orders, the Jesuits and the Oratorians, must be considered as playing an important rôle in the great Catholic revival in France of the XVIIth century. How was it that a mendicant order could make a place for itself and hold it in seventeenth century France? How could the severe asceticism of their rule make any appeal at this time? Their Founder was neither a Saint Ignatius of Loyola nor a Pierre Bérulle, but a hermit from Calabria. The spread of the Order in the home of its Founder is understandable; its severity, its insistence upon "perfection" and the superlative nature of its demands, one can imagine appealing to the Spaniard – especially since the inception of the Order in Spain coincided with the ultimate defeat of the Moors.[2] But it was in France and in the seventeenth century that the Order saw its most prosperous years and the period of its most rapid expansion. Much has been written about the life of Saint François de Paule, but no one has tried to explain why a man so foreign, apparently, to all that the seventeenth century stood for should have had such influence. The seventeenth century was an age of consolidation and relative stability – relative that is to the previous centuries – but it was still a turbulent period,

---

[1] R. Bellarmine, *Conciones*, Venice, 1617, p. 678. The use of the name "Boni-homines" (Bons Hommes) is curious. I am indebted to Mr. A. J. Krailsheimer of Christ Church, Oxford, for drawing my attention to the fact that the title was in use in England some two hundred years before S. François de Paule; it was used c. 1257 to designate Austin Canons of two English houses (Ashridge and Edington). In France the title lapsed in favour of *Minimes*, although the Minimes de Chaillot were often referred to as Bons Hommes until the Revolution.

[2] See Pedro Iayme Tristan, a Spanish Minim, *Enchyridion, o breve chronica ... de la Sagrada Religion de los Padres Minimos*, Barcelona, 1618, pp. 65–67. Minims from the "couvent" of Saint Roch, Toulouse, recommended to the King of Spain, Ferdinand V, by the Founder himself, founded a "couvent" in Malaga in 1492: Ferdinando Sanctissimo Regi per duos fratres Minimos de Mauris octingentis annis Regum occupantibus Victoriam mandat. Dum enim Malacam Granatae, obsideret, nec ullæ spes recuperationis audito per dictos Religioses nuntio animatus est, nocteque ipsa fugientibus Mauris panico tramora libertas urbi et Regno tradita. In cuius memoriam celebre monasterium ab Rege Ordini extructum quod deinceps de Victoria nominari voluit sicut et Fratres dicti Ordinis in anno 1492.

a period of wars and pestilence; it was a philosophical age, at least in appearance, but it required a further century for philosophical ideas to permeate more than a thin upper crust – it was still an age of belief in miracles and in possession by devils and demons; it was still a superstitious age. It was an age of crisis and, as such, was inevitably a tragic age. The initial problems facing the historian of this Order are these: why, in the seventeenth century, should it have developed as it did? What particular accord is there between the spirit of the age and the strange personality of its Founder and the apparently out-moded way of life of his followers?

It is surprising that there should be no account of the development and work of the Order during the seventeenth century other than the transcript of passages from various chronicles by members of the Order. The present state of work on the Order is set out below:

I. PRINTED WORKS

(1) General Histories of the Order

Apart from articles in various Catholic Encyclopaedias there is only one work – G. M. Roberti, *Disegno storico dell' Ordine de' Minimi*, 3 vols., Rome, 1902, 1908, 1922. A work difficult to obtain; there is no copy in the British Museum or in the Bibliothèque Nationale; the copy in the Biblioteca Nazionale, Rome, is imperfect, wanting volume 3; through the kind offices of the Central Library, I was able to borrow this copy; I have been able to consult volume 3 in the Vatican Library.[1]

Roberti has limited himself almost entirely to an adaptation of the four following general histories, written by members of the Order in the XVIIth and XVIIIth centuries, and to the printed reports of the Capitoli Generali.

F. La Noue (Lanovius), *Chronicon generale Ordinis Minimorum*, Paris, 1635.
L. Dony d'Attichy, *Histoire générale de l'ordre sacré des Minimes*, Paris, 1624.
E. Isnard, *Codex minimus*, 2 vols., Lyon, 1631/2.
R. Thuillier, *Diarium patrum, fratrum et sororum Ordinis Minimorum provinciae franciae ... ab anno 1506 ad annum 1700*, Paris, 1709.[2]
J. M. di Laurio, *Acta capitolorum generalium*, 2 vols., Rome, 1916.

[1] Referred to subsequently as Roberti, followed by vol. no.
[2] Two volumes bound in one; referred to subsequently as Thuillier I and Thuillier II.

(2) *Works by members of the Order*

There is no systematic bibliography in Roberti; his lengthy "dé-pouillement" of the early chronicles is of considerable help as a starting point. Provincial bibliographies and biographies published in the XVIIIth and XIXth centuries add greatly to our knowledge since they usually mentioned members of the religious Orders; wherever possible, I have consulted these. The catalogues of the Minims' own libraries are useful in the drawing up of the bibliography since they usually referred to members of their own Order. The catalogues of the British Museum and Bibliothèque Nationale normally indicate whether an author was a member of an order.

Relying on the above sources, I have been able to draw up a Bibliography of works by members of the Order in France of the XVIIth century which contains 364 works.

II. MANUSCRIPT SOURCES

Apparently unknown to Roberti. A few documents have been printed by learned societies [1] and the valuable *Correspondance* of Mersenne is at the moment being published by the *Centre National de la Recherche Scientifique*; otherwise this is an untapped source and comprises the following sets of documents:

I. Papers concerning the lands and revenues of the various "couvents." These papers were seized at the time of the Revolution and suppression of the orders. They now repose in the various dépôts of the Archives Nationales and Archives Départementales, although occasionally in municipal libraries.

II. Transactions between the consuls of a township and the local "couvent": these are often to be found in the Archives Municipales and vary considerably in value as historical material.

III. Papers concerning internal administration within the "couvents": Actes Capitulaires, Registres Capitulaires, Visites etc.: found sometimes in the State or Municipal libraries, sometimes in the Archives. Many appear to have been lost; a few are in private libraries and archives.

IV. Manuscripts by members of the Order: many to be seen in libraries throughout France.

---

[1] The thesis for the diploma of Archiviste-paléographe at the Ecole des Chartes, 1966, by Mlle O. Dresch, is devoted to a study of the archives of the Paris Minims. It is unfortunately too late to incorporate any of her findings in the present study.

V. Catalogues of Conventual Libraries: at the time of the suppression of the Order, the libraries were taken over by the municipalities. There was a good deal of looting but often whole libraries were preserved. Several catalogues are extant and may be found in public labraries and archives throughout France.

VI. Papers relating to the French "Couvent" at Rome, Santa Trinità dei Monti: a few papers are still in the convent and I have been allowed to see these by kind permission of the Mother Superior; others are in the *Pieux Etablissements français à Rome* together with a few documents relating to the history of the Order in France itself. I am grateful to the Curator and to the Librarian at the *Séminaire français à Rome* for help in consulting these archives. There are also many papers concerning the French "couvent" at Rome in the Bibliothèque Nationale, Paris.

The first task in the preparation of the present study was to draw up a bibliography that should be as complete as possible; as far as printed works are concerned this is limited to the seventeenth century, but considerable latitude has been permitted in the bibliography of manuscripts, particularly when dealing with municipal and departmental archives where documents from the XVIth and XVIIIth century are often bundled together in *liasses* with XVIIth century material. The second task was to draw from this bibliography the essential materials to write a history of the Order in France of the XVIIth century. It is necessary to justify the limitation of the study to the XVIIth century; the history of the Order from its beginning to about 1600 is set out in considerable detail in the chronicles which have just been mentioned and which have furnished Roberti with most of his material. The seventeenth century was, however, less carefully documented; there exists the printed *Diarium* of Thuillier but this is no more than a necrology giving, for the most part, trivial biographical detail; it is moreover limited to the Province of France (Paris). It is precisely at the period when the chronicles of the Order were being written that its history becomes of the utmost interest; both spiritually and intellectually it flourished, but the history of its prosperity has remained almost untold. If justification is needed for undertaking a study of any aspect of the religious history of the seventeenth century, it will be found in M. Antoine Adam's *Zaharoff Lecture* for 1959 in which he shows the "actualité" of the subject:

... dans le Grand Siècle qui est déjà, à sa manière, le siècle des Lumières, il existe des hommes qui ne croient pas à l'intelligence, et qui ne verraient dans l'univers qu'un absurde énigme si la Révélation ne venait leur en dire le sens.

... les guerres, les révolutions, les bouleversements de la technique compromettent l'effort des hommes, leur donnent un sentiment aigu des conflits dans lesquels ils se trouvent engagés ... quel temps plus que le nôtre mérite d'être appelé tragique? Il n'est pas étrange que la religion de Bérulle et de Pascal, bien plutôt que celle de Grotius ou que celle de Voltaire soit devenue, si l'on peut ainsi s'exprimer, la religion du XXe siècle.[1]

The Minims may not have had a Bérulle or a Pascal; Saint François de Sales belonged to their Tiers-Ordre, however, whilst Mersenne, Maignan and Plumier made remarkable contributions to seventeenth century science and philosophy. And within the Order, in the small "couvents" as well as in the large, were to be found men and women of a simple piety and an unshakable faith, men who, like Nicolas Barré, forsook everything in order to bring some measure of relief to the poor and needy – men who, in the words of M. Adam, placed no faith in human intellect and could see no point in the enigma of existence without divine aid. It would be wrong to ignore their faults, their cabales and the artificiality and naiveté of so many of their printed works; it would be wrong to overlook the interesting social and political background to their history and to ignore, for example the fascinating question of necromancy and diabolic possession.

The subject may be divided into three parts: the Temporal, the Spiritual, the Intellectual; this division is not without its difficulties since the individual quality of any religious order depends upon the blend of these three. The particular "sagesse" which is to be associated with the Minims is derived in the main from a submission of the intellect to a rigorous form of spiritual and devotional discipline, and from the mortification of the body by means of the harshest of monastic rules. It was the original intention to leave the Temporal out of consideration, but this led to a false interpretation of the Order and, at the same time, excluded some interesting examples of social and ecclesiastical history: the value of money given for a weekly mass to be said in perpetuity, the relations – deplorable on the whole – between the secular and regular clergy over such matters as benefices and burials, the descriptions of conventual buildings with their gardens farms and vineyards – all these have their importance in conditioning the spiritual and intellectual life within the cloister.

[1] A. Adam, *Sur le problème religieux dans la première moitié du XVIIe siècle*, Oxford, 1959, pp. 12 and 17–18.

PART I

THE TEMPORAL

ORGANISATION

(1) DIVISION INTO PROVINCES

Over the whole Order there presided the Corrector General who was elected by a college of the Provincials (Heads of Provinces) every three years – his tenure of office was extended to six years after 1629. The Provincials too were elected for a three-year period, while elections for the office of Corrector of a "couvent" were held annually.

The Founder died in 1507 and on the 28th December of that year the first General Chapter was held in Rome in the refectory of the Convento della Santa Trinità dei Monti which was even then closely associated with French members of the Order. The ascendancy of the French element at this early date may be seen from the following division of the Order into Provinces:

1. Calabria
2. Tours
3. France (Paris) } Known as "Provincia Francia" but already divided as shown; the title "Francia" referring only to the Province of which Nigeon (Paris) was the head.
4. Aquitaine
5. Spain
6. Germany.

Of the thirty "couvents" then in existence thirteen [1] were French:

le Plessis-lès-Tours	Gien	Amboise	Bomiers
Amiens	Toulouse	Grenoble	Bracancour.
Nigeon (Passy, Paris)	Abbeville	Châteliers	
Montgaugier	Châtellerault		

The division of France into the three Provinces mentioned above did not survive the rapid expansion of the Order during the XVIth

---

[1] Fifteen, if one includes Santa Trinità dei Monti, given to the French by the Founder, and Fréjus which had a precarious existence because of malaria from the marshes of the Reyran; it was founded in 1490, passed from the Province of Aquitaine to that of Lyon in 1571 but is not mentioned in the XVIIth Century.

century. The Province of Aquitaine became the Province of Gascony and out of it two further provinces were formed: Lyons, in 1571; and Provence, in 1596. In the same year the Province of France separated into two – France and Champagne.

In 1600 there were in France 38 "couvents" belonging to the Order; by 1623 that number had risen to 112. This rapid expansion, the most rapid in any part of the Order at any time and probably more rapid than for any other order, necessitated the creation of four more Provinces – Lorraine, the Duchy of Burgundy, the County of Burgundy and Auvergne. An attempt at creating a Province of Avignon was quashed on the grounds that it would have led to a Provençal faction and open the door "pour donner l'entrée à une conséquence très dommageable au bien de la France, aux droits des Français et au bonheur de tant de maisons régulières." [1]

This expansion continued at only a slightly slower rate throughout the seventeenth century. The founding of the Couvent des Minimes de Bard in 1673 in the Province of the County of Burgundy may be said to mark the culminating point of the history of the whole Order: it was the 448th "couvent," and the 150th in France. This figure includes Lille which, although in the Province of Flanders-Belgium, was normally considered as belonging to the Province of France and it further includes two houses in Switzerland, Romont and Estavaï, which were administered by the Province of the County of Burgundy; it does not include Nice or Perpignan, since they belonged to the Italian and Spanish provinces of Savoy and Catalonia respectively.[2] Mons is not included: it remained in the Province of Flanders-Belgium and, although it became French by right of conquest and was ceded to the Province of France in 1691, its delegates were refused permission to go to an election in Paris (Nigeon) in 1692.

We may conclude that one third of the whole Order was French (150 out of 448 "couvents" in the year 1673); the other two thirds were distributed over a wide area of Europe, from Calabria to Flanders and from Bohemia to the Atlantic seaboard. The Germano-Bohemian province was, it is true, somewhat isolated from the remainder; it stretched from Leobschutz (east of Prague and now in Poland) to Munich and Neuburg (near Ingoldstadt); there were twelve "cou-

---

[1] Bibliothèque Nationale, Fonds Français, 18938, fol. 184.
[2] Perpignan became French in 1659 with the secession of Roussillon but it seems to have remained within the jurisdiction of the Minims' Province of Catalonia for some time. The archives of the "couvent" are preserved in Perpignan in the Archives Départementales, Pyrénées Orientales, and include many documents from the period before the secession.

vents" in this province. Calabria, the home of the Founder and always closely associated with the Order, provided no less than fifty-three "couvents," or nearly an eighth of the total; these were distributed between two provinces: the one round Paula itself, called the Provincia di San Francesco, was the largest of all with thirty-one "couvents," and the other, Calabria Ulteriore, was amongst the largest with twenty-two. In Spain the distribution was uneven: the Province of Granada was composed of twenty-four "couvents" all south of the Guadalaquivir and along the coastal strip from Cadiz to Vera; there were five in the island of Majorca; but, with the exception of Valencia and Barcelona, both meeting-places on occasion for the General Chapter of the Order, the remainder of Spain contributed little. Central Italy and Lombardy were well represented. The distribution of the French "couvents" is considered later but it will be convient to mention here that the whole country, except Brittany and Normandy was covered more or less evenly. Apart from two "couvents" in Peru, at Lima and Guamanga, the Order was never established outside Eutope.[1]

In Rome there were, and still are, two conventual churches whose jurisdiction covered the whole order and under whose ægis remains the small Order of to-day: these are the churches of San Andrea delle Fratti and Santa Trinità dei Monti. In the XVIIth century the French community which congregated at the latter under the discipline of S. François de Paule could count amongst its members three of the most lively intellects of the time: Mersenne, Maignan and Plumier. This French enclave is an important part of the history of the Order and more than once it was a serious bone of political contention.

(2) THE CONVENTUAL BUILDINGS

When the Minims were established in a town, they frequently resided in a private house while a site was found for them and the buildings completed; this accounts for the discrepancy in so many towns between the date of foundation and the earliest record of any building. At Nantes, for example, the Minims lived in a house which had been given to them by Anne de Bretagne in 1504; in 1589 they took possession of the ancient Chapelle de Saint Antoine de Padoue together with some houses and gardens. It was not until 1593 that

---

[1] A map showing the distribution of the "couvents" at the beginning of the XVIIIth century will be found in the article *Minimi* in the *Enciclopedia Cattolica*, Rome, 1948.

their "couvent" was completed and their church took another forty years.[1] Progress was normally slow and there was a wide range of style and planning, varying from strange neo-gothic imitations to the neo-classical and baroque. Occasionally existing monastic buildings were taken over, and at Aulnoy (Seine-et-Marne) the dilapidated remains of a "couvent" which had once belonged to the Order of Grandmont was taken over and more or less restored, the whole of the interior being "peinte en détrempe;" several of the mediæval monuments and sculptures also survived.[2] The only work that deals with the buildings is the *Codex Minimus* of Estienne Isnard published in Lyon in two parts in 1631 and 1632; it is therefore an extremely incomplete survey and, moreover, his descriptions are little more than lists of superlatives – "Nigeon ... omnia et singula quae in isto conventu sunt regalem redolent magnificentiam, Ecclesia et specialiter Chorus. Sacristia ... Claustrum, exquisitioribus picturis antiquorum SS Martirum passiones ... Refectorium amplissimum picturis penitus ornatum. Bibliotheca illustrissima. Dormitoria religiosa, commoda, recreativa ... Horti amoenissimi et satis dilati ..." [3] – and so on for all the "couvents" in the Order at the time.

A few prints exist which show something of the appearance of the "couvents" and there are several architects' plans and ground plans extant in various Archives.[4] From these we are able to see that the general lay-out of the buildings was traditional but, since the Minims came late to a town, and since virtually all their communities were urban, their sites were frequently small and had to conform to existing street patterns. The buildings were therefore often irregular and the quadrangle became little more than a court-yard, the main gate probably a mere "porte cochère." In all but the smallest "couvents," the traditional component parts were to be found – chapel, refectory, cloister and dormitory; to these might be added a library, pharmacy, infirmary, barns and out-houses. The garden was often separate from the main site.

There are very few remains of the French "couvents". Of the Parisian houses, Nigeon has disappeared entirely even to its name. The Place Royale (now Place des Vosges) remains intact but the "couvent" which took its name lay behind the square itself on the North side and

---

[1] P. M. Grégoire, *Etat du diocèse de Nantes en 1790*, Nantes, 1882, Pt. II, pp. 42–43.
[2] A. Dauvergne in *Bulletin du comité de la langue, de l'histoire et des arts de la France*, No. 6, 1853/4, Paris, 1855, pp. 477–481.
[3] Isnard, *op. cit.*, II, p. 24.
[4] see Bibliography, Manuscripts.

was pulled down early this century to make room for the police barracks which are now on the site. At Vincennes there was also devastation but, since the Minims occupied existing buildings near the château, this has little interest in the history of the Order. Elsewhere it is the same; there are several "Rues des Minimes" but little more than the name has survived. A garage in Pont-Saint-Esprit is remarkable for its seventeenth century aspect – it is the old "couvent des Minimes." In Toulouse a whole quarter is called "les Minimes" and the church still stands; it was, however, almost entirely rebuilt in the nineteenth century. The only extensive remains are of the "couvent" at Rouen which is now the convent of the Benedictine sisters, the churches at Clermont-Ferrand, Toulon and Saint Grégoire de Tours, also fragments at Decize, Aubeterre and Arlay,[1] and of the French "couvent" in Rome at the head of the Spanish Steps; the church of Santa Trinità dei Monti is well known to tourists and the conventual buildings house a prosperous convent school. Its cloisters, with a curious astrolabe erected on the walls by Maignan, and the retro-choir have scarcely altered since the days of Plumier[2] or when Claude painted the view of Rome with Santa Trinità in the middle distance.[3]

For the most part the buildings were the simple and unadorned work of local architects and craftsmen[4]; occasionally members of the Order worked in mediæval fashion on their own buildings and furnishings; Nicolas Boulon was remembered by Thuillier in this respect – "Dum in sæculo degebat peritissimus architectus visus est, unde ex tempore quo Minimorum instituto per professionem publicam mancipatus est in conventu scilicet Ambianensi die 8 Dec. anni 1648. Conventibus non paucis construendis, ornandis et decorandis, præsertim Parisino, Boloniensi et Suessonensi pro monialibus fuit maxime proficuus."[5] Jean Clément was another member of the Order who assisted in the construction of one of the "couvents," so also was Claude Breton, described as "opifex lignarius, qui post professionem suam arte sua multis præfuit domibus."[6] Jean Perceval, who was a friend of Mersenne, was another member of the Order who was also

---

[1] Joan Evans, *Monastic Architecture in France from the Renaissance to the Revolution*. Cambridge University Press, 1964, pp. 121–122 and illustrations 707–719.
[2] See the chapter on Plumier.
[3] National Gallery, London; see reproduction in the Appendix.
[4] An exception must be made for la Place Royale, where the the church was the work of Mansart himself; Archives Nationales, LL. 1564–1565. *Registres Capitulaires des Minimes de la Place Royale*, Vol. II, sub anno 1656. And see the chapter on artistic work.
[5] Thuiller, II, p. 257.
[6] *ibid.*, I, p. 189 and I, pp. 159–160.

an architect. At Tours, where there was something of a tradition of painting and craftsmanship among the Minims during the XVIIth century, a number of stone-masons and wood-carvers who had been employed on the new "couvent" of Saint Grégoire de Tours, took their vows and continued to work as members of the Order on the altar and baldachino of the conventual church.[1] In general, it seems that the Order attracted the skilful artisan and craftsman; some who achieved very considerable distinction are considered in more detail later, in the chapter devoted to the painters, sculptors, engravers and book-illustrators.

(3) ORGANISATION WITHIN INDIVIDUAL "COUVENTS"

Within the cloister the electoral system that obtained in the Provinces and for the selection of the Corrector General was rigidly adhered to. Monthly, or more often if the need should arise, the members would meet and, "capitulairement assemblés au son de la cloche," would proceed to business, each motion being voted upon. The whole domestic business of the "couvent" would come under discussion— from the annual appointments to the victualling and clothing arrangements. The minutes of the meeting ("actes capitulaires" or "registres capitulaires") were kept by a scribe. Once a year the election of Corrector was held and then the election of the other officers followed. It was unusual for a Corrector to be elected for two years running but the same names are wont to crop up at fairly regular intervals in this office; it was also quite common for the Corrector of one "couvent" to be elected Corrector of another within one or two years. Reappointment in successive years in the other offices, particularly in that of Scribe, was common but it seems to have been an understood thing, even if not established by rule, that each member took a fair share of all duties. There are exceptional cases of long spells in one office: Isaac Quatroux was in the Pharmacy at la Place Royale for nearly thirty years (1646–1672), and between them Mersenne, Regnault and La Noue did twenty years in the office of librarian at the same "couvent." [2]

Help from outside seems to have been limited to the appointment

---

[1] During the time that Michel de Coons was Provincial, i.e. 1676; Roberti, II, p. 133 and the Abbé Rolland, *Histoire de Saint François de Paule et de son couvent du Plessis-lès-Tours*, Paris, 1874; pp. 268–270.

[2] Archives Nationales, LL. 1564–1565: *Registres capitulaires des Minimes de la Place Royale*, Vol. II.

of a surgeon and a barber (often one and the same individual, one imagines), and builders and architects – even these jobs were sometimes undertaken by members themselves; all other work was done communally. From the registers which I have been able to consult I have compiled the following list of offices:

Discret – or private secretary to the Corrector. Sacristain. Scribe. Scribe des Conclusions Capitulaires.	Common to all "couvents".

Apothicaire. Bibliothécaire. Claustrale. Clefs. Cuisine. Détrempe – responsible for paints, white-washing etc. Infirmerie. Jardin. Livre des comptes – also called la Bourse. Porte. Provisions. Réfectoire. Registre des baptêmes.	To be found in virtually all the large "couvents" and in some of the small ones.

L'abreuvoir. Chambres. Chantre. Le four. Grainterie – in country "couvents," responsible for the provision of store seeds. Oeconome – a term used only at Arles as far as I can verify. Premier et deuxième senieurs (sic) – a term used in the "couvent" at Serres (Lorraine). Provision des vins.	Used in two or three instances only.

Although there are many sepulchral registers extant, I have been unable to find a single reference to the keeping of them. Since the right to be buried within the cloister was, as we shall see, one that was frequently bought for large sums of money, I conclude that it must have been kept by the Corrector himself or by his "discret."

Monsieur Y. Bizardel, who has transcribed a part of the *Conclusions*

Capitulaires des Minimes d'Aubeterre,[1] speaks of the "petite république où tous étaient élus" within the "couvent"; it is tempting to imagine a life of easy, if monotonous, regularity. But an examination of the available records suggests that there was much privation and hardship – few "couvents" could support themselves when plague struck and the "quête" was suspended because of the risk of bringing contagion into a town. Few "couvents" were large enough to prevent the doubling up of many of the duties set out above; omission of offices in the records of the annual elections suggests that often there were not enough members in a "couvent" to undertake them; sometimes the more necessary but less desirable jobs were given as a punishment for slackness or disobedience.[2] The picture of the self-indulgent cenobite was probably true often enough but so also was the more ascetic picture given by the paintings of Eustache Le Sieur and Jean Jouvenet (the death-bed scene in a "couvent," Musée de Rouen); such illustrations together with some of the biographical details of members of the Order help our reconstruction of what monastic life in the XVIIth century may have been and they form a necessary supplement to the somewhat impersonal "registres."

(4) VISITS

Each Corrector General went on a tour of visits during his tenure of office, making recommendations to the Provincial or to the Corrector of an individual "couvent"; these reports have been preserved in a large number of instances. On the other hand there are few reports still extant of the annual visits which the Provincial made to each of the "couvents" in his Province. Each Corrector was required to give the Provincial free access to all documents that he might hold and was required to sign a declaration that he had nothing to say by way of complaint; this declaration was then signed in turn by each of the members of the "couvent" and handed to the Provincial. A similar procedure was adopted for the "Visite Générale" of the

---

[1] Printed privately in 1942, at Angoulême(?). I am indebted to the Archivist of Charente for drawing my attention to this publication and to M. Bizardel for sending two copies of his pamphlet to me.

[2] See Gervasio Pizzurno, *Manipulus Minimorum canonum omnium regularium ex summis pontificibus olim per R. P. Balthasarem d'Avila eiusdem Instituti Generalem; modo in hac 7 editione per R. P. Gervasium Pizzurnum* ... Genoa, undated. Preface bears date 1677; information contained goes up to 1694. Subsequently referred to as "Pizzurnus."

Corrector Général. The formula adopted was as follows (either French or Latin):

Je ... ayant ... ans et ... ans de profession déclare que je n'ai rien à dire dans les visitations du .... Cependant je suis en tout respect le très-humble et très-obéissant ...

A set of these declarations has been preserved in the archives of the Pieux Etablissements Français à Rome.[1] It covers a "Visitation" of the Province of France (Paris) in the winter of 1676; very unfortunately it is incomplete, otherwise it would have been of unique value in attempting to estimate the strength of the Order at that time.

(5) STRENGTH OF THE ORDER IN FRANCE

There is no precise method of determining the strength of the Order. For the Province of France (Paris) there exists a necrology which we must accept as being complete, the *Diarium Patrum, fratrum et sororum Ordinis Minimorum provinciae Franciae, sive Parisiensis* by René Thuillier. From this I have abstracted a nimonal roll of all members of the Order in the Province who died between 1601 and 1700 – 974 members, of whom 67 were women and who belonged to the Second Ordre de Saint François de Paule. Thuillier gives the age of rather more than a third of the members and the average age appears to have been 48, a surprisingly high average for the seventeenth century. Bearing in mind that there was a rapid expansion during the century, it seems possible that the total number at any one time in the Province of France may have been in the neighbourhood of 200 at the beginning of the period and as high as 450–500 around 1680. For the rest of France the figure is more conjectural; the anonymous author of the *Nombre des ecclésiastiques* (Paris, 1660), gives the number as 2500, on page 39, but then says (p. 46) that it was 2000. The only figures which are reliable are those provided by the Commission des Réguliers which was set up to report on the state of the regular clergy in 1768; the figure of 975 members for the 153 "couvents" then in existence seems likely, and it probably represents about a half of the total strength of the Order at its height in the previous century. Since there

---

[1] Liasse 239. See Bibliography, Manuscripts (Private Archives). The Archivist could offer no suggestion as to how these documents come to be in the Archives of the Pieux Etablissements under the heading of Santa Trinità dei Monti.

In this and subsequent quotations from French the spelling has been modernized.

are no other figures available for the whole Order, it is from this report that the information below is taken.[1]

NAME OF "COUVENT"	NO. OF MEMBERS	"RENTE" IN LIVRES.
Province de Champagne		
Notre-Dame-de-l'Épine, Lépine.	*2	779
Vitry-le-François.	7	3.577
Bracancourt. – Haute-Marne.	4	2.856
Méchineix. – Haute-Marne.	*1	190
Laon.	9	3.284
Metz.	10	7.014
Épernay.	4	1.880
Reims.	8	4.129
Rethel.	5	2.282
Doulevent-le-Château. – Haute-Marne.	*2	770
Brienne.	4	1.979
Villiers-lès-Montmorency.	*1	200
Verdun.	4	1.960
13 maisons	61	30.900
Province de Bourgogne-duché		
Avallon.	4	1.365
Beaune.	9	1.460
La Guiche. – Saône-et-Loire.	6	1.898
Semur. – Côte-d'Or.	*4	529
Vitteaux. – Côte-d'Or.	5	1.361
Chalon-sur-Saône.	13	4.596
Dijon.	12	5.713
Notre-Dame-de-l'Étang. [2]	4	1.194
Tonnerre. – Yonne.	4	589
La Clayette. – Saône-et-Loire	6	1.441
Mâcon.	13	1.466
11 maisons	80	21.615

[1] *Abbayes, Prieurés et Couvents d'hommes en France. Liste générale d'après ... la Commission des Réguliers en 1768*, edited by L. Lecestre, Paris, 1902, pp. 60–65.
An asterisk placed before the number of members indicates that the "couvent" was scheduled for closing by the Commission.
[2] i. e. Dijon II: see Bibliography, MSS, Côte-d'Or. Lecestre inaccurate in placing it in Vosges.

NAME OF "COUVENT"	NO. OF MEMBERS	"RENTE" IN LIVRES.
Province de Bourgogne-comté.		
Arbois. – Jura.	10	2.467
Arlay. – Jura.	*4	1.380
Besançon.	20	4.988
La Consolation. – Doubs.	10	2.412
Dôle.	13	5.001
Morteau. – Doubs.	6	1.545
Ornans.	10	1.963
Rupt-sur-Saône. – Haute-Saône.	10	2.148
8 maisons	83	21.904
Province de Provence.		
Aix-en-Provence.	10	2.372
Pourrières. – Var.	*3	815
Trets. – Bouches-du-Rhône.	*4	1.199
Arles.	6	1.321
Marignane. – Bouches-du-Rhône.	*3	766
Avignon.	10	4.291
Venasque. – Vaucluse.	3	838
L'Isle-sur-la-Sorgue. – Vaucluse.	8	2.779
Draguignan.	3	663
La Ciotat.	8	169
Marseille.	26	6.389
Aubignan. – Vaucluse.	1	240
Mane. – Basses-Alpes.	6	4.405
Bormes. – Var.	*3	951
Toulon.	10	1.394
La Valette. – Var.	5	1.289
Pont-Saint-Esprit.	5	2.593
17 maisons	112	32.444

NAME OF "COUVENT"	NO. OF MEMBERS	"RENTE" IN LIVRES.
Province de Paris ou de France		
Abbeville.	6	2.868
Amiens.	5	6.700
Roye. – Somme.	3	1.642
Douay.	*5	2.728
Beaumont-sur-Oise.	4	2.777
Beauvais.	*3	1.795
Boulogne-sur-Mer.	*3	1.137
Calais.	7	3.655
Guise.	4	2.215
Crécy-en-Brie.	3	1.954
Decize. – Nièvre.	4	3.582
Nevers.	5	2.048
Chauny.	4	2.524
Péronne.	*3	881
Brie-Comte-Robert.	4	1.076
Les Bonshommes ou Nigeon, à Chaillot.	12	14.933
Paris, près la Place Royale.	29	20.056
Vincennes.	11	11.685
Dieppe.	3	3.043
Rouen	*9	9.660
Aulnoy. – Seine-et-Marne.	*3	2.029
Château-Thierry.	*3	335
Compiègne.	5	1.765
Soissons.	6	4.839
Lille.	14	7.948
Dunkerque.	6	818
26 maisons	164	114.691

NAME OF "COUVENT"	NO. OF MEMBERS	"RENTE" IN LIVRES.
Province d'Aquitaine		
Agen.	*3	400
Béziers.	5	400
Notre-Dame-de-la-Consolation.[1]	*4	200
Blaye. – Gironde.	7	1.300
Bordeaux.	25	4.000
Carcassonne.	*6	150
Caumont ou Cazaux. – Gers.	5	800
Samatan. – Gers.	*1	250
Narbonne.	8	900
Aubeterre-sur-Dronne. – Charente.	6	668
Plaignac. – Dordogne.	6	668
Perpignan.	8	900
Vic-en-Bigorre.	6	500
Tournay. – Hautes-Pyrénées.	3	500
Toulouse.	17	3.567
15 maisons	110	15.203

Province de Lyon		
Moulins-sur-Allier.	4	2.814
Grenoble.	8	3.182
La Plaine. – Isère.[2]	*3	1.524
Tullins. – Isère.	4	1.413
Saint-Chamond. – Loire.	4	1.387
Saint-Etienne.	10	2.711
Feurs. – Loire.	4	1.018
Lyon.	28	11.119
Montmerle. – Ain.	5	1.906
Roanne.	9	1.842
Le Péage-de-Pisançon. – Drôme.[3]	6	2.113
Valence.	*4	882
Roussillon. – Isère, arr. Vienne.	4	2.994
Vienne.	*2	618
14 maisons	95	35.553

[1] Usually referred to as "Béziers II"; about two miles from the centre of the town on the southern side.
[2] Usually referred to as "Grenoble, la Plaine," or as "Grenoble II."
[3] Usually referred to as "Romans."

Province d'Auvergne

Beauregard-l'Évêque. – Puy-de-Dôme.	9	5.736
Bard.[1]	3	1.016
Chaumont. – Puy-de-Dôme.	9	8.483
Clermont-Ferrand.	8	3.723
Courpière. – Puy-de-Dôme.	5	1.450
Brioude.	3	1.206
6 maisons	37	21.614

Province de Touraine

Angers.	8	3.278
Angoulême.	*5	1.639
Châteauneuf-sur-Charente.	2	682
Gien.	4	1.495
Blois.	*3	1.138
Bonniers-les-Moines. – Indre.	3	1.568
Bourges.	*6	804
Dun-le-Roi. – Cher.	*2	535
Issoudun.	5	186
Chartres.	4	759
Le Mans.	4	731
Sillé-le-Guillaume. – Sarthe.	*2	973
Nantes.	10	4.019
Orléans.	9	3.243
Champigny-sur-Veude. – Indre-et-Loire.	4	1.492
Châtellerault.	4	1.332
Poitiers.	4	1.439
Surgères. – Charente-Maritime.	6	3.692
La Rochelle.	*3	1.582
Saint-Pol-de-Léon.	*3	835
Rennes.	7	804
Amboise.	*4	1.221
Montgaugier. – Indre-et-Loire.	3	1.200
Plessis-lès-Tours.	18	4.699
Tours.	8	3.074
Morlaix.	*2	2.274
26 maisons	133	44.695

---

[1] Or Bort? Pizzurnus, *op. cit.*, *Conventus* lists it as "Bardensis." No archives are extant to prove the point.

Province de Lorraine

Bassing. – Moselle.	*4	1.407
Dieuze. – Moselle.	6	1.538
Nomény. – Meurthe-et-Moselle.	2	823
Dun. – Meuse.	5	2.815
Bar-le-Duc.	5	824
Notre-Dame-de-Bon-Secours, Nancy.	8	5.000
Notre-Dame-de-la-Consolation. – Vosges.	4	2.000
Épinal.	6	1.395
Lunéville.	6	1.333
Nancy.	21	7.122
Pont-à-Mousson.	5	2.033
Serres. – Meurthe-et-Moselle.	*6	2.446
Vézelise. – Meurthe-et-Moselle.	*3	757
Stenay. – Meuse.	6	1.199
Sainte-Lucie. – Meuse.	6	2.035
Marchéville. – Meuse.	2	645
Saint-Mihiel. – Meuse.	5	1.268
17 maisons	100	34.640

Total général: 153 maisons; 975 religieux; 373.229 livres.

Recruitment into the Order seems to have been fairly universal throughout France with the exception of Brittany and Normandy; along the coast from Bléville,[1] a suburb of modern le Havre, to Morlaix and Saint-Pol-de-Léon there was not a single "couvent." Paris, Tours, Marseille, Aix-en-Provence, Lyon and the whole of Lorraine were the chief centres of recruitment but the 153 "couvents" were evenly spaced out and the membership of the Order was probably representative of France as a whole.

It is also difficult to come to any definite conclusions about the social status of the Members. There were a few representatives of the nobility, two members of the le Fèvre d'Ormesson family and Jacob de Sadirac being the only ones mentioned by Thuillier; many of the names he quotes, however, suggest the Petite Noblesse – Dony d'Attichy, Etienne de Brie, Gilles de Fourmamoir, Jean-Baptiste de Saint-Lô. More humble-sounding names abound which suggest that recruitment was chiefly from the Bourgeoisie and Artisan classes – Jean Potier, Pierre Petit, Marie-Madeleine Gilbert, Pierre Tillot, Antoine Bocquet. There were also a few foreign refugees – Lawrence Ogilbey, a Scot; Francis Binans, said to be English; another Scot, Andrew Baird who , with a compatriot Ian (Jean) Brown (Bruno),

[1] Suppressed before the above list was drawn up.

taught Oriental languages and was a friend of Mersenne; there were
also the brothers Robertson, and Henry More, grandson of the Blessed
Thomas More.

5. LE SECOND ORDRE DE SAINT FRANÇOIS DE PAULE

The female, or Second, Order was never of any importance in
France. It counted no more than 67 members during the seventeenth
century, many of them relatives of members of the male Order; they
were divided between Abbeville, founded in 1621, and Soissons,
founded in 1653. The majority were at the former and their history
has been told by E. Prarond.[1] There were, as we shall see, two teaching
institutions that sprang directly from the inspiration of the Minim
Nicolas Barré and these may well have been detrimental to the
recruitment of nuns into the Second Ordre.

6. LE TIERS-ORDRE DE SAINT FRANÇOIS DE PAULE
AND THE QUESTION OF LAY PATRONAGE

In the thirteenth century at a time when there was developing a
laity which could pretend to both education and leisure, there grew
up around the great orders societies of both men and women who
aspired to the high ideals of the monastic life but who wished to
remain "dans le siècle." These societies also counted amongst their
members a certain number of the secular clergy and the importance
of this element became increasingly important. Such societies were
known as the "Third-Order" of each of the parent orders and received official recognition from the Pope. The most important of them
all was the Third Order of Saint Francis (of Assisi) and, in common with
the Franciscans, the Minims had their "Tiers-ordre." The rule was
strict and there was a ritual to be followed throughout the year which
bound members to a devotion not unlike that of the full members of the
order.[2] The position of all Tertiaries in canon law has been the subject
of a recent study in which, however, the Minims are mentioned once
only [3]; the author, who has drawn largely from the work of two

---

[1] *Topographie historique ... d'Abbeville*, 3 vols, Paris/Abbeville, 1871; Vol. II, pp. 385–426.
[2] *Regola dell Terz'Ordine dei Minimi*, Rome 1917. *La règle du Tiers-Ordre des Minimes, avec
notes*, F. Giry. Paris, 1673.
[3] *Il Diritto ecclesiastico*, Anno LXX, fasc. I, Gennaio-Giugno 1959, pp. 101–207; *La
personalità giuridica dei Terzordini*, by A. di Iorio. The mention of the Minims is merely in a
list of those orders which had Third-Orders attached to them.

scholars, Vromant and Bongaerts,[1] has defined the scope of the Third
Orders under the headings: Lo scopo delle personne morali; Lo scopo
religioso; Lo scopo caritativo. The first and last of these objects need
little elucidation but the second is explained in the following terms:

> Per scopo religioso bisogna intendere, con una certa larghezza, quello
> che ha per oggetto Dio e le relazione da favorire verso di Lui, come, ad
> esempio, la perfezione cristiana da ottenersi mediante i tre voti religiosi ...
> l'incremento del culto publico, scopo delle confraternità, l'esercizio di
> qualche opere di pietà ... l'educazione della gioventù.[2]

The Tiers-Ordre de Saint François de Paule was not merely a "confrérie" like that of the Confrérie du Rosaire, but a congregation
submitting to the same vows and rule as the first and second Orders.
Members undertook a noviciate of a year followed by the public
pronouncement of vows which could be abjured after seven years.
The aim of the Tiers-Ordre was to inculcate a simple devotion within
the home rather than that its members, most of whom were women,
should merely ape the conventual life; in this way it is almost impossible
to judge the full measure of its influence within seventeenth century
France. Its members were urged to succour the widows and orphans,
the infirm, the oppressed, and they were further urged to adopt the
principle "Bless them that persecute you," [3] to refrain from the
popular vice of duelling and to maintain sobriety and moderation in
their daily life.

Much of the popularity of the Minims in the XVIth and XVIIth
centuries must be attributed to its Tiers-Ordre; in the early days of
its existence several Royal persons were members: Charles VIII, who
bestowed special favours on Saint François de Paule himself and who
founded the French "couvent" in Rome; François Ier and Anne de
Bretagne, who were instrumental in founding several "couvents" in
France. This royal patronage continued into the next century when
Chrestienne de France, sister of Louis XIII, received the cordon of
the Tiers-ordre in the Minims' church at la Place Royale; the Duchesse
d'Elbeuf and the Duchesse de la Valette received the cordon at the
same time. Henriette-Marie, wife of Charles I of England, was a
member and so also were the Duchesse de Nemours, several members
of the Aumale family, the Marquise de Villars, the Duchesse d'Ascot
(Flanders) and Jacques Aurillot, Conseiller du Roi. All these names

---

[1] *De fidelium associationibus*, Museum Lessianum, (Théologie), Brussels/Paris, 1955.
[2] *Il diritto ecclesiastico*, loc. cit.
[3] Pizzurnus, *op. cit.*, under *Tertiarii*, and Giry, *op. cit.*, *passim*.

appear, some of them repeatedly, in the acts of foundation or in the lists of donations and "fondations de messes" for "couvents" all over France. But the majority of the members were wealthy bourgeois and bourgeoises who supported the Order with gifts of land, money and occasionally treasures; sometimes they were instrumental in the initial act of foundation itself, as at Semur in the Province of the Duchy of Burgundy, and Arbois in the County of Burgundy which were founded by Elizabeth Léauté and la veuve Pierre Camus respectively, both members of the Tiers-Ordre. It is not possible to obtain accurate assessment of its numerical strength since only one register of membership has survived, and that only of female members.[1] Dony d'Attichy gives a short list of prominent members [2] of whom two, apart from the Royal Family, deserve to be mentioned; they are Mlle de Vivergier, veuve de Monsieur de Bérulle, mother of Pierre Bérulle, Cardinal and founder of the French Oratory, and Saint François de Sales who had always shown great devotion to the Founder of the Minims and who, shortly before he became Bishop of Geneva, received the "cordon" of the Tiers-Ordre and made a pilgrimage to le Plessis-lès-Tours in order to pray at the Founder's shrine.[3] The Order was justly proud of its illustrious member and it was a Minim who, at the Beatification of François de Sales in 1662, composed three sets of Latin odes in his honour. This work, called *Horatii Christiani*,[4] as well as giving an apotheosis of the Blessed François, develops the theme of his attachment to the ideals of the Minims, their charity and their pure love of God; part III, containing fourteen odes, is devoted to the mystical side of the Salesian theology and odes VIII–XII bear the sub-title *B. Franciscus Salesius S. Francisco de Paula tamquam obedientiae Evangelicae typo clarissimo specialiter adhaeret;* here the miracles of the Founder are placed in parallel with the spiritual development of François de Sales. Although the author is obviously carried away by his subject, it is correct to point out a similarity between the Salesian

[1] Arles: *Sœurs du Tiers-Ordre de Saint François de Paule,* 1623–1731; MS register preserved in Archives Départementales, Bouches-du-Rhône, Série H, 31. I am doubtful whether the list of members of the Tiers-Ordre in Dieppe, Archives Départementales, Seine-Maritime, Série H, *Minimes de Dieppe,* liasse 8 (h) (my classification, see Bibliography) is really of the Tiers-Ordre des Minimes.

[2] *op. cit.,* pp. 160 et sq.

[3] L'abbé Rolland, *Histoire de S. François de Paule et de son Couvent du Plessis-lès-Tours,* Paris, 1874, pp. 271–272.

[4] By Jacques Ladore: see Bibliography, Printed works. The beautifully bound copy in the Bibliothèque Nationale is ex-Minimes de la Place Royale, bearing the original shelf-number K 9 18.

interpretation of the Christian message and the "sagesse" of the Order of Minims; there is a similarity in the fusion of mystical and rationalist, or practical, elements of the Faith. This third part of the *Horatii Christiani* is completed by the inclusion of three Latin hymns in praise of Saint François de *Paule*, an ode (No. XIII) in praise of the Pope, Alexander VII, for his wisdom in beatifying François de *Sales* and for his generosity as a protector of the Order of Minims; finally there is an ode (No. XIV) which delights in the fact that the Beatification coincided with the birth of the Dauphin.[1] After François de Sales's canonization, in 1665, his Feast Day (29th January) became a feast of obligation throughout the Order.[2]

Neither Marie de Medicis nor Anne d'Autriche were, as far as we know, members of the Tiers-ordre although they were amongst the prominent patrons of the Order; the former founded the "couvents" at Angoulême and Blois and was amongst the founders of the "couvent" at la Place Royale. This royal patronage from the earliest days of the Order in France may account for the strong gallican tendency amongst the French Minims; in part this was reaffirmed by what seemed to them the almost miraculous birth of Louis XIV. All the historians of the Order emphasise the fact that Vienna di Fuscaldo, mother of Saint François de Paule, was barren for many years and that she and her husband obtained by prayers to Saint Francis of Assisi the gift of the son they desired and whom they dedicated to the service of God under the patronship of the saint of Assisi. Now Anne d'Autriche was also barren, and for many years had assiduously prayed in the Minims' church in the Place Royale, asking that she should not fail France in her duty and invoking the aid of Saint François de Paule.[3] It may also be noted that her confessor, the abbé

---

[1] This is, in fact, stretching a point; the Dauphin was born in 1661 and François de Sales was beatified in 1662. The Minims were, as we shall see, particularly devoted to Louis XIV and extended this devotion whole-heartedly to his son.

[2] Pizzurnus, *op. cit.*, *S. Franciscus Salesius*.

[3] E. Dondé, *Figures de la Vie de S. François de Paule*, in fol., Paris, 1671, gives the following *Extrait*; it occupies a complete page (unnumbered following p. 171) and is surrounded by an elaborate, ornamental frame.

Extrait
des Registres

de la Sacristie du couvent des
Minimes de la Place Royale, où sont
exprimés les vœux à S. François de Paule
par les Têtes couronnées, et autres.

Anne d'Autriche, Reine de France et de Navarre, épouse du Roi Très-Chrétien Louis XIII à présent régnant, ayant été par l'espace de plusieurs années sans avoir lignée, sachant bien comme S. François de Paule était un des principaux Protecteurs de la France, et en

Thiersault, was a member of the "Tiers-Ordre." [1] The birth of the
Dauphin (later Louis XIV) was at once equated by members of the
Order with the birth of their blessed Founder, so that it was possible
for Pierre Duval, when dedicating his *Vie et miracles de S. François de
Paule* to the Queen in 1640, to speak of "les bénédictions abondantes
que la main du Tout-Puissant a départies à votre Majesté en la naissance heureuse de ces Premiers Princes de l'Europe" (Philippe, Duc
d'Orléans had been born that same year, 1640). So that the full import
of this association of circumstances might be felt, he added to his work
what would otherwise seem an irrelevance, the *Cantiques sacrés de
l'épouse sainte au berceau de Jésus Dieu-Enfant.*[2] Another writer who
shows the same attention to the Royal patronage of the Order in
France was the historian Hilarion de Coste whose *Eloges de nos Rois
et des enfants de France* bore, in the edition of 1643, the following dedication "A l'Altesse Réale de Monseigneur le Dauphin l'espérance des
Français, fils aisné du très-chrestien, très-victorieux et très-auguste
Louis XIII ...." [3]

7. THE CONFRÉRIES ASSOCIATED WITH THE ORDER [4]

"Confrérie" in the ecclesiastical sense means a group of men and
women who meet at regular intervals to make some special religious
devotions or who wish to emphasise a particular aspect of Christianity.
The "confréries" in seventeenth century France were numerous and,
although each one had to be under episcopal jurisdiction, several of
the smaller ones were of purely local importance and were probably
never fully recognised at Rome; in this they differed from the Tiers-
ordres.

The association of several "confréries" with the Order of Minims
dates from about the middle of the seventeenth century and continued
in some instances until the dissolution of the Order at the time of the
Revolution. The bonds that existed between the "confréries" and the
Order were tenuous and their inter-relationship ill-defined. There is

possession de lui donner des Dauphins, elle eut recours à lui et voulut bien elle-même
prendre la peine de se transporter souvent les vendredis en ce couvent de la Place Royale,
pour y accomplir les vœux qu'elle avait faits à ce grand Saint. Enfin après avoir imploré
son assistance, elle ressentit le pouvoir qu'il avait auprès de Dieu, ayant obtenu un beau
Dauphin, lequel naquit le 5 septembre 1638.

[1] F. Giry, *La Règle du Tiers-Ordre des Minimes*, Paris, 1683, pp. 285–286.
[2] See Bibliography of printed works, Duval.
[3] See Bibliography of printed works, Coste.
[4] For a general history of "confréries" see F. Beringer, S. J., *Die Ablaesse*; French translation, *Les Indulgences*, Paris, 1890, Vol. II.

probably scope for a full-scale study of the social influence of the Tiers-Ordres and of the "Confréries"; it was through them that the laity was often attached to the Church. The association of "Confréries" with the Order, first recognised by Clement VII,[1] proved to an be important source of patronage and financial assistance; the conventual church was used for devotional purposes and indulgences were granted to those who assisted on certain days throughout the year.

The principal associations in France during the period under review were:

Minimes de Moulins .... Confrérie des Bien-Mourants.
Minimes de Moulins .... Confrérie de la Vierge.
Minimes de Moulins .... Confrérie de l'Ange Gardien.
Minimes de Dieuze ..... Confrérie du Rosaire.
Minimes de Soissons .... Confrérie du Rosaire.
Minimes de Douai ...... Confrérie de l'Ange Gardien.
Minimes de Lille .... Confrérie des Noces de la Sainte Vierge.
Minimes de Lille .... Confrérie de la Dévotion au Saint An-
                        neau.
Minimes de Grenoble ... Confrérie de la Trinité et de la Rédemp-
                        tion des Captifs délivrés.
Minimes de Lunéville ... Confrérie des Agonisants.
Minimes de Lunéville ... Confrérie de Saint Antoine.[1]
Minimes d'Avallon ..... Confrérie de Saint Joseph.
Minimes de Lyon .... Confrérie des Enfants de la ville (Roy-
                        aume de Notre-Dame d'Août). Con-
                        frérie de la Santé.[2]
Minimes de Sillé-le-Gillaume with the Confrérie de S. Sébastien.
Minimes de Sillé-le-Gillaume with the Confrérie de Jésus, Marie et
                                                        S. Joseph.

The titles have a mystical ring about them and the "Confréries" doubtless thrived on their attraction to the imagination of the laity and on the general appeal of the slightly esoteric approach to religion that they promised. Antoine Masson, a Minim writing towards the

[1] Pizzurnus, op. cit., Confraternitas.
[2] Dating back to 1386, this Confrérie is one of the oldest that became associated with the Order. Archives Départementals: Meurthe-et-Moselle, H. 1021–1022.
[3] Both these Confréries of Lyon owe their existence to the Plague. The Minims worked ceaselessly during the several plagues of Lyon; parents founded a Confrérie at their church, seeking protection of Our Lady. The main Feast associated with this was the Assumption (August 15) – hence the itle. The second confrérie was under the dual patronage of Saint Roch and Saint François de Paule.

end of the seventeenth century, stressed the mystical symbolism of both
the "Tiers-Ordre" and of the "Confrérie"; in the former he saw a
living example of the Heavenly Society and in the latter a representation of those "respects que les bienheureux rendent à Jésus-Christ
et à la Vierge dans le ciel." [1]

8. FINANCES AND PROPERTY

Shortly after the establishment of the Order in France privileges
were bestowed upon it, and these have to be considered before an
attempt is made to evaluate the revenue of any of the "couvents."
When Louis XI gave the initial permission for the Minims to build,
he granted immunity from "Péages, subsides de guet, garde et portes" [2]
which is the modern equivalent, approximately, of living free from
rates. In addition he granted immunity from the "gabelle" and
"autres subventions quelconques." In 1515 François Ier granted a
privilege by which their communities and individual members were
"quittes et exempts de payer aucune chose pour raison de péage,
traverses, aides, subsides et subventions quelconques pour le passage
de leurs dits vivres et nécessités et provisions d'eau et de leurs dits
couvents soit par mer, eau douce ou par terre en quelque manière que
ce soit." [3] In 1563 they received a further privilege granted by Charles
IX; they were included in the Edit de l'Aliénation du domaine des
ecclésiastiques,[4] so that their property dealings were free from the
equivalent of modern stamp-duty. A further important concession
made in their favour was in 1609, when Henri IV decided that they
were to count as a mendicant order [5] and freed them from all excise.
In spite of this, they were never generally accepted as mendicants
and were never considered as having the privileged position of the
"Quatre mendiants."

Three times in the years 1623–1633 individual "couvents" appealed
against local taxation and on each occasion the appeal was successful
and immunity was won. Nigeon received its supply of wine by barge
from Auxerre; shipments were liable to a duty levied on the Yonne at
Sens and on the Seine at Montereau. Invoking, one supposes, the

---

1 A Masson, *Les Secrets du Paradis*, Paris, 1693, pp. 312, 318 *et sq.*
2 *Privilèges concédés et octroyés tant à S. François de Paule ... qu'aux couvents et religieux de son
ordre par les Rois de France*, Paris, 1644; p. 16.
3 *ibid.*, p. 6.
4 *ibid.*, p. 23.
5 *ibid.*, p. 29.

privilege of 1515 they were able to free themselves from these dues
in 1623.[1] In Dieppe a sum of 27,000 livres was levied in the town to
build a new parish church; in the same year as the levy, 1625, the
Order won immunity by a petition to Louis XIII.[2] It was also by
direct appeal to Louis that in 1633 the Minimes de Nantes obtained
complete freedom from local taxation on wine, oil and other provisions which they brought downstream from Angers.[3] This included
indemnity from the "trépas de Loire", shipping dues similar to the
ones which the Minimes de Nigeon had appealed against ten years
earlier and which for some reason had not been cleared by the general
privilege of 1515. Over and above these exemptions from dues levied
on the transport of wine, there existed the "baux de vin" which granted
to various religious orders freedom from all other taxes levied on the
sale of wine. In 1717 the "baux de vin" were revoked for the Minims
by an "Arrêt du Conseil d'Etat"[4]; gradually the minor privileges
were in their turn revoked, but the major ones remained, being a
grievous source of envy to the unequally taxed laity.

It is because of all these privileges that the real value of the revenue
of a "couvent" was quite different from the value of a similar sum in
the hands of, say, a bourgeois or a member of the petite noblesse.
Taxes were largely in the form of direct taxation on salt and on the
transport of wine, oil and grain; it was immunity from precisely such
taxation that they had won. Without taking this into due consideration, the figures which follow may be deceptive.

Several account books are extant, but it is difficult to piece together
a statement of revenue for any one "couvent" for the whole period of
the seventeenth century. A compulsory return stating the amount and
source of revenue was not enforced until 1668 and statements even
after that date are apt to be fragmentary. I have chosen three statements on which to base some general conclusions:

I. The return made in 1668 for the small "couvent" at Pont-Saint-
Esprit where there were 11 "religieux."

II. The detailed analysis of the accounts of the "couvent" at Arles.

III. The list of foundations at the Couvent de la Place Royale,
Paris.

---

[1] *ibid.*, p. 37.
[2] *ibid.*, pp. 39–40.
[3] *ibid.*, pp. 41–43.
[4] Bibliothèque Nationale, Fonds Français, 21668.

I. *Etat fidèle et véritable de l'établissement, fonds de terres et revenu, casuel et charges du couvent des religieux Minimes de l'ordre de Saint François de Paule de la ville du Saint Esprit en Languedoc, iceux religieux étant de la province de Provence.* [1]

Fonds de terres

Ledit couvent a été établi dans ladite ville l'an mil six cent trois, le 21 novembre, sous le règne de Henri IV avec permission de Monsieur l'évêque d'Uzès et réception de messieurs de la présente ville.

Le couvent des PP. Minimes de la ville du Saint Esprit en Languedoc possède au terroir de la Motte douze saulmées [2] de terre situées en divers endroits dudit terroir, et au terroir de Bolesne huit saulmées, le tout dans le comtat Venaissin, lesquelles tous frais faits rendent audit couvent douze à treize chargés de froment ou autre grain une année comportant l'autre, le tout étant en megerie.[3]

Au terroir du Saint(?) lieu Corcholes une terre de six minées [4] rentée trente-six livres tous les ans.

Au même terroir, lieu dit les Parrons un jardin de la contenance de deux saulmées ou environ, renté deux cent trente-trois livres.

Pensions annuelles rangées selon l'ordre des mois de l'année

Janvier:

Le premier jour la communauté du Saint Esprit fait audit couvent septante-cinq livres à cinq pour cent.

Le 15 un particulier de Bolesne au comté Venaissin fait vingt et une livres, Monnaie du Pape.

Le 24 au même lieu on fait onze livres.

Le 25 aussi audit Bolesne on nous fait deux pensions, l'une de sept livres sept sols, l'autre de dix-neuf livres.

Le 28 au susdit lieu on fait audit couvent douze livres.

Février:

A la Palud le premier de ce mois un particulier fait audit couvent vingt et une livres de pension, Monaie du Pape.

Le neuf, à Saint-Jean en Vivarais un particulier fait trente-sept livres dix sols au denier seize.[5]

Le quatorze, à Bolesne au comté Venaissin un particulier fait trois livres trois sols, Monnaie du Pape.

---

[1] Archives Départementales, Gard; Série H, 857, fol. 14 *et sq.*

[2] Littré, "salmée." Measurement of area equal to 70 ares (1 are = 100 square metres, roughly .025 acres); the "saulmée" may be taken as 1.75 acres. According to Littré this measurement is found only in Bouches-du-Rhône.

[3] Godefroy, *Dictionnaire de l'ancienne langue française*; megerie, moitié des fruits.

[4] *ibid.*, 1 minée = 40 pas au carré. Rather more than $\frac{1}{2}$ acre.

[5] Au denier seize – see l'*Avare*, I, 5 "... et vingt pistoles rapportent par année dix-huit livres aux sols huit, à ne les placer qu'au denier douze." i.e. one "denier" of interest for every twelve lent, or 8.3%; "au denier seize," the usual rate of interest in the above MS, is equal to 6.2%.

Le vingt, en cette ville du Saint Esprit un particulier fait dix-huit livres quinze sols au denier seize.

Mars:

A Baignols en Languedoc deux particuliers font audit couvent le trois du mois entre eux dix-huit livres quinze sols au denier seize.

Le dix-huit, à Aiguères en Vivarais un particulier fait dix-huit livres au denier dix-huit.

Le neuf, au Saint Esprit un particulier fait six livres au denier dix-huit.

Avril:

Le trente, au Saint Esprit un particulier fait audit couvent dix-huit livres quinze sols de pension, le fonds au dernier seize.

Mai:

Le trois du mois, un particulier d'Aiguères en Vivarais fait douze livres dix sols au denier seize.

Le dix-neuf, à Saint-Martin en Vivarais un particulier fait dix-huit livres quinze sols de fonds au denier seize.

Le vingt-deux, en cette ville du Saint Esprit un particulier fait six livres.

Juin:

Le deux, un particulier de cette ville du Saint Esprit fait septante-cinq livres de pension, le fonds au denier seize.

Le vingt, un particulier de la même ville fait six livres cinq sols au denier seize.

Le vingt et un, un particulier aussi de la même ville fait neuf livres sept sols au denier seize.

Le vingt-cinq, à Pierrelate en Dauphiné un particulier nous fait dix-huit livres au denier dix-huit.

Juillet:

Le quatorze, deux particuliers de cette ville du Saint Esprit nous font entre eux deux huit livres.

Le vingt-deux, au même Saint Esprit un particulier nous fait neuf livres.

Le même jour, à Bolesne, au comté Venaissin, divers particuliers font audit couvent en tout quatorze livres quatorze sols, Monnaie du Pape.

Août:

Le vingt-cinq, en cette ville du Saint Esprit un particulier fait dix-sept livres trois sols.

Le vingt-sept, à Bolesne un particulier nous fait quinze livres, Monnaie du Pape.

Le trente et un, un particulier de cette ville fait six livres cinq sols au denier seize.

Septembre:

Le cinq, à Carpentras au comté Venaissin la communauté des Juifs dudit lieu fait vingt et une livres de pension.

Le douze, à Bedavrides, ville du même comté, un particulier fait au couvent dix-huit livres, Monnaie du Pape.

Le quatorze un particulier de cette ville du Saint Esprit fait six livres cinq sols au denier seize.

Le vingt, en la même ville un particulier fait neuf livres seize sols au denier seize.

Le vingt-huit, un particulier aussi de la même ville fait vingt-cinq livres.

Le vingt-neuf, un particulier de la Palud, comté Venaissin, fait au couvent quinze livres au denier vingt.

Le vingt-trois, à Laudun en Languedoc un particulier fait vingt livres au denier vingt.

Le trente, un particulier de Saint-André de Roqueperthuis fait dix-huit livres au denier seize.

Octobre:

Le six, un particulier de la ville du Saint Esprit fait dix-huit livres au denier seize.

Le vingt, un particulier de la même ville fait dix-huit livres quinze sols au denier seize.

Le vingt et un, à Saint-Marcel en Vivarais un particulier fait trente-sept livres dix sols au denier seize.

Le vingt-deux, un particulier d'Aiguères fait une pension de dix-huit livres quinze sols au denier seize.

Novembre:

Le premier, divers particuliers de cette ville du Saint Esprit font en tout onze livres huit sols neuf deniers.

Le deux, deux particuliers de la même ville du Saint Esprit font en tout dix livres au denier vingt.

Le vingt et un, à Saint-Martin divers particuliers doivent en tout dix-huit livres quinze sols au denier seize. Le trente, un particulier de Saint-Alexandre en Languedoc fait six livres cinq sols au denier seize.

Décembre:

Le vingt-cinq, un particulier du Saint Esprit fait neuf livres de pension.

Le même jour, à Bariac en Vivarais un particulier nous fait quinze livres au denier vingt.

Le trente et un, la communauté de cette ville du Saint Esprit fait bature-vingt-six livres cinq sols au denier vingt.

Le même jour, la communauté du Bourg-Saint-Andio [1] en Vivarais fait en ce même couvent cent livres de pensions, le fonds au denier seize.

---

[1] i.e. Bourg-Saint-Andéol (Ardèche); Saint-Andiol is in Bouches-du-Rhône and could not be described as "en Vivarais."

Casuel
La quête nous rend ou en argent ou en pain cent livres. Le tronc trois cents livres d'autres fois plus ou moins le tout de trente ou quarante livres.

Les Charges
Il faut un quintal de cierges tous les ans. Les réparations qu'il faut faire en ornements de l'église ou à l'entretien d'icelle sont continuelles.
Pour l'entretien des couverts et du reste de la maison, trente livres.
Pour les tailles des biens que nous avons, douze à quinze livres.
Pour l'entretien des chambres en meubles, linge pour les malades ou le réfectoire, soixante livres.
Pour la cotte de notre Révérendissime Père Général, du Rd. Père Provincial et des chapitres ou définitaires [1] ou provinciaux, soixante livres.
De plus, il nous faut acheter sel, huile, provisions de merluche, poisson, vin, vêtements, chaussures pour onze religieux.
Nous soussigné Correcteur du couvent des religieux Minimes de l'Ordre de Saint François de Paule en la ville du Saint Esprit en Languedoc en suite de l'arrêt de la souveraine cour du Parlement de Toulouse ... ce jour d'hui vingt-neuvième août de l'année mil six cent soixante-huit, certifiions le présent état être le plus véritable et fidèle (le plus qu'il nous a été possible de dresser) en foi de quoi ... scellé du sceau de notre office ...
Fr. Jean Bonaud, Correcteur.

II. Livre dit Saint Jacques, ou livre des pensions du couvent des Pères Minimes d'Arles ... dressé en 1668. Refait en 1679 etc.[2].

This gives a fuller account than the one quoted above but it follows the same pattern; in addition to the "terres et pensions" it gives a list of the masses to be said for the departed and the capital sums invested for that purpose. Between 1622 and 1688 a total of 22,485 livres was given for 38 masses; the sums for an annual mass in perpetuity ranging from 3,000 livres to 60 livres, the most usual sum being 300 livres. These figures serve as a point of comparison with one of the richer "couvents," that of la Place Royale, Paris.

III. Annales des Minimes de la Province de France où se trouvent l'abrégé de la vie de Saint François de Paule, les Généraux des vingt-huit couvents ... et en particulier tout ce qui concerne le couvent de la Place Royale ... Paris, 1754. [3]

Below in tabulated form are all the entries for the years 1619–1699.

[1] i.e. Chapitres Généraux.
[2] Nîmes, Bibliothèque Municipale, MS No. 628; see Bibliography (Manuscripts).
[3] Bibliothèque Nationale, Fonds Français, 23126. Another copy in Bibliothèque Mazarine, No. 2429; slight variation in pagination. References given are to the version in the Mazarine.

A. CAPITAL AND INCOME from "Fondations de messes" and donations (pages 109–116 of the manuscript).

Date	Sum in livres	Conditions
1619	8,000	To lodge M. J-B. Marchand and his servant and to say one mass per annum in perpetuity.
1622	3,200	Gift of Zéline Taverine.
	1,600	Further gift of above less a "rente contribuée" paid to her.
1633	300	By will.
1635	1,500	By will and for privilege of being buried in Minims' church (800 livres taken, remainder in settlement of debt).
1638	1,800	Two masses per week and an additional two per annum in perpetuity.
1639	950	Burial in Minims' church.
1652	1,200 ⎱	For saying masses for the departed.
1653	156 ⎰	
	1,000	Gift by will of Mme Lemoyne.
	250	Gift of Mme Lemoyne.
1658	2,200	A mass each Monday in perpetuity.
1665	8,000	A mass each day and a "service" once a year in perpetuity.
?	2,000	Gift to enable "droit d'indemnité" on two houses in the Hôtel des Ursins to be paid off.
1666	6,000	Gift of Marie, Duchesse de Rohan, to pay off "achat" of above houses.
	5,000 [1]	Gift of Catherine de Polignac.
	600	Two "rentes" of 300 livres by Jérôme de Nouveau, Surintendant des Postes.
?	6.000	Settled by widow of above; "rente" ceased.
1668	1,500	Mass each Wednesday in perpetuity.
1669	6,000	Gift of Catherine Girard, in exchange for a "rente" of 300 livres.
1680	1,250	Marguerite du Bois, for burial in Minims' church and one mass per week plus additional ones on each of 3 feast days.
1682	2,000	Two masses a week for husband and wife.
1679	1,000 [2]	A mass each Wednesday.
1689	1,000	Two masses a week in perpetuity.
	1,000	One mass per week in perpetuity.
	100	One mass annually in perpetuity.

[1] This was transferred to the Minimes de Valence; no date given.
[2] Used to buy a farm at Frementeau.

Date	Sum in livres	Conditions
1693	100	"Un salut tous les jours de la semaine de la Passion pour les agonisants."
	50	"Rente."
	150	"Un salut, fête de S. Charles."
1630 [1]	200	"Un obit à perpétuité."
	350	An annual mass.
1631	3,000	Each to Nigeon and la Place Royale by a man and his wife on the profession of their son; burial of wife in Minims' church and 5 masses annually in both places for 50 years.
	1,200	Marie, widow of N. Prevost, Sieur d'Amboise, for two masses a week and a "service" annually in perpetuity.
1696	6,000	Gift of d'Ormesson, successor to the abbé Chaillou.[2]
1632	975	Against a "rente" of 60 livres and three masses annually for 50 years.
1633	600	A "service" on 9th November for 50 years.
	100	Twelve masses a year.
1635	300	"Rente" by Olivier d'Alesso.
	200	For burial in Minims' church; Olivier d'Alesso.
1638	1,000	Annual mass and "service" on 11th January.
1641	450	Mass on Fridays for 50 years.
1651	1,800	Against a "rente" of 100 livres and two "services" annually for 50 years.
1653	600	A mass on Mondays for 50 years.
1669	100	Weekly mass for 50 years.
1675	400	A gift of 200 livres and 200 livres to endow a mass for Anne Proust.
1676	500	Madeleine de Varrège; special conditions, see later.
1678	125	"Rente" given by P. le Fèbvre de Laizeau.
	3,000	Daily mass for 50 years, P. le Fèbvre de Laizeau.
1682	60	Weekly mass and 8 others per year for 50 years.
1684	300	Twenty masses a year for 50 years.
1685	4,200	"Aides et Gabelles" given by C. Mopinot and his wife against a "rente" to them of 200 livres.
	400	Thirty masses per year for 50 years.
	300	Nicole, widow of Nicolas Besche, for Litanies de la Sainte Vierge on Saturdays for 20 years.
1691	4,000	Four masses per week and an annual "service" for 50 years.

[1] There seems to be no reason for the sudden return to the 1630s in this list. The order is the same in both the Mazarine and Bibliothèque Nationale versions of this Manuscript.

[2] The family of Le Fèvre d'Ormesson had many connexions with the Order; see also sub anno 1635, Olivier d'Alesso. Through the Alesso family the Ormessons are connected with Saint François de Paule himself: see Michaud, *Biographie Universelle*, vol. 31 and the *Journal d'Olivier le Fébvre d'Ormesson*, Paris, 1860/1; also the *Bottin Mondain*.

Date	Sum in livres	Conditions
	800	Forty masses a year and two "services" annually for 50 years.
	2,000	Two masses weekly for 50 years.
1695	500	An annual mass for 50 years.
1693	2,000	Three masses weekly and an annual "service" for 50 years.
	500	For burial in Minims' church.
1698	1,000	An annual "service" in perpetuity.
1699	1,000	An annual "service" on 9th May, in perpetuity.

To this should be added a further 9,750 livres from entries on other pages of the manuscript [1] and an unspecified amount from "aides et gabelles."

Total sum, excluding annual "rentes" . . . . 110,541 livres
Annual "rentes". . . . .   1,075 livres

Taking the exchange rate of 13 livres = £1, the sum given for the endowment of masses and in donation can be put at £8,500 (XVIIth Century sterling).[2] The purchasing power of this sum may be judged very approximately from the entries below concerning the purchase of a Turkish carpet for the High Altar steps (126 livres) and the loan of 20,000 livres (i.e. less than 1/5th of the sum of endowment and donations) raised to build the west door of the Church. We may consider that the sum of 6,000 livres donated in 1669 by Catherine Girard against a "rente" of 300 livres as being equal to 5% interest on a capital sum of at least £6,000 (1964), although the modern equivalent is almost impossible to evaluate; what is certain, however, is that by the close of the XVIIth century the Minims at La Place Royale had a very considerable capital sum at their disposal.

B. GIFTS FOR BUILDING – For the Church and its chapels a total of 168,050 livres was subscribed up to the end of the century (see pp. 119–163 of the manuscript).[3] Some idea of the value of this in terms of the cost of building in the XVIIth century may be obtained from an entry on p. 175; a loan of 20,000 livres was raised to cover the total cost of the erection of the main door; this "portail" was the

---

[1] pp. 125, 128, 178 and 179.
[2] Mersenne, *Cogitata physico-mathematica*, Paris, 1644, p. 32. This rate seems to have been constant for we find Locke obtaining the same exchange in 1675–1679; see J. Lough, *Locke's travels in France, 1675–1679*, Cambridge, 1953, p. lxvi.
[3] See *Histoire de la ville de Paris* by the abbé Lebeuf, Paris, 1867, III, pp. 495 et sq.

work of Mansart himself; it was his last work, and can be seen in the engraving of la Place Royale in the Bibliothèque Nationale.[1] During the period 1630–1660 houses in Paris, described as "maisons très communes," varied from 1,000 livres to 3,300 livres.[2]

C. PROPERTY – Many of the provincial "couvents" had extensive lands which brought in a substantial revenue and furnished valuable assets in kind. The Minims at Rheims, for example, held excellent vineyards on the "Montagne de Reims." But, apart from their own site, the Minimes de la Place Royale held little property and none of it of any considerable value; moreover, three of the six sites were purchased during the XVIIIth century out of sums bequeathed in the seventeenth.

(a) A house and chapel, dedicated to Sainte Susanne, in the Rue S. Honoré. The Archbishop of Paris had a lien on this and the chapel was incorporated in the Eglise S. Roch. (Affaire de la Chapelle Sainte Susanne.)
(b) A house in the Rue Marivault.
(c) A house in the Rue des Ursins.
(d) A house in the Rue Saint Claude.
(e) A farm at Frementeau.
(f) An "hôtellerie" at Juvisy.

An analysis of the conditions upon which the sums of money were vested in the Minimes de la Place Royale is of considerable interest. It would have been impossible for them, one imagines, to fulfil to the letter the obligation of saying so many masses. There was sufficient complexity for the main Feast Days, witness a scrap of paper that I found in the fifty or so blank pages at the end of the manuscript in the Mazarine and on which someone had jotted down the masses to be said on these days alone. To this would have to be added all the regular names for, say, the Monday or Friday on which the Feast Day happened to fall. Surely there can have been little more than a calling of names at the daily Celebration? Yet for this privilege such large sums were spent. Two of the conditions which were common are worthy of comment, the first of these being the right to be buried within the conventual church. The extremely high price that people were prepared to pay for this was a bone of contention between the Orders and

[1] See reproductions in the Appendix.
[2] G. d'Avenel, *Histoire de tous les prix*, Paris, 1894–1926, vol. VI, pp. 292 *et sq.*

the secular clergy who lost thereby an important source of personal income. Common burial, even when the departed was fortified by the rites of Mother Church, was a somewhat macabre affair in the XVIIth century; it may have been softened if the inhumation was performed in the privacy of one of the monastic houses and hence it is probable that families would urge the senior members to ensure burial not only in hallowed, but in private ground. The second condition points to the fact that the Order acted as a sort of security not only for spiritual safety but for material prosperity; in short the Order acted as a sort of Life Insurance for the buiyng of annuities. How else is one to explain the entries, and there several of them, which specify that a sum was given to the Minims against a "rente" of so many livres. The rate of interest was also fairly high: thus in 1669, Catherine Girard gave the Order 6,000 livres in exchange for a "rente" of 300 livres (i.e. 5%). The Order can have had little more than the security until the death of the person "insured."

Two of the conditions imposed are of purely local interest for la Place Royale but similar conditions were made in connection with donations to the other houses of the Order. In 1680, a gift of 250 livres was made for the specific purpose of the upkeep of the lamp on the High Altar.[1] The value of this gift can be appreciated by comparison with an entry under 1675: "Grand tapis de Turquie pour mettre sur les marches du Gd. Autel. Il a coûté 126 livres, 10 sols." [2] Then there are the conditions laid down by Madeleine de Varrège in 1676: "... elle nous a donné 500 livres pour aider à bâtir une bibliothèque. Elle nous a permis de nous en servir pour la provision de vin à condition de remettre cette somme tous les ans mais que, si ce bâtiment ne se faisait dans le temps de 6 années, cette somme de 500 livres servirait tous les ans à faire la provision de vin. Elle a demandé d'avoir part aux prières des Religieux." [3] It is quite certain from all the records that the library was not completed within these six years.

There is one reflexion of the financial difficulties occasioned by Louis XIV's costly wars. On page 182, and under the year 1690, we find the following reference to the increase of various "charges par édits" and the obligation to surrender all "argenteries qui excèderaient le poids d'une once [4] pour être converties en espèce; le Roi en donna

---

[1] p. 179.
[2] p. 178.
[3] See above sub anno 1676.
[4] p. 183, reference to a chalice weighing 3 marcs. "Once" – 8 onces = 1 marc. Almost exactly equivalent of English ounce and half-pound respectively. There is very little infor-

l'exemple, les Princes et les peuples suivirent ... comme cela ne suffisait pas encore, il eut recours aux églises qui avaient quelques argenteries." Six candlesticks went from the Place Royale. In this time of economic stress Louis XIV looked with envy and annoyance upon the Orders with their immunities from taxation and their secure income; the document from which I have quoted and which I have transcribed in part reveals the details that lie behind such pungent criticisms that one finds in the pages of La Bruyère's *Des biens de fortune* or *De la mode*, in La Fontaine's *Fables* and in Vauban's *Dîme royale*.

One important source of revenue was the Quête. It has been estimated that rather more than half of the Minims' expenditure in 1660 was covered by the Quête (456,750 livres out of 912,500 livres); there is unfortunately no means of checking this statement which occurs in the anonymous *Nombre des ecclésiastiques*;[1] by no means all the account books are extant. If as much as a half was in fact found in this way, it is some indication that the Franciscan inspiration behind the Order was not extinct. Nevertheless, had the Order followed the Franciscan ideal in its entirety this would have been their sole income. Relatively speaking, the Order was poor and it is interesting to compare their position with that of the older orders; the figures are for 1768.[2]

	"COUVENTS"	RELIGIEUX	RENTES ON LIVRES
Minimes	153	975	373,229
St. Benoît	70	773	1,714,780
Cîteaux	228	1,873	2,235,366
Bénédictins de S. Maur	191	1,917	2,829,313
Capucins ⎫	432	4,397	Nil
Récollets ⎬ i.e. Franciscans	223	2,534	Nil
Cordeliers ⎭	345	2,395	451,536

mation about gold or silver plate and ornaments in the Minims' churches; the only complete inventory that I have been able to find is for the small "couvent" of la Guiche – Archives Départementales, Saône-et-Loire, Série H, 354–356; Monsieur Y. Bizardel in his transcript of parts of the *Conclusions capitulaires des Minimes d'Aubeterre* refers on p. 31 to the scant ornaments, plate etc. that the Minims possessed at Aubeterre.

[1] p. 39. Published in Paris in 1660.
[2] Figures from the report of the Commission des Réguliers already cited.

CHAPTER II

OPPOSITION TO THE ORDER

Opposition to the Order was of three kinds: direct opposition by Huguenots, the burning down and sacking of religious houses; opposition by the secular clergy and opposition by the general populace.

I. DIRECT OPPOSITION

This was confined to the XVIth century and does not come into the present consideration, except in so far as all religious and political questions in the XVIIth century must be taken against the background of upheaval during the Wars of Religion. The Minims had suffered; their "couvents" at Châteliers, Châtellerault, Gien and Bracancour had been sacked, but they had suffered no more acutely than anyone else on either side. During the XVIIth century their encounters with Huguenots amounted to little more than open debate with them in the market-place. E. G. Léonard in his recent history of protestantism [1] has shown how the spirit of controversy was weakened by the Edict of Nantes.[2] He makes a further statement which it will be convenient to discuss here: catholic controversialists in the XVIth century, he says, chose to dispute biblical themes which they knew little enough about but, he continues, these of the XVIIth century were courteous, erudite and skilful, inspired by the example of Saint François de Sales.[3] During the XVIIth century the Minims' encounters with the Protestants amounted to little more than open debate in the market-place. In several localities, notably at Castres and Pont-Audemer, the controversy became more than usually acrimonious, while Chichon's dispute with a minister of the Reformed Church in Poitiers shows

---

[1] *Histoire Générale du Protestantisme*, 2 vols. Paris, 1961.
[2] Vol. II, pp. 312 *et sq.*
[3] *ibid.*, p. 323.

that controversy had reached a low level of debating skill – a long way from the "controverse instruite et courtoise" mentioned by M. Léonard, although they are not perhaps important enough incidents to invalidate his generalisation; we shall return to them later. The generations of the early sixteen-hundreds had too bitter a memory of the previous century to be easily won over by mere eloquence or doctrinal dispute; a challenge to fundamental attitude of heart and mind was required, hence the Salesian and, later, the Pascalian methods of persuasion on the one hand, and recourse to new brutality culminating in the Dragonnades on the other. The Minims had their connexion with both the Salesian and the erudite methods of dealing with Protestant opposition; Saint François de Sales was a Tertiary of the Order of Minims and was, according to his own word, an admirer of Saint François de Paule. In the early years of the XVIIth century the Order made a notable contribution to biblical studies and Mersenne, as will be shown, took the unprecedented step of securing an authorization for the publication of a protestant work of exegesis. By examining the part that the Order played in controversy up to 1630 we have an object-lesson in the major trend of Catholic-Huguenot confrontation at the outset of the century, ranging from Chichon's tirades to the philological exactitudes of Jean Bruno and Mersenne.

II. OPPOSITION FROM THE SECULAR CLERGY

From the information previously given under the heading *Finances*, it is evident that the religious orders became rich at the expense of the secular clergy in that they acquired large sums of money as "fondations" for saying mass for the departed; they also granted burial within their churches and took the burial dues which the parish clergy claimed as theirs – the rapacious habits of the clergy accompanying a body to the grave were mercilessly exposed by La Fontaine in *Le Curé et le Mort*. The feeling of resentment was widespread; one of the first acts after the building of a conventual church was to apply to the Bishop for a licence to inter bodies within the church. Such licences are extant for Tournay, in the Pyrenees, and for Dieppe; they were preserved with other documents establishing the right to perform this office. Disputes between the Order and the secular clergy were numerous and acrimonious; out of disputes such as these came some of the most pungent criticism not only against the orders but against the Church as a whole. It is valuable therefore to be able to examine in some detail a concrete example of this type of dispute. The Couvent de la Place Royale lay within the parish of S. Paul, a large church in the Rue S. Antoine. The curés between 1620 and 1640 were the abbés Ladvocat and Mazure, who both repeatedly arraigned the Minimes de la Place Royale for impinging upon their rights. The case was set out in a printed address [1] to the Parlement de Paris in 1641 and may be summarized as follows:

(a) The original foundation had been for a hospice for 20, whereas there was now a fully established "couvent" with more than 100 "religieux."
(b) The Minims administered the sacraments, even on Easter Sunday.
(c) "... ils attirent le peuple en bénissant et départant eau bénite, cierge, Cendres, Rameaux, Pain Bénit, ceintures, cordons, petits habits et choses semblables, donnant permission de manger de la viande aux jours défendus, lire la Bible et livres censurés, bref en tout donnant toutes les libertés."
(d) Confessions heard out of the confessional; irregularity of ritual; carrying the Host to the sick in their own homes "sur une patente sans ciboire en peril de tomber et d'irrévérance"; administration of last rites without the secular clergy having been informed.
(e) Unseemly behaviour towards the clergy of S. Paul when accompanying the body of those who had chosen burial within the Minims' church.[2]

The Parlement de Paris was therefore requested to see to it that:

(1) There should be no interference with parochial duty.
(2) The Minims should be obliged to make a "reposoir" before the door of S. Paul during the *Procession du Saint-Sacrement*.[3]
(3) They should observe the Patronal and all other feasts appropriate to the Parish.
(4) They should bless *Rameaux* etc. for their own use only.
(5) They should not perform the Churching of Women.
(6) They should pay 50 livres a head per annum for "droits curiaux."
(7) They should pray for the parish clergy in the same way as for themselves.

Of the Minims' defence we know rather less. In 1621 and in 1629 they were defended by the Avocat Fremin, and a résumé of his brief is extant under the title *Avis sur le plaidoyer de l'avocat Desaguetz*.[4] Their

---

[1] Archives Nationales, L. 952. See Bibliography (Manuscripts).
[2] See the *Registres Capitulaires des Minimes de la Place Royale*. Archives Nat., LL. 1564 sub anno 1628, "août, le 28 dudit mois à l'occasion de l'enterrement de M. de la Roche qui avait élu sa sépulture en ce couvent, et prévoyant la violence que pourraient nous faire le curé de S. Paul et les siens ..."
[3] Archives Nationales, LL. 1565, *Registres Capitulaires* etc. sub anno 1644.
[4] See Bibliography, Manuscripts, Bibliothèque Historique de la Ville de Paris, No. 130894. Undated but presumably printed for the defence of the Minims in 1640.

final defence was based on four points: that Desaguetz had wrongly interpreted the Papal Bulls granting the initial establishment at La Place Royale; that he had wrongly interpreted the intentions of the Council of Trent concerning the religious orders; that he had ignored the Clementine "Religiosi" and, most important, that he had overlooked the liberties of the Gallican Church. In a pamphlet, which is undated, but which may have been issued in the hope of influencing the final judgement in the early months of 1646, the Abbé Mazure gave an *Extrait du Concile général Lateran*.[1] The text is set out in parallel columns of the original on one side and a French translation on the other; on the last page the abbé added an extract from the Council of Trent, session 24 under the 13th heading. It was the duty of the bishops, he quotes, to ensure that all the populace within their jurisdiction was divided into parishes, "unicuique suum peculiaremque Parrochum assignent, qui eas (i.e. Parochias) cognoscere valeat et a quo solo licite sacramenta suscipiant. Nonobstantibus quibuscumque privilegiis consuetudinibus etiam immemorabilis." To which, as a parting shot, Mazure has added, "Quant aux privilèges dont les religieux se veulent prévaloir, ils sont tous révoqués ou du moins réduits aux termes communs du droit."

Was this a "cause célèbre" in the XVIIth century? It appears to be unknown but it remained before the Parlement de Paris for many years and the issues at stake were important enough, for the very existence of the orders was in question and the forces mustered became impressive. The clergy of S. Eustache joined the abbé Mazure and the clergy of S. Paul, while every order in Paris joined forces with the Minims and their enumeration takes up two sides of the printed "arrêt." Below is a shortened form of this "arrêt":

Arrêts de la cour de Parlement du 27 mars 1646, portant règlement entre les curés, Religieux et Religieuses, touchant les enterrements des séculiers. Paris, 1646.[2]

Entre Maître Nicolas Mazure, Prêtre, Docteur en Théologie de la Faculté de Paris et maison de Sorbonne, Curé de l'église Parochiale de S. Paul, demandeur en requête du 13 avril 1641 d'une part: et les Religieux Minimes du Couvent de la Place Royale à Paris, défendeurs d'autre: et entre lesdits Minimes ... et ledit Mazure etc ... (there follow two pages of previous cases). Vu par la cour ... (there follows a further citation of cases going back to François L'Advocat, Curé de S. Paul v. Minimes de la Place Royale, 1629) ... ce faisant, que défenses fussent faites auxdits

---

[1] See the general catalogue of the printed books in the Bibliothèque Nationale, under *Mazure (l'abbé N.)*.

[2] Bibliothèque Nationale, *Arrêts* etc. 23668 (652–751) No. 658, 24 mars, 1646.

Religieux de lever ou faire lever les corps des personnes décédées dans ladite ville (de Paris) et faubourgs, et les inhumer et enterrer dans leurs églises sans congé et permission du curé en la paroisse duquel était demeurant au jour de son décès la personne décédée, et lors que lesdits paroissiens ... par leurs testaments ... auraient élu leurs sépultures en aucunes des églises desdits couvents ou monastères situés dans le détroit et limite de ladite paroisse du défunt, le corps ... étant levé et conduit par le curé ou vicaire de la paroisse et les prêtres habitués d'icelle en l'églisse du couvent, icelui curé ou vicaire ne serait tenu faire aucune présentation dudit corps, ni harangue auxdits religieux à l'entrée de la porte de leurs églises, audit cas serait loisible d'entrer avec lesdits prêtres en l'église ... et au milieu de la nef, faire mettre et déposer le corps du défunt, et après avoir fait chanter le pseaume "De Profundis," et les oraisons et prières accoutumées, lesdits religieux feraient le surplus de la sépulture, et après les cérémonies de laquelle appartiendrait et serait pris par ledit curé tout le luminaire qui aurait été porté au convoi et enterrement, et celui qui serait autour du corps, sans que lesdits religieux puissent prétendre aucune chose, fors et réservé s'ils avaient assisté audit convoi les deux torches que d'eux d'iceux religieux auraient portées à côté de leurs croix, lesquelles torches appartiendraient à leur convoi ... (There then follows a further citation of cases.) ... Dit a été, que la cour faisant droit sur les demandes respectivement faites par les parties ... a ordonné et ordonne que toutes les fois et quantes qu'aucun particulier aura élu sa sépulture dans l'église desdits Minimes, ou d'autres religieux ou religieuses de cette ville et faubourgs de Paris, soit que le monastère se trouve construit dedans ou dehors l'étendue de la paroisse du défunt, le curé ou son vicaire lèvera le corps et le conduira avec son clergé jusques à la porte de l'église du couvent ou ledit défunt aura élu sa sépulture, auquel lieu ledit corps sera reçu par le Supérieur dudit monastère ou autre religieux à ce commis, et après que ledit curé ou vicaire se retirera avec son clergé, et seront les cierges et torches qui auraient servi au convoi partagées également par moitié entre le curé et lesdit religieux. A fait et fait inhibitions et défenses auxdits religieux de lever les corps des défunts qui auraient élu leur sépulture en leur église, sinon en cas de refus des curés ou leurs vicaires, et après sommation dûment faite, le tout sans préjudice aux accords et translations faites entre aucuns dedits curés, religieux et religieuses pour raison desdits enterrements lesquels seront entretenus entre eux sans défense. Prononcé le 27 mars 1646.

This was confirmed only after two ghoulish attempts had been made to prolong the affair; whatever the legal rights of the case may have been, the secular clergy certainly lost on the count of moral law.

Arrêt de la cour de Parlement de Paris confirmatif d'autre arrêt en ladite cour le 27 mars 1646.[1]

---

[1] Bibliothèque Nationale, *Arrêts* etc. 23668 (652–751) No. 666.

Vu par la cour ... (summary of above) ... pour éluder l'effet duquel arrêt lesdits curés ont résolu entre eux par un complot prémédité d'envoyer le soir en carrosse les corps de ceux qui auraient élu sépulture dans l'église desdits religieux, ou au moins obliger les parents de ce faire, en refusant de les conduire avec leur clergé jusques à la porte de leur église, ainsi qu'il a été ordonné par ledit arrêt; et de fait ledit curé de S. Paul, le 7 avril dernier aurait envoyé par un de ses prêtres avec un autre ecclésiastique lever le corps d'un petit enfant, décédé le jour précédent en la maison de Messire Jannin de Castille ... lequel devait être apporté en l'église des suppliants où est la sépulture des sieurs de Castille; lesquels prêtre et ecclésiastique de S. Paul conduisirent le corps dans un carrosse jusques au-devant de la porte de l'église des suppliants et de retirèrent à l'instant sans attendre que le Supérieur et les religieux fussent venus recevoir le corps de leur main et leur certifier que l'enfant était baptisé, de sorte que les suppliants furent contraints ... de recevoir le corps et de protester seulement de la contravention qui était faite audit arrêt.

Comme aussi le 12 avril était décédé sur la paroisse de S. Eustache le sieur d'Arses, Trésorier de France en Bourgogne, qui avait désiré d'être enterré en l'église des suppliants, le corps leur fut amené sur le soir dans un carrosse, sans assistance d'aucun clergé ni luninaire, accompagné seulement du vicaire de la paroisse de S. Eustache, revêtu d'une robe longue de deuil, avec un bonnet carré, qui était avec un autre ecclésiastique dans le carrosse avec le corps: lequel vicaire ayant voulu offrir le corps en cette forme ... ledit Supérieur fit difficulté de recevoir le corps, pour n'avoir été conduit par le Curé de la paroisse ou le vicaire avec le clergé de l'église, conformément à l'arrêt. Néanmoins il fut obligé à la prière des parents et pour éviter le scandale de faire lever le corps qui avait été posé devant la porte de l'église de leur couvent ... (There follows a restatement of the original "arrêt.")

Nor is this an isolated case. At the same time as the "affaire Mazure" the Minimes de Sillé-le-Guillaume (near le Mans) were engaged in a lawsuit with the curé de Saint Etienne; their Corrector wrote to the Corrector of la Place Royale asking for advice [1] – evidence enough of the notoriety of the case within the Order. The Minimes de Dieppe were likewise engaged in a protracted dispute with the curé de Saint-Rémy for, amongst their papers, there is a liasse of documents summarising the dispute and containing by way of supporting evidence the printed statements relevant to the "affaire Mazure" and a printed Arrêt du Grand Conseil du Roi, 21 mai, 1647, allowing the Minims to assist at interments.[2] The Minimes de Tournay (on the Spanish frontier) also preserved carefully all documents relating to burial

[1] Archives Départementales, Sarthe, Série H, 1346.
[2] Archives Départementales, Seine-Maritime, Série H, Minimes de Dieppe, liasse 4 (f), (my classification) – see Bibliography.

disputes, for they too had had their difficulties; the Bishop of Tarbes had granted them the right to perform burials in their church but after a lapse of fifty years their right was challenged by Guillaume Capvern, or Cabbert, Archiprêtre de Tarbes, who acted out of "un pur mouvement de malice et de haine qu'il a conçu contre les religieux Minimes." [1] Another case was fought between the Minimes de Blaye (Gironde) and the "vicaires perpétuels" of the parishes of Saint Sauveur.[2] An even longer case than those mentioned was before the Sénéchaussée of Angoulême for forty years; this case had its origins as far back as 1617 when the Bishop of Périgueux annexed the living of S. Quentin to the "couvent" at Aubeterre (Charente). This arrangement called for no adverse comment, "les PP. Minimes remplissant leurs devoirs ... à la satisfaction et édification des paroissiens," until 1690 when the abbé Noël de Rivauger was given the "cure" of S. Quentin. He at once claimed full rights as curé and lodged a complaint with the Sénéchal at Angoulême (8 September, 1690). Shortly after this, a Minim was prevented from saying Mass and from preaching; new representations were made and a settlement reached whereby the Minims paid Rivauger 300 livres annually but retained the benefice granted by the bishop in 1617. An appeal was then made by Rivauger to the Parlement de Paris with a whole host of calumnies from both sides and an invocation of the liberties of the Gallican Church on the part of the Minims; this brought Letters Patent in confirmation of all the Minimes' rights to the benefice (December 1696). The secular clergy was not to be pacified and the dispute went on until at least 1736 when an inventory of the documents from which I have quoted was drawn up.[3] A similar case involved the clergy of Valence, who took by devolution a benefice belonging to the Minimes de Romans; it went successively before the Sénéchal of Valence, the Parlement de Grenoble and the Grand Conseil without any decisive action being taken.[4]

Disputes similar to the ones I have quoted bring no credit to either side, and it was out of such confusion and strife that later critics were

---

[1] Archives Départementales, Pyrénées (Hautes), Série H, 415; see also Série H, 234, the Minimes de Vic-en-Bigorre were granted similar permission in 1611, see Série H, 245.

[2] Archives Départementales, Gironde, Série G, 620.

[3] Archives Départementales, Charente, Série H, xxxii, *Mémoire touchant la fondation du couvent d'Aubeterre et de la cure de S. Quentin unie à icelui et le procès que nous avons eu avec Mre. Noël de Rivauger; avec un inventaire de toutes les pièces nécessaires pour le défendre quand on nous attaquera* ... *1736*.

[4] *Factum pour les Minimes du couvent du Péage* (i.e. Romans, Drôme). Undated, probably c. 1630; in the Bibliothèque Municipale de Valence.

to pour scorn and contempt on the whole Church. It seems on the whole that the Minims were more magnanimous than the secular clergy; they had a more genuine care for the people, taking the sacrament to the sick and dying without bothering about intricate details of ritual, allowing them to read the Scriptures, interpreting with latitude the rules about eating meat on certain fast days – they, who lived in perpetual Lent.

The cases are also interesting in the reiterated insistance upon the liberties of the Gallican Church. The Order enjoyed a uniquely privileged position vis-à-vis French royalty and there is a strong patriotism underlying the writings of many of its members; at a time when the religious orders were held in little repute at Court, the Minims could count upon a measure of support. Their invocation of Gallican rights was therefore well calculated to carry the day when they found themselves the subject of litigation.

III. OPPOSITION FROM THE POPULACE

One hears little enough of the common people in France of the XVIIth century and it is not surprising that there is little evidence of any opposition to the spread of the Order from them. How could they oppose it if the Bishop or Seigneur decided to establish the Order in a town? There would be grumblings at the expense, for the town would have to find some money for the initial foundation and grants would have to be made from time to time, during an outbreak of plague, for example, when the begging for alms would be discontinued, or when the Provincial Chapter was held in the town. The enumeration of the orders in Paris took, as we have seen, two sides of print on quarto pages; in the Provinces too there was the same proliferation of orders and some quite small towns might have upwards of a dozen "couvents." Boze in his *Histoire de l'église d'Apt"* (Apt, 1820) gives the following account of opposition to the establishment of the Order there "... une pieuse dame de Marseille ayant offert mille écus pour l'acquisition d'un local, les Capucins furent reçus d'après une délibération prise en 1612. Quelques particuliers préférant les Récollets ou les Minimes, formèrent l'opposition."

On two occasions at least, the Consuls of a town openly voiced their opposition. The Minimes wished to found a "couvent" in Agen in 1645, but first wished to establish their privilege of exemption from "taille." The Consuls objected and were not to be moved even when they received a letter interceding on the Minims' behalf from their staunch supporter, Anne d'Autriche, the Queen Mother. Opposition continued until 1657 and the "couvent" was recognised at the General Chapter of 1661. Complaints still continued to come up and there were rumblings of it until 1729; Agen was one of those towns where the orders proliferated, causing a disproportionate amount of taxation to be borne by the common people.[1] Opposition of a more general nature was voiced in Valence where, in 1603, the Bishop wished to establish the Order and build a "couvent" on a site near the river. A school had previously stood on this site and the Consuls objected on the grounds that "un bon collège pour instruire la jeunesse" would be a preferable investment. Nothing more is heard of the matter until 1608, when a sum of 1,200 livres was found by the town to help the construction of the Minims' church. The Consuls again objected but, in the absence of further details and in the knowledge that the Minimes de Valence were fully established in the town shortly after this, one has to suppose a quick overriding of the Consuls' objection.[2]

At Béziers there was opposition of a more vigorous kind. During the years of plague 1629–1630 the Minims' "couvent" had been used as an infirmary. When plague was again rife in the town in 1652 it was assumed that the same facilities would be granted. The Corrector refused, whereupon a riot broke out; the Minims were expelled and all their possessions flung into the street. It is an interesting reflexion on the times to note that they were allowed back the next day so that they could celebrate Mass in order to use up a quantity of consecrated Host in the Tabernacle and so avoid its profanation. After this affray, the Minims refused to go back into their original "couvent" and a new one was provided for them on the outskirts of the town, the expense falling on the inhabitants. An added item of expense was the charge made for all their damaged property and a detailed list was drawn up for costing by the Consuls. This is one of very few documents which permit us to know domestic details of one of the smaller and poorer houses. There is no mention of a library; their cooking utensils, beds, linen, refectory tables and benches were exiguous in the extreme.[3] It is only fair to pint out that in many other towns the Minims cooperated

---

[1] Archives Municipales, Agen; Série GG, 190. The original letter from the Queen Mother to the Consuls is extant.

[2] Valence, Archives Municipales, Série BB, 13.

[3] Béziers, *Relations des Consuls du 14 juillet, 1652,* and printed in *Bulletin de la Société Archéologique de Béziers,* 2e série, vol. 14, pp. 223–237 and 257–261.

fully with the civil authorities in time of plague and that several of them died ministering to the sick.

Since both Valence and Béziers were centres of protestantism, one cannot help wondering whether behind these two examples of civil opposition there does not lie a history of long-standing acrimony on both sides.

PART II

THE SPIRITUAL

RELIGIOUS LIFE AND WORK
WITHIN THE ORDER

In his *Journal* for 1956 M. Julien Green wrote:

Un livre sur Bernières-Louvigny. Les austérités du XVIIe siècle, le pessimisme des meilleurs quant à leur propre salut. Si les justes ont tant de peine à eviter l'enfer, qu'en sera-t-il de nous?[1]

A similar reflexion dominates one as one reads the works of devotion and spirituality composed by members of the Order of Minims. How could an Order which demanded from all its members the most rigorous abregations thrive in the easy land of France and, in particular, during the seventeenth century? The East, the desert; these are the proper places, it would seem, for the practice of asceticism.[2] A barren hillside in Provence or in the Gévaudan might be considered as fertile for this sort of austerity; but it was in the valley of the Loire, in the pleasant parkland of le Plessis-lès-Tours, that the Order put down its first roots into French soil and, subsequently, at Nigeon (Chaillot) on the fringe of Paris overlooking the Seine; at Amboise and at Gien. In trying to account for the popularity of the Order, some purely historical reasons have already been suggested – the favour that its Founder received at Court and the long line of Royal Patrons who followed the example of Louis XI. To these reasons should be added the fact that there already existed an ancient tradition of monasticism in Europe and, particularly as a factor conditioning the popularity of an austere religion, the fact that the Wars of Religion forced extremes upon the French nation. But these conditions could just as easily have produced a worldly and easy conformism to

---

[1] *Journal, novembre 1956, Le bel aujourd'hui,* Paris, 1958, p. 264. It was a Minim, Robert de Saint-Gilles, who prepared one of the earliest editions of Bernières-Louvigny.

[2] G. Penco, *Storia del monachismo in Italia dalle origini alla fine del Medio Evo,* Rome, 1961; "L'ideale monastico appare di primi rappresentanti dell' ascetismo orientale come inseparabile dall' ambiente di deserto."

the dominant mood of mundane complacency, so that the answer to the question must be sought in an analysis of the spiritual motive power behind the Order and in its contribution to the religious and intellectual life of France.

Indelibly stamped on the Order was the strange personality of Saint François de Paule himself. The austerity, mysticism and charity of this extraordinary man became a part of French tradition; books telling of his birth, his ascetism in the deserted Calabrian countryside and of his gathering together a few hermits were popular reading amongst the devout. They told of his reputation as a thaumaturge, of a man who, with the wave of a hand and a word of prayer, could prevent rocks from falling on innocent victims below; they repeated stories of his ability to heal, to cast out devils and to raise the dead; they also repeated the more remarkable legends of his having crossed the Strait of Messina on his cloak and of his strange appearance above the ground at le Plessis. The most authoritative of these lives was by Hilarion de Coste, *Le Portrait en petit de Saint François de Paule* [1]; the author was a thoughtful historian, and his work quotes the relevant documents in a carefully composed Appendix and set of foot-notes. Other lives of the Saint such as Du Vivier's, *Vie et miracles de Saint François de Paule* [2] and Pierre Duval's work of the same title [3] were less carefully documented, if at all. The life of François de Paule was, of course, included in the compendious *Les Vies des Saints* by the two Minims Simon Martin and François Giry,[4] while other members of the Order in one way or another gave accounts of his life which saw the press – François Victon, Adrien Roussel, Claude Raffron, Pierre Pijart, Nicolas Lesguillier and Ambroise Granjon.[5] In some ways the most remarkable of all these lives was the one by Etienne Dondé with its engravings and its account of the original portrait of the Saint by the painter Bourdichon [6]; we see a traditional, patriarchal figure with staff and hood, upturned eyes and flowing beard. Or else we see him kneeling in prayer or with a far-off, tortured look; he is seen in all the familiar incidents of his life both in Calabria and in France; he is seen haranguing the King of Naples, curing the sick of Tours.

---

[1] Paris, 1655.
[2] Paris, 1609.
[3] Rouen, 1640. Added to this life was a set of canticles, see Bibliography.
[4] See Bibliography under both these authors and pp. 121 *et sq.*
[5] All referred to in Bibliography.
[6] I have given a short analysis of this work on pp. 221–222 and a reproduction of one of the pages of illustration is in the Appendix, opposite p. 247.

Miracles were not lacking at the inception of the Order in France; but to one in particular, I think, some importance should be attached since it affected a royal prerogative. In the words of François Victon:

Ioannes Lescart, Turonensis mercator, scrophis a quibus per Carolum VIII tactu Regio sanctus non fuerat, Sancti Viri precibus liberatur.[1]

A man who could thus overcome "The King's Evil" was assured of acclaim, and his Royal patrons would have desired him as an ally or else would have seen to it that he was liquidated. There is, therefore, this highly mystical background to the spirituality of the Order. Voltaire has spoken of the necessity of having some miracle in the early stages of a religious movement, and the curing of Jean Lescart in Tours probably stood the Minims in good stead, just as Fox's prediction to the Justice of the Peace advanced the cause of the Quakers. However, the spiritual life of the Minims was not entirely founded on the mystical and supernatural; the Founder's purpose was a practical one – the exercise of charity. The spiritual and practical elements are brought together in the *Rule* of the Order.

This *Rule* was formulated by the Founder himself and it remained inviolable throughout the period under review. The earliest example of the *Rule* in French is the fragmentary document in the Bibliothèque de l'Arsenal; it is of uncertain date but is almost certainly contemporaneous with the earliest stages of the Order's development in France.[2] The Minims' rule was printed as early as 1525 for use in the "couvent" of Nigeon, whereas the rule of the Benedictines which was formulated by Saint Benedict of Aniane in the VIIIth century, on a model of the original rule of Saint Benedict, was not printed until 1661 by L. Holstenius in his *Codex Regularum*.[3] The printed *Regula Fratrum Minimorum* (Nigeon, 1528) is a similar production to the work of 1525 but adds to it sections dealing with ritual and with the privileges conferred upon the Order.[4] The *Rule* contains but four articles – Obedience to the Church through the Correctors and Superiors of the Order; Chastity; Humility; Perpetual Fasting. The first three of these articles are common to all orders but the perpetual Lentern fast of the

---

[1] *Vita et miracula S. Francesci a Paula*, Paris, 1627, p. 167.

[2] See previously, p. 4. There existed an Italian *Regola Prima* approved by Pope Alexander VI in a bull, 26 Feb. 1493.

[3] See G. Penco, *Benedicti Regula*, Florence, 1958, p. xx.

[4] The British Museum has a particularly fine copy (C.29.b.16) printed on vellum and with coloured capitals and a few miniature, hand-coloured illustrations which appear to be either copies of the Bourdichon portrait of the Founder or to have been closely inspired by it; see sig. a i; sig. A i; end of *Praecepta Decalogi* facing sig. a i, and at end, sig. c iiii, verso.

Minims was a distinctive feature and one of which the Order was proud. The meaning of this article has been defined in the *Introduction* with reference to Nicolas Lesguillier's *Rule*, composed when he was Corrector at La Place Royale.[1]

What we may call the "spiritual rule" was confined to a few precepts governing attendance at Mass, observation of the Canonical Hours, partaking of Holy Communion, prayer; the "administrative rule" briefly but firmly laid down the ordening of the conventual life, silence at all meals and after Vespers, the provision of time for study and meditation, the punishments meted out for offences. The *Rule*, no less than the life of the Saint and Founder, became the subject of printed works in the XVIIth century – Giry and Pijart, to whom reference has been made, included the *Rule* in their lives of the Saint; François de la Noue included it in his general history of the Order.[2] The asceticism of the Order and the harshness of the privations that its members accepted were therefore widely known outside the cloister: "Pain, eau, de temps à autre quelques légumes, voici les ragoûts de Saint François de Paule," declaimed Bossuet in his *Panégiriques de Saint François de Paule*,[3] and a recent commentator has shown how Bossuet looked upon this "Minime des Minimes" as a startling example of self-effacement to be followed in an age dominated in certain circles by an invincible amour-propre.[4] Bourdaloue too insisted upon the same point [5]; nor is it surprising that the two most popular preachers of the seventeenth century drew inspiration from the Minims. Had the personality of their founder been less well-known and had the austerities of his followers been less widely recognised, there was still within the Order something which was calculated to appeal in the seventeenth century. By a simple process of attraction of opposites, a worldly society is likely to be struck by extremes of asceticism; more than this, however, there remains in the seventeenth century a good deal of what we may call "mediaeval religion." Fear of death, fear of the machinations of the Devil, an implicit belief in miracles – these survived; at the same time, there arose a sophisticated

---

[1] Arsenal, MSS No. 1074, p. 307. See also a commentary by the Minim Antoine Ruteau, *De vita quadragesimali in Ordine Minimorum ... sub voto servata*, Mons, 1646.

[2] Paris, 1635, pp. 21–39; 54–58; 73–76.

[3] *Oeuvres*, Paris, 1835, vol. IX, pp. 161 *et sq.*

[4] A. J. Krailsheimer, *Studies in Self-interest*, Oxford, 1962, pp. 184–186. Bossuet preached his first *Carême* at the Minimes de la Place Royale in 1660; see C. Cordonnier, *Le R. P. Barré ... Minime*, Paris, 1932, p. 88 and also the article by J. Truchet in *XVIIe Siècle*, Nos. 50–51, Paris, 1961, pp. 64–76, *Bossuet et l'éloquence religieuse au temps du Carême des Minimes*.

[5] *Sermon ... Fête de Saint François de Paule. Oeuvres*, Paris, 1900, Vol. VI, pp. 136–151.

society which tended towards libertinage. Mysticism and rationalism coexisted. Above all there is the great catholic revival in France with Saint François de Sales and Saint Vincent de Paul, with the work of the Oratory and the organisation of the Seminary of Saint Sulpice – and with the attendant religious disputes which, rather than the gradual development of pastoral care in the growing urban communities, tend to be the conspicuous landmarks in the religious history of the century. The Order of Minims was instrumental in many aspects of the revival and yet managed to remain aloof from the famous controversies over Jansenism, Quietism and the Régale.

We have already seen that the Order was staunchly patriotic in France and therefore tended towards Gallican sympathies in ecclesiastical matters. Now, at the bottom of each of the great controversies there was a question of political loyalties: it was under considerable pressure from France that Jansenism was finally condemned at Rome: and it is well known that the sympathies of the Pope, Innocent XII, were with Fénelon rather than with Bossuet in the Quietist controversy.[1] It is not surprising that an Order which could claim Louis XIV as its own child [2] and whose members wrote long and eulogistic works on the Kings and Queens of France,[3] on the glittering feats of arms wrought by command of the King at La Rochelle [4] and on the mystic symbolism of the Fleur de Lys [5] should have conformed to Gallican requirements. There was a long tradition of loyalty to the throne, and this had been rewarded by the bestowal of important privileges. Nevertheless, it is a remarkable reflexion on the age that one of the most difficult theological problems, that of the Jansenist doctrine of grace, should have been solved without question throughout the Order by the purely formal signature of its members to a document of denunciation in June 1661.[6]

Superficially the Order appears to have affinity with the Quietists. The mysticism seen in some of their writings, in Louis de la Rivière's work on Marie de Valence for example and his *Tableaux des quatre amours*, is akin to the mysticism of the Quietists; of greater significance

---

[1] Witness his utterance, "Erravit Cameracensis excessu amoris Dei; peccavit Meldensis defectu amoris proximi."

[2] By reason of his mother's assiduous prayers on Fridays in the Minims' church, see previously.

[3] See the chapter on Historical Studies.

[4] *Lettres d'un solitaire au Roi . . . faisant la guerre etc.*, Poitiers, 1628, by the Minim A. Chavineau.

[5] Hippolyte Raulin, see Bibliography, Printed Works.

[6] *Registres capitulaires des Minimes de la Place Royale*, Archives Nationales, LL. 1565.

is the particular emphasis which the Order placed on "the pure love of God" and on the quest for "perfection." Monastic perfection, as it was understood by the Minims, was a long way from the passive contemplation of the Quietists; there was the harsh discipline based on firm liturgical principles by which the Order escaped from the odium of enthusiasm. This distinction is on the official level; on the individual level, when it is merely a question of temperament, there is obviously a rapprochement to be made. The Minims spent long hours in contemplation and in meditative prayer, and they would have been at one with the Quietists in their desire for passivity and withdrawal from the world. A work which goes a long way towards explaining the similarity of attitude between the Quietists and the Order is *Les Secrets du Paradis* by the Minim Antoine Masson [1] which has the sub-title ... *ou explication générale des differents états des bienheureux dans le ciel*. In this work the author develops the idea of eternal war between Earth and Heaven: it is impossible to escape the effects of this war unless one is pure [2]; this "cloistered virtue," purity, perfection, call it what one will, is a common bond between the Quietists and the religious orders; moreover, one has only to recall Madame Guyon's attachment to the works of Saint François de Sales and Jeanne de Chantal to realise how near she came to orthodoxy in matters of devotion. But if Masson shows clearly this common bond, he also shows the differences; for him the Heavenly Society (la Société des Saints) is not to be found in mere contemplation but in an active and disciplined body – the Tiers-Ordre – which is seen as a living example of the Kingdom of God.[3] Once again one returns to the theme of discipline and rule which curb enthusiasm.

The third of the great controversies, that of the Régale, did not affect the Minims. They had their disputes with the secular clergy concerning benefices, but the question of vacancy never arose.

The Order was, free to develop along the lines that its Founder and the early Superiors had intended when they formulated the strict rules governing the observance of ritual. Although a detail here and there might become altered at a General Chapter, the ritual laid down by the Founder was the one followed throughout the whole of the seventeenth century; the Provincials and Correctors castigated all lapses. Mass had to be heard each Sunday, the Canonical hours were

---

[1] Paris, 1693.
[2] See especially pp. 345–365.
[3] *ibid.*, p. 312.

to be observed,[1] the Litanies of the Blessed Virgin were to be said each evening after Compline [2]; each Friday, special hymns in praise of the Founder were sung. Sundays and Feast Days had their special ritual according to the Roman Liturgy, but Feasts of special obligation for the Order were limited to two – April 2nd, the day of Saint François de Paule, and September 29th, Saint Michael the Archangel, under whose protection Pope Clement X had placed the Order.

All adornment of the Liturgy was repressed. Gregorian chant was forbidden and Mass was to be sung "cum tremore, alacriter, computando, sine notulis"; and with the added instruction:

Voce quadrata, cum pausa in medio, et sine versuum spatio quo possint dici duo verbi Ave Maria, non prolongando vocem cum cauda, nec abbreviando. Idemque faciendum in Missa conventuali, cum cantatur.[3]

It seems that any aesthetic pleasure to be derived from adornment of the ritual was proscribed so that the fullest attention could be paid to the meaning of the liturgical language; this is the counterpart of the severity of the rules imposed upon bodily pleasures; the twin disciplines of external rigorism and liturgical sparseness forced the adherent to inner contemplation. It was no part of the Founder's intention, or of those who followed him as Superiors of the Order, that any extraordinary ritualistic rigmaroles should be followed – rather the opposite. The *Ceremonial* of the Order has few peculiarities; in this way it is distinct from some of the older orders whose ritual was complex and who had made a speciality of embellishing the Liturgy – the use of music, for example, amongst certain Benedictines, particularly at Solesmes.[4] Saint François de Sales, whose admiration for the Minims

[1] i.e. Matins and Lauds at mid-night.
Prime and Terce at 6 a.m.
Sexte and Nones at 9 a.m. (11 a.m. on Feast Days).
Vespers at 2 p.m. (3 p.m. in Winter and during Lent).
Compline at 6 p.m.
[2] C. Cordonnier, *op. cit.*, pp. 58–59 states that this recitation of the Litanies of the Virgin was a self-imposed discipline undertaken as a mark of gratitude for a privilege obtained for the Order by the Comte d'Allais in 1650. In fact we find references to this practice at a much earlier date, see *Ordonnances* for 1621 referred in the next footnote.
[3] G. Pizzurnus, *Manipulus Minimorum*, Genoa 1697(?), p. 20, sub *Cantus*. For these and subsequent details of ritual I have relied on Pizzurnus, *Missa, Communio, Oratio* etc. and on the *Caeremoniale ad communem usum FF. Ordinis Minimorum*, Florence, 1655. I have also made use of *Ordonnances faites par le R. Père Jean du Bourg, Provincial des Minimes en la Province de Lyon en sa visite de cette Province, 22 mai 1621;* this manuscript is in the Archives Départementales, Rhône, and forms part of a collection of similar *Ordonnances* running from 1571–1789, (Série H., Minimes, L. 35 Minimes de la Province de Lyon, Nos. L. 1 and L. 2 (1–3)).
[4] A. A. King, *Liturgies of the Religious Orders*, London, 1955; see for example p. 62 where the author mentions the desire of certain Benedictines to get away from a more complex liturgy, causing a faction (the Cistercian faction) within the order.

and whose membership of the Tiers-Ordre have been mentioned, acted as president to the chapter of the Feuillants and advocated a simple adherence to the Roman Breviary, criticising as "offensive, childish and obscure" parts of the old Benedictine ritual.[1] François Giry, a Minim of great distinction as we shall see, had this to say about the Founder's intention that ritual should be simple and within the competence of the most humble intellects to follow:

> Notre Bienheureux Père, ayant fait sa règle pour toute sorte de personnes ... il n'a rien voulu prescrire qui ne pût être aisément pratiqué par tout le monde.[2]

There were, then, no subtleties to follow but the harshest reminders of Christ's suffering; there was no softening of the stringent message calling all to repentance and to a renunciation of the World. The body was to be disciplined, and we find such precepts that on Fridays even the members of the Tiers-Ordre were exhorted to say five *Pater* and five *Ave Maria* with their arms outstretched, so that they might take some part in the torment which Christ had suffered.[3] Neither was the partaking of a frequent Communion for the comfort of one's soul recommended by the Founder; Christmas and Easter, Pentecost, the Feasts of the Purification and Assumption of the Virgin,[4] these were the five occasions on which members of the Order were originally required to communicate. By order of the Chapter General which met in Malaga in 1526 two more occasions were added, April 2nd and September 29th – the feasts of the Founder and Patron respectively. Punishment for failure to partake of the Sacrament on these days was severe:

> Omittens dictis diebus Communionem sine causa, tali die silentium servet et comedat in terra panem et aquam dumtaxat et prima sequente Dominica se præparet ad Communionem.[5]

We find however that the Founder's original intention was not strictly followed and, at the General Chapter held in Avignon in 1578, Com-

---

[1] A. A. King, *ibid.*, p. 81.
[2] F. Giry, *La règle du Tiers-Ordre des Minimes*, Paris 1683, p. 27.
[3] *Ibid.*, p. 41.
[4] In the Dominican rite four feasts of Our Lady were observed from the XIIIth century onwards, to these four (Purification, Annunciation, Assumption and Nativity) two more were added in the late XIVth century (Conception of the Virgin, Visitation of the Virgin) and yet a further one in the XVIthe century (Our Lady of the Snows). A. A. King, *op. cit.*, pp. 362–366.
[5] Pizzurnus, *op. cit.*, sub *Communio*.

munion on the first Sunday in each month was ordered. Almost exactly a hundred years later and, one feels, in deliberate opposition to the habits of the Jansenists, a much more frequent Communion was insisted upon; in the *Manipulus* of Pizzurnus we find, under the heading *Communio*, an additional instruction, "Nunc singulis diebus Dominicis," dated from the General Chapter held in Milan in 1679. One of the steps towards this modification was certainly the pamphlet by the French Minim Jacques Ladore, *Le bonheur de la fréquente Communion* [1] written as an obvious counterblast to Arnauld's *Traité de la fréquente Communion* (1643). In their long dispute with the Minimes de la Place Royale, the clergy of S. Paul objected to the ease with which the poor and the sick could obtain the Sacrament and they complained about the apparent lack of reverence with which the Host was carried through the streets, "sans ciboire ... et en tout danger de tomber." It is, perhaps, a question of *ease* rather than of *frequency* which is at the bottom of the whole question of *La Communion Fréquente;* Arnauld did not condemn frequent Communion as such, but rather the facility with which it could be obtained by a rapid and merely formal confession.[2] The long and difficult preparation and the need for real penitence before partaking of Communion which were advocated by Arnauld were never questioned by the Order where discipline in the matter of penitence was harsh. But, for those living in the state of perpetual penitence it is logical that frequent, or even daily Communion, may be partaken; indeed we find Nicolas Barré urging almost daily Communion for the Sœurs Charitables whom he chose to instruct in his schools; to one of these he wrote:

Je trouve bon que vous communiiez tous le jours excepté un jour de la semaine ... à condition qu'on se tiendra au-dessous de toutes les créatures, ne méritant pas de servir de marchepied dans la maison.[3]

The Superiors of the Order were constantly faced with two disciplinary problems; on the one hand there were instances of individuals whose rigorism went to such unheard of lengths that they were in danger of the sin of pride, believing that their self-inflicted privations were in themselves sufficient to fulfil their duties as members of the Order; on the other hand there were those lax members who absented themselves from conventual ceremonies. By insisting upon a more

---

[1] Paris, 1656.
[2] H. Bremond, *Histoire littéraire du sentiment religieux*, Paris, 1916, vol. IX, pp. 48 *et sq.*
[3] *Lettres spirituelles*, Paris, 1698, p. 245.

frequent Communion, the Superiors could curb the excesses of the
fervent who might otherwise have started on the path to enthusiasm
in a Jansenist or Quietist form, and they could insist upon a more
corporate activity amongst the less zealous. The greater frequency of
Communion was also in accordance with a directive of the Council
of Trent (Session XXII, 6); the religious orders founded just before the
Council set an example of frequent communion which was followed
throughout the Church.[1]

During the visit which each Provincial made of his Province, a
report was drawn up and its contents promulgated. These reports
usually drew attention to administrative discipline, such as the proper
keeping of accounts and the maintenance of buildings; from time to
time there were severe personal reprimands and orders for incarcer-
ation.[2] Matters of spiritual discipline and ritual were usually summed
up in a general exhortation to follow the sublime precepts of the
Founder. Of interest, therefore, are the more detailed *Ordonnances*
which Jean du Bourg, Provincial of the Province of Lyons made, on
22nd May, 1621, concerning spiritual discipline [3]:

Office selon la pure règle "voce quadrata." Recommandons au Ven.
P. Correcteur d'avoir l'œil à ce que tous les religieux du chœur, prêtres ou
autres et les Frères oblats, aux jours de fête et dimanches à Matins, Grand'
Messe, vêpres et complies y assistent et commandons à ceux qui sans licence
expresse ou légitime s'en absenteront de dire leur coulpe à la communauté [4] ...

Recommandons aussi la continuation de la prédication après complies
avec les Litanies de la glorieuse V.M. à la fin, laquelle méditation nous
voulons ... durer à tout le moins une heure et demi-heure [5] ... sans que
personne s'en puisse exempter comme aussi sortir des autres offices ...
sans licence etc.

L'hymne de Saint François de Paule notre Père Sig. *Brutio natus* [6] avec
l'antienne *Mundi Contemptor*, le verset et l'oraison seront dorénavant chantés

---

[1] *Enciclopedia Cattolica*, Rome, 1948–1953, under *Communione*, quotes the Théatins, Bar-
nabites and Jesuits in this respect.

[2] For example the order to imprison Claude Pithoys, see p. 135 and the acrimonous
"affaire Flasch-Bachelier," see p. 102.

[3] Archives Départementales, Rhône, Série H, L. 35 etc., see p. 65, note 3.

[4] Performance of some act of penance before the assembled brothers was a common
feature, see Pizzurnus, passim.

[5] Does this mean "une heure et demie" or "une heure pour la prédication et une demi-
heure pour les Litanies"?

[6] Brutio natus Pater hic beatus, / Paula quem mundo peperit ruente, / Quemquem
mirac(u)lis retinet coruscum, / Gallica tellus. / Malint terris humilis videri, / Rebus in
cunctis Minimusque dici: / Celsus, ut tandem superum cateruis / Esset Olympi. / from
Cæremoniale Ordinis Minimorum, Florence, 1655, Appendix V.

tous les vendredis de l'année après vêpres dans la chapelle dudit Saint François de Paule pour l'honneur et la dévotion que nous devons à ce grand homme comme Père de pure, sainte relion.

Ayant aussi averti comme au chapitre définiteur tenu par notre prédécesseur ... au mois de septembre, 1619, il avait été ordonné de dire le pseaume *Exaudi Domine* [1] et l'oraison ordinaire pour la conservation de notre Roi très-chrétien Louis XIII [2] nous en ordonnons la continuation à tous les jours de fête après vêpres sans qu'il soit loisible à personne de faire autres suffrages et prières sans l'avertissement et licence du Père Correcteur...

It is characteristic of these reports and ordonnances that the Provincial should the have gone on to emphasise that poverty was one of the most important parts of the Rule and that, as an outward sign of it, members were all to wear identical habits, no one being allowed to have them made "de serge de limestre [3] ou autres étoffes excédant la somme de 4 livres"; boots were not to be worn even by members who had to go across country from place to place. A similar sign of poverty was to be made within the "couvent": "Défendons ... que dorénavant les chambres du dortoir soient garnies de lits tournoyées à la menuiserie, courtines et autres superfluités."

The *Ordonnance* quoted above is also of interest in that it contains one of the few official references to preaching. We know that preaching in public was one of the chief activities of the Order in the sixteenth century, and we know that the preaching of an *Avent* or a *Carême* by a member of the Order might lead to the subsequent foundation of a couvent – this happened at both Saint-Pol-de-Léon and Chalon-sur-Saône. The Chronicles of La Noue and Dony d'Attichy mention several members who carried into the seventeenth century a tradition of eloquence that derived from the previous century, when public harangues with Calvinists were common. Of these, François Humblot is the most remarkable; his *Conceptions admirables sur les Lamentations de Jérémie*, containing a set of sermons for each day in Advent, Christmas Day, St. Stephen's Day, the Circumcision and Epiphany, were published in Paris in 1618 at the end of his turbulent career; at the same time he published *Armes catholiques pour combattre ceux de la religion prétendue réformée*, a work as rigorously anti-Calvinist as his earlier *Phantôme de la Cène ministrale*. The latter work was said to have been occasioned by the conversion of large numbers of Calvinists in Saumur

[1] Psalm XVI. (i.e. Psalm XVII in *Authorised Version*).
[2] An instance of the gallican tendency amongst the French Minims.
[3] *Littré*, "serge fabriquée à Rouen."

and Châtellerault where Humblot had preached in 1611; it is not surprising to read of an attempt to murder him.[1] Gaspar Dinet also belonged to this tradition and became a court preacher before being elevated to the see of Mâcon from his position of Provincial of Lyons.[2] Pierre-André Challuau preached both *Carême* and *Avent* in Montargis and Nemours and, after a disputation with the Calvinist Minister Vitreu, preached a *Carême* in Nantes.[3] John Binans, an English refugee, joined the Order in Dieppe and subsequently moved to many different "couvents" in the North of France and Burgundy; he is credited with being a Hebrew scholar and harangued the Jews in Avignon and Aix-en-Provence as well as a Calvinist minister from Manosque.[4]

Within the "couvent" also, preaching and reading aloud were an essential part of the spiritual activity and were governed by statute.[5] Although several examples of formal eloquence have survived in the form of *Oraisons funèbres* pronounced by members of the Order, little if anything is known of the daily readings and sermons. From what we know of the public sermon and from the more formal oration we may deduce a little; but more important is to attempt an assessment of the Minims' attitude to Scripture and the lives of the Saints, since these, we must assume, furnished the bulk of the substance of the sermons preached. The public sermon was in the nature of a debate, often an open dispute – I am referring here only to the early part of the century, the years of Humblot, Challuau and John Binans – and was aimed at destroying the claims of the Calvinists; emphasis was therefore placed on heresy and false doctrine. It is likely, although the point cannot be proved, that the sermon within the "couvent" was an exposition on a text, a commentary on monastic rule and practice, or else was devoted to extolling one or other of the Saints; in some instances, it may have been more theological and the preacher may have developed some special point of doctrine, but this was probably rarer than the scriptural or hagiographic exposition; the Minims were not especially given to theological subtleties, neither could they claim any particular dogma or cult as their own.

Few of the books listed in the Biblilgraphy deal with Biblical commentary, although Mersenne with his *Quaestiones in Genesim* plays an

---

[1] In Bourg-en-Bresse. Dony d'Attichy, *op. cit.*, I, pp. 454–486; Roberti, *op. cit.*, II, pp. 323–328.
[2] Roberti, *op. cit.*, II, pp. 362–363 and p. 685.
[3] *ibid.*, II, pp. 363–366; Doni d'Attichy, *op. cit.*, I, pp. 374–388.
[4] Roberti, *op. cit.*, II, pp. 396–400.
[5] Pizzurnus, *op. cit.*, *Lectura* and *Praedicatio*.

important part in the history of exegesis in the XVIIth century; this work was not without its forebears in the Order but exceeded in scope anything that had been previously attempted. It was a Scottish refugee who first claims attention in this field of study; Jean, or Ian, Bruno (Brown?) was born in the later XVIth century and joined the Order in either France or Spain. He became Doctor of Theology at Alcalá de Henarez then, for a while, was at Avignon; moving north, he was instrumental in the spread of the Order in Flanders and in the Low Countries and settled at length in Paris, at la Place Royale, where he taught Hebrew to Mersenne.[1] On his death in 1643 he left to the library at la Place Royale a valuable collection of manuscripts. At the same time, another Minim, Théophile Minuti,[2] was corresponding with Mersenne and Peiresc, furnishing them with information about Hebraic and Syriac manuscripts. Jean Bruno may rightly be credited with the initiation of the proper study of Biblical texts within the Order. He relied upon a minute philological examination of the text and the method which he instituted can be found in Rangueil's commentaries on the Books of Kings, Camart's work on the prophecy of Elisha and in Mersenne's *Quaestiones in Genesim*. His own *In Benedictiones duodecim Patriarchum commentaria et quaestiones analyticae*, (Venice, 1605), is an extensive commentary on *Genesis*, XLIX, (Jacob's summoning of his sons); each verse is subjected to a careful scrutiny and the various versions – Hebrew, Septuagint, Vulgate – are compared and contrasted. Thus on pages 39–40, discussing *verse 6*, he has a most illuminating comment to make on the words "in coetu illorum non sit gloria mea." How is it, he asks, that one version has "anima mea," another the astonishingly different "viscera mea," and one commentator of great authority, S. Jerome, has "iecur meum"? The answer that Bruno gives is simple: כָּבֹד, which he transliterates *cavod*, means *glory*, whereas כָּבֵד (*caved*) means *liver*. The question is of some importance since the idea of "glory" is recurrent in Scripture; as Bruno states "Potest etiam gloria *animam* significare, ut sit eiusdem sententiae repetitio per diversa verba. Sicut Psalm: 29 ver. 13." [3] This apparently synonymous meaning of "glory" and "soul" in Scripture throws some light on the word "gloire" in seventeenth

---

[1] There are regrettably few references to him: Hilarion de Coste mentions him in his *Vie de Mersenne*, Paris, 1649, p. 14; Jacquier, a distinguished XVIIIth century Minim, refers to him in his oration *In Laudes Ordinis Minimorum* ... *1764*, printed in J-M. di Laurio, *Acta Capitolorum Generalium*, Rome, 1916.

[2] See p. 201.

[3] i.e. *Psalms*, XXX, v. 12 in *Authorised Version*.

century usage; it is an interesting side-line, but Bruno is more concerned to expose the virtually nonsensical renderings of "viscera" and "liver." It is characteristic of his method that he does this with a minimum of satirical comment on the confusion and on the absurdity of the false rendering; he is content with a simple exposition. Those who followed the Latin translation of the *Septuagint* (he mentions S. Ambrose *De Benedictionibus Patriarcharum*, ch. 3) had been faced with a text "... et in congregatione illorum non contendant viscera mea"; S. Jerome, reading "caved" for "cavod," took the text as "et in congregatione illorum non emuletur iecur meum" (!!). Bruno's close examination and comparison of various texts led to a tradition of scientific exegesis in which his pupil Mersenne forms an important link with "la théologie positive" of le P. Simon and later seventeenth century exegetes. Mersenne, as we shall see, began to apply Bruno's method to the whole corpus of Scripture but got no further, after 1000 pages in-folio, than *Genesis*, IV; Rangueil, also working at la Place Royale, attempted a similar analysis of the text of the *Books of Kings* but after two large tomes [1] had only completed *Book I*.[2] The example of "cavod" – "caved" is not an isolated one; it occupied Bruno for less than two pages in 205. The more extensive works of Mersenne, Rangueil and Camart do not equal him for careful analysis of meaning.[3]

It is notable that such attention as there was to detailed Old Testament studies comes in the early part of the seventeenth century, that is during the time when members of the Order would enter into public disputation with the Calvinists and preach against them in the market-place. Bruno had taken part in this activity in Flanders and he may have accompanied Gilles Camart, the Minim who wrote

---

[1] *Fr. Claudii Rangolii commentarium in libros Regum;* vol. I, Paris, 1621; vol. 2, Paris, 1624, the latter with "Approbatio" signed by Mersenne.

[2] i.e. *Samuel* I in *Authorised Version*.

[3] It is interesting to note that hesitation about the passage in question, *Genesis* XLIX, 6, goes on into modern times: thus Sir L. C. Brenton in his English version of the *Septuagint*, London, 1844 has "... mine inward parts"; Mgr. R. A. Knox in his translation of the *Bible*, London, 1959, has "... this heart of mine." L-Cl. Fillion in the *Sainte Bible d'après la Vulgate*, Paris, 1888, has "gloire," and this seems to have always been uppermost in the minds of English translators from the Greek: thus *Authorised Version* has "mine honour," following exactly the translation of Châteillon (Sebastian Castallion) in his *La Bible nouvellement translatée* (sic), Bâle, 1555. The *Revised Version* reverts to what would appear to be archaic and puts "glory"; the *Revised Standard Version* has "my spirit" ("glory" in footnote). J. Skinner, *International critical commentary*, Edinburgh, 1930, has "mind" ("liver" in footnote with the explanation that this organ is the seat of the emotions(!). He also refers the reader to the same passage in the Psalms as Bruno, (XXX, in *A.V.*, v. 13.) It is perhaps apposite to point out that Joseph Rutter, in his translation of Le Cid, London, 1637, translates "gloire" by "glory." La Bruyère also contrasts "gloire" with "légèreté," *Caractères, Des Femmes*, 48.

Elias Thesbites, a critical work on the text and content of the prophecies of Eliaha. Camart was sent by the Superiors of the Order to preach throughout France; he subsequently went into central Europe and harangued the Hussites in Prague. It is in its friction with Protestantism that the Minims' spirituality found inspiration in the Old Testament and Hebrew studies; Camart himself, commenting on the use of Scripture, wrote:

> Peperit nostra aetas nescio quam fanaticorum hominum sectam qui ex Anabaptistis orti sunt. Ii quorumdam veterum haereticorum de quibus Philastrius, Epiphanius, Augustinus, errores e tenebris revocantes nullo sibi studio opus esse in sacrarum litterarum intelligentia capienda afferunt, sed solis enthousiasmis divinaque revelatione, unde in haereses incidere.[1]

The interesting thing about this is that one has only to change the speaker and leave out "ex Anabaptistis" to make it a diatribe against the Catholics and their ignorance of Scripture, lack of Biblical authority, and so on. When Camart was preaching in Pont-Audemer in 1609 a Calvinist argued with him, but:

> Vix dum sacrilegas voces deprompserat cum in proferentis et maledici pectus veluti retortae, divino eum iudicio humi afflixerunt furioso et amenti similem, qui elatus inde nullis suorum artibus convalescere potuit, sed geminae horae spatio nec longiore intervallo spumas ore iactans, oculos contorquens, toto corpore miserum in modum labefactato et concusso energumeno proprior quam phrenetico ad suorum terrorem, Catholicorum confirmationem et perpetuam Camarti gloriam Deo ita providente extinctus est.[2]

I shall return to this episode later when dealing with the "heroic" type of character that we find from time to time in the Order. For the moment I wish to insist upon a single aspect of this story. Camart probably, and his hearers both Catholic and Protestant most certainly, looked upon his action and the fate of his "victim" as direct evidence of God's power (or Satan's power) depending on the point of view. Are not similar episodes to be found in the Old Testament and, to the men of Pont-Audemer in 1609, therefore true? Dathan and Abiron, Doeg and Achitophel had all met violent ends because of their impiety[3]; why, therefore, not this poor wretch faced by a new-time prophet? Again, one has only to change the scene slightly and one has an episode

---

[1] *Elias Thesbites*, a posthumous work, Paris, 1631, p. 383.
[2] *ibid.*, Introduction by François de la Noue and other members of the Order, sig õ iii (verso) *et sq.*
[3] *Athalie*, III, vi, v. 1037.

in the life of Fox, the first Quaker.[1] It is at least possible that, if someone to-day were to hear one of the sermons preached in the "couvents"
of the Order in the early part of the XVIIth century, he would be
struck by a similarity to the puritanical utterances from this side of
the Channel, or the Biblical diatribes from Geneva or the Low
Countries. One could push the parallel further and show similarities
between Marie de Valence, a heroine in the eyes of some members of
the Order and, say, Antoinette Bourignon the Flemish visionary and
Protestant enthusiast.[2] The constant criticism which Protestants in
general level at the Church of Rome is that it does not base its teaching
upon the Bible – an unjustified criticism when one takes into account
the long traditions of Catholic biblical scholarship. It is true, however,
that no book in the French language played, or plays, the same part
as the *Authorised Version* in English life; the Old and New Testaments
became popular literature in England during the XVIIth century,
while in Catholic countries their counterpart was lives of the saints.[3]
But French preachers kept the Bible in the minds of their flocks and,
even if it was not on the level of "popular literature," it was possible
for a seventeenth century critic to write:

> L'Ecriture nous est plus vénérable et plus familière (qu'aux Italiens);
> je crois que nous en avons l'obligaiton aux Huguenots ... Le long com-
> merce et les fréquentes disputes que nous avons eus avec eux ont fait que la
> France est celui de tous les royaumes catholiques où le goût de l'Ecriture
> est le plus répandu. On l'aime, on la sait; sa simplicité nous pique.[4]

If the sermon preached in the "couvent" is a reflexion of the spiritual seekings of those members who expressed themselves in print, it is
likely that its content changed somewhat in the middle period of the
century. A large number of writers within the Order composed lives
of the Saints and of men and women amongst their contemporaries
noted for their piety; leaving out funeral orations and works which

---

[1] Voltaire, *Lettres Philosophiques, Troisième lettre sur les Quakers*, ed. F. A. Taylor, Black-
well, Oxford, 1946, p. 9.

[2] For Marie de Valence see the biography by the Minim Louis de La Rivière and see
pp. 63 and 324; for Antoinette Bourignon see Bayle, *Dictionnaire*, art. *Bourignon.*
   Throughout, I have used the word "enthusiast" in its literal (XVIIth century) sense of
one who believes he (or she) has direct communion with God without the intermediary of
any sacrament or office of the Church.

[3] G. N. Clark, *The Seventeenth century*, Oxford, 1950; see also H. Bremond, *Histoire littéraire
du sentiment religieux en France*, Paris, 1916, vol. I, p. 239 *et sq.*

[4] Le Cerf de la Viéville, *Comparaison de la musique française et de la musique italienne*, III,
pp. 122–123; quoted by C. M. Girdlestone in *French Studies*, XVI, Oxford, 1962, pp. 222–
223. The work was first published in 1707 but was written at the end of the seventeenth
century or very early in the eighteenth. Le Cerf de la Viéville died in 1707.

were historical rather than hagiographic, these number sixty, mostly written between 1620 and 1680. They are of very uneven quality, ranging from the highly colourful life of Sainte Fare by Robert Regnault [1] to the more carefully documented life of Saint François de Paule by Hilarion de Coste.[2] The veneration of the Saints and their relics was closely associated with the granting of Indulgences. The term *Indulgence* requires some definition since it is not infrequently taken to mean "permission to sin" or a "licence for self-indulgence." According to the Church, *Indulgence* is a remission either partial or total (i.e. plenary), granted to a truly repentant sinner of the temporal punishment still due after the guilt of sin has been forgiven by God. An *Indulgence* is, accordingly, a pardon and, in the traditional meaning of the word which still survives in Brittany, is associated with some special act of veneration – "le pardon d'Auray," for example, associated with the veneration of Sainte Anne d'Auray. The abuses so amusingly described by Chaucer and to which Luther so vehemently objected in the Wittenberg theses were real enough; they were ironed out at the Council of Trent and excommunication was thereafter the punishment for the trafficking of Indulgences. A book devoted to the whole question of Indulgences was composed for the Order by a Minim, Simon Pourré [3], while in the *Manipulus Minimorum* there are two articles [4] setting out the position within the Order. Members were granted plenary indulgence upon taking the habit, on celebrating or assisting at Mass on the principal feast-days, by invoking the name of Jesus "in articulo mortis," by taking part in the special spiritual exercises of the 40-hours prayer. They were slso granted plenary indulgence on going abroad to work in infidel lands.[5] Seculars could obtain plenary indulgence by worshipping in churches belonging to the Order on Sundays in Lent and, in certain churches – those dedicated to Saint Peter, S. Paul and S. Sebastian – on any day between mid-Lent and Easter. At other times of the year Indulgence could be obtained within the Minims' churches on the feasts of the Circumcision, Epiphany, the Conception, Nativity and Assumption of Our

[1] Paris, 1626.
[2] Paris, 1655.
[3] *Le trésor des Indulgences*, Lille, 1663. The copy in the Bibliothèque Nationale (D. 48602) is ex-Minimes de la Place Royale, shelf mark y
[4] Pizzurnus, op. cit., *Indulgentiæ Fratrum* and *Indulgentiae Saeculorum*.
[5] There is little evidence that French members of the Order undertook such work; Roberti mentions only three, and these unimportant, Vol. II, pp. 688–689.

Lady, Nativity of S. John Baptist and on the feast of SS. Philip and
James (1 May). To this should be added the feasts of special obligation
for members of the Order and the tertiaries – 2nd April, associated
with the Founder since his canonization in the early XVIth century,
and the Sunday after 29th January, the feast of Saint François de
Sales, by decree of Alexander VII in 1666 (15th September). Plenary
indulgence could only be obtained from the Pope and a printed form
of authorisation was distributed to the churches in which a particular
Indulgence was operative; collections of these survive for Dieppe,
Douai, Lille and Nancy [1] – for Dieppe the papers relating to
Indulgences are still preserved in the same liasse as those concerning
the attestation of relics and the privilege of exposing them on certain
days.[2] Although the majority of the Minims' "couvents" in France
were dedicated to the Virgin under one or other of the usual styles –
"Virgo Assumpta" being the most common but also "N. D. de Bon
Port" (Dieppe and Blaye), "N. D. de Bon Secours" (Nancy and la
Ciotat) – other dedications were common and were associated with
some local tradition, such as Saint Ferréol at Brioude or Saint Rémi
at Epernay, or to some special benefits received by intercession, such
as deliverance from plague by prayer to Saint Roch at Bordeaux,
Toulouse, Carcassonne and Sammathan.

The Minims' veneration of the Saints is best seen in the lives of Saints
composed by Simon Martin; his writings were ultimately collected and
published by two other members of the Order, François Giry and
Claude Raffron. This collection is called simply *Les Vies des Saints*,
and sprang originally from Martin's small work *Les actions admirables
de Jésus . . . avec un traité pour les fêtes des Saints* (2 vols in-8°, Paris, 1630).
Martin then turned his attention to the production of small tracts,
each one devoted to a Saint; the intention was to provide one for each
day of the year. Of these tracts, a few survive in the Bibliothèque
Nationale and are listed in the Bibliography; few others survive.
His idea was abandoned, however, in favour of a more compendious
volume which he called *Les fleurs de la solitude, cueillies des plus belles vies
des Saints qui ont habité les déserts et qui ont chéri plus expressement la vie
solitaire, tant en l'Orient qu'en l'Occident et particulièrement en France* (2 vols
in-folio, Paris, 1652). Once again we can see the patriotic intentions
of the French members of the Order coming out in this title. Simon

---

[1] See Bibliography, MSS (Archives Départementales) under Seine-Maritime, Nord and
Meurthe-et-Moselle.
[2] Archives Départementales, Seine-Maritime, Série H, Liasse 4, g-1, (my classification).

Martin left much unpublished material at his death in 1653 and from it a second collection of lives of Saints was made under the title, *Les sacrées reliques du désert, composées des vies des saints solitaires qui ont été fort peu connus jusques à présent, découverts par ... feu R. P. Simon Martin*, (1 vol. in-folio, Paris, 1655). The inspiration for these works almost certainly came from the Spanish Jesuit Pedro de Ribadeneira, whose *Flos Sanctorum* had been translated into French in 1633 and again (4th edition) in 1667, when the name of Simon Martin appears in the list of those who augmented the original version. Ribadeneira was one of the earliest Jesuits and his work was entirely eclipsed by that of the Bollandists (members of the Society of Jesus like Ribadeneira himself) who undertook to purge the lives of the saints of all the legendary material that had accrued over the ages. Martin's aim seems to have been more humble, and those who followed him and who produced the definitive edition of his work seem to have had the same idea. The Bollandists have always been renowned for their excellent scholarship: the volumes of the *Acta Sanctorum* were from the beginning monuments to patient resesrch. The first publications were two volumes in 1643 to cover the Saints for January; by the early XVIIIth century (1695–1717) the work had got as far as June (7 volumes); it was completed in 1940 and the revision of the work is in constant progress. In the XIXth century Simon Martin and his followers were referred to as the Petits Bollandistes, a borrowing rightly deprecated by the Bollandists themselves [1] and a title to which the original authors never aspired. Simon Martin was first re-edited and augmented by François Giry, whose commentary on the Rule of Saint François de Paule has been mentioned. He was the son of Louis Giry, one of the original members of the Académie Française and famous for his translation from Tertullian; joining the Order against the wishes of his father, he soon distinguished himself as an able teacher and as an eloquent writer. He was above all a fervent admirer of the Founder of the Order and brought into all his writings something of that curious spirituallity which characterises many of the Minims' writings. It is wrong therefore to have equated him with the Bollandists; his work is not scholarly and analytical, but eloquent, persuasive and calculated to move the less well educated. Hence its importance at the time

[1] See Delehaye, *A travers trois siècles, l'œuvre des Bollandistes*, Brussels, 1920, p. 280; M. Delehaye is wrong, however, in thinking that Mgr. Guérin first used the title for his edition of *Les Vies des Saints* in 1888, he had already used it in 1866 and had obtained Papal authority for the title in 1874: *Catalogue Général de la Bibliothèque Nationale*, under Giry (François) and *Approbations et félicitations* in front of *Les Petits Bollandistes*, vol. I, Paris 1882 by Mgr. Guérin.

of the great Catholic revival in France in the seventeenth century. Further, it was probably these considerations that led Mgr. Guérin to republish it in the eighteen-sixties and in 1870, when a short reprint was made during the siege of Paris.[1]

Shortly before his death, François Giry became the Director of the Ecoles Charitables which had recently been founded by another Minim, Nicolas Barré, whose austerity and zeal went to such lengths that he had to be curbed by one of the Correctors at la Place Royale; there is something of this almost excessive zeal in *Les Vies des Saints* in the Giry edition (Paris, 1638–1685). His main contribution is what the title calls ... *un martirologe des Saints de France qui ne sont pas dans le romain;* to the heading for each day there has been included a list of names of *Autres Saints de France*, which shows a marked independence from Roman jurisdiction, although the *Approbation*, signed by A. Granjon and Claude des Masures, Théologiens de l'Ordre (des Minimes), was careful to distinguish between "Saints de notre France selon le Martirologe" and "Plusieurs personnes illustres en sainteté."

The definitive edition of *Les Vies des Saints* takes us outside the strict limits of the seventeenth century. Giry died in 1688 and Claude Raffron, who had been with him at la Place Royale, wrote, *La vie de François Giry, ancien Provincial des ... Minimes de la Province de France* [2] which he included in a shortened form in *Les Vies des Saints*.[3] Raffron was probably a more scholarly man than Giry and the final edition of the *Vie des Saints* shows evidence of some careful editing, but much of its original flavour remains. Several separate printings of this last edition were made [4] and it was from the one of 1719 that the numerous nineteenth century reprints were taken. So the work had grown in scope and size from the modest beginnings of one whom Thuillier described as "vir inexhausti et immensi laboris" [5] and who died in the mid-seventeenth century, to the three large folios which are almost contemporaneous with the *Lettres Persanes* of Montesquieu.

---

[1] *Les Patrons de Paris: les vies de Sainte Geneviève et de Monseigneur Saint Denis, d'après le P. Giry*, Paris, 1870; the preface speaks of the need for intercession during "la crise épouvantable qui est seulement comparable à une agonie."

[2] Paris, 1691.

[3] Edition of 1719, vol. III, appendix, pp. c-cx; for note on rdition, see below.

[4] The Bibliothèque Nationale lists an edition of 1696 (Paris, R. et N. Pepie, 2 vols); although posthumous for Giry, under whom it is listed, it seems to have been untouched by Raffron. The Bibliothèque Nationale also lists two editions of 1715, one Paris. C. Robustel, 2 vols in-folio, the other, also 2 vols in-folio, Paris, E. Couterot. There is another edition, in the British Museum, Paris, E. Couterot, 3 vols in-folio; pagination for vols II and III is continuous but each has separate title-page; vol. I, pp. 1–1897; vol. II, 1–1227, vol. III, pp. 1228–2176, also two appendices numbered i-ccxlvi and i-clxxvi.

[5] *op. cit.*, II, p. 290.

To convey some idea of the composition of the *Vies des Saints* I give below for two days in January a comparison between the official martyrology of the Church, the *Acta Sanctorum* of the Bollandists (the first two volumes, 1643) and the *Vies des Saints;* the French bias is clearly seen.

JANUARY 10

Le Martirologe Romain [1]:
- S. Nicanor.
- S. Agathon.
- S. Jean Bon.
- S. Paul (Premier Hermite).
- S. Marcien.

Acta Sanctorum:
- S. Nicanor.
- SS. Thecla, Iustina.
- SS. Saturus, Vitalianus, Felicitas, Quintus, Artartes.
- SS. Revocatus, Firmus, Iucundus, and others martyred with them.
- S. Possessor and two others martyred with him.
- S. Paulus Thebaeus (Primus eremita).
- S. Marcianus.
- S. Florida.
- S. Valericus (Walericus).
- S. Domitianus.
- S. Ioannes Camillus Bonus.
- S. Agatho.
- S. Sethrida.
- S. Aldus.
- B. Benincasa.
- S. Guilielmus, Archiepiscopus Bituricensis (i.e. Bourges).
- B. Gonsalvus Amaranthus.
- B. Christiana.

Les Vies des Saints [2]:
All in the *Martirologe Romain* and the following
- S. Guillaume de Bourges (in *Acta Sanctorum* above).
- S. Vaubry (of Limoges).
- S. Floride (of Dijon, in *Acta Sanctorum* above).
- S. Sethride (of Faremoutiers, in *Acta Sanctorum* above).
- Le Très-Pieux Olivier de Sombroste (of Cîteaux).

---

[1] From the 1638 edition prepared by Simon Martin and later incorporated in *Les Vies des Saints.*

[2] In the 1719 (3 Vol.) edition.

Lives of Saints for this day:

 Acta Sanctorum – bibliographical and biographical notice on each Saint
   or group of Saints.

 Vie des Saints – article on S. Guillaume de Bourges only.

JANUARY 16

Le Martirologe Romain:

 S. Marcel.
 SS. Berard, Pierre, Accurse, Adjute, Othon.
 S. Honorat d'Arles, Evêque.
 S. Titien.
 S. Mela.
 S. Honorat, Abbé.
 S. Foursy (abbé de Péronne).
 S. Priscille.

Acta Sanctorum:

 S. Priscilla.
 S. Marinus.
 SS. Saturninus, Faustinus, Nassanianus and seven others.
 SS. Ananus and Marius.
 SS. Milites IX.
 S. Honorius and thirteen others martyred with him.
 S. Danax.
 S. Marcellus.
 S. Melas.
 S. Honoratus.
 S. Jacobus Tarentasiensis (Tarentaise in Savoy).
 S. Faustus.
 S. Valerius.
 S. Titianus.
 S. Liberata.
 S. Honoratus Abbas.
 S. Treverius.
 S. Furseus.
 S. Tozzo.
 B. Ioanna.
 S. Henricus.
 SS. Berardus, Otto, Petrus, Accursus, Adiutus.

Les Vies des Saints:

All in the *Martirologe Romain*, and the following:

 S. Jacques de Tarentaise (in *Acta Sanctorum*).
 S. Faust (of Riez, in *Acta Sanctorum*).
 S. Spur (of Cavaillon).
 S. S. Trivier (of Terouenne, near Lyon).
 S. Meroflette.

Lives of Saints for this day: –

Acta Sanctorum – bibliographical and biographical notice for each Saint listed.

Les Vies des Saints – articles on:

> S. Marcel.
> S. Honorat d'Arles.
> S. Foursy de Péronne.

In addition to the lives given for each day, the *Vies des Saints* had important Appendices of lives of French men and women noted for their piety; most of them belong to the sixteenth and seventeenth centuries; members of the Order of Minims are prominent. Thus, on 16 January, in addition to the Saints mentioned above, one was called upon to remember la Vénérable Sœur, Grâce de Valence, du Tiers-Ordre des Minimes.[1] Because these *Appendices* contain some of the most characteristic features of the Minims' spirituality, a summary of their contents is given below and, later, two of the lives given here will form the basis of an investigation into those personal qualities which distinguished the Minim from his contemporaris.

Les Vies de Saints Appendix I: Table.

January: 7th le Vénérable Louis de Blois, Abbé de Liesse. + 1666.

> 7th R.P. Charles de Condren, Général de l'Oratoire. + 1644.
> 16th la Vénérable Sœur Grâce de Valence, [Tiers-] Ordre des Minimes. + 1606.[2]

February: 2nd la Vénérable Mère Marie de l'Estonac. + 1640.

March: 23rd le Vénérable Claude Bernard, dit le Pauvre Prêtre. + 1641.

> 28th la Vénérable Marie de Maillé. + ?[3]
> 31st le Vénérable Pierre Moreau, de l'Ordre des Minimes + 1626.

April: 2nd M. Jacques Olier, Instituteur du Séminaire de Saint Sulpice. + 1657.

> 18th la Vénérable Mère Marie de l'Incarnation, Carmélite. + 1618.
> 22nd le B. Frère Gilles, Compagnon de S. François d'Assise + 1260.
> 24th Messire Jean-Baptiste, Baron de Renti. + 1649.
> [28th Dom Jean de la Barrière, Fondateur des Feuillants. + 1600][4]

---

[1] *Les Vies des Saints*, Vol. III, Appendix I, pp. xxi-xxviii.
[2] (Tiers –), my addition. Her life had already been composed by a Minim, François Victon, in 1622; see Bibliography.
[3] No date of death given in table.
[4] Not included in table at beginning of Appendix, but see pp. clvi-clxiv.

May: 22nd R.P. Jérôme d'Etienne, de l'Ordre des Minimes. + 1712.
                  23rd Messire Jean-Baptiste Gault, Evêque de Marseille.
                  + 1643.
                  [31st] [1] La Vénérable Sœur Marguerite du Saint Sacrement,
                  Carmélite. + 1648.
                  [31st R.P. Nicolas Barré, Minime et Instituteur des Ecoles
                  Charitables du Saint Enfant Jésus. + 1686] [2]
June: 9th le Vénérable Père Ambrose de Jésus, de l'Ordre des
                  Minimes. + 1541.

[In addition to the above, pp. ccviii–ccxlvi are devoted to the following
lives not given in the Table at beginning of Appendix I]

April: 10th Madame la Baronne de Neuvilette. + 1657.
April: 6th la Vénérable Mère Catherine Mechtilde du Saint Sacre-
                  ment, Institutrice des Religieuses de l'Adoration Perpétuelle.
                  + 1698.[3]

Appendix II: Table
July: 14th le Vénérable Père Gaspar Bon de l'Ordre des Minimes. +
                  1604.
                  16th le Révérend Père Dom Barthelemi des Martyrs. + 1590.
August: 16th la Vénérable Mère Marguerite d'Arbouze, Abbesse du
                  Val de Grâce. + 1626.
                  31st le Vénérable Prêtre Henri Marie Boudon. + 1702.
September: 27th le Vénérable Père Vincent de Paul, Instituteur de la Con-
                  grégation de la mission. + 1660.
                  29th la Vénérable Mère Catherine de Vis, de l'Ordre des
                  Minimes. + 1634.
October: 2nd le Vénérable Prêtre Thomas Elie, Aumônier, de Saint
                  Louis. + 1257.
                  8th le Vénérable Père Yvan [Instituteur de l'Ordre des Reli-
                  gieuses de Notre-Dame de Miséricorde].[4] + 1653.
                  19th Monsieur le Cardinal de Bérulle, Instituteur de l'Ora-
                  toire. + 1629.
                  19th [la Vénérable Mère Agnès de Jésus, Religieuse de l'Ordre
                  de Saint Dominique, au Monastère de Langeac en Auvergne.
                  + 1634] [5].
November: 3rd le Vénérable Frère Martin de Porras, de l'Ordre de Saint
                  Dominique. + 1639.
                  20th le Révérend Père François Giry, de l'Ordre des Minimes.
                  + 1698.

---

[1] [31st], my addition.
[2] Not in table, but see pp. cxciii-cc.
[3] A fuller form of this life by Giry was translated into Polish and published in Warsaw in
1738, see Bibliography.
[4] [Instituteur ... Miséricorde] my addition from p. ix.
[5] Not in Table but see pp. lxxxii-xcvii.

December: 9th le Vénérable Prêtre Pierre Fourrier, Curé de Martincourt. + 1640.

13th la Vénérable Mère Jeanne Freminot de Chantal, Première Religieuse de la Visitation. + 1641.

15th la Vénérable Mère Marie Victoire, Fondatrice des Annonciades Célestes. + 1617.

31st le Révérend Père Louis de Grenade, de l'Ordre de Saint Dominique. + 1588.

[In addition to the above, pp. cxlv–clxxvi are devoted to the following lives not listed in the Table to Appendix II]

July: 29th le Révérend Père Paul Trouchet,[1] de l'Ordre des Minimes. + 1647.

August: 7th la Vénérable Mère Esprite de Jésus de Jossaud, du Tiers-Ordre des Minimes. + 1658.

February: 3rd Frère Nicolas Sage, Religieux Oblat de l'Ordre des Minimes. + 1709.

Of the 35 lives given in these two Appendices 2 only are mediaeval, 3 are of men and women who died during the XVIth century, 28 during the XVIIth century and 2 during the XVIIIth century [2]; 10 are of Minims of the First and Second (female) Order, 4 are of members of the Tiers-Ordre and include M. Olier of the Séminaire de Saint Sulpice and Cardinal Bérulle of the Oratory. The religious life of France of the XVIIth century (with the exception of the Jansenist and Quietist disputes) can be seen in epitome in these lives: Jeanne de Chantal, the friend of S. François de Sales and founder of the Religieuses de la Visitation; Bérulle and Condren of the Oratory; M. Olier and le P. Barré who each furthered the cause of religious education; visionaires and mystics; founders of new orders and simple priests. If the biographical notices for each day in the *Vies des Saints* reveal what was the contemporary taste in popular spiritual reading, the Appendices reveal even more surely the particular qualities that Minims looked for in themselves. The lives of the Saints, taken with the lives of the heroes of the Old Testament, reveal something of those heroic qualities that all XVIIth century Frenchmen tended to admire in the epic poems and tragedies of the age; such qualities underlie the Minims' quest for perfection. The obvious interest and pride which they took in those of their own members who displayed such qualities

---

[1] Whose life was also written by the Minim Antoine Morel, see Bibliography.

[2] Emphasising that the present was as fertile in miracles and exemplary lives as the early days of the Church; cf. *Athalie*, I, i, v. 104, and *Les Vies des Saints*, Appendix I, p. lxii.

will make a starting point for the investigation into the particular characteristics of the Minims' ideals, their teaching and their "sagesse."

When La Noue wrote the preface to Camart's *Elias Thesbites*, he told in some detail the episode of the preaching in Pont-Audemer when the man who had interrupted fell down in a fit and died. It cannot be doubted for a moment that La Noue and other members of the Order and probably Camart himself, thought of the episode in terms of Elijah and the priests of Baal. When members of the Order were engaged on missionary activity amongst the Huguenots, they could associate themselves with Sainte Fare [1] or Saint Martin de Tours [2] who faced the Pagans in the Dark Ages. So great is the variety of material provided by the lives of the Saints that a man could, in any situation, identify himself with one or more of them, their aid could be invoked for help in countless ills and miseries: Sainte Fare for blindness, Saint Louis for deafness [3] and so on. The cult of the Saints was, therefore, a very personal one but, against this, the qualities that were admired in this cult were of a superlative nature so that the Saints also had about them something of that elevation, that "éloignement," which was characteristic of the heroes of antiquity. (The qualities that were praised above all were physical courage, complete faith and unswerving loyalty; the latter particularly noticeable in the French Saints as a loyalty to the land of France, and typified by Sainte Geneviève and Saint Denis, the Patrons of Paris, and by Saint Louis himself.) Saint Martin de Tour came across some Pagans whose shrine was near a large fir tree; he ordered that the shrine should be destroyed and the tree felled. The Pagans defied him saying that, if he had any faith in his God, he could receive the weight of the tree upon his shoulders when it fell. Accordingly St. Martin allowed himself to be tied to the tree and the Pagans felled it in such a way that the Saint was bound to be beneath the trunk as it crashed to the ground. At the critical moment, the Saint spread out his arms in the form of the cross and the tree fell backwards amidst the Pagans.[4] Such robust tales of adventure go to fill up the pages of *Les Vies des Saints* and their popularity was probably unbounded; but there is another characteristic which is of equal importance: the theme of suffering. With the

[1] In the *Vie de Sainte Fare* by the Minim R. Regnault and in *Les Vies des Saints* for December 7th.
[2] *Les Vies des Saints*, for November 11.
[3] Saint Louis, Roi de France, *Les Vies des Saints*, for August 25th.
[4] *Les Vies des Saints*, III, p. 1695, for November 11th.

Church Triumphant goes the Church Suffering; the Christ in Glory is placed in parallel with the Christ in Agony:

Hier [la Toussaint] l'Eglise Militante rendait ses honneurs ... à l'Eglise Triomphante: aujourd'hui elle travaille au secours ... de l'Eglise Souffrante. Hier elle implorait pour elle-même les prières et les suffrages pour la première; aujourd'hui elle offre ses vœux et ses supplications pour la seconde. Hier elle se réjouissait de la gloire et du bonheur de l'une; aujourd'hui s'afflige des peines et des douleurs de l'autre.[1]

War, poverty and pestilence were the lot of the majority during the XVIth and XVIIth century. The records of the Order are full of references to the most abject misery, particularly in Lorraine and in Provence. It is not surprising that the lives of the more extrovert Saints should have provided material for the only form of "divertissement" permitted to members of the Order, nor that the more spiritual Saints should have served as models of conduct in an afflicted world; the adventurous and legendary martyrs of the early Church stood in relationship to the Order and to a large number of believers who held the theatre in abhorrence much as, say, the Cid stood to the world at large. Those who sought a more inward way of life turned rather to a different type of ideal – to Saint Francis of Assisi or the Other Saint Francis, founder of the Minims, or again, to Saint François de Sales. Their lives were no less surrounded by an aura of sanctity and even of the "merveilleux" – this has been seen already with reference to the more extraordinary episodes related in the life of Saint François de Paule – but they corresponded more closely to a known reality. The heroes of Corneille may correspond to a certain swashbuckling, heroic type bred of the Thirty Years War; the reality for the majority of Europeans was, however, something different. The mass of the civilian population had suffered apallingly both directly and indirectly because of the ravages of war; plague too was rife. Faced with these, the more introspective – and it is surely wrong to emphasise the extrovert nature of the seventeenth century character to the exclusion of everything else – turned to the themes of humility, poverty, penitence and intercession; that is to say they turned to precisely those aspects of Christianity emphasised by the hermit type of Saint, to the "fleurs de la solitude, cueillies des plus belles vies des saints qui ont habité les déserts et qui ont chéri plus expressement la vie solitaire." (It will be remembered that this quotation is in fact the title of one of the books

[1] *ibid.*, III, pp. 1587, 1588, for November 2nd, *la Mémoire des Fidèles Trépassés.*

by Simon Martin which led to the *Vies des Saints*). The theme of solitude sounds strange in an age which found the aspirations of Alceste to find "un endroit écarté" as amusing as they were incomprehensible. Yet, for a large part of the seventeenth century the austere orders flourished in France and the most austere of all, that of la Trappe, was founded at the height of this century on ideals which stem from the Order of Minims.

We are concerned here with the ideal of perfection as exemplified in the lives of the Saints, an ideal which we shall find again in the mystic writings and in the New Testament commentaries composed by members of the Order. Perfection, nothing less, was the ideal of the Founder; the "rule" aimed to inculcate the desire for perfection in all its members and the very title "Fratres Minimi" shows how the Founder pushed his adherents towards superlatives. Until the founding of la Trappe, the Order had not its equal for austerity and its emblem and motto was the single word "Caritas," the Pauline imperative. For all monks the life of Saint Anthony must be taken as the archetype; *la Vie de Saint Antoine, Abbé*, is from this point of view, the most important and most significant in the *Vies des Saints*.[1] Thus the following passage tells us a great deal about seventeenth century monastic ideals:

> Comme il se trouvait souvent en conférence avec ses Religieux, il leur donnait diverses leçons pour la pratique des vertus. Une fois entre les autres il voulut avoir leur opinion sur les vertus, et leur demanda laquelle de toutes leur semblait la plus nécessaire à la vie religieuse. Les uns donnaient le premier lieu à la pénitence, par laquelle les appetits sont mortifiés; les autres au silence et à la solitude qui retranchent les occasions du péché; les autres à la miséricorde ... et les autres à d'autres vertus. Mais Antoine comme le plus expérimenté en cette sainte pratique, donna le premier lieu à la discrétion, comme à la guide ... de toutes les autres, sans laquelle la vie spirituelle est aveugle, confuse et en désordre. C'est ainsi que par ces conseils et autres semblables, le saint Père formait ces religieux *à la perfection de la vie monastique*.[2]

Next to Saint Anthony comes Saint Francis of Assisi [3] as an example of perfection. The well-known story of his life is retold in *Les Vies des Saints* as is the less well-known life (to anyone outside the Order) of Saint François de Paule.[4] In these two lives the reader is forced to

---

[1] *ibid.*, I, pp. 281–292, for January 17th.
[2] *ibid.*, I, p. 286. (My italics). "Discrétion" is used here in its more literal meaning of "an ability to distinguish, to discern" (Discerno ... Discretum, whence Discretio, -onis) and leads to an important consideration in the "sagesse" of the Minims.
[3] *ibid.*, III, pp. 1285–1311, for October 4th.
[4] *ibid.*, I, pp. 963–1013, for April 2nd.

consider the steps by which perfection can be achieved; for the member of the Order such reading becomes an exercise, retracing the steps in the spiritual ascent; the rule to which his vows bound him helped him to achieve the example of his spiritual masters. He had, like them, to abjure the world; if he could not go into the wastes of Calabria like Saint François de Paule, his Founder, he could find sequestration in his "couvent" and his isolation was merely heightened by living in proximity to the world, yet not in it; his enforced silence, the locked gate, these provided for him the remoteness of the desert.[1] He had to renounce the Devil; like his Lord and Master, like Saint Anthony his architype and like the two Saints Francis, he had to come to grips with the power of Satan before he could achieve any measure of perfection; hence in nearly all the lives of prominent members of the Order there comes a sory of exorcism or torment. It was the period of Elizabeth Ranfaing,[2] of the Devils of Loudun and of the Witches of Salem, and any attempt at rationalisation of such problems as witchcraft and possession was held in some suspicion – Mersenne, who undertook just such a rationalisation does not feature, for all his saintliness, in the pages of Les Vies des Saints. A Minim had to renounce the Flesh; in this he was aided by the strictures that his Order placed upon all indulgence of the senses. He took vows of chastity; he was vowed to vegetarianism; drunkenness was severely punished.[3]

The true hero of the Order was therefore the man who could combine the courage and vigour of the early martyrs, who could show the quality of "discrétion" and who could, aided by the discipline of his rule, aspire after the example of the Founder and those other Saints whose inner conduct had led them towards spiritual perfection. In the pages of Thuillier's Diarium Patrum Ordininis Minimorum Provinciae Franciae (Paris 1709) and in the lives of members of the Order appended to Les Vies des Saints one can trace this spiritual quest and see what particular qualities were held by the Order to have been admirable and conducive to perfection.

The lives of two members of the Order will serve to sum up these qualities; two lives which, in a sense, are complementary since they belong to different periods of the seventeenth century and since one (le P. Moreau) represents the tendency to see perfection as its own end, whereas the other (le P. Barré) represents the tendency to see no point

---

[1] Pizzurnus, op. cit., Silentium, Egressio, Ianitor.
[2] See pp. 134 et sq.
[3] Pizzurnus, op. cit., Castitas, Quadragesimalis Vita, Ebreitas.

in perfection unless it is made to work for improved social conditions outside the cloister. This does not mean that Moreau did not have an acute feeling for the victims of the world's injustices; his compassion and his charity were unbounded but remained on a personal level. Barré, on the other hand, progressed from a personal compassion to a corporate sense of urgency in the need for social reform, believing that prayer, fasting, intercession and sequestration within the cloister, important as they were for those who taught, were not ends in themselves.

Pierre Moreau was born of wealthy parents in Soissons in 1552. His childhood and early manhood were spent in the tense, turbulent atmosphere of the Wars of Religion; Soissons was a centre of trouble, witnessing successive expulsions and returns of the Huguenots and the passage of several "processions blanches." [1] Henri III had organised in Picardy and in Champagne a Confrérie des Pénitents whose white habits had been blessed by the Papal Nuncio; the "pénitents" processed through the countryside, covering distances of 20 to 30 leagues, carrying relics and a consecrated Host. This Public display of guilt was intended to draw down divine favour on France and to ward off the ills which beset the land. Soissons became a centre for these processions, which not unnaturally attracted the mob of unemployed and down-and-outs, who used them as an excellent occasion for begging bread and wine. Plague, which these processions were intended to ward off, was spread from place to place and Soissons suffered particularly harshly, a fact attributed to the return of some Huguenot families rather than to the insanitary mendicants. This, then, is the background of Pierre Moreau's life, the story of which was often retold in the seventeenth century [2]; the following account is based on details from Les Vies des Saints (vol. III, Appendix I, pages lxii-lxxix).

He was breast-fed by his own mother (an unusual feature at this time amongst the wealthier classes from which he came) so that he might "sucer la piété avec le lait"; he spent an extraordinary childhood, giving his food to the children of the poor and, when he had none to give, "il les obligeait au moins de souffrir qu'il nettoyât leur vermine sans se mettre en peine qu'il attirait sur lui l'incommodité

---

[1] Claude Dormay, *Histoire de la Ville de Soissons*, 2 vols, Soissons, 1663; see Vol. II, pp. 464–466, 496–499.
[2] Dormay, *op. cit.*, II, book VI, ch. LI and ch. LXVIII, refers to a life "par un autre"; this was in 1663 and refers presumably to a biographical note in La Noue's *Chronique*. François Giry wrote a life of Moreau (Paris, 1687) and it is adapted for the *Vie des Saints*, Appendix I, pp. lxii-lxxx.

dont il tâchait de les exempter." This, says the author of his life, is so
surprising in a child that it can only be a sign of divine inspiration,
"... on ne doit point douter qu'elle lui fût inspirée [cette action] par
celui qui s'est chargé volontairement de nos ordures pour nous en
délivrer." His education was such as one would expect – the Humanities, philosophy, the sacred languages (it will be necessary to recall
this detail later), mathematics, medicine. These he studied at Soissons
and later at Paris; on the completion of his studies he went back to
Soissons to aid his mother who had been widowed. Next he went to
Orléans to study jurisprudence and became "avocat" at Paris. He
returned again to Soissons where the wealth left by his father could
easily have procured for him a high position in the judicature; he
preferred, however, to remain an "avocat," "s'estimant plus heureux
d'être le défenseur de la justice que d'en être arbitre, et de plaider pour
l'innocence que de condamner le coupable." His professional conduct
seems to have been remarkable in its probity; he never let a case hang
on in the courts so that he could gain fees thereby, and he gave
free legal aid to widows, orphans and the poor, in imitation, one is told,
of Saint Yves, the Patron Saint of the legal profession. He was consider-
ate also to his servants and became esteemed throughout Soissons.

   There then occurred the decisive event of his life, his presence at a
series of exorcisms in the cathedral. He had been deeply disturbed by
the rampant heresy in the town and wished to have tangible proof of
God's power against the powers of hell. Demons, in this age of human-
ism, usually spoke garbled Greek or Hebrew and the presence of one
who could act as interlocutor was of importance.[1] Pierre Moreau
intervened and drew upon himself all the wrath of Satan:

> Le serviteur de Dieu qui avait un désir incroyable de voir le S. Sacrement
> se confirmer lui-même en triomphant de toutes les puissances de l'enfer y
> [i.e. aux exorcismes] était extrêmement assidu, d'autant plus qu'ayant
> l'usage des langues savantes, il y pouvait servir à donner l'intelligence des
> mots grecs et des mots hébreux que les esprits des ténèbres prononcent assez
> souvent par la bouche de ceux qu'ils possèdent ... Son zèle excita la rage
> de ces monstres contre lui.

He returned after the exorcism to his "cabinet" and found all his books
and papers strewn about the place and at the same moment there was
an onset of violent physical pain. This obsession [2] lasted for forty years

---

[1] See the chapter on the Minim Claude Pithoys.
[2] *Possession* is defined as the inhabitation of a body by the Devil; *Obsession* is an attack
by the Devil upon the exterior causing torment "de même qu'un bourreau tourmente un

and left such a mark upon his face that the Bishops, clergy and the whole populace of Soissons were assured that the obsession was real: "il n'y avait personne qui ne regardât ce saint Athlète comme un autre Job et *comme une copie vivante de Jésus Christ souffrant sur le Calvaire.*" Like Saint Chrysostom's monk Stagirus, [1] he was drawn towards monastic life by obsession, while the presence in Soissons at that time of Pierre Nodé was a decisive factor in determining his choice of the Order of Minims. This Nodé (or Naudé) was prominent in the Order and was at one time Provincial of the Province of France (Paris). He was the author of a work on exorcisms, a fact it will be useful to recall later. He was uncle of the famous Gabriel Naudé who, although not a member of the Order, was closely connected with it through his friendship with Mersenne and through his interest in the library at the Place Royale. Moreau's entry into the Order was through membership of the Tiers-Ordre; his mother died shortly after his obsession, leaving him free to dispose of the family fortune as he chose. After a journey to Rome and to Loreto, he turned his home into a hospice and each Sunday and feast day brought into it a beggar whom he would serve himself and whose feet he would wash; he gave wine and food to the participants in the Processions Blanches and it is recorded in his life that: "Les misères publiques ne le touchaient pas moins que les particulières. Dans un temps de famine, où les marchands de blé fermaient leurs greniers pour attendre une plus grandre cherté, il ouvrit les siens, vendit son grain à un prix raisonnable et en donna une partie gratuitement aux pauvres ... Il faisait cuire plusieurs fois la semaine de grandes fournées de pain que l'on distribuait tous les matins à sa porte."

Moreau was the author of a translation into French of an Italian life of Saint François de Paule which, together with a few other writings on Demons, the Antichrist and Heretics, does not seem to have survived. From the moment that he joined the Order his whole life was devoted to the quest for perfection rather than to any intellectual activity. He was thirty-six years old when he became a novice but he gladly accepted all the menial tasks that a novice had to perform, such as the sweeping out of the conventual church. He fulfilled admirably, says the author of his life, the ideals of Saint Anthony – silence, modesty, austerity. In his patient suffering there is also a strong reminder of the temptations and torments of Saint

criminel et qu'un barbare tourmente un ennemi qui est devenu sa proie"; *Les Vies des Saints*, *loc. cit.*, p. lxvi.
[1] *Les Vies des Saints, loc. cit.*, p. lxvi.

Anthony: "Le démon ... déchirait ses habits, le jetait contre la terre, lui ensanglantait le visage ... lui cassait les dents ... Lorsque l'heure de l'office divin approchait, ce fervent serviteur de Dieu se mettant en chemin pour y être des premiers il (le démon) lui faisait paraître devant les yeux tantôt les abîmes, tantôt des troupes de bêtes sauvages qui faisaient mine de le vouloir dévorer." Similar horrors occurred to him in the refectory, in the dormitory and at Mass; but the inner torment was more hideous than the external. He was tempted to renounce his vows, to blaspheme, to abandon hope, to renounce all religion; but he merely exulted in his torments, abandoning himself entirely to the will of God and keeping everything to himself and to his confessor.

It is not the purpose here to suggest any sort of diagnosis of his ills any more than it is to find out how something kept strictly between himself and his confessor should have found its way into what was tantamount to popular reading. The interesting thing for the moment is to see how such a life was held up as an example and how the events could be reported in a work of piety; the importance of it is the object lesson it gives in seventeenth century monastic ideals and in religious fervour. It is against this background that the intellectual activity of the Order – and indeed all intellectual activity in the seventeenth century – must be judged.

Moreau, then, the wealthy and successful lawyer who practiced to the utmost the ideals of Christian charity, found his spiritual home within the Order of Saint François de Paule. After serving his noviciat, during which time, be it noted, his Correctors had to curb the excesses of his asceticism, he took his full vows and was ordained priest. He was known for his special devotion to the Passion of Our Lord and for his fervent devotion to the Founder and Patron of the Order; he was five times elected Corrector of the "couvent" at Soissons and was visited by Louis XIII and his Jesuit Confessor, le P. Arnoult. His torments did not cease, however, until the very end; blindness was added to all his other hardships for the last two years of his life. In 1626 he died after three days of peace, "le démon tant de fois vaincu ... fut contraint de se retirer." There were, as one may well imagine, the wildest death-bed scenes; the populace stormed the Minims' church to touch his body and to get snippets of his habit "pour servir à la guérison des malades": the Biship of Soissons himself pronounced his funeral oration and is reported as saying as he entered the church, "Nous allons enterrer un Saint."

It is difficult not to see in this life of Moreau an attempt by the authors at having him canonized or at least beatified; the same is true of the life of Nicolas Barré, and indeed in more recent times attempts have been made to reopen the case for canonization of Barré, but the modern author has to declare that his writings are not intended to prejudice any "procès de canonization" that may ensue [1]; nevertheless we find the Abbé Bremond speaking of Barré as "un des grands saints de ce temps–là ... que nous ne désespérons pas de voir un jour sur les autels." [2]

Barré, like Moreau, came from a wealthy provincial family. He was born in Amiens in 1621 and, also like Moreau, his childhood was one of singular piety and devotion – the authors of his life in the *Vies des Saints* go into some detail on this point. A Jesuit education in the College Saint-Nicolas doubtless heightened his religious inclinations and disciplined his already active intelligence; without any of the emotional storms that led Moreau into the Order, Barré simply made his choice at the age of 19 and served his noviciat in the "couvent" at Aniems. He was quickly translated to Paris: his vows were pronounced at Nigeon in 1640, and early in 1644 he was at la Place Royale, the intellectual centre of the Order. He fulfilled several functions including that of "garde" of the splendid library, sharing the office with Hilarion de Coste, the biographer and friend of Mersenne; however, the attractive intellectual activity of la Place Royale seems to have made no appeal to Barré. He exercised his office of "lector in philosophia" [3] with diligence but it was as a teacher of theology that he really distinguished himself. Like Moreau, his asceticism knew no limits; he spent long hours in meditation and, unkwnon to his superiors would spend all night prostrate before the Tabernacle in the conventual church, finding in the severity and harshness of the Order the necessary discipline for his spiritual ascent but supplementing these severities by others, of his own making, to force himself into the way of "perfection." He also, according to Thuillier,[4] indulged in an active mortification of his flesh to such an extent that his superiors had to intervene – another

---

[1] In order to conform with a decree of Urban VIII, (Pope, 1623–1644). In 1642 he issued *Decreta servanda in canonizatione et beatificatione sanctorum* and modern Catholic writers dealing with biographical material preface their work by a printed declaration of adherence to this decree. The Minim authors of the two appendices to *Les Vies des Saints* seem to have been content with a more tacit acceptance of it, although Simon Martin himself inserted a formal declaration in *Les Fleurs de la Solitude*, Paris, 1652.

[2] Bremond, *op. cit.*, vol. IX, p. 118.

[3] Archives Nationales LL. 1573, sub anno 1645.

[4] I. pp. 226–227.

point in common with Moreau. Suffering, real or imagined, external or self-inflicted, acquired an almost sacramental value; although the Superiors of the Order were always ready to curb any undue excess which might have led to hypocrisy in this matter and therefore to sin; all those who wrote about their fellow members of the Order seemed to exult in pain since, one infers from their writing, without it, true *imitation* of Christ (i.e. perfection) was unattainable.[1] If Moreau's suffering was that of a man obsessed by diabolic machinations, Barré's suffering is that of a man suffering because of man; his austerity had as its end to make him a better confessor and director and, later, to make him a more fitting example for those who were to work under him. His suffering was largely that of the religious man who finds himself struggling to convert the hardened libertine (a problem quite beyond the ken of Moreau). Again, it is not the intention here to question whether a less introspective nature might not have succeeded better; the important thing is to see the ideals of the Order in operation and to note how they affected a particular type of religious sensibility. One of the main differences between Moreau and Barré comes from the difference of their age, leading to a difference of ambience: Moreau was essentially a child of the upheavals of the Wars of Religion, an era of fanaticism and violence: although it would be wrong to minimize either the fanaticism or the violence of the seventeenth century, Barré belongs to a more stable age and the problems he faced were those of the beginning of the age of urbanism.

It is not surprising that Barré fell ill. His Superiors sent him back to Amiens to recuperate [2] from the effects of fifteen years incessant mortification of the body and senses. He spent two years in his native town and was thence transferred to Rouen, where the decisive action of his life took place. Rouen was an extremely busy city in the seventeenth century; its industry and port were flourishing, but a social problem of the most urgent and pressing kind was at once apparent to Barré. Industry and prosperity had caused over-population and the mass of lower class children lived in squalor and ignorance. It is a matter of history how Barré founded at Rouen his first charitable

---

[1] See for example Thuillier, I, pp. 191/2. Writing of the Minim Abraham Patron, he says: "Primum tentata est eius valetudo tremore nervorum, ad quem averruncandum nihil profuerunt aquae medicatae, balneaque calida ... inutilia quoque fuerunt quaecumque alia remedia ... donec demum in absolutam paralysim incidit ... etc. Virum hoc in statu pro Christi amore patientium exemplar, vera dolorum ... victima; dicam melius, perfectissimus Provinciae nostrae Job, integris plusquam octo annis innumerabilium dolores morborum ... toleravit."

[2] Le Chanoine Farcy, *Le R. P. Barré, religieux Minime*, Paris, 1942, p. 34.

organisation for the education of these children and how this organisation spread to Reims, Dijon, Chalon-sur-Saône and to Marseille. It
is likewise a matter of history that Barré returned to Paris and there
founded another institute in the Rue St. Maur and how Madame de
Maintenon chose from amongst the sisters of this institute the first
"institutrices" for her own charitable organisation at Saint Cyr.[1] Le
P. Barré has therefore his place in the history of education, and it is
interesting to see what his foundations owe to the example of other
similar organisations in the seventeenth century and what they owe
to his own personality – particularly in so far as his personality was
shaped and moulded by the ideals of the Order.

Le Chanoine Cordonnier has pointed out [2] that numerous attempts
had been made in Paris and elsewhere to tackle the problem of educating the illiterate masses, but these attempts had two faults; either
they were initiated by individual curés in parishes and therefore
lacked cohesion and system, or else they were in the hands of monastic
organisations – one thinks particularly of the Ursulines – and were
therefore in some measure thwarted by cloistral discipline; the sisters
could not, for example, go out into the streets to find the children but
had to wait for those who presented themselves. Barré's system com-
bines both the organisation and discipline of the one and the freedom
of the other – hence his originality and his success. He realised that,
although this was a job only for women with vocation, it was not a job
for those who had bound themselves to monastic vows; his organisation
is on the lines of a Tiers-Ordre. The female Order of Minims was
never strong in France; it had two "couvents" only and played no
conspicuous part in either education or nursing; Barré's own sister
Louise [3] was a member of this Order and so also were the sisters of
several other members whom Barré may be presumed to have known,
but it was not from amongst them that he recruited his "institutrices";
he found them from amongst members of a "confrérie" that had been

---

[1] See Le Chanoine Farcy, op. cit. and also L'Institut des Sœurs du Saint-Enfant Jésus ...
des origines jusqu'à nos jours, Rouen, 1938. For the loan of these two books I am endebted to
the Reverend Mother Superior of Annecy Convent, Seaford, Sussex, whose institution is
a direct offshoot of le P. Barré's foundation. See also H. de Grèzes, la Vie du P. Barré ...
fondateur de l'institut des écoles charitables, Bar-le-Duc, 1892; C. Cordonnier, le R. P. Barré,
Paris, 1932; Y. Poutet, l'Influence du P. Barré dans la fondation des Sœurs du Saint-Enfant Jésus de
Reims, article in Revue d'Histoire de l'Eglise de France, vol. XLVI, No. 143, Paris, 1960. I am
also endebted to the Reverend Mother Superior of Saint Maur's Convent, Weybridge,
Surrey for lending me a copy of Charitable Mistresses of the Holy Infant Jesus, Dornach, 1925,
a book dealing chiefly with XIXth century developments of the Institute founded by Barré.
[2] op. cit., pp. 153 et sq.
[3] Thuillier op. cit., II, pp. 151–152.

established for some time in Rouen, the Confrérie (or Famille) du Saint-Enfant Jésus attached to the church of the Oratorians in the town. The cult of the Holy Childhood, together with the cult of the Sacred Heart, became increasingly popular in seventeenth century France; before the followers of le P. Eudes had made a speciality of the latter, the former cult was widespread; its origins went back to the early Church and in particular to the mediaeval nativity scenes, but it was revived in a distinct form (i.e. distinct from Italian worship of "Bambini") and in a particularly mystic form during the early seventeenth century by a Carmelite nun, la Sœur Marguerite du Saint-Sacrement, in Beaune. The Infant Christ is already the Christ of the Passion and, in so far as the Minims espoused any particular devotional cult, it was this.[1] Le P. Giry wrote a *Traité de la Sainte enfance*,[2] and several "confréries" were attached to the Order which had as their object devotion to the Holy Family or to the Holy Child. We know from Barré's devotional writings that he was himself much attracted to the cult; we know also from all that the Minims wrote that they were attracted to humility, poverty and charity. All this Barré eloquently preached from the pulpit of the Minims' church in Rouen, urging that action be taken to save the children of the urban masses. The appeal "nisi conversi fueritis ... sicut parvuli" was immediate and calculated to strike particularly deeply with members of the Confrérie du Saint-Enfant. Le Chanoine Farcy has collected the documentary evidence to prove the point: six of the first members of Barré's institute were members of the Confrérie and several more of its members helped. The Charitable Sisters who bound themselves to Barré were subject to disciplinary measures which belong to the Minim tradition of austerity. In one respect they were less fortunate than members of the Order who had a long established organisation behind them and one which allowed the monastic houses to accept gifts of property and in kind to assure their stability; Barré, on the other hand, insisted from the first that his Institute should subsist solely upon Providence. A rigorous programme of devotion and a heavy time-table made demands upon the sisters which seem exorbitant to-day; they were, however, in keeping with the superlative nature of the Minims' ideals, but at the same time show an interesting departure from them: a departure,

---

[1] Their devotion seems to have been universal with the exception that the Minims of Beaune opposed the beatification of Marguerite; this seems to have been merely a local objection. See l'Abbé Deberre, *Histoire de la Vénérable Marguerite ... de Beaune*, Paris, 1907.
[2] Paris, 1670.

that is, from the belief that perfection could be obtained only by separation from the world. We find here that Barré sticks closely to that primitive conception of "Caritas" which was in the mind of Saint François de Paule and which was ever present in the mind of Barré's near contemporary, Saint Vincent de Paul. Barré is doing more than commenting upon the Minims' device [1] when he wrote in the statutes for the Ecoles Charitables "C'est une erreur de croire et de s'imaginer qu'en travaillant par charité pour autrui on se perd soi-même, et qu'on se ruine en enrichissant les autres." As well as charity he urged obedience, disinterestedness, a total abandonment to Providence and an "esprit de famille"; his Sisters therefore had to refuse all gifts from parents or from the children; had to give themselves up entirely to the day's work; were forbidden to speak about the station which they held in the world. The routine, based as one may imagine upon monastic practice, was monotonous but not, compared with the general practice of the day, unenlightened; against the background of the most horrible squalor an attempt was made at teaching decency and cleanliness – the elements of house-keeping were taught and a monthly roster of domestic duties adhered to by the pupils. The educational work of the Order is considered briefly in the chapter on the place of studies in the Order, while the history of the spread of Barré's charitable organisation leads us away from the history of the Order itself and must be considered irrelevant here. The Order admired Barré as an example of the highest ideals for which it stood (witness his life in Thuillier's *Diarium Patrum* and in *Les Vies des Saints*). It also provided a successor, le P. Giry, as head of the charitable foundations, but it did little else to espouse the cause of its illustrious son. Le Chanoine Farcy attributes this lack of continued interest to a motive of jealousy amongst members of the Order.[2] They were, according to him, glad enough to have in their midst a brilliant preacher and confessor but considered that his work detracted from the central purpose of the Order. There may be some truth in this, but all members of the Order who wrote about Barré after his death eulogise him; it is more likely, therefore, that the Order realised, as Barré had done initially, that the work called for workers who were not sequestrated by monastic vows and so were content, when le P. Giry died in 1688 only two years after Barré, to allow the direction of the Institute to pass into the hands of the secular clergy.

---

[1] The word Caritas emblazoned.
[2] *l'Institut des Sœurs charitables* p. 89.

To have died well is probably the most important outward sign of inner spiritual peace. Thus Thuillier insists upon the point for the least known as well as for the most famous; an unfortunate Irishman, Francis Hebron, joined the Order on the 28th of March 1617 and died of consumption at Nigeon on the 24th of May in the following year: "... ex vitio pulmonum, cum gaudio et magna animi ad voluntatem Dei submissione suscepit, consecutus est." [1] Of the death of Nicolas Barré he gives a minute description occupying four pages,[2] lingering day by day with the dying man, exulting in his final serenity and in the attraction that the news of his death had for the Paris crowd:

Eo vero temporis, quo nobiscum superstes extitit, articulo, ita tranquillo fuit animo, quieta mente, et fronte serena, ut manifestare videretur Deus se Servi sui jam remunerare labores, et praemia meritis elargiri. Post haec ... emisit spiritum. Vicinis de illius mortis luctuoso campanarum sonitu admonitis, omnium sermone per universam urbem percrebuit Hominem sanctum in Conventu Minimorum modo diem clausisse supremum.

The perfect death, calm and serene, was possible only to those who had forced themselves to contemplate death and who had no earthly connexions at the time of their agony.

The essential qualities of the Minims' beliefs and attitudes are summed up in the following quotations taken from a little known work by one of their Provincials, André Chavineau,[3] called *Le tableau de la mort, pris sur la religieuse fin de Père Ange de Joyeuse, Capucin*, and printed in Tours in 1609:

Obsession with the thought of death and naïveté of its presentation:

L'idée de la mort ... nous la retrouvons étrange en mourant et non seulement à notre sujet, mais si quelqu'un de nos amis, nos femmes, voire et nos enfants (que nous avons aimés lorsqu'ils respiraient) change d'habits et de face, nous les avons en horreur et fuyons et leur personnes et le lieu qui les contient, lorsque cette fille de la nuit se présente à nous, sans yeux, sans oreilles, sans chair, peau, tendons, veines, muscles et nerfs, et que nous la considérons en squelette tenant une faux en sa main portant cette devise "Memini Parco," nous frémissons.[4]

Total belief in the worthlessness of man and in his imperative need of redemption by the Cross:

---

[1] *op. cit.*, I, p. 214.
[2] *ibid.*, I, pp. 247–250.
[3] See also pp. 167 and 176.
[4] *op. cit.*, pp. 6–7. A "Baroque" obsession.

Combien de fois me fussé-je précipité dans les abîmes de l'enfer si mon Dieu ne m'en eût retiré? Comment un pauvre ver de terre pourrait s'effleurer jusques au ciel, s'il ne rencontrait pas l'arbre de la Croix? [1]

Fear of the World:

Mais quoi dira quelque homme attaché à la cuisine du monde et vivant aux gages des voluptés? [2]

Again, in the letters which Barré wrote to his Sœurs Charitables, we find the same belief in the "anéantissement" of man's condition on the one hand and the possibility of his Glory on the other:

Pour donner des règles à la Nature corrompue ... vous devez vous comparer à un cheval que l'on ne nourrit que pour travailler ... à un âne, animal pesant et paresseux, que l'on nourrit de chardons et auquel on n'épargne aucunement les coups ... à une brebis toute prête à être tondue, égorgée et écorchée, et cela sans bruit. Vous travaillerez à vous rendre silencieuse et muette comme une carpe ... petite comme une souris ... mais sur la pure miséricorde de Dieu vous aurez à cœur de vous rendre comme un Ange et comme un Saint du Paradis, c'est-à-dire, présente à la Majestueuse grandeur et souveraineté de Dieu par une adoration amoureuse, profonde, silencieuse, continuelle et sans relâche autant que faire se peut, au moins dans les temps prescrits et déterminés chaque jour.[3]

This forgetfulness of the body was doubtless heightened by the severity of the rule and by the particular mortification that living in perpetual Lent must have inflicted. There is an ecstatic fervour about the way in which they lived and about their joyful self-effacement which often bordered, it seems, on the masochistic. When Barré wrote: "l'amour propre qui nous est plus intime que le mœlle de nos os", [4] it is difficult not to make a comparison with La Rochefoucauld in the *Maximes;* but the comparison is nothing more than superficial. If there is a temptation to call the fortitude of members of the Order "stoical", one should remember that, unlike the hero of the great classics and unlike the ideal of the "honnête homme" seen in the pages of the *Maximes,* the Minims' conception of the perfect life owed little if anything to Seneca or Cicero but a great deal to Saint Anthony and Saint Francis of Assisi. If there is a temptation to see in their self-effacement a parallel

---

[1] *ibid.,* p. 47.

[2] *ibid.,* p. 10.

[3] N. Barré, *Lettres spirituelles,* Rouen, 1697, pp. 143-145. In substance a truly Pascalian expression of the infinitely miserable and infinitely great; in style, however, it is far from Pascalian, particularly in the near bathos of the ending.

[4] In a recently printed letter; *Un texte inédit du P. Barré* by Y. Poutet in *Revue d'Ascétique et de mystique,* No. 143, Toulouse, 1960, pp. 350-356.

with the classical exclusion of self, one should remember that, by the practice of his vows and by frequency at the confessional, a Minim was forced towards a self-examination of the most rigorous and searching type; he appears as an introvert in an age which tended to admire a more impersonal analysis of the human condition. This is partly brought about because the commonly received idea of the seventeenth century tends to reside too much upon the judgement of a few masterpieces; but more particularly it is due to this, that whereas the heroism of the classical hero and the idea of "honnêteté" stem from philosophical and aesthetic theories, the introspection of the Minim comes from his having rubbed shoulders with harsher realities of life than those met with in the comparative ease of Parisian and Court life. His apparent stoicism is not a philosophical attitude at all, but a sharp reaction to conditions as he found them and to the disparity between these conditions and the spiritual ideals held up for him to follow. He was nearer to La Bruyère than to La Rochefoucauld, if one is to make a comparison with the well known figures of the century. "Le motif seul fait le mérite des actions," wrote La Bruyère in *Du mérite personnel*,[1] and La Rochefoucauld would have agreed; but, La Bruyère goes on, "le désintéressement y met la perfection" – surely meaningless to the author of the *Maximes* but very close to the authors of *Les Vies des Saints*.

---

[1] *Les Caractères, Du mérite personnel*, No. 41, Paris (Garnier) 1963, p. 110.

GALLICAN TENDENCIES OF THE
FRENCH MINIMS

As a token of respect for the Order which his father had established in France, Charles VIII founded a "couvent" in Rome, Santa Trinità dei Monti, for the benefit of the French Minims; immediately Saint François de Paule, then Corrector General of his own order, granted a special privilege: "en l'an 1501 ... ordonna par privilège spécial et prérogative octroyée à la nation française que de là ci-devant ledit couvent des Minimes de Rome serait apprêté aux religieux français et gouverné par eux et non par autres." [1] At the same time, the French were given the right to exclude members of the Order of any other nationality; these privileges were confirmed by Julius III at the request of Henri II in 1553 and were further implemented by Paul III. The sumptuous church and extensive conventual buildings are intact and virtually unchanged since the day Claude did his *View of Rome*.[2] The site is magnificent, one of the best in the whole of Rome, on the leading edge of the Monte Pincio and with the woods of the Villa Borghese behind. This French enclave in Rome was quite naturally an object of envy to the other nations and a privilege jealously guarded by the French Minims. Any attempt at gaining access was looked upon as a move of deep political significance, even if it were made by French members who had taken their vows abroad or by peripheral Frenchmen, such as the Provençaux. Several such attempts were made during the seventeenth century and they became magnified out of all proportion because of the acutely sensitive nationalism of the French. It is impossible to distinguish patriotism from Gallicanism; the Minims had every encouragement to adhere to the French throne since, from the earliest days of the Order, Kings and Queens of France had

---

[1] *Instruction pour le couvent royal des Minimes français à Rome;* Bibl. Nat., Ancien Fonds Français, 4055, fol. 22–23.
[2] Reproduced in the Appendix.

bestowed privileges upon the Order and had themselves been members of the Tiers-Ordre. Later, in the section devoted to Historical Studies, we shall see the extent of the Gallicanism of such writers as Hilarion de Coste; it is also as well at this point to recall the intensity of patriotic feeling in Du Val's *Vie et miracles de Saint François de Paule,* dedicated to Anne of Austria and referring to the birth of the Dauphin (Louis XIV) in terms which leave no doubt that the author thought of it as miraculous. Hippolyte Raulin's *Panégyrique orthodoxe, mystérieux et prophétique sur l'antiquité des Fleurs de Lys* and Chavineau's *Lettres d'un solitaire au Roi* further emphasise this patriotic fervour. It is also apposite at this point to recall that the "couvent" of Santa Trinità dei Monti was frequently styled "Couvent *Royal* des Minimes français à Rome." No other order and no other nation could so blatantly emphasize its autonomy in the very heart of Rome. By and large, the religious orders received little official support in France during the seventeenth century; there were strong reasons why the Minims enjoyed a privileged position.

For many years attempts were made to weaken the French position in Rome. The "Royal" and "French" "couvent" became more than an object of envy; it became the symbol of French intrusion into Roman affairs. François de Paule was a Calabrian and, perhaps because he had signified quite clearly his preference for the French, it was the Calabrians, under Cardinal Spada, who in the XVIIth century were particularly irritated by this intrusion. It was therefore a longstanding controversy that le Sieur d'Aubeville was ordered to settle when he took up his appointment as Ambassador in Rome 1661.[1] The various phases of this quarrel can be found in Mgr. Fourier Bonnard's history of the "couvent" [2]: the sources of his history are the relevant documents in the archives of the Pieux établissements français à Rome and the relevant files in the archives of the French Embassy at Rome. He makes no reference, however, to certain other documents which throw a different light on the dispute and show that the crux of the matter was a domestic quarrel which was merely acerbated by foreign dissension. The documents are:

(a) A complete memoir of the "affaire Flasche-Bachelier" in 1645. (Bibl. Nat. F.F. 17588, fol. 235–258).[3]

---

[1] *Mémoire pour servir d'instruction au Sieur d'Aubeville ... s'en allant à Rome par ordre de sa Majesté ... 5 mai, 1661;* printed in *Recueil des instructions données aux Ambassadeurs et Ministres du Roi; Introduction et notes par G. Hanotaux,* Paris, 1888; Vol. I, pp. 87–89. See also Mgr. J-M. Vidal, *Les droits de la France à la Trinité des Monts à Rome,* Paris, 1933.

[2] *Histoire du Couvent Royal de la Trinité du mont Pincio à Rome,* Paris, 1933.

[3] The catalogue entry gives no indication of this set of documents.

(b) Part of a collection called *La sédition en Normandie*. (Bibl. Nat. F.F.
18938, fol. 184–187).
(c) A letter to the King from the Minimes d'Avignon, undated.
(Avignon, Musée Calvet, MSS 2397).
(d) A printed *Discours au Roi* by F. Ogier, 1629. (Bibl. Nat. F.F.
15769).
(e) The printed works of Nicolas Chichon.[1]

The "affaire Flasche-Bachelier" was probably in the first place a
clash of character: Bachelier had, as Corrector General, already met
opposition. He was stern and inflexible and singularly lacking in
"Caritas" – the motto of his Order. During his "visite générale" in
1627, he deprived three Minims of St. Etienne of the right to vote in
their assemblies; he ordered that they should scourge themselves in the
refectory while the Miserere was said and that they should be imprisoned in the "couvent" at St. Chamond. The Provincial of Lyons,
le Père le Bourg, objected to the severity of the punishment and
voiced his complaint at the General Chapter in 1629. He was supported
by several other Provincials. Bachelier faced opposition of a more
serious nature when he was again Corrector General after the election
of 1637.
At the General Chapter held in Rome in 1623 two important
administrative changes were made. It was decided that, for the purposes
of voting, the provinces of Germany, Flanders, Lorraine, Burgundy,
Savoy, Switzerland and the Comté d'Avignon [2] should form a bloc
with France – "ces provinces étant gauloises et plus voisines de la
France que de l'Italie et l'Espagne." (We have here a miniature object
lesson in France's territorial aspirations in the XVIIth century). At
the same time it was decided that if a Corrector General were to die
while he was in office, two members of each *nation* should meet with
the late Corrector's "Collègues" to elect the successor. The resolution
was, obviously, a weak one since it relied on such a dubious term as
"nation." In 1635, at Marseilles, this rule was altered so that the
Provincials of the fifth and sixth Provinces of each country should

[1] In the Bibliothèque Municipale, Poitiers. See the Bibliography under Chichon, N.
[2] There are very few other references to Avignon as a *Province*. It was always considered
as forming a part of the Province de Provence. There is, however, a memoir concerning an
attempted separation, Bibl. Nat. F.F., 18938, fol. 184–187. The memoir condemns this
separation as "dommageable au bien de la France, aux droits des Français et au bonheur
de tant de maisons régulières," undated, but presumably c. 1620. See Bibliography. The
Minims of Avignon also petitioned the King to be allowed to enter Santa Trinità on the
grounds that they were French: Avignon, Musée Calvet, MSS 2397.

act as electors with the Provincials of the seventh and eighth as their
"commis."

In January 1637 the Corrector General died. The court of electors
was to meet in Genoa on the 25th of September. For France, the
Provincials of Lyons and Provence were nominated as electors and
those of Flanders and Champagne as "commis." The Provincial of
Champagne was Bachelier whose previous election to Corrector
General had been made by the influence of the Spanish faction. He
proceeded to obtain "lettres de cachet" to exclude the Provinces of
Flanders and Germany so that Champagne became the sixth in seni-
ority and so that he, Bachelier, should go forward as an elector. The
Spanish and Italian electors together with one of the French electors
who was in Rome at the time, met in Genoa. The others failed to turn
up. In the case of absence, they were supposed to postpone the election;
Bachelier and the other French electors met in Lyons and deliberately
delayed. The court in Genoa proceeded to elect Pizzurno corrector;
Bachelier managed to prove the invalidity of the election and got
himself nominated instead.[1]

In June 1640 Bachelier set out from Nevers on his "Visite Générale"
of the Province de France (Paris) of which le Père Flasche was then
Provincial. By August he was in Calais where he was taken ill and was
unable to continue the visit until Christmas; by Easter he still had not
finished. In spite of this long delay, he foolishly prevented the Provincials from going on their annual visits until he had completed his
own tour; he caused considerable inconvenience thereby and infringed
a rule which stated: "Correctorium visitationes breviori quam com-
mode poterunt tempore; peragant ne ex eorum prolixia visitatione
incommoda patiantur conventus et fratres." During this time he
ordered several transfers between "couvents" without letting the
Provincial know; he insisted that a brother at Vincennes should vote
in spite of the fact that he had been deprived of the right by his own
Corrector; he accepted novices into the Place Royale and into Fublaines without informing the Provincial – all this is set out in an
indictment drawn up by Flasche and seems quite in keeping with
what we know of Bachelier's character. Flasche also added that during
the period fron Christmas to Easter Bachelier had lived in the Place
Royale and had lived "vie commune" [2] and that he had prevented

---

[1] Bibl. Nat., F.F. 17588, fol. 257–258. Memoir of the "affaire Flasche-Bachelier." This
document is referred to in subsequent footnotes as *Mémoire;* the term "affaire Flasche-
Bachelier" is of my own coining and is not to be found in the catalogue of MSS.

[2] "C'est-à-dire mangeant de la chair," added in margin.

two members of the Order, Michel le Vayer and Jean Segrétier, from going to Rome – violence had been done to them on the road.[1]

Because of the indictment that le Père Flasche made, Bachelier wrote threatening letters to Flasche ordering the Provincial to appear before him within eighteen hours. This was an illegal action since the rules required the presence of six other superiors who could not possibly have come together in so short a space of time. Flasche then appealed to the secular arm and Bachelier, invoking the bull of Gregory XIII which forbade such appeals, at once excommunicated him and ordered him to retire to Decize. But Flasche pointed out that he had appealed to the King as "protecteur contre les violences" and that Bachelier's accusation was not covered by the bull which aimed at curbing appeals "pour opposition et résistances par voies de fait et non de droit." [2] As well as calling upon the King, Flasche also appealed to the Pope, thus fulfilling his duties as a Gallican [3]; he also set out his proposals for the reform of the Order, reforms which also savour of gallicanism – that there should be no further division of the Order into Provinces and that there should be one Corrector for the whole of France.[4]

It is Nicolas Chichon who connects this involved dispute with Santa Trinità dei Monti. He was a Provençal by birth but had spent a number of years in the Province of Tours, mostly at Poitiers. I am unable to agree with Mgr. Fourrier Bonnard that he was "saint homme et savant théologien." [5] He was one of several members of the Order to enter into open debate with Calvinist ministres; two of his harangues with a M. de Curville were published in Poitiers in 1619 and 1620 – strange mixtures of "préciosité" and the most facile sophistry: the reader is invited to accept the first of these harangues as "un déjeuner avant un dîner"; the second, attempting to prove the atheism of the Reformed Church, culminates in the following syllogism: –

> Nul infidel est Catholique et Chrétien;
> M. de Curville est infidel –
> Donc M. de Curville n'est ni Catholique ni Chrétien.

The only other work on which his literary fame might have rested was deemed to be seditious and was burnt by the Corrector of Poitiers by

---

[1] *Mémoire*, fol. 235–236.

[2] Flasche relied on the text-book of canon law as concerning the Orders, *Dubia Regularia*, Lyon, 1629. (Several editions).

[3] *Mémoire*, fol. 236–238.

[4] *ibid.*, fol. 247 and the amplification of his whole position, fol. 238–245.

[5] *op. cit.* p. 71. Mgr. Bonnard associates neither Chichon nor Bachelier with the controversy over Santa Trinità.

order of the King.[1] He was imprisoned in the "couvent" of Tours, but escaped: "ayant trouvé moyen de forcer les prisons, il s'est retiré à Rome au couvent de la très-sainte Trinité du mont." [2] He once again began a seditious work, *Occidando Tyranno*, and this in its turn was suppressed by the French embassy in Rome. He stirred up trouble by having Pizzurno ejected from the "couvent" on the grounds that he was Italian, while at the same time he managed to gain the admission of others (Provençaux?). Bachelier, it seems, was the instigator [3]; Pizzurno was, as we have seen, his chief rival for the correctorship of the whole Order and, in 1637 when he was elected, Chichon used his influence to reverse the decision and to get Bachelier elected in his place: "et afin que le Général de l'Ordre souffrît de ses (i.e. de Chichon) violences aussi bien que les particuliers, il a sous l'autorité dudit ambassadeur disputé l'éléction du Collègue Général français et puis celle du Général (Pizzurno) et, ayant obtenu sur lui que par divers artifices on ait défendu par lettre de cachet aux Provinciaux de France de reconnaître ledit Général jusqu'à ce que notre Saint Père ait jugé sur le différend; ce qui met l'ordre des Minimes en grand hasard, attendu l'impunité des discoles faute de Supérieur auquel on puisse avoir recours." [4]

If we can analyse Chichons plan, we can see something of the problems of the age. He was a Provençal and yet he managed to get an Italian excluded from Santa Trinità – an excellent way of getting himself accepted as "French." In addition to this he excluded from the correctorship an Italian and secured the election of a Frenchman – again, on the face of it, proving his French sympathies: but, far from making for French unity, his intrusion weakened it. The paradox of French unity being by a Frenchman is the paradox of a newly integrated nation composed of many related but contrasting elements. The suggestions put forward by Flasche are strikingly "modern" for the period 1620–1640 in the insistence upon national, rather than provincial, centralization: there is, in addition, one observation which he makes that is a reflexion of his Gallicanism and which has a more permanent interest and value as an object lesson in French unity and disunity:

[1] *Mémoire*, fol. 255.
[2] *ibid.*
[3] *ibid.*, fol. 249.
[4] *ibid.*, fol. 255. Discole – qui est non doctrinable: La Curne de Ste Palaye, *Glossaire de la langue française*, Vol. V. Littré: dyscole, difficile à vivre, de mauvaise humeur.

Or, tant s'en faut que cette poursuite nous soit avantageuse, au contraire elle est préjudiciable à notre nation parce qu'elle la met en haine des autres desquelles elle a toujours été si considérée que, de 38 généraux, il s'en trouve 22 de Français; de 36 procureurs généraux, 26 de Français. Et les Italiens et les Espagnols vinrent en cette assemblée de Gênes en intention d'élire un Français pour Général et l'eussent effectué si l'absence des nôtres ne les eût irrités. Et jamais en aucunes assemblées ne se sont détournés des Français que par l'induction des Français mêmes.[1]

The name of Chavineau has not yet been mentioned in this "affaire." He was the author of an extremely patriotic work on the successful outcome of the siege of La Rochelle,[2] published in Poitiers in 1628. He is named in the memoir as the Corrector who burned Chichon's seditious work and he is further referred to [3] as the Provincial of Tours whom the French Minims in Rome approached to obtain a letter from the Ambassador to prevent further incidents. The memoir ends ". . . ce qui a donné sujet à quelqu'un (à nous inconnu) de calomnier d'ambition ledit Père Chavineau."

Further trouble did in fact occur; in 1645 the King ordered the expulsion from Santa Trinità of a Minim called Ferrand who, although French, had made his profession in Italy, at Bologna. A few Minims petitioned the King in Ferrand's favour, amongst them Simon Bachelier.[4]

The seat of the trouble in these two disputes is not really Italian jealousy; it is much more a domestic matter and, like most religious problems in seventeenth century France, can best be interpreted in terms of gallican interests. We do not know what the motives of Chichon and Bachelier were – personal ambition and self-agrandizement as likely as not – and as for Ferrand the question of motive does not arise. But what is quite clear is the reaction which their behaviour provoked; from a clash of personalities (Flasche-Bachelier) and from the assertiveness of an insignificant monk (Chichon), there blows up a controversy which compromises the whole organisation of the Order, which leads to an invocation of the rights of the Gallican Church and which involves the King himself and his Ambassador in Rome to whom an *Instruction* (undated) was drafted, outlining the history of the autonomy of Santa Trinità.[5] The full significance of the *Instruction*

[1] *Mémoire*, fol. 257–258.
[2] *Lettres d'un solitaire*, Poitiers, 1628.
[3] *Mémoire*, fol. 257–258.
[4] Bibl. Nat., F.F. 15721, fol. 700–706. Apparently unknown to Mgr. F. Bonnard.
[5] Bibl. Nat. Ancien Fonds, 4055, fol. 22–23, previously quoted.

is contained in the last two paragraphs in which the Ambassador is required to:

Supplier (le Pape) en tant que urgent plaid de confirmer lesdits privilèges et pouvoirs de rendre convenable à l'entretenuement (sic) de l'exemption dudit couvent ... et d'en prendre la protection envers sa sainteté *comme de chose concernant l'intérêt du Roi et de la Nation française.*

Pour tailler l'herbe sous les pieds de la partie adverse et maintenir le Roi en ses droits, aussi la religion en sa perfection, faut constituer un cardinal français ... protecteur de la nation française.

From the whole *Instruction* and particularly from the two passages in italics in the quotation, it is clear that, whatever motives Bachelier and Chichon may have had, ultramontane tendencies were imputed to them.

PART III

THE INTELLECTUAL

CHAPTER I

THE PLACE OF STUDIES IN THE ORDER

Shortly after the foundation of the Order the question of "studies" was raised at a General Chapter. To what extent should members of the Order study the Humanities as distinct from Theology? What should be the amount of time spent upon such studies? Should members of the Order acquire academic distinctions at the Universities? These and many others were the questions that occurred from time to time throughout the sixteenth century and during the whole period under review. The position is clarified by Pizzurnus in the *Manipulus Minimorum*, under the heading *Studium*.[1] In 1523, at the General Chapter held in Rome, the following exhortation was made, "Praecipitur Provincialibus studii continuatio sub poena suspensionis officii." This was followed by the stringent *Coactio* (Malaga, 1526); "Cogantur studentes impigre bonis litteris vacare. Negligentes puniantur inedia panis et aquae pro una vice et ad studium frequentandum moneantur. Et si ter moniti cum debito intervallo, contempserint; priventur per annum utraque voce et per mensem faciant coquinam." More practical are the decrees governing "Lectores":

Forment suas lectiones omnes lectores quod eorum auditores ad edificatoriem prædicandum et confessiones audiendum – idoneos aptos efficiant. (Paula, 1535 and Avignon, 1599).

Provideat quilibet Provincialis in sua Provincia de idoneo, aut pluribus, lectoribus, secundum uniuscuiusque spiritus capacitatem. (Avignon, 1599).

Legere lectores debent a Festo Omnium Sanctorum ad Nativitatem Sancti Ionnai Baptistae. (Avignon, 1599).

The Lectores seem to have been largely occupied with reading during meal-times when silence had to be observed [2]; they also had

---

[1] pp. 199–201; paragraphs 1255–1270.
[2] *ibid.*, p. 134, *Lectura;* p. 197, *Silentium,* and p. 188, *Refectio.*

their place in educating the novices by reading and, we may believe, in teaching some to read. It was not until the beginning of the seventeenth century that a definite rule was formulated concerning the establishment of centres of instruction within the Provinces, and then at the rate of one per Province, (Decree of Clement VIII). The seventeenth century rules governed for the most part such things as the prohibition against receiving university distinctions, except at Salamanca and Alcalá (by decree of the General Chapter, Genoa, 1646); the languages that were to be taught – Latin, Greek, Hebrew and, "in scolis celebrioribus," Arabic, (Decree of Paul V). There was also the interesting rule passed at Barcelona in 1661 and confirmed at Milan in 1679, which established the teaching of thomistic principles as "de rigueur" throughout the Order. It is quite clear from Pizzurnus that studies were a privilege and that punishment followed any abuse: "Abutentes studiosi privilegiis concessis acriter puniantur. Et si non se emendant priventur studio a Provinciali." Bread and water and cookhouse duties for the slackers and those who indulged in intellectual delights – the whole tone seems a little minatory to the modern reader. It is not possible to speak of the Minims as an intellectual body as it is of the Jesuits, the Oratorians, the Benedictines of the Congregation of Saint Maur or the Dominicans. Impressive as the intellectual activity of the Order undoubtedly is, it must be considered against the austerity of their spiritual discipline; the majority of members would probably have agreed with one of their Correctors, Nicolas Lesguillier, who wrote in his *Ratio Studiorum* the following quotation from Seneca:

> O hominem eruditum!
> Simus autem nos hoc titulo rusticiore contenti;
> O virum bonum! [1]

The austerity and the puritanical rejection of all that did not tend towards the advancement of spiritual perfection were not only noticeable in the devotional life within the cloister, but were also a feature of the intellectual activity that was carried on there, we therefore find Lesguillier mistrustful of the human intellect and speaking of the blemishes on the face of human knowledge: "humanae scientiae naevi sex." These blemishes are:

---

[1] N. Lesguillier was Corrector at la Place Royale; his *Ratio Studiorum* was published in Paris in 1639. Quotation from p. 92. There is no evidence of any direct influence, other than in the title, perhaps, of the Jesuit *Ratio Studiorum*, Rome, 1586 and subsequently many editions; the Jesuit work deals with organisation of classes, marking exercises and so forth. The quotation from Seneca is from a letter (*Epist.* 88. 33) on philosophy and education.

(a) Exilitas seu tenuitas.
(b) Easdem obtenendi difficultas interdum impossibilitas.
(c) Insipidia et ingrata illarum possessio.
(d) Quin et exitialis in nobis sua proles.
(e) Earumdem ex accedenti facilis iactura.
(f) Etiam per se usuræ brevitas.[1]

He considers that all time and effort spent on such imperfections should merely fill in those odd moments of the day which would otherwise have been idle. Intellectual pursuits come therefore at the bottom of the scale of importance; moreover, he is mistrustful of books, thinking with Callimachus, "magnum librum magni mali instar esse." [2] He backs up his arguments with repeated quotations from Seneca and from the Fathers of the Church, coming to the somewhat stark and minatory conclusion:

Licet sapere, sed sine pompa, sine invidia, sine ambitione, semper memineris Minimitanum te esse et de Minimorum Ordine, apud quos sub gravissima censura cautum est, ne ulla doctrinæ praeferantur insignia, nulla doctoralis ambiatur laurea.[3]

This leads him to a general reflexion upon the place of "studies" in the Order with reference to its Rule:

Caeterum perperam impensum liberalibus disciplinis (quæ solam excolunt intelligentiam) videretur esse studium, si quod ad salutem spiritualemque profectum apprime necessarium est, quodque quotidianis colendum officiis, alta quodammodo defossum iaceret ignorantia, utique Regulae nostrae laboraretur inscitia.

Quapropter operae pretium facturum me existimavi, si communibus praeceptis ac generalibus studendi discendique; prioribus regulis, opera nostra speciale quoddam aliud documentum accederet de ea qua possit optima ratione et sciri et servari. Minimitana Regula ab his quos ad illius sollicitam custodiam sua addixere data fides et vota. Haec autem optima ratio, ex regulae spiritus pendet intelligentia, cuius quidem et vocis et naturae facilis, et aperta proxime sequetur explicatio.[4]

The *Ratio studiorum* is prefaced by a schematic synopsis which is given below and from which we may deduce, in addition to the austerity

[1] *op. cit.*, p. 6.
[2] *ibid.*, p. 62.
[3] *ibid.*, p. 93. Here there is possibly an example of influence of the Jesuit *Ratio Studiorum*, editions after 1599; the *Regulae Provincialis* lay down, section *a*, that studies are a privilege to be enjoyed only by the humble.
[4] *ibid.*, pp. 96–98. The "explicatio" which follows is entitled [*Tractatus*] *de speciali ac propria Religionis nostræ virtute, seu dote, quæ spiritus Regulæ Vulgo nuncupatur.*

already mentioned, the elements of a theory of education which is also remarkable for the austerity of its outlook: "Qui litteris *navat operam*... "He who slogs away ..." (Operam navare – a phrase used by Livy and Caesar) – libri pauci et primarii ... the essentials of rudimentary book learning ... to be stored in the memory ... et in ingenium transmutanda": to which we may add his advice, "moneo ut saepe morosa sit lectio, intercisa et identidem." (see diagram on p. 115)

Lesguillier advised that all reading should be "morosa" (attentive, scrupulously careful), "intercisa" (in small parts, cut up into small digestible fragments), "identidem" (often repeated). This simplification of learning and the reduction of Knowledge to rudiments is not unlike the precepts of Descartes; Lesguillier was probably influenced by the fact that the standard of education of the average novice that had to be educated within the Order was very low. It is known that some members were illiterate and that, when they were appointed to the post of, say, Scribe or elected to the keeping of accounts, they had to go the Corrector to confess their inability to read or to calculate.[1] The deplorable state of the *Résolutions capitulaires* often betokens a less than modest pretention to literacy amongst many others. Among the books written by Minims during the century, a number were obviously intended for use by those who had to teach the novices; such, for example, was the *Quintessentia Magistralis* which bore, appended to the title, the phrase: *in quatuor secta partes succinctis solutionibus praecipua in theologorum scholis controversa solvens*.[2] The four parts deal respectively with God and the Trinity; Creation and Man's disobedience, Sin and the Law; the Word Incarnate, the New Law; the Sacraments: at the end of each section there are a number of *Assertiones*, or dogmatic summaries, which could be committed to memory. For the teaching of Philosophy there were several summaries and two complete *Cursus Philosophiae*[3]*;* further, the Magister or even the Corrector himself often made up compilations from which lessons were given, a set of these from the early eighteenth century remains intact at Marseilles,[4] while other manuscript fragments may well have had a similar origin.

A case of extreme simplification such as was urged by Lesguillier

---

[1] *Résolutions Capitulaires des Minimes d'Aubeterre;* MS in the private archives of M. Y. Bizardel and transcribed by him in part, Angoulême(?), 1942(?).

[2] Sanmihiel, 1614; by the Minim Cyprian Rouyer.

[3] Printed summaries by A. Boucat, A. Dupro, J. Durelle, A. Estienne; complete *Cursus* by E. Maignan and J. Lalemandet. See Bibliography, Printed works.

[4] Ten volumes, Bibliothèque Municipale, MSS 1259–1268.

QUI LITTERIS
NAVAT OPERAM
DUO PRAE
OCULIS HABEAT
ET IDENTIDEM
RECOLAT.

TEMPORIS INOPIAM
AC CITISSIMAM
ILLIUS FUGAM,
IDCIRCO.

SEDULO AGENDUM.

NECESSARIUS INCUMBENDUM.

NULLUM TEMPUS OTIO
PRAETEREUNDUM.

DISCENDORUM MULTITUDINEM
AC VARIETATEM IDCIRCO
COMPENDIO STUDENDUM, AD
QUOD NECESSARIA.

INGENIUM (Quale).

EUISDEM CULTURA
AD QUAM
NECESSARIA SUNT
TRIA.

DOCTOR.

LIBRI PAUCI ET
PRIMARII.

LECTIONIS RATIO.

NON PRAECEPS AUT FESTINA

QUIN ET SUBINDE STATIVA.

MEMORIAE MANDANDA

IN INGENIUM TRANSMUTANDA.

is to be found in the Hebrew Grammar [1] produced by the Minim
André Réal, primarily for use within the Order; the lessons would
lend themselves admirably to a system of instruction by adherence to
the principle of "lectura morosa, intercisa, identidem" advanced by
Lesguillier. The aims which are stated for this grammar were to foster
a desire to understand the Biblical texts and to thwart the alleged
misuse of a knowledge of Hebrew by Protestant scholars. If the whole
educational system within the Order looks starkly utilitarian, it is
perhaps some relief to find that Réal advocated a study of Hebrew
because of the intrinsic beauty of the language, "Linguae Sanctae
captus dulcedine, pro deliciis habet."

Works on simple surgery and medicine and an elementary arithmetic have been mentioned later. It is not certain that any of these
was written specifically for use within the Order, but rudimentary
education in these subjects was given.

The Order had little educational interest outside the cloister –
there is the notable exception of the Ecoles Charitables of Nicolas
Barré. At Serres, in Lorraine, the Minims were given charge of a
school which prepared entrants to the University of Pont-à-Mousson.
The "couvent" at Serres was founded by Jean de Lenoncourt and
Barbe, his wife; Lenoncourt was styled "Conservateur des privilèges de
notre Université du Pont" in the *Diarium Universitatis Mussipontanae*,[2]
and it was appropriate that at the time of the foundation of the "couvent" he should have linked it with an interest in the university which
served all Lorraine. According to Lepage, *Les Communes de la Meurthe*,[3]
the Minims ran a small school for the sons of the lower classes; quoting
the original charter he says: "afin que la jeunesse et autres puissent
être catéchisés et enseignés en la foi et crainte de Dieu et instruits des
lectures et premiers fondements de grammaire ... gratis et sans
aucun salaire pour être rendus capables d'aller au collège du Pont-à-
Mousson, pour servir tant à l'église qu'à la république." In neither
the *Résolutions Capitulaires* for the "couvent" at Serres nor in the records
of the University of Pont-à-Mousson is there any mention of those
pupils who passed through the hands of the Minims, nor is there any
mention of a member of the Order being elected to a post in this
school.

At Avignon the Minims taught for a while; a grant of 25 écus was

---

[1] *Brevis ac facilis introductio ad linguam sanctam*, Lyon, 1646.
[2] Paris, 1911, p. 87; the *Diarium* is transcribed direct from the original registers.
[3] Nancy, 1853, Vol. II, p. 528.

made by the consuls of the town because 120 pupils received instruction
in mathematics and what was referred to as "la physique"; this was
in 1608, but there appears to be no other mention of their teaching
activity in the town.[1]

The Minims can therefore make no claim to have been "un ordre
enseignant"; when, in fact, they had the opportunity to have become
one, by taking full charge of Barré's "Ecoles charitables", they preferred to allow the responsibility to pass to the secular clergy. If,
however, the term "education" be taken in a wider sense than the
mere giving of instruction in classes, the Order plays a not insignificant
role in the education of the seventeenth century. A few of their members
played an important part in the diffusion of new ideas and in the
teaching of specific skills such as book illustration, turning, the construction of sun-dials and other bits of scientific apparatus.

To a limited extent the spirit of Lesguillier's work is to be found
with the truly erudite members of the Order. The idea of "libri pauci
et primarii" subsists; there is evidence of wide reading in Maignan,
while Mersenne's knowledge is encyclopaedic; but what characterises
their work is not the insistence upon a vast fund of book knowledge –
a failing with much seventeenth century erudition – but rather an
ability to investigate at first hand and to experiment. If also behind
the work of Mersenne and Maignan there is the same moral earnest-
ness as that evinced by Lesguillier, their attitude to human knowledge
is no longer that of the "naevi sex" but rather of the imperative need
to use the ability of the human intellect to behold God in the revelations
of contemporary (Galilean) physics. "Studies" for them are not just
the fatiguing business of learning by rote, but the necessary investigation into the nature of things; an investigation which has been
imposed upon man by the New Science. "Studies" must become the
defence of and not the opponent of orthodoxy. The old verities are,
of course, immutable but they require a restatement in the light of
new discoveries, and the articles of the Faith must not be trammelled
up with an outmoded concept of the physical universe: such are the
views of Mersenne and Maignan and the few other members who
made intellectual activity the main substance of their contribution to
the well-being of the Order; with them the narrow strictures of
Lesguillier become a stimulating discipline, fertile for the production
of some of the most important contributions to seventeenth century

[1] Avignon, Musée Calvet, MSS 2381, *Recueil de plusieurs pièces sur les églises, couvents . . .
d'Avignon. Collection Massilian;* fol. 180.

science and for the dissemination of some of the most recent discoveries. The attitude of these men shows a way towards the balance between Faith and Science, a balance which has constantly wavered since their day. The first objective was to overcome superstition. In the previous century the Order has been preoccupied with the question of the conversion of the Huguenot population, and their activities had been directed to this end; although this opposition of contending forces was to be maintained during the whole of the seventeenth century, there arose the further question of the conversion of atheists and deists. There is therefore a move away from polemical towards scientific writing; away from controversy, towards instruction. In the minds of the more enlightened members of the Order prime importance was accorded to the conquest of superstition by the reconcilation of science with the tenets of the faith, in such a way that the ground would be cut from under the feet of genethliacs, astrologers, dabblers in alchemy, manichaeans, rosicrucians and the like. In this respect the works of Claude Pithoys and the early works of Mersenne are paramount, and belong to the period 1620–1630 approximately. Subsequently, attention to purely scientific material developed and, with it, a desire for encyclopaedic knowledge. This was long before the age of specialisation; a belief in an attainable sum total of knowledge which could be divided into comparatively few component sections was commonly held. The true significance of Mersenne's work can only be appreciated if it is considered as a whole. The formless mass of its totality, the half-formed ideas, the originality of much of his scientific research, the ingenious but often inconclusive arguments that abound in it, all these betoken an attempt at setting down within a single corpus of writing a readily accessible summary of knowledge – hence the fact that numismatics and problems concerning pendulums rub shoulders in the compass of a single work, the *Cogitata*. I shall return to this question later when dealing specifically with Mersenne, but I have insisted on it here to show that the idea of encyclopaedic knowledge was prevalent during this period, and that the aims of those members of the Order who advocated the propagation of scientific knowledge were akin to those of a later generation. This forms an important link between the mediaeval and renaissance thinkers and the philosophers of the "enlightenment." To a great extent this "enlightenment," in the eighteenth century sense, was the secularisation of knowledge, but impetus for this move was undoubtedly being provided from within as well as from without the Church – and from the Order of Minims as much as anywhere else in France. Here we may draw attention to a significant rapprochement with Raymond Lull; faced with the problem of converting the Mahometans, Lull attempted a synthesis of science and faith similar to the attempts of Mersenne and Maignan over 300 years later when facing the problems of the conversion of erudite libertines. Lull's works were to be found in several of the the libraries belonging to the Order, and extracts from his works are conspicuous feature in the ten volumes of notes made by a Minim of Marseilles, previously referred to. His mysticism, renunciation of the world and the fact that he became a Tertiary of the Order of S. Francis of Assisi were additional points in favour of his acceptance by the Order as a figure of some importance.

A reflexion of all tendencies is seen in the composition of the conventual libraries and, before going on to consider the contribution of individual members to the intellectual life of the Order, I have devoted a short chapter to this question. Intellectual activity was associated chiefly with the "couvents" of la Place Royale (Paris) and Santa Trinità dei Monti (Rome). During Mersenne's lifetime the former "couvent" became a centre for the exchange of ideas for the whole of Europe, as the successive volumes of his correspondence prove.[1] The number of members concerned at any one time was small and most of them were either in direct contact with Mersenne, like Niceron, or, like Plumier, were inheritors of his influence through the intermediary of one of his pupils and through the influence of the "couvent" in Rome, which exerted some measure of unifying influence and acted as an entrepot of knowledge for the French members.

---

[1] "From Mersenne's cubicle Sir Kenelm (Digby) could watch the scientific work of western Europe unfold. It was still another vantage-point ... from which to enrich his vision." R. T. Petersson, *Sir Kenelm Digby*, London, 1956, p. 123.

CHAPTER II

THE LIBRARIES OF THE ORDER

The composition of the libraries that were available to members of the Order is an important consideration; it enables us to assess the particular quality of the Minims and to see more clearly the place of intellectual activity in the Order. Within the cloister the object seems to have been spiritual "perfection"; without, the principal activities were preaching and caring for the sick. A little teaching was also done in a few localities. Preaching, and this often included open discussion in the market-place with a Calvinist minister, called for a considerable mastery of subject matter to which eloquence, the art of persuasion, had to be allied; Pizzurnus also pointed out that the hearing of confessions called for as wide a learning as possible.[1] We find that nearly all the libraries had a large section devoted to history, particularly of the schism, and another section, usually fairly representative, devoted to the Greek and Latin authors who were considered as having the almost exclusive gift of the sublime in style. These sections together with the Biblical and devotional works provided the main substance of the numerous sermons and harangues that were pronounced all over France by members of the Order. Most libraries had in addition sections devoted to mathematics, science and pharmacy.

The catalogues of a dozen or more of the libraries are extant and from an analysis of their contents and the balance of their composition, I have come to the following conclusion, expressed below in diagramatic form, concerning the place of the library in the life of the Order. I have also drawn on Pierre Blanchot's *Idea Bibliothecae Universalis* [2] which was written in the "couvent" of La Place Royale in 1631; that is, during the formative years or the library.

---

[1] *Manipulus Minimorum,* under the heading *Studium* already quoted on p. 111.

[2] See bibliography of works by members of the Order. This work is, unfortunately, incomplete; it shows, however, even in its fragmentary form, the desire to systematize knowledge.

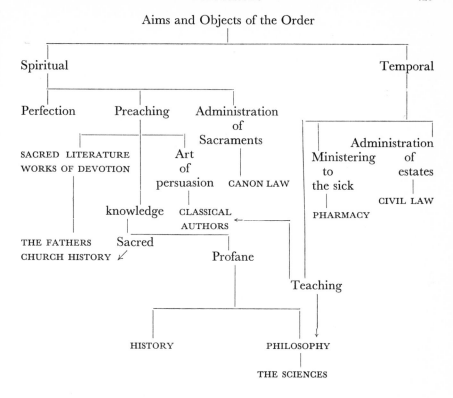

Within this general framework there is room for a wide diversity in the composition of a library: at La Place Royale the library was particularly rich in historical works; at Marseilles, in mathematics, travel and navigation (a reflexion of local interest); the library at Toulouse inherited the rich collection made by Sponde, Bishop of Pamiers, of works on the Greek and Latin authors, commentaries on scripture, history.[1] Of the small libraries, few catalogues are extant; Lunéville had a library of 1,026 volumes [2]; Bassing had 336, of which one is given as "Pensée (sic) de Paschale (sic)" [3]; La Valette had no more than 200.[4]

Librarians were appointed annually at the conventual chapter and changes seem to have been frequent. At La Place Royale, where the library contained over 17,000 books in the XVIIth century, we find

---

[1] 3,000 books according to P. Frison in the life of Sponde prefaced to the *Annalium C. Baronii*, Paris, 1647.
[2] Archives Départementales, Meurthe-et-Moselle, H. 1028.
[3] *ibid.*, H. 981.
Carpentras, Bibliothèque Inguimbertine; MSS No. 1769, fol. 713/4.

that Mersenne, La Noue (the historian of the Order) and Regnault (the translator of Acosta's history of the Indies) had all done duty as librarian.[1] In other "couvents" the task was left to chance which probably accounts for the haphazard nature of so much of the cataloguing: some catalogues were drawn up on the basis of format only [2]; others omitted dates of publication and even authors' names on occasion.[3]

The Corrector was empowered to buy books for the library and to sell duplicate copies and useless books. Losses seem to have been frequent. At the Chapitre Provincial, Lorraine, in 1693, the Provincial found it necessary to decree that books should not be lent to outsiders and that all libraries were to be searched for books which did not belong there. The reason for this last directive is that the Minims were frequently transferred from one house to another taking, it seems, books from the library with them. This moving from place to place must also have enabled a member of the Order to gain access to a larger number of books than if he had remained all his life at, say, Bassing. Notwithstanding Lesguillier's strictures concerning books, their libraries were amongst the richest in France and a few members of the Order made notable contributions to the discoveries of the age: one has only to think of Mersenne, Maignan and Plumier. It seems unlikely from an examination of the catalogues of the libraries where these men worked that they relied upon them to any great extent; a possible exception being the library at Santa Trinità dei Monti in Rome. There is evidence to show that these men were allowed to possess books of their own – a modification to the rule of poverty. The description of Louis XIV's visit to Maignan at Toulouse and of Martin Lister's to Plumier at the Place Royale make their cells appear more like laboratories and libraries than traditional cells.

CHARACTERISTICS OF SOME OF THE MORE
IMPORTANT LIBRARIES

Nigeon, Vincennes and La Place Royale

An account of all the conventual libraries in Paris can be found in A. Franklin's *Les anciennes bibliothèques de Paris*.[4] The one at Nigeon,

---

[1] *Registres Capitulaires des Minimes de la Place Royale;* Archives Nationales, LL. 1564.

[2] Metz. This was the second largest of twelve conventual libraries in the town; Bibliothèque Municipale, MSS No. 1450/1, liasse 8.

[3] The large and valuable library at Lyon; Archives Départementales, Rhône, Série H., L. 10. Also the library at Lunéville; see above.

[4] 3 vols. Paris, 1867–1873.

called by Franklin "Passy," was the oldest and there are references to it in the middle of theXVIth century.[1] Its collection of 10,000 volumes forms an important part of the Bibliothèque de l'Arsenal, where the catalogue dating from the mid-XVIIIth century is preserved.[2] The proportions of the collection do not show any particular trends. All works by members of the Order were clearly indicated, however, and it was helpful in drawing up the bibliography of works published by Minims.

The library at Vincennes was much smaller. Franklin seems unaware of the existence of the catalogue of this collection, preserved in the Bibliothèque de l'Arsenal.[3] Drawn up in the mid-XVIIIth century, this catalogue, in common with many others which belonged to the Order, contains a declaration of the census of books at the time of handing over to the Revolutionary Tribunal: "Bibliothèque des Minimes de Vincennes – recensement fait le 12 février 1792. Nous avons trouvé 2,926 volumes."

Many authorities speak of the rich collection of books built up at the Place Royale. This library was started as late as 1614 but rapidly became the most important conventual library to which, a singularly liberal gesture, the public was admitted.[4] The wealth of this collection was due almost entirely to donations and legacies, the most important being the Jean de Launoy legacy of historical works in 1677. Several catalogues are extant in the Mazarine, the Arsenal and in the Archives Nationales; Franklin has given a chronological survey of them beginning with the catalogue of 1722, and ignores the composition of the library in the XVIIth century.[5] There is, however, a catalogue anterior to the one of 1722 which dates in all probability from the middle of the XVIIth century [6]; although incomplete, it shows quite clearly the arrangement that the early librarians intended to maintain. Their system was different from that of the other catalogues which have survived and might well have proved the basis for a more scientific approach to librarianship had the work continued. Works on librarianship were rare in the early and mid-seventeenth century; one, however, *Avis pour dresser une bibliothèque*, by Gabriel Naudé, is of

[1] *ibid.*, Vol. II, p. 62.
[2] Arsenal, MS, No. 5763.
[3] Arsenal, MS, No. 6493, fols. 194–197.
[4] Franklin, *op. cit.*, II, p. 326. There were only three public libraries in Europe in 1620 the Ambrosiana, Milan, opened in 1608; the Bodleian (1612); the Angelica, Rome (1620); A. Bonneau in preface to G. Naudé's *Avis pour dresser une bibliothèque (1644)* Paris, 1876.
[5] *ibid.*, II, pp. 323–335.
[6] Mazarine, MSS No. 4146.

interest since the author was a friend of Mersenne's and frequently visited the "couvent" at la Place Royale during the years when Mersenne and Regnault were the librarians; the first edition was in 1627, and there was a second edition in 1644 as well as an English translation by John Evelyn, London, 1661. In this work, classification by subject rather than by author is advocated, and the libraries which he arranged for Mazarin, for le Président de Mesmes and for Christina of Sweden all have this type of classification. Naudé does not go any further towards suggesting the actual division but, in another work, he pleads that liberal studies should not be lumped together under the heading *Humanitas* but should be divided:

angustis ex finibus circumscribitur quemadmodum in scholis ... sed decem partes comprehendit videlicet:
    Linguarum Latinae, Graecae
    Eloquentiam
    Poeticam
    Geographiam
    Chronologiam
    Historiam
    Antiquitates
    Fabulas
    Criticam.[1]

Instead of large sections under generalised headings such as "Libri historici profani," this catalogue of the Minims' was drawn up on a similar basis of large numbers of sub-sections, but splitting up even further the divisions we find in Naudé:

1. Historical method.
2. Geography.
3. Voyages, navigation.[2]
4. Universal history, chronology.
5. Martyrology.
6. Genealogy.[3]
7. Episcopal, Pontifical history.
8. Hagiography.
9. Monasticism.
10. Annals, ecclesiastical.

[1] *De studio liberali*, Urbini, 1632, p. 33. Naudé was also a compiler of Bibliographies, publishing two specialised works: (a) *Bibliographia Politica*, Wittemburg, 1641; (b) *Bibliographia Militaris*, Jena, 1683.
[2] 234 volumes in this section, the second largest.
[3] Sacred, i.e. of Christ, the Virgin, S. John Baptist.

11. Ancient History: Greek.
12.   „   „   : Greek and Byzantine.
13.   „   „   : Roman.
14.   „   „   : Roman antiquities.
15. Modern History: English.[1]
16.   „   „   : Spanish.[2]
17.   „   „   : French, up to early XVIth century.
18.   „   „   :   „   , XVIth century.
19.   „   „   :   „   , Henri IV, Louis XIII.
20.   „   „   :   „   , Royal Family, Salic Law, General history
                             of early XVIIth century.
21.   „   „   :   „   , Provinces.
22.   „   „   :   „   , Paris.
23.   „   „   ’   „   , Burgundy, Franche Comté.
24.   „   „   :   „   , Normandy, Brittany.
25.   „   „   : Savoy.
26.   „   „   : Switzerland.
27.   „   „   : La Grande Belgique. Bar, Luxembourg, Lorraine.
28.   „   „   : Flanders, Brabant, Hainault.
29.   „   „   : Holland [3].
30.   „   „   : Belgium, Brabant, Flanders.[4]
31.   „   „   : Genealogy, Heraldry.
32.   „   „   : German provinces.
33.   „   „   : Hungary.
34.   „   „   : Muscovite kingdom, Denmark, Northern States.
35.   „   „   : Ottoman Empire, Tartars.
36.   „   „   : Italy, States and Dukedoms.
37.   „   „   : Laws and customs.
38. Political History I.
39.   „   „   II.[5]
40. Political theory.
41. Letters.

Extensive as it is, this plan represents only a part of the complete collection. There was a separate catalogue of Bibles and works of devotion [6] and it is remarkable that there are no sections devoted to mathematics or science, although these are a prominent feature in the catalogues from 1722 onwards; the date of accession of these works must therefore remain conjectural. It is, however, certain that this library is the supreme expression of all that was best in the intellectual

[1] 74 works in this section.
[2] Includes the Spanish colonies and Aethiopia (i.e. India) also the Portuguese colonies.
[3] A vague term at this period. The section includes all annals etc. in which the adjective "hollandais" occurs.
[4] A probable error in cataloguing: this reduplicates section 28.
[5] The distinction between this section and the previous one seems slight.
[6] Bibliothèque Nationale, Fonds Latin, 16818.

activity of the Order in the XVIIth century. The arrangement of the catalogue invites comparison with the Bodleian catalogue which had the great merit of being printed and became, therefore, an important bibliographical guide. The first edition, Oxford, 1605, was a subject catalogue, having the following divisions: Expositores S. Scripturae: Libri Medici: Libri Iuris: Libri Artium: Interpretes librorum Aristotelis. Within each section the arrangement was in alphabetical order of authors. The later editions (i.e. from 1620 onwards) were by alphabetical arrangement throughout.

The library was enriched by the works of several Minimes: it housed for a while the precious collection of Plumier's engravings and notes; the printed works of Mersenne and Maignan were on its shelves. Most regrettably the notes and scientific instruments of the former were sold shortly after his death [1]; it is some compensation that a collection of letters addressed to him from all parts of Europe was compiled by Hilarion de Coste, several times Corrector of La Place Royale and Mersenne's first biographer.[2]

At the time of the Revolution, the library had fallen into disrepair and the collection was in danger; many of its printed books and manuscripts now enrich the libraries of Paris.

Reims, Marseille and Lyon

Although the catalogue of the Minims' library at Reims [3] dates from 1740 or shortly after, it serves as a good guide to the composition of one of the richer libraries in the XVIIth century since, out of nearly 6,500 works listed, less than 20 are from the period 1700–1739. Classification was under sixteen headings to each of which a letter was assigned to aid cataloguing; the works were then numbered, two or more volumes of one work usually bearing the same number.[4] This attempt at a systematic method of shelf-marks seems to have been rare at this period; only the catalogues of the library at La Place Royale subsequent to 1722 went as far in classification. An interesting feature of this collection at Reims is the very high proportion of early printed

---

[1] *Registres Capitulaires de la Place Royale*, Vol. II; see under September, 1648: Archives Nationales, LL. 1565.

[2] Bibliothèque Nationale, Nouvelles Acquisitions, Nos. 6204–6206, bound with the arms of the Order and the library mark of La Place Royale. Now printing in Mersenne *Correspondance;* see p. 142 n. 2.

[3] Reims, Archives Municipales.

[4] Exceptions occur in sections A, B and C and also in E where is a lacuna of 180 numbers.

books that it contained and it seems likely that a third of the whole was anterior to 1600. The proportions of the collections under the various headings are also of interest:

– Scriptura Sacra – 122 works:
   including the *Biblia Sacra Gothica.* Lyon, 1527;
   Sacra Vetustissima exemplaria castigata, Lyon, 1569.
A. Scriptura Sacra Interpretes – 268 works.
B. Sancti Patres – 334 works:
   particularly rich in XVIth century editions amongst which
      Ambrose; Paris, 1551 & 1569.
      Origen; Paris, 1574.
      Bede; Paris, 1532 & 1554.
      Gregory; Paris, 1562 & 1571.
      Jerome; Paris, 1524–1526 & 1546.
C. Theologi Scholastici – 214 works.
D. Libri Polemici – 605 works.
E. Libri Iuris, canonici et de ritibus – 600 works.
*E. Libri Iuris, civilis – 586 works.
F. Theologi morales et casuistae – 418 works.
G. Loci communes et Miscellanea – 325 works:
   Essais de Montaigne; lettres du Cardinal d'Ossat; Lettres de Gui Patin; Oeuvres de Boileau.
I̵H. Historici sacri cum Cosmographis – 660 works.
H. Historici prophani – 186 works.
 I. Concionatores – 178 works.
L. Libri ascetici seu Spirituales – 749 works.
M. Philosophi, Medici, Mathematici – 495 works:
   this section contained one of the earliest works in the whole collection
      Marsilius Ficinus, *De triplici vita cum textu Salerni,* Paris, 1489. Also rich in Natural History – Edward Wootton, *De diversitate animalium,* Paris, 1552; *Icones animalium,* Zurich, 1560; *Histoire de la nature des oiseaux écrite en six volumes,* Paris, 1555. This section contained the printed works of Mersenne and Maignan but was otherwise poor in XVIIth century works.
N. Grammatici et Humanisti – 592 works:
   dictionaries (French–Italian, French–Spanish); polygot dictionaries; dictionaries of the ancient languages. Text books on foreign languages. Latin and Greek authors.
O. Libri prohibiti et Hæretici – 144 works:
   list headed by the *Augustinus.* Many Jansenist works; Pasquier Quesnel, Pierre Charron; the *Koran.*

The catalogue made no special reference to manuscripts of which the library possessed but few – an anonymous *Compendium Theologiae Veritatis,* dated 1275 and *Praxis electionum,* Guillelmi Handagoli of 1310.

Neither of these appears to be extant. Two manuscripts of no importance by members of the Order, Robert and Jean Mopinot, have
remained at Reims and so has an undated printed book, Roderic de
Zamora, *Speculum vitae humanae*.[1]

The library at Reims lends itself to comparison with the one at
Marseille as far as size is concerned: the latter contained just over
7,000 volumes.[2] Allowing for the fact that the library at Marseille
contained many XVIIIth century books, the number of works on
Mathematics and Science (673) and on Voyages and Travel (183) –
a subject untouched by the library at Reims – shows the more liberal
proportions of this collection. Even more liberal was the library at
Lyon [3] which included the works of Pierre Bayle on the open shelves –
there is no mention of *libri prohibiti*! Admittedly this catalogue is of
later date, 1784, and the freshening wind of criticism was being felt
within the cloister as well as without; but, by confining our attention
to the XVIth and XVIIth century works that it contained, we can
see how practical this collection was. The section on Pharmacy and
medicine listed 136 works in-folio and 200 in-quarto – and exceptionally large selection from which the following have been drawn *:

* Dates and places are lacking throughout the catalogue and authors' names are frequently omitted.

Pharmacopœia Lugdunensis.
Pharmacopœia Bruxellensis. (1641; 1671 etc.)
De arte medica infantium.
De venenis et antidotis.
Methodus medicinæ componendi, Sylvatii. (i.e. *Opus pandectarum medicinæ* by
    Mathæus Sylvaticus: many editions Bologna and Venice in the XVth
    and XVIth centuries. Also Lyon, 1534.)
Herbarium Italice, Durante. (Castore Durante: printed in Venice, 1636,
    several editions).
A medical work by Lister. (Martin Lister, work unidentified).
Ophthalmolographia, Vopisius. (Unidentified.)
Centuriæ chirurgicæ. Fabricius. (Wilhelm Fabricius: Several of his works
    might be thus called; none given that are identical.)
The works of Campanella. (Thomas Campanella: *Medicinalium principia* . . .
    libri septem. Lyon, 1635.)
A work by Santorelli called *Methodus*. (Probably A. Santorelli, *Antepraxis
    medica*, Naples, 1633.)

[1] M. 45 in the Minims' catalogue. See *Incunables de Reims*, Reims, 1889.
[2] Based on a count made in the 1776 catalogue, Bibliothèque Municipale, Marseille,
MS No. 1485. The earlier (?) catalogue, No. 1484, is missing.
[3] *Inventaire de la Bibliothèque des Minimes de Lyon;* Lyon, Archives Départementales, Rhône;
Série H., L. 10.

Rome: Santa Trinità dei Monti

None of the historians of the French "couvent" in Rome has given more than a passing reference to the library, a strange omission since it was here that the intellectual life of the Order was fostered. This library must have had its influence on Mersenne, J-F. Niceron, Plumier, Maignan and Feuillée who had all elected to come to Santa Trinità for the purpose of study. One catalogue only exists and everything conspires to keep it secret: it is in the Archives Nationales, Paris,[1] under a heading that is misleading: *Catalogue de tous les livres dans tous les couvents de l'Ordre des Minimes, par Jérôme Durand: 1600*. The title inside the book, however, makes it clear that this refers to the Italian "couvents" only; Durand was at the time Corrector General and it may have been his intention to have made a catalogue of all libraries in the Order – if it was completed, it has not survived. To make it even more obscure, the binding (XIXth century) bears the inscription "Catalogue des Minimes de la Place Royale."

It is interesting to have such an early catalogue; it shows that the library was rich in renaissance works and it also shows that a representative selection of herbals and pharmacopoeias had been collected by the beginning of the century; they were the best books of their kind and were to have a considerable influence on the pharmacists and botanists in the Order who came from France to work in Rome. In the chapter on Plumier, I have again referred to the botanical work carried on at Santa Trinità and the opportunities that residence there gave for this particular study. The list of medical works includes the following:

Avicenna, *Canonis libri quinque*, Venice, 1582 (?)
Bartolomeo Traffichetti, *L'arte di conservare la sanità.* –, 1562.
A. Cornelius Celse, *De medicina libri VIII*, Florence, 1478.
Castore Durante, *Herbario nuovo ... con figure*, Rome, 1585.
    Tesoro della sanità, Venice, 1589.
    Trattato di dodici bagni singolari, Perugia, 1595.
Dioscorides, *De medicinali materia libri sex*, Lyon, 1550.
Garcia del Horto (Orta), *Due libri dell'historia dei semplici*, Venice, 1576.
Mesué (i.e. Yahya ibn Masawaih) – entered in catalogue is a work "*de consol. medic. simpli*, Venice, 1497"; I am unable to find a work which corresponds exactly.
Jean Lébault, *Trésor des remèdes secrets pour les maladies des femmes*, Paris, 1585.
Pietro Andrea Mattioli, *Discorsi della materia medicinale*, Venice, 1573.
Nicolò Mutoni, *Luminare maius omnibus cum medicis tum aromatoriis pernecessarium*, Venice 1553.

[1] LL. 1563.

The library was also rich in historical works some of which are now in the library of the French Seminary in Rome; during a whole morning's search with the librarian I have been unable, however, to find a single one of the valuable herbals and scientific works which, in theory, should have passed into this library. During the XVIIIth century the museum, which had been built up during the previous hundred or more years, was sold and one can only assume that with it went a large part of the library. So far, it has been impossible to throw any light on the possible strength of the library during the XVIIth century; all that one can state with certainty is that in 1600 the foundations of what may have become a most interesting and valuable collection of books had already been laid.

It is pertinent to ask how these libraries compared with other collections of books during the seventeenth century. In 1644 a Carmelite friar, Louis Jacob, made a European survey of the best libraries [1]; apart from some of the Royal libraries and some of the private collections (Bodley's being singled out for special comment), those belonging to the Minims seem to have been amongst the most considerable. Of the Dominicains de la Rue S. Honoré he writes, "édifice somptueux, de moindre qualité en livres," and of thoses of the Rue S. Jacques (whence the name Jacobins), "belle pour ses livres"; of the Capucins de Paris," de considération pour la quantité et la qualité de ses livres." There are unfortunately few statistics in his work but "considérable" seems to indicate approximately 4,000 books. He gives the size of the Oratorian's library – 6,000 books – and of the Minims of the Place Royale – 8,000 – remarkable since Jacob's survey dates from only 30 years after the foundation of the Library. In the provinces we find the same sort of comparison; of the library of the Minims of Amiens he writes "réputée une des principales (bibliothèques de Picardie)"; Tours had 6,000 books and therefore bears comparison with conventual libraries of other orders in the capital; Toulouse, enriched by Sponde's bequest, had become one of the best libraries in Aquitaine. Further proof of the wealth of the Minims' libraries comes from modern catalogues of municipal libraries and from catalogues of incunabula. From the latter we find that the town of Marseilles derived a richer inheritance from the Minimes d'Aix than from any other single source,[2] an inheritance which included the

---

[1] *Traité des plus belles bibliothèques*, Paris, 1644.
[2] *Catalogue des incunables de la bibliothèque de la ville de Marseille*, Marseille, 1897.

remarkable work on astronomy by Abou-Maschar, printed in Augs-
bourg in 1489,[1] and the works of Raymond Lull in the edition of
Paris, 1499.[2] The small library at Roanne has eight manuscripts which
came from the Minims of that town [3]; Besançon lists eleven of its
incunabula as ex-Minim [4] – and so on throughout France. But the
collection of rare books, illuminated manuscripts, sumptuous missels
and the like was only a small part of the librarianship of this order [5];
they started late in comparison with the others and the mere accumu-
lation of rich relics from the middle ages had no relevance in their
conception of what a library should be.

---

[1] Listed No. 1. in the above catalogue.
[2] No. 85 in the above catalogue.
[3] *Catalogue des incunables de Roanne*, Paris, 1900.
[4] *Incunables de Besançon*, Besançon, 1893.
[5] See however the article by A. Auriol *Missel des Minimes* in *Mémoires de la Société archéologique du Midi de la France*, Paris, 1934, Vol. II, p. 208. (Minimes d'Aix) and p. 309 (Minimes
de Paris).

CHAPTER III

CLAUDE PITHOYS

A belief in the Devil was as fundamental to seventeenth century religion as a belief in God. When Sir Thomas Browne wrote that he knew that witches existed,[1] he was not being arch but merely expressed the common belief of the age which could be both rational and thaumaturgical at one and the same time. Reason and mysticism were not thought of by the majority as opposites, but rather as complementary parts of knowledge or as different facets of the same truth. To deny the Devil was atheistic, and reasonable arguments could be adduced to prove the point. Exorcisms were therefore common and important events and, although the actual ritual which accompanied them was a specifically Roman catholic function, the underlying theological implications were common to both catholic and protestant interpretations of the faith. We may quote in substantiation of this point the Devils of Loudun and the Witches of Salem, which have both furnished modern authors with material to illustrate the folly of persecution and "witch-hunting" – manifestations alike of fear and mass hysteria.[2] It is against this background that the case of Claude Pithoys must be judged, although it was a little earlier than either of the famous episodes quoted above.

Pithoys, because of his apostasy, received no recognition from his contemporaries [3] and Roberti dismisses him with the curt remark, "Di questo religioso francese, autore di parecchie publicazione, non ho potuto raccogliare alcun dato biografico." [4] Biographers outside the Order have helped to save him from oblivion – A. Calmet in his

---

[1] *Religio Medici*, I, sect. xxx.

[2] Aldous Huxley, *The Devils of Loudun*; Arthur Miller, *The Crucible*, better known to the French in the film version, *Les Sorcières de Salem*.

[3] a. Mersenne, a very guarded reply to an inquiry from Rivet, 12 March, 1634; *Correspondance*, Vol. IV, p. 70. b. La Noue, the merest mention in his *Chronicon*.

[4] *op. cit.*, II, p. 612.

Bibliothèque Lorraine and P. Norbert in his *Histoire de Sedan* both mention him; J-B. Boulliot devotes a short article to him in the *Biographie Ardennaise;* the article in Michaud, *Biographie Universelle,* gives the essential details of his life and work; there remains, in addition, an unsolved problem posed by a reference to him in a manuscript in Metz. His work has not so far attracted the attention that a systematic criticism of sorcery and witchcraft deserves, especially when it comes from the pen of one who was born as early as 1587 and who survived until 1676, that is to say, long enough to have known the first generation of those whose onslaught on such superstitions is of vital importance to the theories of toleration and liberty current in the decades after his death. He is one of those interesting characters who join the two periods of enlightenment, the sixteenth and eighteenth centuries.

His life is easy to relate; born in 1587, he entered the Order at an early age. He published, with the full approbation of his Superiors, a pungent criticism of what he considered to be a case of false possession by devils and gave a fearless account of what happened when he had been arraigned before the bishop of Toul on the 7th, 8th and 9th of February, 1621, for doubting the validity of the exorcism in this case. He subsequently went to one of the "couvents" in the Province of Champagne and became Corrector of Verdun; suddenly, in 1632, he left the Order, became a protestant and retired to the Academy of Sedan where he became Professeur de Droit, Professeur de Philosophie and Garde de la Bibliothèque Publique. He was succeeded in the second post by Pierre Bayle in 1675, and in the next year he died.

The details of the possession by devils which ended at the exorcism at Toul make distressing and gruesome reading. Elizabeth Ranfaing, a young widow of Nancy, fell into the hands of an unscrupulous doctor who, having tried to seduce her, had recourse to maleficious medicines. The doctor and his assistant were eventually burnt, but not before Elizabeth had endured for many years physical torments of which the details are luridly told by H. M. Boudon in *Le Triomphe de la Croix* [1] and, with much attenuation, by Hélyot in his *Histoire des Ordres.* [2] During the worst of her suffering she never ceased to cry out to God to deliver her, so that it was generally believed that she was the innocent victim of a spell cast upon her by the doctor; in short, she was possessed. She therefore underwent an exorcism at Toul at the hands of Porcelets, the bishop. Now Pithoys was present and he had

[1] Liège, 1686; pp. 119 *et sq.*
[2] Paris, 1718; Vol. IV, pp. 344–361.

serious doubts, not about the validity of exorcism as such, but about the genuine nature of the possession in this case. Members of the Order believed in the reality of the Devil; Dondé's illustrations of exorcisms at the hand of the Saint and Patron of the Order himself should be taken as an adequate expression of an idea commonly held within the Order.[1] But, for whatever reason, Pithoys was persuaded that Elizabeth Ranfaing was not a victim of the Devil. His criticism, succinct and penetrating in itself, goes far beyond the purely local interest of the case he saw for himself. He urges that profane words as well as sacred should be used in the ritual to catch out the subject who might be expected to "respond" to an invalid pronouncement and thus disclose the false nature of the possession. If this were of no avail, insignificant words of Greek and Hebrew might be used in the hope of tricking the subject once again into discovering the falsity of the possession; should both these fail, then unconsecrated Hosts should be mixed with consecrated ones and administered as the Sacrament to see whether the possessed could distinguish between them. In other words, Pithoys is suggesting that exorcism was frequently perform-ed upon "poseurs" and "poseuses" who, out of masochistic delight or in connivance with the clergy, who benefited from such public displays, caused the public to be hoodwinked into thinking that the Devil had been beaten. An examination of his work shows that, far from denying the possibility of real possession, he was careful to show a proper respect for the Devil. By a process entirely understandable to a seven-teenth century mind, he was able to reaffirm his belief in God by fearing the profanity and blasphemy of a faked exorcism and irrever-ence for Satan's power. He also insisted on a thorough and independent medical examination which should form a part of any exorcism, so that a false subject should be eliminated before the theological ex-amination. Such, then, is a brief analysis of his first work: *Découverte des faux possédés, très-utile pour reconnaître et discerner les simulations, feintises et illusions d'avec les vraies possessions diaboliques.* With this he published an account of his arraignment before the bishop of Toul and of his three interviews with him; the second part of the work merely reiterates the same criticism but adds the significant thrust that the bishop withheld the manuscript minutes of the inter-views. Both parts of the work were published in Châlons in 1621 and received, it is interesting to note, a eulogistic stanza and an approbation

---

[1] See previously, p. 60.

signed by Simon Niclot, then Correcteur des Minimes de Bracancour, the senior "couvent" in the Province de Lorraine; there were also "approbations" from the Universities of Dôle and Paris.

For a while we hear nothing more of Pithoys; nothing, that is, except for a reference in a manuscript at Metz, in the Archives Départementales de la Moselle, where, following up various references to the Visite Générale made by Simon Bachelier, I found *Constitutiones factae a Patre Generali in Conventu Bracancursi post visitatem generalem in provincia Campania; Simon Bachelier, 1627.*[1] The manuscript is difficult to read and I am indebted to the Sous-archiviste for help in deciphering the following extract from pages 2–3:

> Reverendumne etiam Patrem F. Claudium Pitoys nostri praedecessoris sententia et obedientia quibus illum utraque voce per annum ob (sub?) prelo mandatum librum ab eo compositum sine licentia superiorum cui annexa est conferentia, et litterae non approbatae privabat et in provinciam vestram Turonensem sub precepto non paruisse; quae sententiae et obedientiae per Apostolicos notarios nonnullis conventibus provincialibus notificata,
> ? in ? capitulo provinciali Remensi intermedio publicata fuit ex textu capituli, usquemodo revocata. Audito super his dicto fratre Claudio Pithoys inauditus se condamnatus asseruit quare visi visendis reperimum illum culpabilem et poenas a nostris generalibus constitutionibus latas incurisse, ipsi a nostro praedecessiori iustitias; declaramusque illum non potuisse in correctorem nostri conventus Virdunensis eligi cum provincia non esset localis nec legitime officium exercuisse, precepimusque illi virtute sanctae obedientiae ut praecepto cui usquemodo parere nolluit intra 15 dies anotitiam praesentiam pareat et post octavarum Sanctissimi Sacramenti conciones statim in provinciam Turonensem cum fratre Dominico Uberto oblato se recipiat; assignantas in correctorem nostri conventus Virdunensis, P. F. Nicolaum Mahuet.

It is tempting to see in this the beginning of Pithoy's apostasy but unfortunately more problems are posed by it than are solved. What writing of his is referred to as "ob (sub?) prelo" without the authority of his Superiors? Two works appeared in 1628 – *L'horoscope, roue de fortune et bonne aventure des prédestinés* and *L'Amorce des âmes dévotes.*[2] Since both these bear approbations signed by members of the Order (including the above-mentioned Simon Bachelier and Nicolas Mahuet), it is impossible that these are the works referred to unless he managed to argue a case in their defence. Is it possible to assume that the events took place at a later date than 1627? The only indication given is that they

[1] Archives Départementales, Moselle; Série H., 3749; *Privilèges, Règlements, Statuts.*
[2] Both Paris, 1628.

took place after the Visite Générale of that year but Pithoys is referred to as already condemned and as having failed to obey an order to go to Tours "sub precepto." A further difficulty occurs in the declaration that he was not eligible for the correctorship of Verdun; the *Horoscope, roue de fortune* specifically mentiones him in this office in 1628; does the interdiction refer to his re-election at some later date or to his election in, say, 1627/8? A possible solution may be that he overcame the interdiction in the same way that he may have overcome the ban on his book; in view of the severity of the tone of the condemnation this seems unlikely. There remains the following intriguing possibility, it seems: the statement that he was "Correcteur des Minimes de Verdun" in the *Horoscope* together with the approbations in the names of Bachelier and Mahuet are forgeries [1] and that Pithoys spent a season in the Province of Tours as a prisoner, "sub precepto," whither Frère Dominique Hubert had escorted him. However this may be, it is certain that in 1632, renouncing his vows and abjuring his faith, he placed himself under the protection of the Duc de Bouillon as a protestant at the Academy of Sedan.

The *Horoscope, roue de fortune* deserves to take its place amongst the literature of debunking. In it Pithoys begins with a general statement on superstition and then leads on to a popular scientific argument aimed at demolishing all astrological predictions:

> Il n'est pas au pouvoir humain de noter infailliblement ric à ric les aspects de toutes les étoiles qui se rencontrent au juste point de la nativité d'un homme. Chose indubitable, puisqu'un signe de Zodiaque en l'équinoxe fait en une heure quinze degrés qui reviennent à 420,000 lieues françaises qui, divisées par 60, donneront à chaque minute 70,000 lieues de chemin.
>
> Arrière donc dérechef ces alambiques de cervelle! au feu ces Almanachs et leurs auteurs! [2]

How similar this is to the more famous argument in the *Pensées sur la comète* in which Bayle shows that the exhalations and emanations of a comet could in no wise affect the earth and its inhabitants! Yet, where Bayle introduces a small amount of popular theory concerning atoms and "tourbillons" into an elaborate argument to refute the accepted ideas of historians and philosophers, Pithoys turns his argument into a theological and moral one couched in a near mystical language that

---

[1] It may be worth while to point out that all Pithoy's other works were printed in the eastern provinces of France (i.e. locally). There seems no reason for this to have appeared from Paris.

[2] pp. 53–54.

would seem strange in Bayle, but which is not unlike the writings of
many of his contemporaries in the Order. Thus, having demolished
sign by sign the significance of the Zodiac, he builds up an allegorical interpretation of it which he calls "Phénomènes de la première
(deuxième, troisième etc. ...) maison *évangélique*." He then proceeds:

Rejetant donc cette fatalité monstrueuse sur les choses inanimées ...
avouons avec les sages de tous les siècles que les nobles actions de l'homme
tiennent de la liberté; que la volonté humaine est une cause non violentée
mais agissant librement avec délibération; qu'elle commande puissamment
sur les mœurs; et que de sa résolution et conduite dépendent la plupart
des accidents humains ... Il ne faut pas la conjonction de Vénus avec
Mercure en la sixième maison des infirmités spirituelles pour enfanter des
maladies incurables; il ne faut que la rencontre d'une mauvaise compagnie
pour corrompre le mieux morigéné. Une seule cajolerie réduira en poudre
les plus constantes résolutions.[1]

During the many years that he was at Sedan, Pithoys wrote only
two works – *Traité curieux de l'astrologie judiciaire, ou préservatif contre
l'astromantie des généthliaques*,[2] *L'Apocalypse de Méliton* [3] and a short work
on geography.[4] He was in his eighty-eight year when Bayle took his
place, so that it seems unlikely that there was any opportunity for
more than a purely formal succession of duties. Did Bayle know of his
predecessor's work? There is only one marginal reference to it in the
Oeuvres Diverses [5] and none in the *Dictionnaire;* on the other hand the
Traité curieux is a striking work and one with which Bayle would have
been in agreement.

The germ of the *Traité curieux de l'astrologie judiciaire* is contained in
the earlier *Horoscope, roue de fortune* but the author has embellished the
arguments and has extended the whole scope of the work, particularly
in the use he makes of arguments drawn from the Fathers of the
Church, Philosophers and Savants, also in the arguments drawn from
the political dangers of astrology and in his delight in exposing purely
nonsensical predictions. All this is familiar to anyone who has read
Bayle, and the grouping of his subject-matter into brief paragraphs
and sub-sections, each with a résumé, is equally familiar. The student
of Bayle is at home amongst such outbursts and indignant questions as:

[1] *Horoscope* etc., pp. 198–199 and 203–204.
[2] Sedan, 1641 and a second edition, Montbelliard, 1646.
[3] Saint-Léger, 1662.
[4] See Bibliography.
[5] *Réponses aux questions d'un provincial*, LXVII, vi; *Oeuvres Diverses*, III, p. 629.

L'astromantie a été inventée et cultivée par de célèbres Magiciens idolâtres.

L'astromantie dangereuse à un Prince et à ses domestiques.

Que l'expérience dont se vantent les généthliaques ne justifie pas leurs inventions ridicules.

Si les astres peuvent agir sur l'âme raisonnable ...

It would be surprising if the Philosophes did not find in his work powerful arguments to further their own attack upon superstition and ignorance.[1] What is remarkable, however, is the extent to which Pithoys the protestant uses the same material as Pithoys the Minim; the only difference between the *Horoscope* and the *Découverte* both of which received the approbation of the superiors of the Order, and the *Traité d'astrologie judiciaire*, published after his apostasy, is one of intensity and enlarged scope.

Bayle states that the *Apocalypse de Méliton* is not Pithoy's own work[2]; he claimed rather that it was an adaptation of an anti-monastic work by J-P. Camus, Bishop of Belley. Certainly it is hard to believe that it is not from the pen of a member of the secular clergy rather than from a protestant, witness the following passage from the preface: "Les artifices dont se servent ces bons frères pour attirer les colombes dans leurs colombiers, je veux dire toutes les dévotions des peuples dans leurs églises et toutes leurs charités dans leurs cloîtres, au grand préjudice des Eglises Parochiales qui en sont désertées et désolées comme chacun sait."[3] Throughout the work he evokes the image of the ancient austerity of the orders compared with their contemporary luxury; he criticises the comfort of the monastic houses, the richness of their food, the pomp of their ritual[4]; he is against the acquisition of all their privileges and the protection of their patrons.[5] It is a pamphlet of regret for past glory rather than a scurrilous attack on monasticism.[6] Only at the end can one discern anything remotely protestant as distinct from being anti-monastic; this is the criticism of the ideals of perfection in which he casts doubt on the intrinsic validity of vows and observances in general.[7]

---

[1] In an appendix I have put a summary of the chapter and section headings of this little known work; in content and in style he seems to anticipate Bayle.

[2] Marginal note already referred to, *Oeuvres Diverses*, III, p. 629.

[3] Préface, p. 5.

[4] pp. 29–57 and 132–161.

[5] p. 145.

[6] The frontispiece is an exception: a monk is seen running out of a farm with a plump chicken, ready for the pot, halfhidden in his cowl.

[7] pp. 190–191.

Pithoys seems to have had no qualms about his apostasy; he married three times and was survived by a son (a minister in Guernsey) and a daughter who struck Bayle as good-looking (she was in her early twenties when Bayle succeeded her father). He retained his gay and impetuous nature until the end of his long life [1] and was engaged in outspoken controversy shortly before he retired, when the *Mémoire*, which he had prepared for the press in 1670 or 1671, was banned by the Moderators of the Académie de Sedan who saw themselves libelled.[2]

Previous historians of the Order have not been interested in its intellectual activity and have been shocked by Pithoys' lack of submission. He has been included here for several reasons: his work both before and after his apostasy is of considerable intrinsic interest; he shows certain traits of character which are not dissimilar from those of Mersenne and Maignan, namely a refusal to accept the mere appearance of things as their true nature, and a delight in investigation; he shows also the effects of monastic discipline on a temperament unsuited to it, a strong, unsubmissive individuality. Those who came after him in the Order and whose intellectual activity is such a remarkable feature of the history of the French Minims differed from him in temperament rather than in intellect; with Mersenne, Niceron, Maignan and Plumier there is the same spirit of interrogation but it overlays a profound "sagesse" which is the most characteristic feature of the Minims' way of life.

---

[1] These biographical details are taken from Bayle, *Nouvelles Lettres*, La Haye, 1739, vol. II, pp. 37–38.
[2] Boulliot, *op. cit.*

CHAPTER IV

MARIN MERSENNE

In 1632 Galileo published the *Dialogo sopra i due massimi sistemi del Mondo* in which he stated his adherence to the Copernican system; Urban VIII, a friend of Galileo, saw himself satirized as one of the speakers in the fictitious dialogue, a benevolent but unenlightened supporter of the Aristotelian system. Galileo's subsequent arraignment before the Inquisition has become one of the most symbolic events in the history of the freedom of thought: experimental science was threatened with extinction by pure theory. The diffusion of Galilean physics was undertaken in the face of the most stubborn adherence to Aristotelian principles. Of those who worked to propagate the new system none was more important or better informed than Mersenne; dedicating his translation of a selection of Galileo's findings to Monsieur Melian, Thrésorier Général de la France, he wrote [1]:

Monsieur, Après avoir considéré plusieurs effets de la nature, et quelques difficultés dans les sciences, qui arrêtent les plus savants, j'en ai voulu proposer un certain nombre dans ce livre que je vous présente, afin de vous témoigner l'estime que je fais de votre excellent esprit, et d'exciter les doctes à la recherche des raisons qui peuvent satisfaire à tous ceux qui ne ferment pas les yeux à la lumière.[2] Je ne doute nullement que vous ne sachiez très bien qu'il est mal aisé de rencontrer les vraies raisons dont on croit souvent envisager l'éclat et la splendeur, encore que l'on n'ait trouvé que l'ombre et l'obscurité, qui *font souvent paraître le mensonge sous l'habit de la vérité . . . il semble que la capacité des hommes est bornée par l'écorce et par la surface des choses corporelles* et qu'ils (ceux qui s'efforcent de trouver la vérité) *ne peuvent pénétrer plus avant que la quantité, avec une entière satisfaction.* C'est pourquoi *les anciens n'ont pu donner aucune démonstration de ce qui appartient aux qualités, et se sont restreints aux nombres, aux lignes, aux figures,* si l'on excepte la pesanteur dont Archimède a parlé . . .

---

[1] *Questions physico-mathématiques et les mécaniques du Sieur Galilee . . . nouvellement traduites de l'italien par L.P.M.M.* (Mersenne), Paris, 1635; epistle dedicatory, (my italics).

[2] As well as the obvious metaphorical meaning, is this an oblique reference to the professor at Padua who refused to look through Galileo's telescope?

Or j'espère ... que vous vous rangerez librement du parti de Socrate, qui tenait que l'on ne peut rien savoir si l'on ignore Dieu; car puisqu'il n'y a rien de possible si Dieu n'est, et que la possibilité de tous les êtres dépend absolument de l'être actuel de Dieu, comme la puissance de l'acte, il est certain que l'on ne peut avoir la parfaite connaissance d'aucune chose, si l'on ne connaît pas la source dont elle prend son origine. Et comme l'on aurait sujet de blâmer un Philosophe qui voudrait connaître la nature des couleurs sans savoirc elle de la lumière qui leur donne l'être et la subsistance, puisqu'il est impossible qu'il y ait des couleurs sans elle: de même l'on peut justement mépriser celui qui s'applique aux sciences, s'il n'essaye pas par leur moyen de s'avancer à la connaissance de Dieu, puisqu'elles sont comme des rayons de la divinité, qui démontrent par leur grande étendue son immuabilité ... C'est donc en cette manière que tous les chrétiens doivent envisager les sciences, et qu'ils s'en doivent servir comme de puissantes machines pour élever leur amour qui est le centre de pesanteur de toutes leurs affections.

In this he is attempting to reconcile an experimental approach to the scientific problem with a belief in a First Cause – a synthesis of Galilean and Thomistic principles. The scope of Galilean physics must have appeared unbounded; traditional beliefs in the perfection of the celestial bodies and their movement in circles were swept away because they had been *seen* to be false – it was the observation of blemishes (sunspots) on the sun's surfaces that had given Galileo his first indication that the earth was in motion around the sun. Likewise the Scholastic notions of natural motion and natural place were deemed to be erroneous; but it was no use substituting theory for theory, Galileo had to go up the Leaning Tower and measure the speed of falling bodies of different weight; hence Mersenne's insistence that the Ancients could give no demonstration of the nature of things beyond the quantitative and the linear.

The motion of the stars, sun and moon, the properties of pendulums and falling weights, discoveries concerning the nature of musical sounds, all these were in Mersenne's mind when he wrote of "plusieurs effets de la nature" in the above epistle dedicatory; more important than the discoveries themselves was their practical application to everyday problems such as navigation, time-keeping and the tuning of instruments – this is surely the significance of Mersenne and those members of the Order who followed him. It is also arguable that the attitude of mind is even more important than any step taken towards what we should call technology to-day. Unhindered by the dogmatic assertions of antiquity, he was free to range over the whole field of scientific investigation; he was more truly a scientist than Bacon, but had something of the same desire for an encyclopaedic system of knowledge; he was often surer in his pronouncements than Descartes, but adhered to similar standards of mathematical exactitude.

It is difficult at this moment to write about Mersenne; le Père Lenoble's *Mersenne ou le Mécanisme* [1] gives such a complete exposition of his work and influence that it will remain the definitive work at least until the edition of the *Correspondance* [2] is complete; even then it is unlikely that any new material will come to light which will alter the findings of Lenoble. There has, however, been considerable interest taken in this most interesting of all members of the Order; the year 1948 saw the publication of several articles in commemoration of the tercentenary of his death. In January of that year the *Osservatore Romano* [3] published an article by il Padre Moretti, author of the article on the Minims on the *Enciclopedia Cattolica*. The article, entitled *Marin Mersenne alle origini della nuova scienza*, is an interesting "post-Lenoble" summary, but nothing more; of greater interest are the articles collected and published by the Centre international de synthèse in the *Revue d'histoire des sciences*.[4] Since then, more and more attention has been paid to Mersenne and the neglect of nearly two centuries has been rectified. In a study of this nature one is tempted to say with La Bruyère, "Tout est dit" and to pass on to the lesser known writers. There remains a certain amount of reassessment to be done concerning his position within the Order and the use made of his intellectual legacy to his successors. It is apposite to ask whether his work conformed to the ideals of Lesguiller's *Ratio studiorum* and whether scientific investigation was not held by him in higher esteem than the spiritual purposes and the ideals of perfection for which the Order existed. During a visit to St. Peter's he took advantage of the height of the gallery in the dome to conduct experiments with pendulums and falling weights – scarcely, it would seem, pious reflections.[5]

[1] Paris, 1943.
[2] The history of the publication of this is rather complicated. It forms part of the publication of the correspondence of Descartes, Peiresc, and Fermat.
The first volume, prepared by Madame Tannery, appeared in 1933 and the second in 1936; the war then interrupted publication and the last volume to appear, No. IX, came out in 1965. This brings us up to 1640 so that a further eight years of his letters await publication. The notes were begun by Paul Tannery and later by his widow; Cornelis de Waard began to work on the notes and publication from vol. II–vol. VII but died in 1963 shortly before the publication of vol. VIII; B. Rochot has now taken over the task. The publishers are the Centre National de la Recherche Scientifique.
[3] Rome, 28 January 1948.
[4] Paris, 1948, Vol. II, pp. 5–100. Articles by P. Sergescu, C. de Waard, P. Humbert, L. Auger, le Père R. Lenoble and J. Itard. Subsequently referred to as R.H.S.
[5] Lenoble, *op. cit.*, p. 51.

The amount of time spent on research into the properties of musical instruments, on abstruse mathematical calculations, on speculations about submarines,[1] on ballistics,[2] on optics ... on preparing for the press long and diffuse works on all these topics and many more; above all, on writing letters and more letters to all the leading geniuses of Europe, could this possibly be in accordance with the dictates of his erstwhile Corrector Lesguillier, "Licet sapere, sine pompa, sine invidia, sine ambitione?"

One cannot consult the *Registres Capitulaires* of the Place Royale [3] without being struck by the fact that certain names, well-known in the Order, recur in one office or another at the annual elections. We have already seen that Mersenne's name was coupled with that of Robert Regnault and François La Noue in the office of Librarian; in the office of Corrector we find Lesguillier (1621), Hilarion de Coste (1622 and on several subsequent occasions) and Dony D'Attichy (1626) – both prominent as historians of the Order; we find Etienne Dondé, author and illustrator of a life of Saint François de Paule, named as Cook at the same time as Mersenne was Discret, or private secretary to the Corrector (1628). Each of these men in his own way enriched the life of the Order by his contribution to its intellectual activity, and none more than Mersenne's friend Jean-François Niceron who became Scribe to the "couvent" in 1642. He was therefore amongst contemporaries whose alert and inquiring minds were in sympathy with his own genius. It was also a member of the Order who taught him Hebrew, the Scotsman Jean Bruno who had published in Venice, in 1604, *In Benedictiones XII Patriarchum commentaria et quaestiones analyticae*, a work which, by its title and intent, is in anticipation of Mersenne's work on *Genesis*. Another member, Théophile Minuti, a friend of Peiresc, furnished him with details of Arab music and instruments and gave him information about the Coptic script. The Order, then, provided not only the necessary security that any man of learning required if he had no patron but it also provided the stimulus and the sympathetic ambiance for the maturing of his abilities. He remained

---

[1] *Cogitata (Hydraulica)*, pp. 251–259 and see Le Noble, p. 491; also R. Triger, *Mersenne et les sous-marins*, Le Mans, 1912.

[2] See inter alia a curious work, not cited by Le Noble, *The compleat Gunner ... to which is added the Doctrine of Physics by the late famous authors Galilaeus and Torricellio ... together with some excellent observations out of Mersennus ... (Military and Maritime Discipline, Book III)*, London, 1672.

[3] Archives Nationales, LL. 1564–1566.

faithful to his Order and his Order revered his memory.[1] More than this, it becomes apparent when one takes Mersenne's work as a whole – in so far as it is possible to do so – that there is no clash of interests or loyalties; it takes its place in a tradition among the French members of the Order. A scathing attack on superstition had been made in the sixteenth century by a Minim, Pierre Nodé. His short pamphlet [2] published in 1578 made the claim, significant enough if one remembers the acrimony of Catholic-Protestant relationships at the time, that "les sorciers maléficiers ... sont pires que tous les autres hérétiques, plus à fuir et punir" [3]; the arguments that he used were all theological identifying sorcerers with the Antichrist and urging the death penalty for all who were convicted under the order made by the Faculty of Theology in the University of Paris in 1398.[4] Mersenne was convinced that the new learning had brought with it new problems and new threats to religion, new heresies more powerful and dangerous than those which had occasioned the great schism. The perennial interest in the occult sciences continued unabated and had even found added vitality; the increased knowledge of Hebrew opened up to the initiated the whole field of cabbalistic tradition of which Robert Fludd may be taken as the greatest exponent. Astrology had similarly received a fillip from the genuine advances in astronomy and Jérôme Cardan reflects the strange and complex mixture of true leaning and quackery that was possible within one individual.[5] Fludd and Cardan, representatives of tendencies, all the more dangerous because they were cloaked with science, were the true opponents of the faith; the Order which had been, according to Bellarmine, so prominent in the counter-reformation and whose preachers had so assiduously done battle in the market places with Calvinist ministers, was now to come to the forefront of the struggle against necromancers and charlatans while, at the same time, it had to face the more subtle threat from the intelligent and sophisticated libertines of Parisian society. In order to overcome the arguments of the superstitious, the atheists and deists, it was necessary not to defend oneself behind the old scholasticism but to use the new science to win over those who abused it. In this way the cause of science became the cause of God.

[1] See H. de Coste, Mersenne; Thuillier II, pp. 90–113 Roberti II, 552–560.
[2] *Déclamation contre l'erreur exécrable des maléficiers, sorciers, enchanteurs, magiciens, devins et semblables observateurs des superstitions: lesquels pullulent maintenant publiquement en France ...,* Paris, 1578.
[3] p. 8.
[4] pp. 24–29 and the title-page; pp. 51–55 and 64–66.
[5] See the article on him in the *Dictionnaire* of Bayle. Plumier acknowledges him as a source of his work on lathes.

Mersenne's work comprises twenty-four original printed works, several containing synopses or even first editions of the works of his friends – Galileo,[1] Hobbes,[2] Roberval [3] and Niceron [4] amongst them – several editions of his letters and a number of manuscripts. Of the printed works two are works of devotion, six are specifically aimed at the conversion of deists, atheists and libertines, while the remainder comprise in themselves an almost complete synopsis of scientific knowledge of the time. Few people would now agree with Thomas De Quincey that "Mersenne was obviously no match for Fludd either in learning or polemic wit." [5] Mersenne now appears as one of the great men of learning of his age, whereas Fludd has largely been forgotten. The controversy between Fludd and Mersenne which, before it died down involved Gassendi and two members of the Order, Jean Durelle and François de Lanoue, as well as the inevitable partisans on both sides that all controversies attract to themselves, is nothing less than the cause of magic confronting the cause of true leaning. The starting point is Mersenne's voluminous *Quaestiones in Genesim* [6] which, in spite of its digressions and the general prolixity of its rambling columns, is a landmark in the history of Biblical exegesis. Leaving aside the sections on ancient music and prosody, the latter with its strange phonetic alphabet, and forgetting for the moment the encyclopaedia of the *Arts libéraux* contained in columns 1479 to 1510, it is at once apparent to the reader that he has before him a work of profound scholarship referring him to the Hebrew as well as to the Greek and Latin texts, and giving comparisons with the Chaldean paraphrase. He demolished the cabbalist divinations with the arguments of modern philology; these divinations depended on giving numbers to the letters of the alphabet and then taking the "total" of a word or phrase and finding its equivalent in another context; his criticism is all the more pungent because he could play this not very advanced word-game to his advantage when occasions suited.[7]

---

[1] *Les mécaniques de Galilée*, Paris, 1634; *Nouvelles pensées de Galilée*, Paris, 1639.

[2] First edition of the *Tractatus opticus* of Hobbes in *Universae geometriae synopsis*, Paris, 1644.

[3] Passim in *Ars navigandi*, part of the *Cogitata*, Paris, 1644.

[4] The posthumous edition of the *Perspective curieuse*, called *L'Optique et la Catoptrique du R. P. Mersenne*, Paris, 1651. This list of inclusions is intended merely as an indication and is in no sense exhaustive.

[5] De Quincey, *Works*, 1871, Vol. 16, p. 407; referred to by J. B. Craven, *Doctor Robert Fludd*, Kirkwall, 1902.

[6] Paris, 1623. The pages are divided down the middle and the columns are numbered, 1–1892.

[7] An example of this was furnished by the rabbinic scholars who tried to show that the phrase "Silho cometh" (Genesis, XLIX, 10) was Messianic; Mersenne himself refuted them

Fludd replied to this criticism in two pamphlets printed together, *Sophiae cum Moria certamen* and *Summum Bonum, quod est verum Magiae, Cabalae, Alchymiae et Fratrum Roseae Crucis subjectum*.[1] Far from giving up the struggle and relying on the defence of his friends within the Order and sheltering behind Gassendi, the whole of the rest of Mersenne's work may fairly be said to amplify and bring up to date his basic objections; it is the continuation of the struggle, and not the throwing in of the sponge as Craven suggests.[2] The prolongation of the struggle was not against Fludd as an individual, for he had no real significance, but against everything that Fludd stood for. In the first place Mersenne's Biblical exegesis heralded the movement sometimes called positive theology, that is to say a theology based on an exact scriptural interpretation; in the second place all his scientific work was directed towards the demolition of such pseudo-science as the cabbalists could muster.

It is here necessary to make two short digressions. The first concerns the connections between Mersenne and Richard Simon, an important and highly significant quarter in which to find evidence of his influence. In the Preface to the *Histoire critique du vieux Testament* le P. Simon pays a tribute to Mersenne for his efforts to get Louis Cappelle's *Critica Sacra* through the press. Cappelle was a protestant and his work was considered even by his coreligionists as being too fundamental in its criticism. Mersenne, realising the need for scientific exegesis, urged that it should be published and, with a Jesuit, le Père Pétau, and an Oratorian, le Père Morin, managed to acquire the Royal assent for its publication; this in fact it took so long to secure that Mersenne had been dead two years before the work appeared.[3] According to le P. Simon, the Holy See was much dusturbed by this unprecedented appearance of a work by a protestant "avec privilège du Roi," and the Huguenots were no less distressed. Cappelle's *Critica sacra* belongs to the main trend of seventeenth century Biblical studies which find their highest expression in the enlarged version of Cappelle undertaken by John Pearson, Bishop of Chester, and published in Amsterdam in 1698. Mersenne therefore forms an important link in this tradition of scholarship running from Jean Bruno to the scientific exegetes at the close of the century.

by using the same method to show that $S(18)$ $i(9)$ $l(11)$ $o(14) = 52$ and that $I(9)$ $e(5)$ $s(18)$ $u(20) = 52$ ∴ SILO = IESU!! See Lenoble, p. 102.

[1] Frankfort, 1629.
[2] *op. cit.*, p. 132.
[3] Published by Cramoisy, Paris, 1650.

The second of these digressions concerns the pamphlet entitled *Effigies contracta Roberti Flud* (sic). It appeared as part of the defence of Mersenne in 1636 under the pseudonym Eusebius a Sancto Justo; it seems likely that it was the work of the Minim Jean Durel or Durelle, a friend of Mersenne's and who will be mentioned again in the chapter on medical work in the Order. Evidence for ascribing it to him resides first of all on the testimony of Hilarion de Coste, who states that Durelle defended Mersenne [1]; further evidence is, I think, provided by the use of arguments derived from a knowledge of medicine in which Durelle had some grounding and of which La Noue, to whom the pamphlet has also been ascribed, was ignorant.[2] It is remarkable in nothing more than its vitriolic and contradictory phraseology and in the assertion (pages 42–43) that Fludd was a Manichaean. In view of the importance of manichaeism in the works of the Philosophes from Bayle to Voltaire, it is perhaps worthwhile drawing attention to the remarkable (and very English) modification of the traditional Dark-Light dualism which characterises this belief; according to Fludd, North represented a "coagulating influence" and South a "rarefying influence." The following extract illustrates the tone of the work:

> Multicolor inquam est Fludus ... est enim togatus et sagatus; oplomachus et ophthalmicus ... est enim mendax et inconstans ... cabalista et alchimista. Est astrologus et magus, chiromanticus et geomanticus; deista et atheista; est Lutheranus, Manichaeus, Calvinista, Priscillianista, Sophista, Tautologus, Stultiloquus, Plagiarus ...! [3]

Whilst his defence was thus venting its spleen, Mersenne himself was deeply engrossed in propagating his own work. The central point at variance between him and Fludd and the cabbalistic school – and even between himself and Descartes and some of the most enlightened men of the age – is the separation of science from metaphysics. This makes him at once more "modern" than Descartes and in many ways a truer progenitor of the philosophers of the succeeding generations. In some ways his attitude is remarkably similar to that of Bacon in his desire to rid science of the impedimenta of metaphysics, by placing them on a plane above scientific investigation, so that the latter can

---

[1] *Vie du R. P. Mersenne*, Paris, 1649, p. 31.

[2] Bibliothèque Nationale, *Catalogue Général*, lists the work under Lanoue, François. The copy, Z^{12} 17167 has a MS note (XVIIth century?) stating, "Confutatio dogmat. Rob. Flud a Jo. Durel."
The British Museum lists the work under Eusebius a Sancto Iusto, adding the note that this was a pseudonym for F. Sanovius (sic) or J. Durelle.

[3] *Effigies contracta*, pp. 2–3. Sagatus-wearing a sagum or military cloak.

proceed untrammelled. In a most telling passage in the *Questions harmoniques* [1] he does just this and it is interesting to see how diametrically opposed he is to the opinion expressed by Sir Thomas Browne that music is divine.[2] Music for Mersenne was a scientific pursuit, a thing that is capable of explanation and analysis; if it gave pleasure, it was because of its action on the nerves of the ear. No passage in all his work explains better what is meant by his "mechanism" and no passage, with one exception, serves as a better introduction to his use of the philosophical position of sensationalism [3]; moreover, no passage goes further to explaining the underlying harmony of sound and colour. He brings Raymond Lull up to date and even anticipates modern poets, musicians and psychologists who attempt to define sound in terms of colour and so on:

Mais *sans entrer dans les considérations de l'éternité,* qui sont capables de faire trembler tout le monde, l'on peut prouver que la Musique ne peut apporter nul solide contentement à l'esprit, car *il n'y a dans l'harmonie que les sons et leur proportion;* quant aux sons, *ils ne diffèrent point des battements de l'air,* comme je prouverai dans un autre lieu, et conséquemment ils ne peuvent donner du plaisir, au contraire, toute sorte de son, qui tient longtemps ferme, est désagréable, comme l'on expérimente aux sons des tuyaux d'orgues que l'on accorde.[4] Et quant à leurs rapports, ils ne sont autre chose que des accidents que l'on appelle relations ou les raisons des dissonances, car il n'y a pas moins de plaisir à considérer et à comprendre la raison septule de 7 à 1 que la double 2 à 1 quoique celle-là soit la raison d'une dissonance celle-ci d'un accord.

Et s'il y a quelque plaisir digne d'un honnête homme dans la Musique ce n'est pas de dire qu'elle est divine, charmante et ravissante comme font les ignorants, mais il consiste à considérer la raison pourquoi deux battements qui entrent dans l'oreille et qui frappent tellement son petit tambour, que quand l'un le frappe deux fois l'autre ne le frappe qu'une fois, sont plus agréables que deux autres, dont l'un le frappe quatre fois pendant que l'autre ne le frappe que trois fois etc. et pourquoi les battements qui sont des dissonances ne sont pas agréables.

---

[1] Paris, 1634. The work dates from 1629 as the "Approbation" shows.

[2] *Religio medici,* "For myself ... even that vulgar and tavern-music ... strikes in me a deep fit of devotion and a profound contemplation of the first Composer. There is *something in it of divinity more than the ear discovers.*" (My italics).

[3] Particularly in so far as Maignan also took up this position. The philosophy of sensationalism has obvious attractions for anyone who was interested in sound and light; it is not a mere reliance upon Aristotle and a reaction against the new philosophy. See subsequently in the chapter on Maignan.

[4] Mersenne was interested in all problems connected with the tuning of instruments particularly in the spread of the overtones in the exact calibration of the scale. He is a forerunner of Bach in this respect and may be considered as one of the precursors of Fourier and the whole idea of harmonic analysis.

Car quant au ravissement que l'on attribue à l'harmonie,[1] il est imaginaire, puisqu'*elle n'a rien de plus excellent que les couleurs et la lumière qui ne ravissent pas les bons esprits* quoiqu'elles les excitent à rechercher les raisons de leurs effets.[2]

It is worth while pointing out that the *Questions harmoniques*, from which this quotation comes, belong properly to the complete work *L'Harmonie universelle*, but that Mersenne saw fit to publish this introductory material separately. An analysis of the *Harmonie universelle* is beyond the scope of this study but it is important to point out that it stems from ideas which had already been expressed in the *Quaestiones in Genesim* (columns 1479–1510) and that the work deals with problems of accoustics as much as with music in the more usually accepted sense; it deals with the physics of sound, the vibration of strings and those produced in tubes; the whole question of overtones and the spread of these in tuning instruments is tackled with the most minute attention to mathematical and experimental detail [3]; his analysis of the capabilities of musical instruments was probably the first attempt at a scientific approach to the problems of orchestration [4] and is furthermore remarkable in that the potentialities of oriental instruments and harmony are also explored [5] – an anticipation of very recent interests. In this way the *Harmonie universelle* is very much a continuation of his controversy with Fludd and it refutes the absurdities of his *Monochordum mundi symphonicum*, but the *Questions harmoniques* mark a division in Mersenne's work; the exegetical and polemical works give place to purely scientific works, the content of which has been admirably summarised by Lenoble and, in a more succinct form, by Léon Auger in the *Revue de l'histoire des sciences*.[6]

If his main contribution to scientific progress was in the realm of accoustics which, after him, became properly a branch of physics, it would nevertheless be a travesty of his thought to interpret him as a specialist. He was for ever mindful of the way in which a scientific

[1] Mersenne is doubtless thinking of Fludd who reiterated the theory of the so called "harmony of the spheres" and who drew an extraordinary diagram to illustrate it, showing the hand of God tuning a viol across the string of which moved the paths of the celestial bodies; reproduced from *Monochordum mundi symphonicum*, Frankfort, 1623, by J. B. Craven, *op. cit.*, p. 153.

[2] *Questions harmoniques*, pp. 17–20, (my italics).

[3] See H. Ludwig, *Marin Mersenne und seine Musiklehre*, Halle, 1935 and R.H.S., *loc. cit.*, pp. 39–51.

[4] R. E. Chapman, *Harmonie universelle and the books on instruments*, The Hague, 1957, and passages in *Correspondance, passim*, especially Vols. II, IV and V.

[5] Also in letters to and from Peiresc and the Minim Théophile Minuti, *Correspondance, ibid.*

[6] R.H.S. *loc. cit.*, pp. 33–52.

discovery in one field will be of value in another. When he is dealing with the tuning of stringed instruments, he shows how a piece of gut can be used as a rudimentary hygrometer [1]; when he is writing about hydraulics, he envisages a submarine from which marine life could be observed and which could travel, undisturbed by tide and tempest, from pole to pole [2]; during the conduct of experiments to determine the speed of sound his mind turned to problems of ballistics and the possibility which he foresaw of a supersonic projectile.[3] Hence the unity of his work: each piece of information, each idea, fits into the generalised scheme of knowledge. He must therefore be considered as one of the originators of the "haute vulgarisation" of scientific information: the diffusion of Galilean physics; the publication of Niceron's work on optics in a more definitive form than had been possible during the author's lifetime; the insertion in his own publications of synopses of discoveries made by his friends – all this makes of his work taken as a whole something of an encyclopaedic journal. By temperament and ability Mersenne was clearly cut out to be the permanent secretary to a scientific academy; he never became one; although, some time before 1635, he founded the Academia Parisiensis. The exact date is unknown because it was decided to preserve a measure of clandestinity about its functions; this is not surprising when we bear in mind the recent sentence on Galileo and the hanging, in 1631, of the chemist, Chanloux. Mersenne's ideal in having an academic institute had been outlined as early as 1622 in the *Quaestiones in Genesim* when, referring to the Academia Musica of Charles IX, founded in 1570, he wrote:

Quod ita peragere voluerunt (i.e. J-A. Baïf and J. T. Courville, the founders), nihil ut in Academia deesset, quod ad virum perfecte tam quoad animum, quam corpus instituendum faceret. Idcirco viros in omni scientiarum naturalium genere versatissimos huic Academiae destinarunt et instituerunt praefectum illius, qui μεγαλοδιδάσκαλος diceretur. Omitto reliquos scientiarum, linguarum praesertim, musicae, poetices, geographiae, caeterarumque partium, et picturae magistros, qui animi bona promoverent, et militiae praefectos, qui ea docerent, quae ad militiam, et omnia honesta exercitia attinent.[4]

[1] *Harmonie universelle*, Paris 1636. *Les instruments*, Livre III, Proposition XI, Déterminer de combien l'air est plus sec ou plus humide chaque jour par le moyen des sons et des cordes.
[2] *Questions inouies*, pp. 84–89; *Cogitata, Ars navigandi et hydraulica*, pp. 259–251. cf. other ideas concerning the submarine in the XVIIth century, Cornelis van Drebbel's in England inter alia; cf. also scientific dreams of Cyrano de Bergerac for example, his journey to the moon. An article on this theme by J. Knowlson appeared in *The Listener*, B.B.C. Publications, London, Vol. LXIX, February 7, 1963.
[3] R.H.S., *loc. cit.*, p. 42.
[4] *Quæstiones in Genesim*, col. 1683.

Mersenne's academy attracted Etienne Pascal and Mydorge, Huygens, Descartes and Carcavi as well as Habert de Montmor, whose own Academy was of equal importance. Mersenne may fairly be said to have made two distinct contributions to the academic spirit coming into full vogue; he conceived the notion of the academy as a Great Teacher, μεγαλοδιδασκάλος, anticipating perhaps the time when the man of learning would have to specialise and knowledge would be departmentalised. His other contribution was to maintain a close interest in the arts and crafts and in the application of purely academic or theoretical knowledge.

Official recognition of the Academia Parisiensis was not made until 1666 (eight years after Mersenne's death) when Colbert granted it the title Académie des Sciences and placed it under Royal patronage. The early history of the Académie Royale des Sciences has been carefully studied by P. Cauja and he has fully explained Mersenne's part in its inception.[1] Proof of Mersenne's pride in the Academia Paresiensis is borne out by a letter which he wrote to Peiresc on the 23rd of May 1635 – "(Si Gassendi vient à Paris) il verra la plus noble académie du monde qui se fait depuis peu en cette ville car elle est toute mathématique." [2] In the same year and to this same academy a young genius was introduced – Pascal, then twelve years old.

The relationship of faith to scepticism has been the subject of several recent studies, and the meaning of scepticism in the context of Pascal's writings has received special attention. Recently Professor R. A. Popkin in an article in *Modern Schoolman* under the title *Father Mersenne's war against pyrrhonism* [3] made out a case for considering Mersenne as opposed to the spread of "practical scepticism" while advocating it "theoretically" [4]; or, "as an epistemological sceptic, opposed to the spread of the application of scepticism to religious and scientific questions but not to philosophical ones," [5] What I think Professor Popkin means is that Mersenne opposed the libertines of his age but at the same time allowed his own mind a free and untrammelled investigation into the nature of the physical universe. In this sense I accept his judgement and accept with reservation the idea that he was

[1] R.H.S., 1948, pp. 292–310. M. Cauja was Secrétaire Perpétuel de l'Académie des Sciences at the time of writing the article.

[2] *Correspondance*, V, p. 209.

[3] No. 34, January, 1957, Saint Louis U.P., pp. 61–78.

[4] *ibid.*, p. 78.

[5] Quotation from a summary of above in *Critical Bibliography of French literature*, Syracuse U.P., 1961, p. 846, No. 4341.

an epistemological sceptic, if by that one means that he acknowledged certain limitations to the capabilities of the human intellect. But, baldly stated, the argument may well be confusing. Mersenne belonged to a generation for whom there need be no conflict between revelation and natural reason, between conscience and Christian morals; for them the supernatural did not contradict the findings of science but crowned them. What was his "mécanisme" (as we have seen it applied to music) if it was not the application of the principles of scepticism to science? And in a certain sense is not his positive theology, based upon philological exegesis, a parallel movement to his "mécanisme"; is it not carrying the principle of scepticism into the realm of religion – at least for someone of this generation? The argument seems to lack historicity and to deny the unity of Mersenne's thought by trying to force a distinction between Religious, Scientific and Philosophical ideas. It is possible that such unity was only conceivable at this moment in history when, to use Lenoble's phrase "Dieu était sensible au cœur du scientiste." But, in common with all those who before and after him attack superstition from a scientific standpoint, Mersenne was bound to adopt an attitude that is sceptical, in the sense that all criticism is sceptical if it is to be fruitful. Unlike many sceptics, both before and after him, he was not prepared to believe in the absolute validity of the processes of his own scientific inquiry, admitting that there was always something beyond the limits of his investigation. In this respect we may make a comparison with the image of the plumb-line in Locke; and this very limitation gives one of the most characteristic features of his scepticism, since it leaves room for an adherence to Lesguillier's maxim "Licet sapere sine pompa." At the same time, it allows him to reflect something of the spirit of the Order and of the Founder's clear distinction between what was necessary and what was superfluous. Scientific truth, once established on a basis of demonstrable certainty, could be applied to man's needs and, more important, could convince him of his own insignificance and dependence upon the Author of so many natural phenomena; "Dieu sensible au cœur du scientiste." Those that followed him in the Order were particularly interested in the application of his ideas to practical problems, and we have seen how Mersenne himself missed no opportunity for showing the practicability of his theoretical knowledge. Here too he bears comparison with thinkers of a later age who urged man to occupy himself with the urgent and obvious necessities of life rather than with idle speculations. We may return to his early *Quaestiones in*

Genesim and to the miniature "encyclopaedia" that it contained in the passage dealing with the arts and crafts [1]:

Genesis, IV, xx. Genuitque Ada Jabel, qui fuit pater habitantium in tentoriis, atque pastorum.

Ecce primae uxoris filius primorum papilionum pastoralium inventor et scenitarum.[2]

De artibus tam mechanicis quam liberalibus an ad salutem animæ conducant?

De mechanicis artibus et earum divisionibus – Lingua, Tropus, Ratio, Tonus, Angulus, Astra; Rus, Nemus,[3] Arma, Faber, Vulnera, Sana, Rates.

Sequentes scientias vel alicui dictioni nostri symboli, vel alicui Evangelio quispiam applicare poterit; ideoque dictionem apponam, tam ex symbolo quam ex Evangelio desumptam, cui celeberrimus Nostri Ordinis concionator sequentes scientas accomadabat, licet aliis Evangeliis eas applicare possis, prout congrum iudicaveris.

There then follows the division of arts and crafts into – Those necessary for life; Those useful for life; Those useful for adornment; Those which lead to voluptuousness; Those which are useful for the establishment of truth. The vast list which he gives under each division allows us to see something of his vision of what can only be called a "République des arts": a vision in keeping with the value he attributed to a scientific academy.

It is on account of this attention to what was practical and demonstrable that his purely philosophical ideas fall into the background; they are not however, without their significance. During the many years that he was engaged in correspondence with Descartes questions of a speculative nature were often the subject of discussion between them. The Minims tended to follow thomistic principles in their teaching [4] and Mersenne's thirty-six proofs of the existence of God which he inserted in the early part of the *Quaestiones in Genesim* [5] may owe something to his reading of Aquinas. Also following Aquinas, he declared that God could have created an eternal world but that the authority of Scripture tells us that it was made in time [6]; other in-

[1] *Quaestiones in Genesim*, columns 1475 *et sq.*
[2] Papilionum pastoralium, i.e. tents for shepherds (Papiloinum > pavillon); Scenitarum, a transliteration of the Greek σχηνιτες – tent-dwellers.
[3] Nemus-oris, a grove or clearing in the forest for grazing.
[4] This became a rule of the Order in 1661, Pizzurnus, *op. cit.*, p. 201.
[5] Columns 15–670, "Quaestio prima – An Deum esse, contra Atheos probari possit." See the list of these proofs cols. 25–26.
[6] See Lenoble, *op. cit.*, p. 261.

stances of the closeness of his thought to thomism could be cited.[1] It is on the question of sense perception that he seems to be most characteristically thomistic, and this is important because of the obvious opposition to Descartes that it implies. It will be more convenient to deal with sensationalism as an alternative to the cartesian doctrine of innate ideas in the chapter on Emmanuel Maignan, but it is important to discuss it briefly here since the connexion between Mersenne and Maignan is a close one. Writing to André Rivet he asked whether he thought that the soul, or understanding, had any operation which was independent of the senses. His reason for asking was, he said, that several people had written books to prove that the immortality of the soul depended on the fact that it was independent of them.[2] Two reasons for wishing to adhere to the doctrine of sensationalism in opposition to Descartes might be given; in the first place it could be a mere adherence to the traditions of scholasticism or, in the second place, it could be a fruitful development from a thomistic premise.[3] To think that the first of these reasons could have been Mersenne's is absurd, in spite of the fact that in his letter to Rivet he quotes Aristotle's "nil in intellectu nisi prius in sensu"; neither is it necessary to overemphasise the thomistic origins of his reliance upon sense-data. His interest in optics and accoustics leads logically to a consideration of the receptivity of the mind to sensations transmitted to it by the nerves. It has been suggested that the passage from the *Questions harmoniques* already quoted serves as an introduction to this aspect of his thought. In the context of the philosophy of both Mersenne and Maignan it is an important consideration underlying their approach to the problem of explaining the physical universe in a way that was strictly opposed to the animism of the superstitious detractors of the new science, and which did not have to depend on such an undemonstrable proposition as the innate ideas of Descartes. It also prepares a way for the increasing interest in man as a biological entity dependent upon the acuity of his senses. The following chapters on Niceron, Maignan and Plumier show that each of these members of the Order had much in common with Mersenne but that they also made a distinctly individual contribution to the intellectual activity of the Minims and of the century.

[1] *ibid.*, inter alia, pp. 248–253; 275–276; 551.
[2] 20 January, 1638; *Correspondance*, VII, pp. 22–30.
[3] The place of sensationalism in thomistic philosophy is summarised by Father F. C. Copleston in his *Aquinas*, Pelican books, London, 1959, pp. 25–26 etc.

CHAPTER V

JEAN-FRANÇOIS NICERON

What harmony was to Mersenne, perspective was to Jean-François Nice-ron. It is the underlying law of the visible world just as harmony is the law of that which is audible; both supply the rational basis for ana-lysing the communication of the external world to our senses. Con-sidered purely mathematically harmony and perspective are similar, being merely practical applications of the abstract laws of mathe-matical proportion. Aesthetically, Mersenne's analysis of harmony and Niceron's work on perspective represent that search for balance and degree which, in the seventeenth century, all critics considered as conducive to the sublime; Nature itself was bound by the laws of proportion, and therefore all art had to observe like laws.[1] Aesthetic consideration meant more to Niceron than to Mersenne and there is dis-cernible in this most attractive man some sign of an attenuation of the rigorous ascetism of the Order. His intellectualism had a creative outlet.

Jean-François Niceron must first of all be distinguished from his famous great-nephew, the author of the *Mémoires*. He was born in 1613 and joined the Order before he was eighteen. He soon distin-guished himself as a mathematician and as an artist and was sent to Santa Trinità dei Monti where, in common with so many other members of his Order, he was able to find the greatest scope for his young talents. In both his work and in Maignan's we find Santa Trinità not only mentioned affectionately, but actually furnishing the pictorial background for the illustrations of some of their technical drawings. It was there that he acquired a first-hand knowledge of the masters of the Italian renaissance and that he met Maignan and other

---

[1] Shakespeare, *Troilus and Cressida*, Act I, sc. iii, "The heavens themselves observe degree ... Take but degree away, untune that string and, hark! what discord follows." This idea is also the basis of the *sublime* in the treatise by Longinus translated by Boileau.

scientists [1] with whom he conducted experiments and spent many hours in conversation. His stay was short and he returned to Paris, to La Place Royale, in 1640, staying there until shortly before his death. He took part in a "Visite générale," travelling as "commis" to François La Noue; we know from the preface to one of his works that he was at Grenoble in 1646 and we know that he fell ill and died at Aix-en-Provence in the same year, at the untimely age of thirty-three.

His earliest work, undertaken during his noviciate, was a portrait of Jacques Auzolles de Lapeyre, the author of the *Mercure charitable*, who spoke of the artist as being "très-excellent esprit et très-savant homme (si alors on le devait appeler homme, n'ayant que quelque dix-huit ans) en tout ce qui dépend de l'optique; ce gentil esprit lors que moins j'y pensais s'avisa de faire de mon portrait la suivante figure (see Appendix p. 249), laquelle semble plutôt un monstre qu'un homme, mais y appliquant un cylindre et le mettant sur le rond qui y est marqué cela me représente si naïvement bien, qu'il ne s'est fait portrait de moi qui soit plus semblable." [2] There was nothing new in drawing distorted portraits on a plane surface in this way; in the National Portrait Gallery, London, there is the portrait of Edward VI by an unknown Flemish artist, a contemporary of Holbein, which is mounted in the bottom of a box and has to be viewed through an aperture made in one end. The principles of linear perspective required for this type of projection were known to the ancients and were arrived at empirically. Even by the time of Holbein the scientific study of perspective was still in its infancy; distance in a painting was often achieved merely by gradation in colour. The theory of spherical projection was developed in Italy, and a knowledge of it was required by the artists and architects in France as the influence of the Italian renaissance spread and the dome became an architectural feature of importance. Niceron's portrait of Auzolles is, therefore, in the nature of an interesting and novel experiment in an art form which had direct bearing on the problems of interior decoration, while the theoretical work which he produced leads to improvements in the projection of maps in which there is some evidence that he was interested. Other portraits that he did were distorted and required some

---

[1] Torricelli, writing to Galileo, "Ritrovandomi io in Roma l'anno 1640, hebbi occasione per via di amici communi di conoscere il Padre Francesco Nicerone ali convento della Trinità dei Monti ... questo padre è vero professore di lettere e scienze di molti sorti." Quoted by A. Favaro, *Amici e correspondenti di Galileo Galilei* in *Atti del R. Istituto Venetio di scienza*, Vol. LXXVI, Serie 9, Vol. I, Parte secondo, Venice, 1917, p. 80.

[2] Auzolles de Lapeyre (or "A Lapeyre"), *Le mercure charitable*, Paris, 1638, pp. 72–73.

special view-point before they could be seen: Dézallier de Dargenville in his *Voyage pittoresque de Paris* refers to two "morceaux d'optique – une Madeleine et S. Jean à Pathmos" [1] in La Place Royale. This Madeleine is also referred to as "en perspective" in the annals of the "couvent" [2]; unfortunately neither this nor the S. Jean nor the original of the Auzolles portrait seems to have been preserved. There was also the extraordinary allegorical painting which hung in the library at La Place Royale and which is described in the Appendix, page 251.

His published work consists of *La Perspective curieuse* (Paris, 1638) and *Thaumaturgus opticus* (Paris, 1646) which is an enlarged version of the former and translated into Latin; even this is an unfinished work and Mersenne entrusted the publication of the final, posthumous version to Roberval who edited it with Mersenne's own *Optique et catoptrique* (Paris, 1651). From the bibliography which Niceron gave in the *Thaumaturgus opticus*, we find only two works on perspective printed in French in the XVIIth century before Niceron – Salomon de Caus's *La Perspective* (London, 1612) and le sieur de Vauzelard's *Abrégé ... de la Perspective par l'imitation* (Paris, 1635).

The sub-title of the *Perspective curieuse* is *Magie artificielle des effets merveilleux de l'optique, la catoptrique ... la dioptrique*, a choice of title which Niceron justifies in the preface; this goes a long way towards explaining the importance that the enlightened members of the Order placed upon scientific work as a means of combatting witchcraft, sorcery and the like:

> Quant à ce qui touche l'inscription du livre, je l'ai appelé "Perspective Curieuse," non pas qu'elle ne soit très-utile mais d'autant qu'avec l'utile il mêle le délectable ... je le nomme aussi "Magie Artificielle" car encore que ce mot de Magie sonne mal aux oreilles du vulgaire, les doctes néanmoins savent assez que, si par corruption il a été attribué aux pratiques et communications illicites qui se font avec les ennemis de notre salut, il n'est pour cela en rien déchu de sa propre signification ... d'où vient que Strabon dans son premier livre dit que μαγι vaut autant que σοφια ... Philon le Juif au livre "De Specialibus legibus" dit ... que la vraie Magie ou la perfection des sciences consiste en la Perspective qui nous fait connaître et discerner plus parfaitement les beaux ouvrages de la Nature et de l'Art ... Il est vrai qu'il prend en cet endroit la Perspective assez généralement, néanmoins il est certain que la vraie perspective dont nous traitons fait une bonne partie de celle-là. [3]

[1] Paris, 1757, p. 285.
[2] See later in the chapter on Maignan who finished the painting.
[3] *Perspective curieuse*, Préface, unnumbered page. It is interesting to note that Niceron chose to translate this sub-title, rather than the full title, into Latin for the 2nd edition.

This passage also helps to distinguish Niceron from his fellow Minims; few would have voiced a commonplace of seventeenth aesthetics – "mêler l'utile et le délectable." If Mersenne was his master in mathematics, his artistic masters were Dürer, Michelangelo, Raphael and Volaterra; this is borne out in one of the interesting passages devoted to art criticism which intersperse the purely technical instructions in the book. One such passage is in the preface of the *Thaumaturgus opticus:*

Pictoria denique quam artium principem esse dicimus quid est aliud quam mera Scenographiae, sive projectionis Opticae praxis, citra quam nullus aliquando pictor aut excellens fuit, aut audivit; cum ex illustribus prioris aetatis monimentis satis constet summos illius temporis artifices praecipuam sub huius scientiae praesidio laudem in arte sua fuisse consecutos: non est quod Albertum Durer, Michael Angelum Buonarotam, Danielem Volaterranum, Raphael Urbinatem et infinitos alios in exemplum adducam; satis enim per de loquuntur, authorumque celeberrimorum studium et industriam ostentant elegantissimae tabulae, Romae et in pluribus aliis Italiae locis intelligentium oculis admirationi expositae.[1]

In another passage from the *Perspective curiese* Niceron describes the whole effect of "trompe l'œil," although he does not use the term; it was then in its early stages but became a recognised art form during the later years of the century and throughout the Rococo period. There is added interest in the passage in the description of some of the interior decoration in the "couvents" at La Place Royale and at Santa Trinità dei Monti:

Ce n'est pas encore sans admiration que nous voyons en quelques tableaux plats fonds (sic) ou voûtes certaines figures, dont les parties antérieures semblent faire une saillie vers ceux qui les regardent, de quelque côté qu'elles soient considerées. Et de cette façon j'en ai vu chez nous deux assez gentilles, l'une est le pied d'un S. Mathieu peint en la voûte de l'un des offices de notre couvent de Vincennes-lès-Paris, qui semble toujours avancer sa partie antérieure hors le fond de la voûte vers celui qui le regarde en quelque part qu'il se mette pour le voir: l'autre est un tableau peint à frais, en une chapelle de notre couvent de la Trinité du Mont Pincius à Rome, auquel est representée une descente de Croix, où le Christ, qui en est la principale figure, est tellement disposé, qu'étant vu du côte gauche, il semble couché et incliné sur le travers du tableau, et son pied droit faire une saillie du même côte; et vu de l'autre côté, tout son corps paraît presque droit; on en peut voir l'effect au grand Autel de notre église de la Place Royale où nous avons une copie de ce tableau assez bien faite.

[1] *Thaumaturgus opticus*, Preface, sig ĩ ij.

A la vérité il est difficile de rendre raison de ces merveilleuses apparences, et encore plus de faire des précepts pour y arriver infailliblement, vu qu'-elles ne dépendent pas seulement du dessein, mais encore du coloris et des ombres, des rehaussements et des refondrements dont l'Art s'acquiert plus par l'habitude en travaillant que pour aucune maxime de science qu'on en puisse prescrire; et on peut dire que ce sont des coups de maîtres inventifs pour le dessein, et savants dans le coloris, tel qu'était celui qui a fait l'ori-ginal de cette descente de Croix, Daniel Ricciarolle de Volaterra, avec encore un autre tableau de l'Assomption de Notre Dame, qui est de même le premier peint à frais dans une autre chapelle de notre Eglise de la Trinité du Mont Pincius ... [1]

Niceron's technique stems directly from Salomon de Caus whose work on linear perspective, although short, is amply illustrated and extremely clear in its explanation. Caus, however, had little interest in the decorative arts but was chiefly preoccupied with the problems of foreshortening due to looking up or down from the horizontal; thus he gives excellent instruction in the art of lettering on a high wall so that all the letters appear the same size to the beholder on the ground. He is also an expert on the question of linear projection and illustrates this by examples of plans of forts and gardens drawn by someone who is looking down on them; Caus was, after all, chiefly an engineer and architect. His influence is noticeable in the technique of illustrating a manual of instruction and is, therefore, more noticeable in Plumier's pictures of the interior of a workshop than in Niceron's work, although it would be a mistake to minimize his influence. There is also the question of Jacques Besson, an engineer of the XVIth century whose work, *Théâtre des instruments mathématiques et mécaniques* (Lyon, 1579), was in Mersenne's own collection of books and which is also acknowledged as a source of Plumier's work. It is safe to assume that Niceron had consulted this book and made use of Besson's tech-nique of illustration. There is in Caus's work only one example of spherical projection but the method he shows is the name as that adopted by Niceron, namely to draw the figure on a plane surface which is then divided into squares; the procedure is then identical to that taught in the British Army for the enlargement of a map by using the grid squares, and may be seen by consulting figure 5 in the Ap-pendix. The difficult part of spherical projection is to determine the shape that the square will adopt when projected onto a given curved surface. Niceron, if we are to believe Auzolles de Lapeyre, could do

[1] *Perspective curieuse*, p. 72.

this intuitively and with great rapidity; but for those who had not the gift, the instructions that he gives show how each of the original squares becomes delineated by segments of the circumference of the sphere or cylinder onto which the picture or pattern is to be projected, and the edge of the picture becomes a tangent to that circumference produced to the eye of the spectator; we may discern in this the influence of Descartes' geometry of tangents. Niceron knew both Descartes and Fermat and received from the former a copy of the *Principia*, a mark of the author's esteem for the young Minim [1]; while from Mersenne, with whom he was in close contact during most of his life, he acquired a knowledge of the mathematics of proportion which underlies the whole question of perspective.

Niceron's originality lies in his combining an interest in the arts, and even art criticism, with a profound knowledge of plane, and circular and spherical geometry, especially the latter. His most complicated designs exceed anything that his contemporaries were capable of undertaking; if we tend to think of the distorted portrait as more suitable for the children's Christmas Annual than being a serious art form, we should remember that without such a work the painting of the interior of a dome would have been a task beyond any but the few who could do it intuitively; moreover, it has a strong connection with the designing of various scientific instruments, the astrolabe for example and the terrestrial globe. This book had a direct influence on Maignan's *Horographia* and on Plumier's treatise on the art of turning wood and metal; both authors acknowledge their debt to their fellow Minim. Indirectly, therefore, it has an influence on the technique of producing the illustrations for technical manuals. The work is an essentially practical one; Niceron included a section on the casting of metal for the manufacture of mirrors, and gave details concerning their polishing. In this also he anticipates Maignan who included a chapter on the polishing of lenses in his work on sun-dials and dialling.

One interesting and, it seems, hitherto unreported fact about Niceron is that he had at La Place Royale a map of the moon. We have this on the authority of Olivier le Fèvre d'Ormesson whose brother, Nicolas, was a member of the Order and a contemporary of Niceron's at La Place Royale. Olivier wrote in his diary:

---

[1] A. Baillet, *Vie de Descartes*, Paris 1691, vol. II, pp. 300–301. Baillet mentions Descartes's distress on hearing of Niceron's death.

Dimanche, 29 novembre (1645) ... aux Minimes, où le Père Niceron me fit voir une carte faite à Bruxelles d'un monde dedans la lune, où toutes les terres, montagnes, îles, étaient nommées des noms des rois et grands de ce siècle, et fort proche celui de la Reine de celui de Mazarin.[1]

As far as I am able to ascertain, the only map of the moon published in Brussels was that of Michel-Florent van Langren; this appeared in February, 1645, and according to a description of it in the *Biographie Nationale de Belgique* it corresponds closely with the above account: "Les cirques et les points isolés portent des noms de rois ... des noms familiers, des noms de ministres (Mazarin) et enfin des noms de savans." [2] Credit for the naming of the features of the moon in this way is usually given to Hevelius who worked in Danzig and whose *Selenographia* did not appear until 1647; certainly his *Tabula selenographica* (Danzig, 1645) names the features according to terrestrial geography – thus "Mare Adriaticum," "Mons Aetna" etc; there is, however, a "Mons Dalanguer" and a "Mons Cragg" [3] neither of which seems to fit his original system of nomenclature and may anticipate his later system. Nevertheless it is quite clear that Niceron had at La Place Royale a new and highly original map.

That which was distorted or "hidden" must have had a particular fascination for Niceron for we have seen the part that this played in his works on perspective. His only other publication was an adaptation and translation of a treatise on the deciphering of codes by the Italian A.M. Cospi. It shows something of the same love of the enigmatic [4] and something of the diligent application to detail that is a hall-mark of his other work. Niceron's contribution to the original is to examine the differences between Italian, French and Spanish with special reference to the question of the frequency of double consonants, double vowels, monosyllables and other features of the written

---

[1] *Journal d'Olivier le Fèvre d'Ormesson; publié par P. A. Cheruel, Collection de documents inédits sur l'histoire de France.* 2 vols., Paris, 1860–'61. See Vol. I, p. 333. This diary contains several references to the brother Nicolas referred to above and to the Minims at La Place Royale in general. The Ormesson family is connected with S. François de Paule through Anne d'Alesso, a great-niece of the Saint.

[2] *Biographie Nationale de Belgique.* vol. II, p. 280. See also *Ciel et terre*, vol. 14, Brussels, 1884, p. 313.

[3] The former in the extreme S. (bottom of map), the latter near the centre S of the Mare Adriaticum and the Mare Sipylum.

[4] The illusory and enigmatic as themes in XVIIth century art and literature have recently been the subject of an article by R. L. Colie, *Some paradoxes in the language of things*, in *Reason and Inspiration. Studies in the History of Ideas 1600–1800*, by J. A. Mazzeo, London, 1962. The author refers to both Mersenne and Niceron but calls them both "Minorites" (i.e. Frères Mineurs), p. 114, and refers to the Minims' church in the Place Royale as "the Franciscan church in the Palais Royal," p. 115.

language which may help to betray a code based upon any simple substitution of letters; all such codes, he contends, can be broken when one analyses the frequency of letters but, he points out, this frequency is different for Italian, French and Spanish. He claims in the introduction that it has value in military and political circles, but apart from this, there is little significance in the work; it does, however, as I have already suggested, help to throw some light on the attractive personality of the translator.

The career of Jean-François Niceron invites that useless speculation "What would have happened if ...?" He was, of all the members of the Order, the one nearest to Mersenne and the one whose intellectual abilities most suited him for continuing his work and interpreting it to the next generation; as it was, Mersenne survived him by two years and died leaving no immediate intellectual successor. The history of the diffusion of Mersenne's ideas within the Order passes to Maignan who, working at Rome and Toulouse, was more remote than Niceron from the direct influence of Mersenne.

CHAPTER VI

EMANUEL MAIGNAN

In the first edition of the *Dictionnaire Historique et critique* Bayle included a short article on le P. Maignan; in the second and subsequent editions the article was enlarged by copious borrowings from a life of Maignan by his former pupil, the Minim Jean Saguens.[1] This and an account of his fourteen years at Rome contained in the manuscript history of Santa Trinità dei Monti [2] are the only sources of our knowledge of his life and of his distinguished career. For the rest, his works have to speak for themselves. It is strange that little interest has been taken in him, since there is ample evidence that he was rated amongst the best philosophers of his time. Baillet [3] in his *Vie de Descartes* considered him greater than Mersenne; Bayle, introducing his article, referred to him as one of the greatest philosophers of the seventeenth century; Niceron devoted a short article to him in the *Mémoires*.[4] Since then, however, this "philosopher," whose universal knowledge would have placed him amongst the encyclopaedists had he lived a century later, has been almost forgotten. Michaud includes him in the *Biographie Universelle*, but his article is merely an adaptation of Bayle and Saguens; recently interest has been shown in him, firstly by the German F. Sander [5] and secondly by the Spanish Jesuit R. Ceñal.[6] More recently J. S. Spink has written about his position as a philosopher in the tradition of free-thought running from Gassendi to Voltaire,[7] and there is a

[1] *De Vita, moribus et scriptis R. P. Emanuel Maignani, Tolosatis, Mathematici praestantissimi elogium*, Toulouse, 1697.
[2] By le P. Martin; see Bibliography, Manuscripts – Private Archives, Rome, Santa Trinità dei Mohti.
[3] Vol. II, pp. 379–380.
[4] Vol. XXXI, pp. 346–353.
[5] *Geschichtliche Forschungen zur Philosophie der Neuzeit; Band 3, Die Auffassung des Raumes bei E. Maignan und J-B. Morin*, Paderborn, 1934.
[6] Two articles: (a) *Revista de Estudios Politicos*, Madrid, 1952, pp. 111–150. (b) *Revista de filosofia*, Madrid, 1954, pp. 16–68.
[7] *French Free-thought from Gassendi to Voltaire*, London, 1960.

brief mention of him as a forerunner of Torricelli in *The Rise of Modern Science*.[1]

Emmanuel Maignan came from a well-to-do Armagnac family; his father was Doyen de la Chancellerie de Toulouse. He was born in 1601 and we know little of his early life, save that nothing would amuse him so much as a book when he was a child.[2] He entered the Order when he was 18 and soon distinguished himself as a young man of outstanding intellect. He spent his noviciate in Toulouse, his native town, and it was there that he died in 1676. During his noviciate he studied philosophy under le P. Ruffat and lost no time in arguing against his master who was a confirmed aristotelian.[3] During this period also he acquired his great love of mathematics in which, we are told, he was self-taught; so remarkable was his ability that the Corrector General sent for him to teach at Santa Trinità dei Monti.[4] He remained there for fourteen years, this being the formative period of his life; it was here that, in 1647, he published his first and in some ways his most interesting work, a treatise on sun-dials, perspective and optical instruments (a work largely ignored by those who have so far written about him). He was elected Corrector of Santa Trinità shortly after his arrival,[5] but his heart seems to have been in his teaching and in his experimental work rather than in administration, although he is reputed to have fulfilled all duties connected with this and later appointments with diligence. Maignan has left one pleasing reminiscence of his time there: Santa Trinità stands at the very edge of the Monte Pincio and commands one of the finest views of Rome [6]; he was always seeking information about natural phenomena and the following is his vivid description of the echo that can be produced by clouds: –

Hic vero ex occasione ad propositum est, ut addam, facile accidere, ut ex illo multiplici repercussu eiusdem fragosæ commotionis, plurimi, uno tantum dato ictu, resultent ictus in ipso solo circumstante aere, quando hic est nebulosus. Sic namque sæpius observavi Romæ degens in Monte Pincio (ubi noster præstat conventus Sanctissimi Trinitatis dictus) cum explodarentur in arce S. Angeli, bellicæ machinæ, ut solet, fere innumeræ plausu,

---

[1] Vol. 3, *From Galileo to Newton, 1630–1720*, by A. Rupert-Hall, London, 1963, pp. 250–251.

[2] Saguens, quoted by Bayle.

[3] *ibid.*, We know nothing of this Père Ruffat unless he is to be identified with the P. Pierre Ruffat, sometime apothecary at Santa Trinità dei Monti; see Mgr. F. Bonnard, *op. cit.*, p. 187.

[4] Saguens/Bayle.

[5] Mersenne, *Correspondance*, Vol. VII, pp. 110 and 381.

[6] See the reproduction of Claude's view of Rome; Appendix, p. 247.

ad præcipua per annum festa, matutino: scilicet observavi singulis explosis machinis respondisse plurimos per nebulas ictus, cum erat aër nebulosus crassior; sed nullo tali responsu facto, unicum ab unica machina bombum exauditum, quoties erat aër serenus, ac purus, excepto quod ad ædificiorum aliquas maiores moles, ut S. Petri et Palatii Vaticani, prout erat oppositio ad eo reflectendum accommodata; bombus idem semel reddebatur, ac sic audiebatur geminatus.[1]

Later, Maignan also showed how water can act as a mirror.[2] The affection that he felt for the French "couvent" at Rome may also be seen in the *Perspectiva Horaria* for in it he describes his work on an astrolabe which may still be seen there on the wall of the North wing of the cloisters; he also illustrated two of his practical experiments in this work with engravings of the interior of the "couvent" – two are reproduced in the appendix. It was also in Rome that he met the German Jesuit A. Kircher, whose work has a strong affinity with his own. He also met and worked with Gaspar Berti and Magiotti whose barometric experiments intrigued him and led him to doubt the veracity of Descartes's theory of the plenum. From his time in Rome also dates his interest in "Fontaines de vent" – springs from which air as well as water issues from the earth. Having investigated this phenomenon he constructed a device on the same principle for blowing a furnace.[3]

On his return to Toulouse he was elected Provincial of Aquitaine; it has been the tendency from Bayle onwards to ignore his work as a Minim. His theological work was hesitant and submissive compared with the boldness of his philosophy,[4] but that is not perhaps the last word. He was an eclectic in whom faith and reasoning should not be considered as conflicting or contradictory; like Mersenne, he saw the greatest threat to the Faith in superstition and ignorance, and his scientific investigation into the nature of things was in no sense a merely deistic affirmation of belief. We possess fragments of his prayers and some sermons, also some advice that he wrote out for the benefit of his pupils about to dispute their theses; he was sincere in his devotion to the Order and did not look upon it solely as a refuge.[5] Moreover, it is an over-simplification of his somewhat complex person-

---

[1] *Cursus Philosophicus*, Lyon, 1673, p. 726. All further references to this work will be to this edition unless otherwise stated.
[2] Toulouse, Bibliothèque Publique, MS 752, fol. 113/4. Subsequently referred to in this chapter as MS T.
[3] MS T. fols. 152/3; reproduced and in part transcribed in the Appendix, p. 265–266.
[4] Professor Spink *op. cit.*, p. 77.
[5] MS T, *passim*.

ality to impute his refusal to accept a post in Paris to mere humility. Louis XIV, on his way back to the capital from his marriage in Saint-Jean-de-Luz, visited him in his cell in Toulouse. He found the Minim in a room which, if Saguens's description is true, must have been a cross between workshop and laboratory for, among many other things Maignan made his own apparatus on his own lathe, and had his own optical benches and equipment in the "couvent" itself. Mazarin, who returned the day after the visit to press the offer of a post was probably met with a strong "crainte d'être attaché" – a veritable "Loup et Chien" type of situation. He did, however, visit Paris on his own initiative and attended the scientific salon of M. de Montmor, Maître des Requêtes.[1] We also know for certain that he painted a picture of the Madeleine on the wall of the gallery at the "couvent" of La Place Royale – presumably where he stayed in Paris. This painting had been started by Jean-François Niceron who, as we have seen, was a friend from the days in Rome; it may have been a desire to complete this work which took him to the capital. The suggestion that he should do it seems to have come from him rather than from anyone in the Parisian "couvent"; the Annales des Minimes de la Place Royale give the date of this visit as 1661 [2] whereas all authorities on Maignan have dated his visit as 1657.[3] It seems likely that this was a second visit and was perhaps in the nature of a pilgrimage to the place where his friend, who had met so untimely a death, had worked.

His earliest published work – the curious Perspectiva horaria, sive de horographia gnomonica tum theoretica tum practica – was printed in Rome in 1647,[4] that is, during his stay at Santa Trinità dei Monti. It at once establishes him as one of the foremost experimentalists of the day. Before Maignan there were several treatises on sun-dials and the art of dialling, but the Perspectiva Horaria breaks new ground in the presentation of the material and is well in advance of all previous work on the subject with the possible exception of the Gnomonices libri VIII published in Rome in 1581 by C. Clavius, and to which was added, in 1599, the Horologiorum nova descriptio, also printed in Rome. Clavius had been commissioned by Gregory XIII to investigate the inaccuracies of the Calendar; the above works were the direct outcome of his

---

[1] Bayle/Saguens.
[2] Registres capitulaires du Couvent de la Place Royale, Vol. II, sub anno 1661, Archives Nationales, LL. 1564–1566. Also Mazarine, 2429, Annales etc. p. 172, "le P. Maignan a peint la figure de Sainte Magdaleine en perspective que le R. P. Niceron avait tracée."
[3] Saguens, Bayle, Ceñal, Spink.
[4] 1648 according to Bayle.

investigation. Maignan's work, which runs to 702 pages in-folio, anticipates by several years the *Elliptical and azimuthal horologiography* (204 pages in 8vo, London, 1654) by S. Foster, who refers to him in the preface, and *La gnomonique* of P. de la Hire (196 pages and tables in 12mo, Paris, 1682) adds nothing to Maignan, while the scant illustrations, limited to a few line drawings in the text, are vastly inferior. Only J. Wells, with his *Sciography, or the art of shadows*, may claim some originality as far as English works are concerned; it was published in London in 1635, an extensive treatise of 427 pages in 8vo giving many tables and diagrams which are, however, cramped and indistinct compared with those in the *Perspectiva horaria*. Athanasius Kircher, the German Jesuit whom Maignan met in Rome, also wrote a treatise on dialling which is certainly the best of the works so far quoted. His *Primitiae gnomonicae catoptricae, hoc est Horologiographiae* was published in Avignon in 1635, the same year as Wells's *Sciography*. These two are the nearest works to Maignan's in time, but the difference between them is surprising; not only is his the fuller and clearer study but it is also the most practical, showing in detail how to make the instruments for constructing the dials (pages 121 et sq. and, in particular the illustration facing page 121) and how to construct a simple piece of apparatus for determining the angle of refraction of glass; he also gives an important section on the polishing of lenses (pages 687–704) and the construction of the buffing instruments required. Recently the work has been called "one of the fullest and most finely illustrated of early works on dialling, which contains the earliest (sic) theory of the refraction of light. One section treats of the grinding and polishing of lenses for dials and telescopes." [1] This practical approach can be seen from the following rapid analysis:

pp. 1–104; Pars theoretica – the meaning of time and the notion of time amongst the nations. Systems of measurement of time. The refraction of the sun's rays by the atmosphere. Theory of shadows and the projection of them onto plane and spherical surfaces.

pp. 105–278; Optice horaria – how to obtain a plane surface and how to erect the gnomon at right angles to the plane. (Note this preoccupation with the most elementary practical detail, it is lacking in all the other works on the subject quoted above.) How to construct inclined planes; how to calculate the meridian and how to determine the elevation of the sun. (All this section copiously illustrated.)

---

[1] *British Optical Association Library Catalogue*, vol. III, London, 1957, p. 133.

pp. 279–550; Catoptrice horaria – projection onto spherical surfaces with detailed instructions on the construction of the instruments required. The sun-beam projected onto a vaulted roof; the "spot dial" and the extension of its use in tall buildings (illustrated with diagrams representing cells in the cloister of Santa Trinità dei Monti); the astrolabe in the Palazzo Spadani, painted on the ceiling which enabled 22 different observations to be made, lunar as well as solar, by means of rays projected upwards onto the ceiling from a mirror on the floor (illustrated by a plate 20″ × 12″ facing p. 391); the problems of perspective that such projections cause.

pp. 551–705; Dioptrice horaria – the linking of optical instruments to the sun-dial; determining the angle of refraction; construction of the bowl type of dial which was aligned by means of a magnetic compass, the first step towards the miniature portable dials which became so important as navigational aids in the eighteenth century.
Polishing of lenses.

It is above all in the illustrations that Maignan is supreme; they are chiefly the work of one P. Guerin whom I am unable to identify unless he is the same P. Guerin, Minim, author of the *Eloge des Ursulines* who is mentioned by Thuillier.[1] A few are by Claude Goyrand (1620–1662) a minor artist who painted religious subjects; one, of a small hemispherical sun-clock, is by P. Gagliardi.[2] The inspiration behind these illustrations undoubtedly comes from Maignan's interest in the practical exposition of subject matter, and one can also discern an affinity with the excellent illustrations in Niceron's *Perspective curieuse*, which have already been described; they show the same admirable sense of form and the same outstanding ability to clarify what must so often remain obscure even in the best of text books on technical subjects, if there is no visual aid to the written word. To emphasise this point I have given in the Appendix a reproduction from Kircher (a complete page with line drawing from the text) and invite comparison with Maignan's work, illustrated in the same appendix by some examples of his plates and line drawings. It is also fruitful to compare at the same time Maignan's illustrations from the chapter "De formandis poliendisque lentibus crystallinis" with the illustrations in Plumier's *Art de tourner* and to compare them both with other technical manuals of the XVIIth century on the one hand and with illustrations from the *Encyclopédie* on the other.

The end of the XVIIth century saw the first stages of the cheap

---

[1] *op. cit.*, II, p. 115. See also Bibliography.
[2] Thieme und Beker, *Allgemeines Lexicon der Bildenden Künstler*, gives brief reference to these artists but does not refer to the engravings in Maignan's book.

production of clocks and the advent of the pocket watch. Nevertheless, throughout the next century, sun-dials played an important part in everyday life and their use as a navigational aid was developed considerably. One other Minim, Joachim Rigaud, of Marseille, prepared a treatise on the subject with illustrations drawn by himself and engraved by Louis David (1667–1718); it was never printed, but the plates together with the manuscript are preserved in the Bibliothèque Publique at Marseille [1]; the influence of Maignan is clearly visible.

It is unfortunate that Maignan did not continue to produce technical books; a similar treatise to the *Perspectiva horaria* on, say, hydraulic engineering and another on optics would have been well within his competence; instead, he turned to speculative work and made important but not outstanding contributions in the fields of theology and philosophy although, in both of these, one can discern the influence of what was surely his true bent – experimental and applied science. He left a number of fragments in the Toulouse manuscript of which some were incorporated in his printed work.[2] His application of Archimedes' principle to a quick test for debased currency and his study of the phenomenon of the sea's acting as a mirror are two such fragments, and are typical of his desire to explore natural phenomena and to explain them mathematically by the principes of harmony, perspective and proportion. Coming midway between his experimental and his speculative work is the account which he gave in the *Cursus Philosophicus* (pp. 718 et sq.) of Sir Samuel Morland's megaphone or "Tuba Stentorophonica", an account which shows many traits in common with other French scientific writings of the later seventeenth century. It is a work of vulgarisation and, like the rest of his output, might have been more significant had it been in French rather than Latin. Like so many other scientific reports it comes from a foreign source, the work of a member of the Royal Society [3]; this internationalism of scientific outlook is furthered by references to his own researches in Rome with Kircher. In common also with works of vulgarisation at this period, there is a marked historical approach to the subject, drawing on classical and scriptural sources.

Sir Samuel Morland was well known in France. He had been sent

---

[1] See Bibliography, Manuscripts, Marseille Nos. 960–962. Reproduction of two plates in the Appendix.

[2] See MS T. and notes thereon in Bibliography, Manuscripts, Toulouse.

[3] For example, the constant reference to the Royal Society by Bayle in the scientific reports in *Nouvelles de la République des Lettres*.

on a fact-finding mission to Savoy to report on the persecution of the
Vaudois and, in spite of his relief work amongst the refugees in Geneva
and in spite of his strongly worded report which inspired Milton's
sonnet on the persecution in Piedmont, was accepted in French
scientific circles and also at Court. His abilities as a hydraulic engineer
commended him to Louis XIV who employed him on the difficult
problems connected with the supply of water for the fountains at
Versailles. His megaphone was made by a firm of trumpet-makers in
London who advertised the product in French (as well, one supposes,
as in English, although there is not a copy of the English advertisement
extant) quoting a price of £2 = 15 = 0 each. Since the firm saw fit
to advertise in French one may presume that Morland had sufficient
demands in France for his invention, possibly from the Army. Maignan's interest in the megaphone was manifold; he was, following
Mersenne, interested in accoustics; he was interested in the actual
production of scientific apparatus and instruments; he had previous
knowledge of the subject and he admired Morland's skill, although he
doubted his originality as an inventor. He states that 25 years before
Morland's announcement in French of the megaphone, he had been
with Kircher in the Vatican Library and that they had examined
together "in pervetusto codice" a reference to a similar device which
Alexander the Great had had from his master, Aristotle. And what,
asks Maignan, if not a megaphone is referred to by S. John in the
Apocalypse when he wrote, "audivi post me vocem magnam tamquam
tubae?" [1] His other reasons for doubting the originality of Morland
is also curious and of particular interest to the English reader; quoting
from Camden's *Britannia* he says:

> ... quem Anglia in provinciam redacta Severus Imp., tota quam late
> patet insula, intervallo fere 50 leucarum a mare ad mare, construxit in
> eius tutamen adversus barbarorum incursus: ei namque muro secundum
> spatia, quibus ab invicem turres eius castella distabant, insertus erat plum-
> beus; ut alii volunt, tubus aereus, per quem verba facta custodum, a prima
> in secundum turrim, et sic in omnes momento perlata significarent, qua
> parte, insultus hostium timeretur. Et addit hic autor eius modi quoque
> miraculum de turribus Bisantii in vita Dione referri a Xiphilino. [2]

The account ends with a description of an experiment which Mersenne

---

[1] IV, 1. Maignan also refers to XIX, 1 and 6, in error, however, for the word "turba"
not "tuba" is used.

[2] Camden, *Britannia;* see under *Cumberland, Wall against the Picts.* In the English translation of 1695, p. 839. A number of pipes (*tubus* as opposed to *tuba*) have been found along
the Wall; their purpose is dubious – drainage, rather than speaking tubes or megaphones?

conducted between the steps of the "couvent" at Vincennes and the Arsenal to calculate the speed of sound; the result, although in excess of calculations made with modern instruments, is more accurate than the calculations of his contemporaries.[1]

The speculative part of Maignan's work is contained in two works, the *Cursus Philosophicus* and the *Philosophia Sacra*. The first of these went through two editions during the author's life, while his pupil Jean Saguens made what is virtually a third edition after his death.[2] At first sight the work appears to be no more than just another "Cursus," a folio volume giving a compendium of philosophical knowledge. It is for this reason, perhaps, that Prof. Spink heads his chapter on Maignan *Between Aristotle and Epicurus;* to classify Maignan so fairly and squarely amongst the ancients places the emphasis in the wrong direction and leads one to overlook his real significance; neither is it true to say that he is entirely forgotten to-day; Prof. Spink seems to be unaware of Padre Ramon Ceñal's two articles. Having regard to the highly experimental nature of Maignan's philosophy, it would give a more accurate assessment of his importance to place him "Between Descartes and Locke." Maignan was affected by the cartesian upheaval and became one of the leading adversaries of the system, not because of a mere conservatism but because he found it scientifically unsound.

Of the 742 pages in-folio of the second edition, 124 are taken up with "Philosophia entis" and the remainder with "Philosophia naturae, alias Physica"; the whole balance of the work is therefore significantly different from the contemporary "cursus," Oviedo's for example, Arriaga's [3] or Lalemandet's.[4] Three points stand out: the first, admirably stressed by Ceñal, is the influence of the experimentalists with whom Maignan worked in Rome during his stay at Santa Trinità dei Monti; here he met Mersenne who visited the "couvent" in 1644 and here also he spent ten months in the company of Niceron, studying mathematics together and learning Hebrew; there is the influence of his association with Gaspar Berti, Raphael Magiotti and Athanasius Kircher, to each of whom he refers in the pages of his

---

[1] See Lenoble, *op. cit.*, pp. 485–486. Lenoble does not refer to Maignan who gives a readily accessible account of the experiment.

[2] These editions are: Toulouse, 1653 and Lyon, 1673. Saguens's *Philosophia Maignani* was published in Toulouse in 1703. All references in this chapter are to the second (Lyon) edition.

[3] Both published in Lyon, the former in 1640, the latter in 1661.

[4] The Minim Jean Lalemandet, *Cursus Philosophicus*, Lyon, 1656. His work of 890 pp. in-folio makes no mention of any contemporary scientific or medical advances and relies on formal, syllogistic logic and a reiteration of Thomist and Scotist principles.

Cursus. The second point is the rejection of cartesian philosophy, not on the grounds of its incompatibility with the tenets of orthodox religion but because of its irreconcilability with the facts of science – Maignan's is, perhaps, the most *scientific* rejection of Descartes in the XVIIth century. The third point is the interest he shows in the sensitive nature of the living organism and his sensationalism as a philosophic standpoint; here again he is not merely reiterating the ancient adage "Nihil est in intellectu quod prius non fuerit in sensu," but is showing, in a way which anticipates Locke and even Condillac, what the living being owes to its senses individually and collectively.

The rôle of experimental scientific inquiry in Maignan's philosophy is prominent in the section *De motu ex metu, ut dicitur, vacui* (pages 489–517) in which he describes the now famous experiment of the bell ringing in a tube and becoming inaudible as the air is pumped out. This experiment, a popular one in any school physics laboratory, was

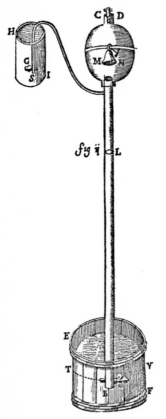

difficult to perform in the XVIIth century because of the inadequacy of air pumps; Maignan and Berti therefore constructed the apparatus shown in the inset. He envisaged the void in the first instance in terms of the space at the top of a barometric tube; when we consider that the atmosphere will support a column of water of thirty feet we can assume that his unwieldy apparatus was at least thirty-five feet high. The following description comes from page 509 and the tracing of the apparatus was made from the unnumbered page of illustrations at the front of the book:

Eximius vir quem dixi Gaspar (i.e. Berti) plumbeam fistulam oblongam ut AB (vide fig.) erexit foris ad parietem domesticae turris in qua scala sunt, et constabilivit adhibitis funibus aptisque confibulis. Longitudinis, ingenue dico, non memini examussim. Os fistulae superius A[1] respondebat uni e fenestris, quas habet turris: os infimum B non multum a terra exstabat clavi aenea seu epistomio R munitum, et quidem intra cuppam EF ad id muneris aptatam aqua plenam. Ori supremo

[1] Not shown. It is top of vertical pipe.

A coaptavit et optime copulavit ac solidavit, comparatum ad hoc; vas vitreum in modum lagenae, satis magnum sed bene firmum, et duo habens colla et ora alterum latius a parte inferiori, quod ori fistulae pyxidatim inseruit in A; alterum angustius in C a parte superiori plumbo sive stanno ut solet, bene instructum, quo arcte et apte exciperet striactam aeneam cochleam D affabre laboratam, genus obturamenti solidissimum, atque ad rem propositam maxime idoneum.

He continues describing the apparatus and gives an account of various experiments and observations that he and Berti made; then, on page 510, he goes on:

Non omnino displicuerunt hae rationes viro physicis et mathematicis versatissimo; subjunxit tamen, ut audivit de magnete, venisse in mentem sibi, quin et insinuatum ab amicissimo tum sibi tum etiam mihi patre Athan. Kirchero, ut ad maiorem de vacuo sive admittendo intra dictam lagenam, sive e contra reiiciendo evidentiam, experimentum denuo tentaret, disposito intra lagenam tintinabulo ut M, una cum idoneo malleolo ferreo N qui posset a magneto deforis proxime applicito attolli, et mox remoto eodem magnete decidere et percutere; si enim audiretur, inquit, ex ea percussione sonus; actum esset de vacuo, quandoquidem sonus fieri nequit in vacuo; sed id quamvis cogitasset, reliquisse tamen infectum.

Ad quod ego, ut bene memini, statim respondi, non posse quidem sonum in vacuo fieri, vel per vacuum propagari; sed causam soni bene posse esse in vacuo ut campanulam et malleolum in lagena vacua; et insuper inibi potuisse malleolo percuti campanulam, et ex percussione concipere tremulum illum motum quo sonant (ut videbis cap. 25 [1]) ac praeterea motum illum a campanula suas in vacuo edente vibrationes potuisse communicari fulcro ad ipsam in lagenae aluo sustentandam disposito, et ita consequenter ipsimet lagenæ, cui contiguum est fulcrum; tum lagena mediante aëri externo, ac per hunc tandem propagari ad aurem; eumque motum sic propagatum, esse id quod vocamus sonum, et ut dicam citato cap. 25 num 23 [2].

He also repeats in this section on the void the findings of Pascal's famous experiment with barometric readings at different altitudes; he states on page 501 that "in horto conventus nostri Minimorum" the mercury stood at "26 pollices, 3 lineas," while at another place "150 hexapedes" [3] higher it stood at "25 pollices" and in a third place "500 hexapedes higher" it stood at only "23 pollices." Maignan is talking about the "couvent" at Clermont-Ferrand, chosen because it stood at

---

[1] i.e. in the chapter *De sensibus*.

[2] *ibid.*, The section *De auditu*.

[3] Hexapeda, approximately 2 metres; pollex = pouce = .27 m; linea = ligne = 1/12 pouce. The initial reading is therefore approximately 72 centimetres of mercury. I have taken these equivalents from Le Noble, *op. cit.*, p. LXIII. A reading of 72 cms indicates a considerable depression.

the lowest part of the town. Two Minims took part in the experiment; one, le P. . Chastin, stayed in the garden all day to observe the check barometer; the Corrector, le P. Bannier, was amongst those who accompanied Périer to the summit of the Puy de Dôme. Maignan looks upon this experiment and upon his own as an investigation into the void in the macrocosm: in the microcosm he found evidence of the same thing. In the chapter *De causa efficiente* he is discussing the possibility of an infinite series and has just quoted Lalovera [1] to substantiate his hypothesis; he continues on page 204:

> Cum ergo iste autor talem affirmet non hypotetice (ut ego tunc) sed absolute, divisibilitatem; necesse est, ut concipiat quantulae possit esse molis particula, quae infinite minor est, quam totum ex quo etsi parvulo (ut posset esse granula papaveris) extracta est cum sibi aequalibus multitudine infinitis; et potest idem cum proportione dici de proportionalibus; etsi non requiro tantam in spiritibus animalibus sensationi servientibus parvitatem; sed talem tamen singuli habere censendi sunt, qualem seorsim nullus possit sensus distincte percipere et ne ipse quidem oculus lynceus quovis licet instructus microscopio.

He returns to the theme of the infinitely small and the revelations of the microscope on page 277, in the chapter *De continuo*. In physics he was an atomist and describes as "pores" the vacant spaces between the smallest particles that he was able to see: "Hinc praeterea explicabis, cur aliqua corpora nunc ad maiorem locum extendi apta sunt, nunc ad minorem contrahi; vides enim *rete* (cuius contextus simile quid habet cum hamis) cum distenditur maiore pandere foramina, quae relaxato reti contrahuntur." His observations here and on pages 239–241 lead one to suppose that his conception of the atomic structure of matter was remarkably modern. His idea of the "net" with "space" between the particles and of his space contracting and expanding according to variations in temperature is borne out by the examination of matter under microscopes thousands of times more powerful than the one Maignan could have used. Had he been able to relate these observations with his others on the void in the macrocosm, he might have reached conclusions that anticipated experimental work years later. As it stands, it is remarkable evidence of an inquiring mind and proves the essentially empirical nature of his philosophy; one may substantiate this further by referring to his practical knowledge of electromotive forces [2] which he considered as flowing ("mea sententia

---

[1] He is presumably quoting Lalovera's treatise *Quadratura circuli*, Toulouse, 1651. Maignan was in the habit of quoting authorities by name only.

[2] His chief source of information was N. Cabeo, *Philosophia magnetica*, Cologne, 1629.

motus electricus fit ut magneticus, effluvio scilicet electrico sollicitante ac determinante festucas, alique corpuscula" (page 400)); or his use of the assymptote, described on page 224 and drawn in the illustrations at the beginning, as part of his mathematical inquiry into the meaning of infinity (pages 220–225); or again, his long article on ballistics (pages 373–385) to prove various points in the chapter *De gravi et levi* – a chapter based largely on the findings of Galileo, Fabri and Mersenne; there is also his interest in the problem of suffusion (page 333); in the Royal Society (pages 206–207 and in the account of Morland's megaphone); and in the contemporary theories of the propagation of light and sound.

The second point to emphasize about the *Cursus philosophicus* is Maignan's rejection of cartesian philosophy; this can only be fully appreciated when the third point – his sensationalism – has been discussed, but the question of the senses and of the void were far from being the only points of variance. The position is summarised in the *Cursus* in a note on page 634, "Typographus lectori," which serves as an introduction to the chapter *De vorticum hypothesibus*. Maignan disagreed with Descartes on the theory of magnetism concerning the striated particles [1]; on the "vis elastica" [2]; on the diffusion of light [3]; on the Eucharist [4] and on the theory of "tourbillons." [5] His dissatisfaction with certain parts of the cartesian physics went back to his stay in Rome; Carcavi, writing to Descartes in 1649, said that there was in Rome a philosopher more intelligent than Mersenne and who hoped to correct certain points in his (Descartes's) *Principia*.[6] Whereas the theologians on the whole objected to Descartes, because they saw a threat to their faith in his rationalism, Maignan objects to him on purely scientific grounds, and yet it is a highly cartesian process of criticism, accepting nothing as true that cannot be proved such, that leads him to his refutation of Descartes's own findings. In his lengthy refutation of the theory of the "tourbillons" Maignan is not so much

---

[1] *Cursus Philosophicus*, pp. 394 and 399 with special reference to Descartes, *Principia*, IV.

[2] Appendix to the *Philosophia Sacra*. The copy of the *Philosophia Sacra* in the British Museum is imperfect, being composed of two editions; volume I is from the first edition (Toulouse, 1661) volume II from the third edition (Lyon 1672). It is not possible in this copy to consult appendices II–IV.

[3] Descartes, *Lettres*, Paris, 1657–1667, Vol. II; letter No. 17, pp. 139–145. Here Descartes affirms that light is diffused instantaneously and in straight lines; Maignan on p. 664 of the *Cursus Philosophicus* and in the Appendix to the *Philosophia Sacra* accepts Vitellione's theory of the speed of light and of its spherical diffusion.

[4] Passim – see later.

[5] *Cursus Philosophicus*, pp. 635–718; one of the longest sections in the whole book.

[6] Baillet, *Vie de Descartes*, II, pp. 379–380; Descartes, *Lettres*, ed. cit., II, letter No. 76, pp. 439–442.

interested in returning to his own theory of the void as in exposing the impossibility of the plenum and the "tourbillons"; for this reason phrases such as "... ratio Cartesii non conformis est legibus bonae mechanicis" are recurrent. Maignan voices three objections – that the "tourbillons" do not conform to the rules of mechanics which govern bodies moving in an eliptical orbit; that all vortices would inevitably merge into one chaos; that the refraction of light from astral bodies is such that it accounts for the refraction due to the terrestrial atmosphere but nothing more – an argument which he adduces with great certainty since he had worked on this very problem in the *Perspectiva Horaria*. Bayle agreed that his objections were valid, and Bayle at that time was a convinced cartesian as far as the plenum was concerned.[1]

Maignan's doctrine concerning the Eucharist led him into a long and violent controversy, the history of which has been summarised by Ceñal.[2] The chief references to his doctrine are contained in the section of the *Cursus Philosophicus* called *De speciebus eucharisticis* (pp. 583–590) and in the lengthy Appendix to the second volume of the *Philosophia Sacra*. Ceñal correctly points out the error of M. Grabmann[3] in supposing that Maignan is one of the leading exponents of Descartes's doctrine of the Eucharist; in fact it would be true to state that Maignan is the leading exponent of a doctrine which depends on the philosophy of sensationalism for its explanation, and is therefore anticartesian by this very premise. His doctrine had some vogue during the later seventeenth century and at the beginning of the eighteenth, particularly in Spain. The clearest explanation of this doctrine is the one given by Rohault in his *Entretiens sur la philosophie*[4]:

Sachez donc ... qu'au lieu que la Philosophie qu'on a enseignée depuis quelques siècles dans nos écoles place les qualités sensibles dans les objets mêmes, la nôtre en fait des impressions de nos sens ... Voyez donc ... qu'il n'y a rien de si facile que d'expliquer de quelle manière les accidents du pain et du vin subsistent sans le pain et le vin: car il n'y a que dire en un mot que le pain et le vin étant ôtés, Dieu continue de faire dans nos sens les mêmes impressions qu'ils faisaient avant qu'ils fussent changés. Aussi c'est en cette manière que le P. Magnan (sic), célèbre théologien de l'Ordre des Minimes, explique ce mystère non seulement dans quatre volumes de philosophie qui sont imprimés à Toulouse in octavo (i.e. the first edition)

---

[1] *Nouvelles de la République des Lettres*, mai, 1686, art. I; *Oeuvres Diverses*, I, p. 548.
[2] In the article in *Revista de Estudios Politicos*, pp. 128 *et sq.*
[3] In *Die Philosophie des Cartesius und die Eucharistialehre des Emmanuel Maignan* – *Raccolta di philosophia neoscolastica;* Supplement to Vol. XIX, Milan, July 1937, pp. 425–436.
[4] Paris, 1671, pp. 50–59.

mais aussi dans un volume de théologie naturelle qu'il a appelé *Philosophia Sacra*, imprimé aussi à Toulouse in folio ... ce bon religieux a enseigné la théologie à Rome, au couvent de la Trinité et ... son livre est approuvé par ses Supérieurs et par un grand nombre de Docteurs de Toulouse.

An excessively prolix defence of Maignan was undertaken by a Minim of the Province of the Duchy of Burgundy, Jacques Salier, whose *Historia de Speciebus Eucharisticis* appeared in three volumes between 1687 and 1704.[1] His method is to confuse rather than to elucidate; he examines historically the ideas of matter and substance, showing how little accord there is between any pair of writers. In all this he succeeds as an iconoclast, ruining the traditional scholastic position and, at the same time, casting doubt on the cartesian system with special reference to Maignan.[2] On the positive side, as an exposition of Maignan's doctrine, the work is less successful than Rohault's short statement that the Eucharistic species produce sensible effects that are normal to bread and wine but that, on Consacration, divine causation produces other sentiments – a remarkable anticipation of Berkeley's theory of sensations.[3] Indeed, the emphasis which Rohault placed upon the senses raises the whole question of Maignan's reliance upon sense data; this marks him as anti-cartesian more surely than any of the points of variance listed in the note *Typographus lectori* already referred to. Neither Prof. Spink nor Ceñal seems to have shown the interest in this part of his philosophy which it undoubtedly warrants. Philosophical systems tend to contain the germ of their own destruction; this was never truer than in the case of Descartes whose "méthode" leads to a sceptical criticism of all things and, perforce, of itself. Cartesian physics were soon held up to the searching light of criticism by Mersenne, Maignan and others; and his philosophy (as distinct from his physics) is vulnerable in two further respects – the absolute postulation concerning thought and matter, and the theory of innate ideas. The first of these is prone to attack from the modern empirical philosophers and the second cannot be proved by the very canons which Descartes himself formulated for the conduct of a philosophical inquiry. The further the seventeenth century recedes into the past the more apparent it becomes that the great break with tradition comes with Locke and Newton at the period so aptly called

---

[1] Vol. I, Lyon 1686; Vol. II, Dijon, 1691; Vol. III, Dijon 1704. The author's name is spelt Sallier in Vols. II and III.

[2] Vol. I, pp. 298–299; Vol. II, pp. 199–201; Vol. III, pp. 342–345.

[3] Vacant, Mangenot, Amann, *Dictionnaire de Théologie catholique*, Vol. V, Paris, 1924, sub *Eucharistiques (Accidents)*.

"la crise de la conscience européenne." Descartes prepares the way; during the years that separate him from Locke and Newton there were several men of outstanding ability who had serious doubts about some of his findings. Pascal and Boyle together with Maignan and the Italian scientists already mentioned in this chapter anticipate Newton on the question of the void; Willis, the English surgeon, with his detailed study of the nerves and brain, invites an investigation of the ways in which a man acquires knowledge through his senses and consequently invites rejection of innate ideas; Malebranche and the Cambridge Platonists considered that Descartes had taken no account of spirituality and intuition. Yet the interesting thing is this: they had all used arguments and scientific methods which might fairly be called cartesian; Bossuet, fearful of the impending attack on the Church in the name of cartesian rationalism, nevertheless uses the doctrine of the "bête-machine" to prove the divine spark latent in mankind.[1] Having shown that all human problems are essentially a question of human consciousness, Descartes left the way open for a critical approach to the study of knowledge which, henceforth, had to be in the realm of demonstrable truth. Briefly then, the most important part of the influence of Descartes was to furnish a system that acted as a basis from which scientists and philosophers were to proceed to conclusions that were frequently at variance with his findings. In this way and, possibly, in this way alone is it permissible to speak of the connection between Descartes and the Philosophes of the eighteenth century. The significance of Maignan's *De materia ex qua anima brutorum* in the Toulouse manuscript and of its incorporation in the *Cursus*,[2] together with his general investigation into the operation of the senses, should be considered against this background, and against the possibility that he had previously discussed the question with Mersenne.[3]

Maignan believed that an animal could think because it was possessed of the necessary instruments – the senses; it could enjoy things or suffer in proportion as it received pleasant or unpleasant sensations. Maignan's originality is to analyse the meaning of *sensitive*. At first sight it appears that he is doing no more than reaffirm the threefold nature of the soul – vegetable, animal and human – of the aristotelian philosophy; his chapter-headings for this part of the *Cursus* are: De corpore animali; De corpore vegetali; De corpore sensitivo; the

[1] In *la Connaissance de Dieu et de soi-même*.
[2] MS T. fol. 145 and *Cursus Philosophicus*, pp. 554–558.
[3] See previously, p. 154.

important De sensibus externis; De appetitu animalis; De motu animali; De animali irrationali; De animae rationalis immortalitate; De anima rationali ut operante moraliter. It is not clear what are the sources for this part of his work; he quotes Cornelius ab Hogellande, *De existentia oeconomia corporis animalis* [1] and shows on several occasions an acquaintance with some of the medical works of the age – F. Ranchin, J. Riolan and G. Ader for example [2] – but this is insufficient to explain the considerable anatomical knowledge he displays. There was a selection of books on medicine in the library at Santa Trinità and also in the "couvent" at Toulouse; a further possible source is the Toulouse physician François Bayle [3] whom he quotes on pages 614–615 on the question of sympathetic movement. François Bayle also refers to Maignan in his works [4] and it seems at least possible that they had discussed problems concerning the nervous system. The influence of Mersenne is again apparent, although tacitly expressed in this part of the *Cursus;* his interest in light and accoustics (particularly in harmonic analysis and in the tuning of instruments) had led him to study the minute variations in the number of vibrations per second which go to make the difference between one semi-tone and the next; he had studied the similar set of variations that goes to make up the visible scale of colour. All this is obviously at the back of Maignan's mind when he says that "Obiecta sensuum sunt ipsa sensibilia; id est ea quorum actiones sunt sensu perceptibiles ... actiones *solas* ease immediate per se sensibiles ... hactenus ea quae vulgo consentur nomine accidentium ut calor, frigus, etc. non esse aliud quod actiones substantiarum." [5] Although there are diverse sense organs, there is properly speaking only one sense; heat, light and sound are only motions in matter and these motions are transmitted to the brain along the nerves – this is the sense of touch. All the other senses are but modifications of this sense which is found throughout the body, "sensus tactus toto corpore viget intus et extra." [6] One by one Maignan enumerates the senses, working from the most generalised, touch, to the four particular senses which he arranges in the order: taste, smell, hearing, sight. In each instance he describes briefly but accurately and

---

[1] Amsterdam, 1646 and quoted by Maignan on pp. 339–340.
[2] The first two on p. 537 and the last on p. 541.
[3] Referred to subsequently as François Bayle to distinguish him from Pierre who will be referred to as Bayle.
[4] *Opuscula*, Toulouse, 1671, pp. 180, 226 and in the preface.
[5] p. 540, from the preamble to the chapter *De sensibus.*
[6] p. 541, *De sensibus – De tactu.*

graphically the organs of sense and the effects that can be produced
upon them – thus his description of the ear:

In intima aure, sinuoso ac sursum oblique verso meatui obtenditur
membrana tenuissima in modo telae araneae, densa tamen et maxima sicca,
quin et diaphana, quam vocant tympanum: mox consequuntur tria ossicula,
quorum unum dicitur malleolus, secundum incus, tertium stapes: et no-
mina conveniunt figuris potius quam usibus: incumbunt haec ossicula
tympano, eique cohaerent colligante funiculo tenuissimo, qui illi sicut in
bellicis tympanis subtenditur. Demum occurrit nervus e quinta conju-
gatione, qui dicitur auditorius, qui videlicet per meatum auditorium e
cerebro procedens ad tympanum porrigitur; ibique in plurimos divisus
ramulos, unum ex eis in linguam et laryngem mittit.[1]

This quasi-medical approach is comparable with Locke's own sensationalism which owed something to his medical studies and to the
celebrated treatise by Willis *Cerebri nervorumque descriptio* (London,
1664) – a work which was well known in France and which was referred to by Maignan's most illustrious pupil, Charles Plumier,[2] who
also undertook the dissection of the hearing apparatus of several
animals.

When Descartes objected to accepting sense-data as the basis of
knowledge his argument was this: Scholastic philosophy and my
senses tell me that the sun moves round the earth; modern science tells
me that I have been deceived in this respect; therefore I reject the
validity of sense-data. Maignan's argument in favour of reestablishing
this validity is not a return to Scholasticism which he had whole-
heartedly and systematically rejected by the force of his experimental
science. His reasoning is as follows: we know that we see, hear and feel
but our senses are uncapable of seizing everything; think of the
difference in appearance of a single hair of your head when viewed by
the naked eye and when viewed under a microscope; think of the
revelation brought about by Galileo's telescope. The microscope
and telescope are merely extensions of our senses; if we could but see
like an eagle or a lynx, what further revelations might not be made.[3]
We are here close to Locke's comparison of the human mind to a
plumb-line which, if it will not reach the very bottom of the ocean,
is yet a useful instrument when we are near the rocks. Our senses are

---

[1] *Cursus Philosophicus*, p. 543.
[2] See the next chapter and Appendix IV, p. 268.
[3] *Cursus Philosophicus*, pp. 541 and 557. This idea is developed by Saguens, *Philosophia
Maignani*, IV, p. 212 – Nos aper auditu, Linx visu, Simia gustu, Vultur odoratu, Præcellit
Aranea tactu.

adequate for our needs; even if we extend their scope by the use of instruments and probe further into the nature of the physical universe, we are nevertheless limited by the ultimate power of the eye and ear:

Hactenus autem non sunt observati sensus diversi, nisi externi quinque et internus unus cuius quidem unitatem quoad se, et sentiendi communitatem cum externis, ostendi cap. 24 num. 40 (pp. 534 et sq) Sunt vero solum quinque externi; non quod illi prorsus sufficiant ad omnia omnino sensibilia sentienda (quasi certo constet quinque illos ad id sufficere) sed quia sapientissimus rerum artifex iudicavit eos tantum esse necessarios, aut simpliciter et absolute; aut ad suavius vitam ducendam: alioqui enim plurima sine dubio sunt sensibilia secundum se; ad quae tamen sentienda nullus a natura constitutus est in animali sensus. Siquidem constat ab animalculis minutissimis plurima distincte et clare cerni, quae prorsus fugiunt oculos maiorum etiam perspicacissimos ut aquilae aut lyncis: unde colligere licet non omnia visibilia cerni oculis ipsis minutissimorum; sed posse etiam ob sui parvitatem illis pariter improportionatam, fugere eorum oculos. Idem autem servata proportione dicendum est de aliis sensibus, non solum propter parvitatem sensibilis; sed etiam propter sensibilitatis eius proprium genus, seu modum agendi: v.g. actio qua magnes movet ferrum, nullo sensu animalis (quod nos sciamus) cognoscibilis est immediate in se: et ita suspicari licet de multis aliis.[1]

Another point here which bears a remarkable similarity to a passage in Locke is the "quod nos sciamus" – "as far as we can tell" – there is no association of thought with the particles of iron in the magnet: "We ... possibly shall never be able to know whether any mere material being thinks or no." [2] For both philosophers these questions lie beyond the confines of our probable knowledge. The most obvious result of the attention to the sense organs and sense-data is the rejection of yet another element of cartesian philosophy, and perhaps the most fundamental and characteristic part of the whole cartesian structure – duality. Thought by itself is no proof of immateriality and, consequently, cannot be used as a proof de se of immortality [3]; thought is provoked by the senses which engender an appetite (Maignan's own word, see the chapter De appetitu); the appetite stimulates motion. All this is carried out purely in the media of matter; a feeling, a movement in the nerves, is transmitted to the cells of the brain. Both man and the beasts think in this way but their appetites are not always satisfied in the same way; there is the purely reflex action which Maignan calls

[1] Cursus Philosophicus, p. 541.
[2] Essay concerning Human understanding, IV, 3.
[3] cf. Mersenne, Correspondance, VII, p. 24; letter to Rivet of 20 Jan., 1638, already quoted p. 154.

"sympathetic action" and there is the motion which leads a dog and a man to food when they are hungry; there is the motion which leads man to moral action and there is an ascent from the knowledge of mortal things to the knowledge of immortal things – God is revealed in Nature [1] as well as by the Angels [2] – and this ascent is by the grace of God ("Gratia Medicinalis," according to Maignan), "Voluntas humana ex naturali conditione coniunctionis sui cum appetitu sensitivo corpore praecise ut sic et absque auxilio indebito non se movet ad appetitendum bonum . . . ." [3]

The boldness and originality of Maignan's philosophy contrast with his religious orthodoxy; even so, he is far from being a purely submissive theologian – one of his last acts was to have to write to the Congregation of the Holy Office explaining his position concerning the Eucharist.[4] The *Philosophia Sacra* is remarkable for the extensive use of scientific arguments so that, although there is an acceptance of the essential postulations of the old scholastic philosophy – the metaphysics of "Ens et existentia" – there is a feeling that the adherence to the traditions of the scholastic system of explanation is no longer satisfactory. Maignan defends orthodoxy against incredulity by calling science to his aid; as with Mersenne, the cause of science and the cause of God are one. Much of the *Philosophia Sacra* is a restatement of positions taken up in the first edition of the *Cursus Philosophicus* especially in the first part, devoted as it is to *Philosophia Entis*, and in the chapter *De speciebus Eucharistics*. In the widest sense of the word Maignan's position is that of the neo-thomists.

Maignan's only other work is a short treatise in Latin called *De usu licito pecuniae* (Toulouse, 1673); in the same year and also at Toulouse there appeared a French translation. Two years later another Minim, André de Colonia published *Eclaircissement sur le légitime commerce des intérêts* (Lyon, 1675 with further editions in 1676 and, Bordeaux,

---

[1] *Existantiae Dei ratio demonstrativa naturalis*, MS T. fol. 109–110 incorporated in the *Philosophia Sacra* chapter III.

[2] The ever recurrent use of "angels" in the *Cursus Philosophicus* may seem to clash with the modernity of much of the experimental science that is displayed in its pages; "angels" symbolise the ascent from the material to the immaterial.

[3] *Philosophia Sacra*, Lyon, 1672, Vol. II, p. 437. I was convinced that there must be in Maignan's work some such explanation as the one given above; had there not been, it would have been impossible to defend him from materialism as is so often the case with the empirical philosophers from Locke onwards.

[4] 2nd May 1675, MSS Biblioteca Nazionale, Rome, Fondi Minori, 1851, fol. 92–93; quoted by J. M. Perrimezzi in *In sacram de Deo scientiam dissertationes*, Rome, 1739, Part VIII, pp. 106–110. See also Ceñal who makes no separation between Maignan's philosophy and his theology.

1677). It is interesting to note that Colonia had been at the "couvent" at Toulouse, and it is not surprising to find a similarity of argument (as well as of title) in both works. It seems likely that Colonia may have been one of Maignan's pupils and that he may well have been a contemporary of another Minim, Arnaud Capdeville, who wrote a book on mathematics, *L'arithmétique en son jour*,[1] which bears to some extent the stamp of Maignan, being a highly practical guide to commercial arithmetic. To the Minims of Toulouse then should go the credit of fostering an interest in trade, an aspect of their work which seems to have been overlooked; Ceñal merely mentions the sharp rebuke that Maignan received from the bishops. Maignan's arguments may be summarised as follows [2]:

I. Un homme qui peut faire valoir honnêtement une chose qui lui appartient n'est pas tenu de le bailler à un autre (envers lequel il n'est pas obligé par aucun devoir) pour s'en servir dans toute l'étendue de son usage.

II. Il est permis à un homme qui peut faire valoir honnêtement ce qui lui appartient, de ne pas le bailler gratuitement à un autre pour s'en servir: et d'en retenir le domaine de propriété.

III. Le profit que par mon industrie je puis retirer d'une chose qui m'appartient, il n'est pas défendu de la retirer par le travail d'un autre, en lui payant exactement ce qui lui est dû pour son travail et ses soins.

IV. Il est permis en conscience de bailler une chose à quelqu'un pour la faire profiter à ses perils et fortunes et de s'en réserver quelque profit, en compensant à proportion les risques que celui à qui on la baille peut courir et l'industrie qu'il emploie pour la faire profiter.

V. L'usage de l'argent ne consiste pas seulement en l'emploi de ce même argent en espèce mais encore dans le trafic des choses qui en proviennent.

VI. Un homme qui donne son argent à un autre pour le faire profiter à ses perils et fortunes, en s'en réservant néanmoins la propriété quant aux fonds, peut, par un droit naturel, et en conscience, retenir pour soi le tiers du profit, si l'industrie de celui à qui il le baille et les risques qu'il peut courir ne sont estimés que les deux tiers, et ainsi à proportion selon l'estimation des personnes prudentes.

The objections made to this by the Ecclesiastical authorities may be judged from the following *Réponses à des objections* which Maignan appended to the French translation:

---

[1] I first found a reference to this work in the manuscript catalogue of the library of the Minimes de Passy (i.e. Nigeon) now in the Arsenal, No. 5763; it is here listed as 1678. The Bibliothèque Nationale has example of the 3rd edition, Toulouse, 1691 and there is a copy in the Bibliothèque Municipale de Toulouse, Toulouse, 1700.

[2] Selection of headings etc. taken from the French translation by M.B.D., Toulouse, 1673.

I. On pretend qu'il y a une différence entre l'argent et les choses qui portent profit d'elles-mêmes ... se soi il est infructueux et ne porte aucun profit que par l'industrie des hommes.

II. Objection qui met l'argent au rang des choses usuelles, et soutient qu'il se consomme par l'usage.

III. Objection fondée sur ce qu'on prétend que le contrat que nous établissons ouvre la porte aux opinions relâchées de la morale.

IV. On veut prouver que notre contrat est un contrat de prêt et que par conséquent il est sujet à la rigueur du decret d'Alexandre VIII, du 18 mars 1666.

V. Objection qui suppose que l'argent est une chose usuelle, selon S. Thomas, l'argent ne produit d'autre argent. (Avec preuve tiré des sacrés canons).

VI. Objection prise des paroles de Jésus-Christ (Luc, VI, vv. 30 and 34).

We have seen that the Minims were chiefly recruited from amongst the bourgeoisie and that many of them were artisans and craftsmen; this expression of a belief in capitalist enterprise is not surprising when we consider how closely it comes to the moment of Colbert's great financial reforms and of his efforts for commercial expansion. The Minims in France were always patriotic, and it is apposite to note that Colonia's works besides his defence of commerce included a panegyric of Louis XIV.

Little has been written about the possible influence of Maignan. Professor Spink states that his philosophy passed without comment or controversy [1]; Ceñal in his two articles went deeper, but he was interested almost exclusively in the controversy over the Eucharist and in Maignan's influence in Spain throughout the eighteenth century. What concerns us here is his influence in France and within the Order. First of all he was instrumental in perpetuating the tradition of scientific studies amongst the Minims and he is the link between Mersenne and the next generations – Plumier, Feuillée and Jacquier.[2] As a teacher of philosophy both at Rome and at Toulouse he must have exerted an influence on several generations of novices; it is a pity that we know nothing of his methods of instruction apart from the most fragmentary notes on the presentation of theses. As a teacher he probably displayed the same delight in graphic presentation that we find in the *Horaria Perspectiva;* it is also interesting to

[1] *op. cit.*, p. 84.
[2] François Jacquier, Minim of the XVIIIth century; editor of Newton's *Principia* in edition of Genoa, 1739–1742.

note that one who spent much time in instructing others should have shown a preference for the philosophy of sensationalism.[1] Few of his pupils have spoken about him; Plumier paid tribute to him in the preface of one of his works, telling us that he went to Toulouse from Marseille in order to work under his directions; Saguens, the chief source of all our knowledge about Maignan, edited the works of his master under the title *Philosophia Maignani* which was placed on the Index in 1707; André de Colonia backed up Maignan's theories on money. During the decline of the Order in the eighteenth century his influence naturally waned, although we find Joachim Rigaud imitating part of his work and Jacquier referring to him in his own mathematical works. Outside the Order his influence is intangible and diffuse. Opinions were changing rapidly and in the direction that Maignan anticipates, but he was superseded almost immediately by the two great influences at work on eighteenth century thought, Locke in the realm of sensationalism and Newton on the void. It is easy to see a latent significance in most of his writings; the Oratorian, Jean-Baptiste Lagrange, placed him in the forefront of those who dispelled the haze of scholasticism, "Maignan raisonne plus mal que Descartes et Gassendi. Ce qu'il y a de particulier, est qu'il amuse son lecteur et ordinairement ses opinions sont les plus mal choisies de toutes et le plus mal débitées ... il se moque perpétuellement des formes accidentelles des Péripatéticiens." [2] There would be no point in this vitriolic attack had his influence not been felt. Then there is the testimony of Bayle in the *Dictionnaire;* the article *Maignan* would have brought him to the notice of the erudite world, for the *Dictionnaire* was a most popular work.

Bayle's admiration for Maignan dated from letters to his elder brother in 1675 and 1678 [3] in which he shows a preference for Maignan's philosophy:

... plus sûr pour ces nouveaux philosophes (Chouet et Rohault) de s'en venir au biais et à la pensée du P. Maignan ...

Le petit in-12 du P. Vincent contre Descartes ne me fait pas grand peur; j'ai vu de cet auteur un gros volume de philosophie ... où il y a beaucoup de fatras. Le Minime *est un autre personnage*, et je prétends avoir un jour

---

[1] cf. Locke and Fénelon, and also Glanvill. See my article *Bayle and Locke*, in *Pierre Bayle*, ed. P. Dibon, Amsterdam, 1959.
[2] *Les principes de la philosophie contre les nouveaux philosophes Descartes ... le P. Maignan.* Paris, 1675, p. 40.
[3] *Nouvelles Lettres*, Vol. I, pp. 258–9 and 381; my italics.

toutes ses œuvres et surtout sa Philosophia Entis Sacra, avec les appendix
qu'il y a ajoutés de temps en temps.

It seems from these references that Bayle's first interest in Maignan
was in his theory of the Eucharist (hence the mention of Rohault)
and that it developed into a wider interest; the appendices to the
Philosophia Sacra contain many of his anti-cartesian ideas, as we have
seen, and it may well be that Bayle's ultimate rejection of cartesian
philosophy in favour of sensationalism was conditioned by his reading
of Maignan. But the fact that Maignan wrote in Latin, that he was a
monk and that his work might appear heavily pedantic would not
have encouraged the reader of the eighteenth century who was
demanding another style of philosophical writing. There is nevertheless
in Maignan much that should be admired: he made a fearless and
systematic attack upon erroneous ideas; he was instrumental in the
vulgarisation of newly discovered scientific facts, and was international
and modern in outlook. Perhaps his most enduring influence, however,
is in the simple scientific experiment and in the production of an
admirable illustrated manual; Niceron – Maignan – Plumier – The
Encyclopédie – there seems to be a direct chain of significance in the
importance placed upon the visual aid as a means of achieving the
vulgarisation of ideas. Is this not also, perhaps, a further point which
connects the sensationalism of the philosophers with their knowledge
of education?

CHAPTER VII

CHARLES PLUMIER *

Posterity has done less than justice to Plumier. He deserves to be remembered on three accounts: as an experimental zoologist and biologist, as an engraver of excellent illustrations for technical books, and as a craftsman. As a biologist he is the forerunner of Buffon, Linnaeus and Lamarck; as an illustrator and craftsman he anticipates the Encyclopaedists who attached much importance to clear illustrations and to the technical skills of "Arts et métiers."

He was born in Marseilles [1] on the 20th April 1646 and probably learnt some of his technical skill as a turner and engraver from his father. At the age of 16 he entered the Order; at this time his main interest seems to have been mathematics for he was sent, at his own request to Toulouse to work under Maignan where he had further opportunities for studying perspective, painting and also turning, for Maignan was adept at these.[2] By the time, therefore, that he went to Rome, to the "couvent" of Santa Trinità dei Monti, he must have been a young man of exceptional promise. The Minims there possessed a complete set of joiners' tools; they would have been sold had not Plumier's skill been mentioned to the Corrector who asked him to undertake the construction of the choir stalls. This is the only example of his work I have been able to find. These stalls with tip-up seats and simple panel work form a retro-choir behind the high altar and are in daily use by the nuns of the Istituto della Santa Trinità dei Monti; the design is of admirable simplicity and good taste, bespeaking a good craftsman rather than a flamboyant designer.[3]

* The following chapter is based on notes which I made between 1948 and 1954 and which provided material for my short note in the *Modern Language Review*, July 1959.
[1] See Michaud, *Biog. Universelle* and C. F. Achard, *Dictionnaire de la Provence*, 4 vols. Marseille 1786. Vol. IV pp. 95/8 and p. 422.
[2] Bayle, *Dictionnaire*, art. *Maignan*, remarque G, refers to his lathes and other machines.
[3] For this information and for allowng me to inspect Plumier's work I am indebted to the Reverend Mother Superior of the Istituto della Santa Trinità dei Monti. I am also

He continued to practice his skills while acquiring a new interest –
Botany. We have already seen that the library at S. Trinità was rich
in herbals and medical works. The connexion between the French
Minims at Rome and Botany is an interesting one: another Provençal,
Philippe Sergeant,[1] had a keen interest in Botany and devoted much
of his time to the excellent garden in the precincts of the "couvent".
Each year, on Trinity Sunday, the patronal feast in this house, the
Minims organised a flower-show to which the populace of Rome had
free access. It was Sergeant's idea that this show should be something
more than a mere spectacle; he arranged a special display of medicinal
plants to attract attention to the work of their pharmacy.[2] Because of
the interest which he took in this display, Plumier was alowed to
work for a while with a distinguished Italian botanist, Paolo Boccone
and, on his return to France, he worked under Pierre-Joseph Garidel,
Professor of Botany in the University of Aix-en-Provence. Up to this
point he had had little experience of practical work and his first
"herborisation" was no further away than the Iles d'Hyères. In the
preface to one of his works *Solum, Salum, Caelum* he pays tribute, to
those who taught him and confesses that he was unable to distinguish
between such things as basil and thyme until his visit to Rome.[3]

His first important assignment came to him in a round-about way:
Michel Bégon [4] had been the French Governor in Saint-Dominico;
he decided that a full botanical survey of the Antilles should be made
and, with Royal consent, he invited Surian, a *médecin-chymiste* of
Marseilles – where Bégon was now Intendant de la Marine – to undertake this job. Surian asked Plumier to accompany him not only on
account of his capabilities as a botanist but also because he valued his
great skill as an engraver. It was Plumier apparently who took charge
for, on his return, he was given a pension and the title "Botaniste du
Roy."

He made two further journeys in 1693 and 1695 to America and
the West Indies to carry out a more detailed study of the flora of the
French possessions. It was after his return from the second of these

indebted to her for showing me *Histoire du Couvent Royal des Minimes Français de la très-sainte
Trinité sur le Mont Pincio, à Rome,* 3 books bound together, late XVIIIth century manuscript
by le P. Charles Martin? Book III, pp. 170/1 gives details of the Corrector's decision and
of Plumier's work.
    [1] See Achard, *op. cit.,* vol. IV, p. 96.
    [2] Other French members of the order who worked in the pharmacy during the XVIIth
Century are referred to in the chapter on Medical Work, pp. 226 *et sq.*
    [3] This preface is given in full in the Appendix.
    [4] Or "Begon": in giving him the é I am following Balteau, *Dictionnaire Biographique.*

that Martin Lister met him in his cell at la Place Royale.[1] Lister was probably already known to many French scientists at the time because of his publications on zoology and on mineral springs.[2] His account of Paris and his reflexion on the arts and sciences are of considerable interest in that they anticipate the criticism that Frenchmen of the next generation were to level at their own institutions: criticisms that were sometimes unfairly balanced in favour of England.

Lister gives the following details about Plumier: he had been shipwrecked and had lost all his specimens; his papers and drawings, however, were on another ship and were safe; he had dissected a crocodile, a sea-tortoise and a viper [3]; he had described and drawn many birds and fishes, and had discovered some new varieties of snake and lizard. Lister was disappointed in that he had brought back but few shells but it was some compensation that Plumier copied for him on the spot a drawing that he (Lister) had much admired, that of a murex [4] which Lister reproduced (Tab. 4) at the back of his book. He mentioned also the beautiful drawings of ferns and other plants, wild gooseberries, currants and vines. "He told me," Lister continues, "that these drawings would make 10 books as the one he had already published [5] and two books of animals. He had often been at Versailles to get them into the King's "imprimerie," but as yet unsuccessfully, but hoped 'ere long to begin the printing of them ... the Booksellers of Paris are very unwilling, or not able, to print Natural History, but all is done at the King's charge and in his Presses." [6]

During a conversation with the Marquis de l'Hôpital, a member of the Académie des Sciences, they discussed Newton, his "preferment" [7] and the *Philosophical Transactions* [8]; the war had prevented the delivery of these in France and the Marquis de l'Hôpital said that he hoped to

---

[1] M. Lister, *A Journey to Paris in the year 1698*, 2nd edition, London, 1699.

[2] Bayle, *Nouvelles de la République des Lettres*, March, 1684. *Oeuvres Diverses*, I, p. 15.

[3] Crocodile? Alligator intended? Sea-tortoise, i.e. turtle.

[4] Murex brandaris, from which "Tyrian purple" is extracted. Plumier was always interested in dyestuffs, see later his work on cochineal and note also that Mersenne in *Questions Physico-mathématiques* had also shown interest in dyes: – *Question XXXIX* (pp. 183 et sq.) De quelles matières se servent les teinturiers ...

[5] *Description des plantes de l'Amérique avec leurs figures*. Paris, Imprimerie Royale, 1693. The manuscript of this beautiful book was kept in the library at the Place Royale and is now in the Bibliothèque de l'Arsenal, No. 2875. Plates bear inscription "Fr. C. Plumier, Minime, Botanicus Regius, delineavit "or abbreviations of the same.

[6] Lister, *op. cit.*, pp. 72–75. "Presses" – reference to "Imprimerie Royale" in previous note.

[7] *Ibid.*, p. 95. Lister presumably means his election to the Royal Society, 1672; his appointment as Master of the Mint was not until 1699.

[8] A French version of articles from this were published under the title, *Journal d'Angleterre*. Bayle made use of them, *Nouvelles de la République des Lettres*, passim.

be able to import a full set. As for the monthly mémoires, these had ceased to be published because of the small membership of the Académie des Sciences. "Why not enlarge your Academy then?" said Lister, ". . . why not amongst others elect Father Plumier?" "Because," said the Marquis, "he is a monk. He belongs to an order; the Académie is closed to members of the regular clergy." Lister's final reference to Plumier is also revealing: on his return from the Indies Plumier was only skin and bone, "and yet by the rule of his order could not eat anything that was wholesome and proper for his cure, nothing but a little slimy, nasty fish and herbs . . . I never heard him complain but what will not blind prejudice do against all the Reason of Mankind?" [1]

I have reported Lister's account at length because he gives us about the only first-hand report we have of Plumier and because he raises the question of prejudice against the religious order from two different points of view. A discussion of these prejudices will find its place in the conclusion to the present study.

Plumier spent the rest of his life at the Place Royale compiling notes and preparing books for the press, but his achievement in this respect is modest: besides the *Descriptions des Plantes*, already mentioned, there was the *Nova Plantarum Americanarum Genera*, (Paris, 1703) and the work he had ready for press when he died and which was printed posthumously in 1705, *Traité des Fougères de l'Amérique*. He also published a short paper on cochineal in the *Journal des Sçavans* [2] and fragments of botanical and biological interest in the *Journal de Trévoux*.[3] The full extent of his intended publication is not known but the manuscripts he has left behind are numerous: there is an elementary course in botany which he composed by interleaving Pitton de Tournefort's *Eléments de Botanique* with plain paper and adding his own notes, which include a detailed analysis of the structure of a flower, a description of the flowers illustrated by Tournefort and, since there were many pages only half-filled, he added a dictionary of botanical terms and a treatise on anatomy.[4] Then there is the large collection of his drawings in the Bibliothèque du Muséum d'histoire naturelle in Paris,[5] the copper plates of which passed to Jussieu. Of these 6,000

---

[1] Lister, *op. cit.*, p. 134. Plumier referred to Lister's visit in a letter to the *Mémoires de Trévoux*, Trévoux, September, 1703, pp. 1671–1692; a copy of his drawing of the Murex is facing p. 1692.

[2] 19 April, 1694; undertaken on behalf of the Gobelins who were interested in this dye.

[3] Trévoux, Nov. 1702, pp. 112 *et sq.*; Sept. 1703, pp. 167 *et sq.*; Jan. 1704, pp. 165 *et sq.*

[4] MSS. Arsenal No. 2502.

[5] See the *Catalogue général des MSS.*, Paris 1914, Vol. II, *Muséum d'histoire naturelle*, pp.

engravings, 1,200 are of animals; 822 of the plates were sold as late as January 1858.[1] Other unpublished collections of his work include a *Historia Plantarum per Americanas insulas annis 1689–1697 observatarum a R. P. C. Plumier*,[2] an English translation of the *Descriptions des Plantes de l'Amérique* dated 1693; an imperfect *Delineationes plantarum Americanarum*,[3] and a work in the Bibliothèque Municipale, Marseilles [4]; the latter, said in the Catalogue to be of doubtful origin, is unmistakably in Plumier's hand and the illustrations likewise are undeniably his.

While Plumier was occupied with his notes and drawings, he also found time to write and illustrate the first comprehensive manual on the art of turning, one of the most important of all arts and crafts. Here again Plumier must be considered as an innovator: many of the articles in the *Encyclopédie* are devoted to industry and to the skills of craftsmen – in fact the whole idea of the *Encyclopédie* evolved from a description of "arts et métiers" ervisaged by a Société des Arts (1729–1737) who were dissatisfied with the slow progress of the work done by the Académie des Sciences. Diderot, himself the son of a cutler, spent many hours learning about the intricate details of various trades and the tools that the craftsmen used. The articles in the *Encyclopédie*, *Tour*, *Tourner* and *Tourneur*, show the prime importance of this art; the illustrations by Lucotte (in some instances taken straight from Plumier) are more numerous for these articles than for any other.[5]

L'Art de tourner ou de faire en perfection toutes sortes d'ouvrages au tour (Lyon, 1701) is obviously the result of Plumier's lifelong hobby. It would be interesting therefore to know at what date Plumier wrote his name in the curious XVIth century collection of drawings *Dessins de mors de chevaux: Modèles de selles* [6]; the technique employed in this work for showing clearly the mouldings and faces of metals would appear to have influenced him. The full manuscript of Plumier's work is not extant but the original pen and ink drawings for the illustrations are

1–4, MSS. Nos. 1–37 also pp. 196 and 222, MSS. Nos. 1176 and 1335.

[1] *Catalogue de la bibliothèque scientifique de MM. de Jussieu*, Paris 1857, Sale No. 4016.

[2] Paris, Bibliothèque de l'Institut, Nos. 966–1000 [XIV, 979] with XV–XVII 980–982, *Americanarum plantarum icones*, 3 vols.

[3] British Museum, *Sloane Manuscripts* Nos. 2337 and 4107. The British Museum has also got a MS of *Nova plantarum Americanarum genera*. Additional MSS, 28, 609.

[4] MS 913. See Bibliography (Manuscripts) and reproduction of illustration in the Appendix.

[5] *Dictionnaire des Sciences des Arts et Métiers; Planches*, vol. X, Paris 1772. See *Tourneur* and particularly Plates LXI and LXII. There are 18 pages of explanation and 87 plates to illustrate the article.

[6] Arsenal MS No. 3104. Plumier's signature on p. 2.

in the Arsenal [1] and provide an excellent study in the preparation of an illustrated technical manual. Illustrated books on machines were rare at this time: Plumier, always punctilious about giving sources of information, refers in the preface to an unpublished work by Cardan and to the published works of Jacques Besson,[2] Salomon de Caus [3] and Joseph Moxon.[4] Plumier's work is at once more detailed and more authoritative than those of his predecessors; he emphasises the practical approach to the subject, the lay-out of the workshop, the disposition of the treadles, bows and benches, the arrangement of the tools hanging on the wall, the details of jigs, taps, dies, eccentrics and so on, whereas the other works were devoted to finished machines rather than technique and practice. Besson and Caus have already been mentioned in relation to J.-F. Niceron and their influence on Plumier is identical. As far as Salomon de Caus is concerned I have quoted his *Forces mouvantes avec diverses machines* as the source acknowledged by Plumier; in fact this is by no means certain since Caus is only mentioned by name, and it may well be that his work on perspective, which influenced Niceron, had an equally powerful influence on Plumier. Salomon de Caus' machines are for the most part fanciful designs: water organs; machines which play tunes every day at noon, or at sun rise; landscape gardening and fountains – these all play an important part in the work. For all that it is a much older work (1579), Jacques Besson's book gives a far better idea of the practical application of mechanical devices: his mechanical hammer (plate XI) and the belt conveyor (plate XXXIX) are excellent, so also are the two plates which illustrate turning (nos. VII and VIII). But with Plumier one reaches a different level of illustration and a different purpose in writing; one comes suddenly to the clarity which characterises the *Encyclopédie*, to the precision of its drawings, and to its intensely practical purpose. He has obviously learnt well from his predecessors in the Order – Niceron on the need for perspective and Maignan in the need for clarity in mechanical drawing. Previously, the skills of the craftsman were handed on from one generation to the next by father instructing son at the work bench; although this system can never be surpassed, we have with Plumier's work the beginning of a new era, that of instruction by means of the illustrated manual.

[1] MS No. 3078.
[2] *Théâtre des instruments mathématiques et mécaniques avec des figures*, Lyon, 1579.
[3] *Les raisons des forces mouvantes avec diverses machines tant utiles que plaisantes*, Frankfort, 1615.
[4] *Mechanick excercises, or the doctrine of handy-work*, London, 1683.

L'Art de Tourner was favourably received by the *Journal de Trévoux* [1]:

"Les planches sont en très grand nombre, gravées en taille-douce de la grandeur du livre [2] et aussi chargées qu'il a été possible en évitant la confusion. Le P. Plumier en a fait tous les desseins avec un soin et une exactitude charmants. Il y a fait entrer tous les outils, toutes les machines, en un mot toutes les pièces qui ont quelque rapport à son ouvrage. Il les a représentées suivant leurs différents côtés, tant par les hauteurs tant par les longeurs et épaisseurs. Il a gardé la perspective autant qu'il a été possible dans les plans géométriques et dans les profils qu'il a donnés, et cela d'une manière si nette et si aisée à concevoir que la plupart des planches n'ont pas besoin d'explication."

In the same review Plumier is praised for the generous acknowledgment that he makes in his preface to Maubois, Tourneur du Roi, whose work ranged from turning the "colonnes torses" in the Eglise des Invalides to producing bronze vases for the gardens at the Château de Choisy and making the screws for the "balancier de Suède" and the "balancier des médailles." [3] The review is illustrated with an example of Plumier's work (taken from the title-page). Skill on the lathe was required for all the fundamental crafts and for the elements of industry; it was also required in the decorative arts where the complex curvatures in wood, ivory and metal that one associates with the neo-classical and baroque styles would have been impossible had it not been for improvements in the techniques of turning. Previously carving and moulding had been the basic requirements, now it was to a great extent the age of the turner. The finished work he illustrated was made in the workshop of a famous turner, Grollier de Servière [4]; Plumier acknowledged his indebtedness in the preface and notes the fact at the bottom of each drawing of finished work. The fantastic vases illustrated cannot be taken seriously as works of art, they are merely grotesque assemblages of all the points of turning which he mentions in the title of the book:

L'Art de Tourner ou de faire en perfection toutes sortes d'ouvrages au tour dans lequel, outre les principes et éléments du Tour qu'on y enseigne méthodiquement pour tourner tant le bois, l'ivoire etc. que le fer et tous les métaux on voit encore plusieurs belles machines à faire des outils tant simples que figurées de toutes grandeurs; la manière de tourner le globe parfait, le rampant, l'excentrique, les pointes de diamant, les facettes, le

---

[1] Trévoux, May 1702, pp. 3-16: Amsterdam, September 1702, pp. 183-190.
[2] in-folio.
[3] See *Comptes des Bâtiments du Roy sous le règne de Louis XIV*, Paris, 1896, vol. III, pp. 109, 296, 924 and vol. IV, pp. 1076 and 1177, i.e. between 1688 and 1705.
[4] He published a work on engineering, *Recueil des ouvrages*, Lyon, 1719.

panier ou l'échiquier, la couronne ondoyante, la rose à raiseau, les manches de couteaux façon d'Angleterre, les ovaires, la torse à jour ondée, la goderonnée, les globes concentriques, la massue à pointes, les tabatières barlongues de toutes figures, le bâton rompu, les cannelures, les écailles etc. et généralement toutes les méthodes les plus secrètes de cet art, avec la disposition des tours, etc. Ouvrage très curieux et très nécessaire à ceux qui s'exercent au tour, composé en Français et en Latin en faveur des étrangers, et enrichi de près de quatre-vingts planches ...

This virtuosity is exactly what was required for the intricate details of the "rocailles" – the incrustations one finds in rococo decoration. It is interesting to compare Plumier's list of skills with the following passage from Louis Grillet's history of French art; describing the highly decorative style of furnishing in the XVIIIth century he writes:

... c'est à qui, des deux bords d'un cadre, s'éloignera d'avantage de l'autre, fera la nique à la symétrie; de là cette habitude des contours chantournés, des parafes, des lignes contournées, brisées, affrontées, balancées, formées d'une succession de cédilles et de virgules comme un flot chatoyant de vaguelettes crespelées où se déferaient des bouquets et des fleurs.[1]

The book is something of a bibliographical curiosity. The copy in the Bodleian Library, Oxford, passed through my hands in 1948; I found it in a relation's house where it had been left in a deplorable condition[2]; as far as I am able to ascertain, this copy had been in use by wool-staplers who had set up their own business in the early XVIIIth century, but several members of the family were also amateur craftsmen. A. Holtzappfel in his *Turning and mechanical manipulations*[3] pays tribute to Plumier: "The execution of his work," he says, "is honourable to its author from the industrious care and exactness which it exhibits, especially when one considers that it is almost the first[4] work published on the subject ... it formed the basis of the article on turning in the *Encyclopédie*." Some attention is also paid to Plumier in the catalogique of a recent exhibition at the Conservatoire des Arts et Métiers[5]; although the author of the Catalogue speaks of the

[1] *Histoire des Arts* in G. Hanotaux, *Histoire de la nation française*, Paris, 1922, vol. XI, p. 386.
[2] Wanting all before sig. a.4. There is an excellent copy in the British Museum from which the illustrations in the Appendix have been made. A copy of the 2nd edition, Paris, 1749, was being offered for sale in Paris at 750 NF in 1962.
[3] 3 vols, London, 1846; see vol. I, pp. 4–7.
[4] "The *first* treatise written exclusively on turning" – a few lines previously.
[5] *Les techniques au siècle de l'Encyclopédie et la collection des maquettes de Madame de Genlis*, Paris, June 1963–December 1963.

"planches" in the *Encyclopédie*, article *Tour*, as "presque toutes inspi-
rées du célèbre *Art de tourner*," [1] he has failed to point out that one of
the reproductions (No. 240 in the Exhibition) was of a "planche" taken
by Lucotte directly from Plumier, (i.e. the "planche" LXII already
referred to). He is also doing less than justice to Plumier and to
seventeenth century turners such as Maubois when he says that only
wood, not metal, could be turned on a lathe at that time [2]; Plumier,
however, expressly refers to the turning of metal and ivory on several
occasions – in the title, in the *Préface* [3] and in the chapter entitled
Comment il faut tourner le fer etc.[4]

Plumier's work is also remarkable in that it was translated into
Russian by Peter the Great who supervised the translation; two other
works were translated into Russian at the same time – L. C. Sturm's
Architectur militaris (from the German) and S. Leclerc's *Traité d'architecture* (from the French).[5] It is no exaggeration therefore to claim
Plumier as one of the very first "westernisers" in Russia or to trace
some of the French influence in the architecture of St. Petersburg to him.

Plumier is in some ways a complex character; he can dwell on the
wonders of the Universe and the way in which they proclaim their
Creator in language that has much in common with John Ray,
Wisdom of God in the Universe, and Derham's *Physico-Theology;* it is close
to the language of the deists and is in remarkable contrast with the
pietistic and mystical obscurities of the majority of his fellow Minims.
At the same time there can be no doubt that he remained faithful to
the strict obedience of this rigorous order. He was generous in praise
of others, as we have seen in his acknowledgments in the preface to
the *Art de Tourner*, and in the *Traité des Fougères* where he gives unstinted
praise to Ray, the English botanist, for the clarity of his illustrations;
he also praises Grew and Malpighi for their biological work. Plumier
was an experimentalist: this comes out most clearly from his *Art de
Tourner*, but the dissections and collections to which Lister refers also
bear witness to this same spirit – and so does his fearless habit of tasting
all the new plants he found; in the *Description des Plantes de l'Amérique*
he describes the colocasia ...

[1] Catalogue of the above, Paris, 1963, p. 50.
[2] *ibid.*, p. 49. He attributes the beginning of metal turning to Vaucanson, mid-XVIIIth
century. He is also inexact in giving, on p. 50, the date of Plumier's work as 1707. The first
edition was Lyon, 1701, and the second, Paris, 1749.
[3] *L'Art de tourner, Préface*, sig ï.
[4] *ibid.*, pp. 11–19.
[5] See C. Martini *Nachricht aus Russland*, Leipsig, 1731, p. 19. and P. P. Comte de Ségur,
Histoire de Russie et de Pierre-le-Grand, Paris, 1829, p. 502.

... cette plante est une violente caustique; je voulus la goûter, mais à peine eus-je mordu le bout de la tige que ma bouche s'enflamma si fort qu'il me fut impossible de pouvoir parler de près de deux heures de sorte que je fus obligé de tenir la bouche ouverte et même de tirer la langue en dehors autant que je pus. L'oxicrat dont je me servis abattit bien cette inflammation, mais je fus pendant dix jours sans connaître le goût de ce que je mangeais à cause que l'acrimonie de ce jus m'avait grossi la langue et le palais. C'est pour cette raison qu'on l'appelle vulgairement "la liane brûlante." [1]

This same fearlessness comes out also in the admirably detached style of his letters to Bégon when he describes an encounter with wolves in Provence or with a crocodile – surely one of the most dangerous creatures – in the Antilles.[2] To Plumier also must be attributed the delightful custom of naming plants after people; before him there is the isolated example of the *Nicotiana* (tobacco plant) which was named after Jean Nicot, the French Ambassador in Portugal, who sent samples to Catherine de Médicis. Among the well-known, and now common, plants that owe their names to Plumier are the *Begonia*, after Michel Bégon; *Lobelia*, after Lobel the curator of the Botanick Garden at Oxford; the *Magnolia*, after Magnol; and the *Fuchsia* after the German botanist Lenhard Fuchs. Writing as late as the middle of the eighteenth century, Burmann was able to say of the fuchsia which now adorns most suburban gardens:

> Rarissima hac planta est. Caeterum in memorium Leonardi Fuchsii hoc plantarum genus a Plumier FUCHSIA dictum est.[3]

Plumier found the plant growing in the Antilles, and it is only in the last 100 years that it has become commonplace in Europe. The first known description of the fuchsia is indeed Plumier's, under the title *Fuchsia Triphylla Coccinea*, with drawings, in the *Nova Plantarum Americanarum Genera;* the drawing, plate 14, is not quite accurate in the number of stamens it shows, but it was on this description that Linnaeus based the genus *Fuchsia* in 1737.[4] It is also interesting to note that the first fully accurate description of this plant was made by another Minim, Feuillée, a pupil of Plumier, in his *Journal des obser-*

---

[1] *Description des Plantes de l'Amérique*, plate 52. The episode is related on the page facing and is repeated in the critique of the work in the *Journal des Sçavans*, 20 July, 1693.

[2] Letters, transcribed from MSS in the Bibliothèque Publique de La Rochelle, are given in Appendix.

[3] J. Burmann, *Plantarum Americanarum*, Amsterdam, 1755–1760. The importance of this work is discussed later.

[4] I am indebted to Mrs. J. Smith of the British Fuchsia Society for this information.

vations botaniques. The full range of Plumier's work as a classifier and namer of plants is the subject of a detailed scientific paper [1] and his own name was perpetuated by Linnaeus in the genus of frangipanier *Plumeria* – a fitting tribute since this is one of the most beautiful of tropical plants.

During his last years, Plumier was often ill and was justly anxious about the publication of his work; nevertheless he found time to undertake a Latin translation of Perrault's *Hommes Illustres*,[2] and was contemplating a visit to Milan and Nuremberg to view the work of several turners of renown. In 1704, at the instance of Fagon, the King's physician, he was about to embark on another journey of discovery, with the special task of investigating the culture and properties of quinine. He died, however, of a sudden attack of pleurisy in the Minims' "couvent" of Santa-Maria, near Cadiz. Had he lived to see his voluminous work through the press, he would have been re-membered as an earlier Buffon, as an important forerunner of the encyclopaedists. Even so, his influence on the whole school of descriptive botany, and even on Linnaeus, is profound; he transformed the *herbal* into the detailed and well illustrated text-book. Interest in his work continued throughout the eighteenth century and on into the nineteenth; writing in 1819 in the *Cyclopaedia* (Volume XXVII), A. Rees wrote under *Plumier:*

Vast treasures of his drawings have remained in the French libraries, for the most part unpublished. The Earl of Bute obtained copies of a great number of these which, after his Lordship's death, passed into the hands of Sir Joseph Banks. Boerhaave had previously procured copies of above 500 of these, done by the accurate Aubriet [3] under Vaillant's inspection [4] which were, in part at least, published by John Burman (sic) at Amsterdam between 1775 and 1760. These plates are executed with tolerable but by no means infallible accuracy, being inferior in neatness and correctness to what Plumier himself had done.

This reference to the Earl of Bute, Sir Joseph Banks and Burmann is of outstanding interest in that it connects Plumier with the eighteenth century botanists. It is not clear what led John Stuart, Earl of Bute, to be interested in Plumier's manuscripts, but it seems likely that he knew of the existence of copies of his drawings amongst the Sloane

---

[1] *Repertorium novarum specierum,* Biehefte Band V, Dahlem bei Berlin, 1920, pp. 100–158.
[2] Never published and MS lost(?); *Archives historiques de la Saintonge et l'Aunis,* Saintes, 1930, Vol. XLVIII, p. 101.
[3] A miniaturist, 1665–1742, employed in the Jardin des Plantes.
[4] Sebastien Vaillant, 1649–1722.

Manuscripts, now in the British Museum; a note inserted in the bound volume, *Delineationes plantarum americanarum* (Sloane 4017), states, "This is not a complete set but only some duplicates which belonged to Dr. Sherard." Dr. Sherard (1659–1728) worked with the English botanist Ray and with the above mentioned Vaillant who was a demonstrator in the Jardin des Plantes in the early eighteenth century.[1] Whether or not it was through Sherard's copies that Bute knew of Plumier, he had in his possession a large store of copies at the time of his death and these form the first five volumes of the Banksian Manuscripts in the Natural History Museum, Kensington [2]; there is a duplicate copy in the library at Kew.[3] Boerhaave and Burmann did more than the English botanists to see that Plumier's work was not forgotten; the former published no less than 6,000 illustrations from the Plumier manuscripts, and the latter, between 1755 and 1760 brought out ten parts of a work devoted entirely to the American flora, *Plantarum Americanarum continens plantas quas olim Carolus Plumierus, Botanicorum Princeps, detexit, eruitique atque in Insulis Antillis ipse depinxit.*[4] As further evidence we may quote repeated references in Lamarck's *Encyclopaedia*, 1783–1797; Descourtilz's *Flore pittoresque des Andes*, 1821–1827 and minor references in A. von Heller, Martius and Petiver. In addition to the direct influence that he had, there remains the fact that his life and work emphasise the important scientific role that the foreign missionary has fulfilled since his time.[5]

The beautiful drawing that Plumier made of a passion-flower, a transcript of all that remains of his correspondence and the preface to one of his manuscript works, *Solum, Salum, Coelum*, are given in an Appendix.

[1] See *A Sketch of the life of Dr. W. Sherard*, in *Journal of Botany*, London, 1874.

[2] C. Plumier, *312 original (sic) watercolour and pen-and-ink drawings*.

[3] I am indebted to the Librarian of the Natural History Museum for drawing my attention to the existence of these copies at Kew.

[4] A. D. de Virville, *Histoire de la botanique en France*, Paris, Société d'éditions d'enseignement supérieur, 1954 (hors commerce), pp. 58–59 deals in some detail with Plumier's influence.

[5] A. D. de Virville, *loc. cit.*, and P. Fournier, *Encyclopédie Biologique*, Paris, 1932, Vol. X pp. 53–59.

CHAPTER VIII

MINOR SCIENTIFIC WRITERS

(1) ESTIENNE OCTOUL, 1589–1655

Octoul's name occurs in the long list which Hilarion de Coste gives of Mersenne's correspondents.[1] He was an active member of the Order and reached some prominence in the administration of the Province of Provence since he signed the "approbatio" for André Réal's admirably clear introduction to the study of Hebrew.[2] His name is to be found in biographical dictionaries of the Midi [3] and in François de Lalande's *Bibliographie astronomique*.[4] He was the author of a single printed work, *Inventa astronomica ... terrae meridianis per observationem cum pyramidis astronomica comparandis ...* (Avignon, 1643), a strange mixture of astrology and highly practical details of aids to navigation. It is possible that Octoul was amongst those friends to whom Mersenne refers in the *Cogitata;* they urged him to publish his *Ars navigandi* as a part of this work rather than in the *Universae geomatriae synopsis*.[5] It is at least apposite to note that the *Ars navigandi* bears a separate "épître dédicatoire" to the Bishop of Marseilles where Octoul was known. His book contained information that Mersenne would have found of interest; "Il propose," says Lalande, "un instrument pour prendre la hauteur (du soleil); c'est un secteur à pinnules [6] dont il faisait tourner le limbe dans une coulisse circulaire concentrique placée dans le plan du méridien." This early sextant may be considered as having some claim to originality; Robert Hooke first described one

[1] Coste, *Vie de Mersenne*, p. 96. Mersenne. *correspondance*, vol. IX.
[2] *Brevis ... introductio ad linguam sanctam*, Lyon, 1646. Réal was another of the Order to correspond with Mersenne; see Coste, *op. cit.*, p. 96.
[3] C. F. Achard, *Dictionnaire de la Provence*, Marseille, 1786, Vol. Iv, p. 17; C. F. H. Barjavel, *Dictionnaire historique ... de Vaucluse*, Carpentras, 1841, Vol. II, p. 215.
[4] Paris, 1804, p. 216.
[5] Lenoble, op. cit., p. xxix and Mersenne, *Cogitata (Hydraulica)*, p. 225.
[6] i.e. with a sighting vane.

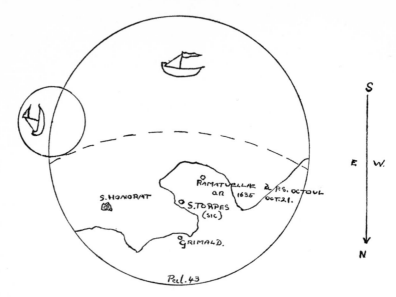

to the Royal Society in 1667,[1] twenty-four years after Octoul's publication. He may also have been amongst the first Frenchmen to have
observed sunspots.[2] His own account of the observation is contained
on pages 70–72 with a diagram (reproduced above) which is reasonably
accurate; the 43rd parallel passes to the South not to the North of
Saint Tropez and the Ile Saint Honorat is far to the East of the
situation given by Octoul. The essential detail is, however, accurate
and can easily be checked against a map.

... mihi anno 1635 die 21 Octobris occurrit res omnino nova, et simili
experientia difficilis, quod scilicet in horto fraterno divinum officium ante
solis ortum recitaturus, ipsum sine fulgentibus radiis viderim, pauloque
post, in duas, limbo superiore discindi partes, quas, fratris uxore eiusque
ancilla etiam me admonentibus, existimabam sine telescopio, maculas, de
quibus Aquis Sextiis in Collegio Borbonio habueram disputationem, vel
esse astra Borbonia, vel esse maculas.

What in fact did Octoul see? Was it a mirage? I am inclined to think
so: he mentions that the sun rose "sine fulgentibus radiis," while a

---

[1] *Chambers Encyclopaedia*, London, 1956, Vol. XII, p. 444. The problem of accuracy in
measurements of angles exercised Kepler and Tycho Brahe some years before Octoul, but
their instruments were large quadrants rather than small pices of apparatus; see C. Singer,
History of Technology, vol. III, Oxford, 1957, p. 640.
[2] Reference in Lalande, loc. cit. Galileo had already observed sunspots in 1610, from the
apparent movement of which he deduced the fact that the sun rotates. There is also the
treatise *De maculis solaribus* of C. Scheiner, Augusta Vindelicorum (Augsburg), 1612.

calm morning in mid-October would favour a mirage over the sea. On the other hand Octoul was a native of this part of the world and would have been aware of the likelihood of such an occurrence. A considerable eruption of sunspot activity is in fact visible to the naked eye, particularly in conditions such as those which he described. He also places the sunspots in the upper segment of the sun (5°–45°), the most prone to such activity.

Octoul was one of a small number of members of the Order who were friends of Peiresc at Aix-en-Provence; through him they were attached to the intellectual activity that we have already noticed at La Place Royale in Paris. He died in the small "couvent" of Pourrières which lies some 30 miles to the East of Aix on the far side of the Montagne Sainte Victoire.[1]

(2) THEOPHILE MINUTI, 1592–1662

Another friend of Peiresc whose contribution to the intellectual life of the Order was considerable was Théophile Minuti. He travelled to the Levant with Henri de Gournay, Sieur de Marchéville, the French Ambassador at Constantinople.[2] Henri de Gournay was himself devoted to the Order and may have been a member of the Tiers-Ordre; he gave relics to the "couvent" at Marchéville in the Province of Lorraine.[3] Minuti's name occurs frequently in the correspondence of both Peiresc and Mersenne; his chief occupation was the collection of oriental manuscripts and he became an authority on Egyptian hieroglyphics and on the Coptic alphabet.[4] He was therefore valuable to both of them as a source of information about the languages of Holy Writ and about conditions in the lands of the Bible. Mersenne obtained from him a considerable amount of information about Arab music and musical instruments.[5] He was also interested in astronomy [6] and botany. Plumier, naming a genus of plants after Peiresc, wrote in praise of Minuti: –

---

[1] Roberti, Vol. I, p. 200, describing this "couvent" makes the following statement, "Perrier (sic) è una piccola città del dipartimento del Orne, nella diocesi d'Aix."!!

[2] See inter alia letter of Minuti to Peiresc in Bibliothèque Méjanes, Aix, MSS, 201–215, *Correspondance de Peiresc*, Vol. VII, fol. 201–203.

[3] Paris, Bibliothèque de Sainte Geneviève; MSS, 714, fol. 24, *Attestation de reliques* etc. See Bibliography, Manuscripts.

[4] Octoul, *op. cit.*, p. 75. See also Bibliography, Manuscripts, Carpentras, Nos. 1821, 1871, 1874, 1876.

[5] Mersenne, *Correspondance*, Vols. III, IV and V passim. He is not mentioned by Lenoble.

[6] He watched an eclipse with Peiresc, Mersenne, *Correspondance*, Vol. V, p. 380.

PEIRESKA

Bibliothecam eius et hortum ditaverat R. P. Th. Minuti Ordinis Min. Prov. Prov(enciae), Linguorum Orientalium peritissimus et ad Orientem ter peragratus, Pentateucho scilicet Samaritano Manuscripto et quam aliis sacri voluminibus, nec non rarissimis plantis quarum et praesantia ita et odore omnes superavit Hyacinthus ille Indicus odoratissimus, tuberosa radice (vulgo tuberouse) quem primus ille ex Indiis Orientalibus in hortum Belgenserianum (Boisgencier) propre Telonum adportavit.[1]

This is an able and concise summary of his contribution to the Order. The tuberose was first described in French by Vigneul Marville in 1699 and it became a favourite hot-house plant; the Romantic poets also favoured it as an exotic image.

(3) JEAN FRANÇOIS, 1606–1666

A third member of the Order who was also known to both Peiresc and Mersenne was Jean François. There is little information concerning him: Thuillier included him in his necrology of members of the Order in the Province of France (Paris) [2] but his chief associations were with the Province of Provence and with Chalon-sur-Saône.[3] He is referred to frequently in Mersenne's correspondence during the years 1626 to 1629.[4] He achieved some prominence in the Order by composing a poem in praise of the Founder, *Ode panegyrica in laudem S. P. N. Francisci de Paula, Ordinis Minimorum Instutoris* (Chalon, 1632). He was one of the first Minims in Chalon and attracted sympathy to the Order in that town by his preaching; later he became Provincial of Provence [5] and entered into corrrespondence with Peiresc who asked him for information on various historical questions. Apart from his letters, nothing of his work seems to be extant and there is no information about his identity except a marginal note in a manuscript, *Elucubrationes Massilienses*, in the Bibliothèque Publique at Toulouse; this manuscript contains several references to the Minims in various towns in Provence and gives some details concerning the correspon-

[1] See previously p. 190, *Nova plantarum americanarum genera*, Paris, 1703, p. 35. Boisgencier: Plumier is inexact. Peiresc's house was Belgentier, near Toulon as Plumier states. For an illustration of the gardens see G. Cahen-Salvador, *Un grand humaniste, Peiresc*, Paris, 1951, facing p. 144.
[2] Thuillier, I, p.148. He was for a while at Vincennes.
[3] The Minim L. Bertaut refers to him in *L'Illustre Orbandale*, Chalon, 1662, Vol. II, p. 174.
[4] Mersenne, *Correspondance*, Vol. I, *passim*.
[5] Not "Provincial des Minimes d'Espagne" as in the Index to the *Lettres de Peiresc*, (Collection des Documents inédits), Paris 1888–1898, vol. III, p. 787. The phrase "de ce pays" in Peiresc's letter, vol. II, p. 101, and which refers to *Provence*, has caused this error.

dence of Peiresc, "Une lettre du P. Jean François, Pro(vinci)al des Minimes du 18 (8?) Mai, 1629; une autre du 16 Mai 1629" and in the margin, "Nota que c'est le P. Jean François Carrière." [1] The name Carrière certainly occurs in and around Aix-en-Provence; but since he probably came from the Paris region (Thuillier vaguely says, "Apud Neustrios natus est") and since the names is of some currency throughout France, this note does not materially help with his identification.

(4) PIERRE MACAIRE, Fl. 1630–1650?

Amongst the manuscripts which came from the library of the Minimes de la Place Royale and which are now in the Bibliothèque de l'Arsenal, is a voluminous and ill-written work of 419 closely packed folios called *Lexicon hydrographique et historique*.[2] It is by Pierre Macaire who was, for a while, scribe of the *Conclusions capitulaires* at the "couvent" at Vincennes [3]; no other information about him seems to have survived. The fact that Thuillier does not list him in his necrology suggests that he came from another province and that he did not stay long within the Province of France (Paris).

His work deserves to be remembered as a monument to patient and laborious effort. He lists some 8,000 rivers, creeks and harbours in all parts of the world; I have tested its accuracy by looking up three insignificant rivers in my native Staffordshire, the Churnet, Dane and Dove, and was surprised to find them listed and to find that the information, although scant, was accurate. His sources were the various atlases of the day and a work by the Jesuit, Louis Coulon.[4] The method adopted by Macaire for giving references was, however, clumsy and the reader finds at the foot of each entry a set of references such as "KKK,ooo,ψψψ," and so on. The accumulated result for, say, the Thames or Seine is an inextricable mass of symbols, and it may well be for this reason that the work, useful in its theme and scope, never saw the press. The purpose of the work and Macaire's qualification for undertaking it remain unknown.

---

[1] MSS 631, fol. 162. These letters are preserved in the Bibliothèque Méjanes at Aix (MSS 203) and others are in the Bibliothèque Inguimbertine at Carpentras (MSS 1816); his letters to Mersenne have been published in *Correspondance*, Vols. I etc.
[2] MSS 2909. Bound with arms of the Order and Place Royale shelf mark 7/IR/15.
[3] Archives Nationales, LL, 1577.
[4] *Les rivières de la France*, Paris, 1644.

(5) LOUIS FEUILLEE, 1660–1731

Lalande wrote of Feuillée under the year 1694, "Cette année le P. Feuillée, Minime, observa à Avignon l'éclipse du soleil du 22 juin: il continua d'observer à Marseille jusqu'en 1700, qu'il alla au Levant; en 1703, en Amérique: ces observations sont imprimées à la tête de son premier voyage." [1]

He belongs properly to the XVIIIth century, the observations referred to by Lalande being published in 1714 [2]. The formative years of his life were spent at Santa Trinità dei Monti and at Marseille, under the direction of Plumier, and he, like his master, became Botaniste de Sa Majesté. He was a truly encyclopaedic genius having a wide knowledge of mathematics botany and astronomy, a fact which is stressed by P. Fournier in the *Encyclopédie biologique*.[3] It is interesting to note that this pupil of Plumier's should also have been a craftsman, using for his astronomical observations instruments which he had made himself.[4]

[1] Lalande, *op. cit.*, p. 329.
[2] *Journal des observations*, Paris 1714 and *Histoire des plantes médicinales*, Paris, 1714–1725. 13 volumes of his manuscript notes are preserved in the Bibliothèque publique, Marseille, MSS 943–955.
[3] Paris, 1932, Vol. X, pp. 60–67.
[4] *ibid.*, p. 61.

CHAPTER IX

HISTORICAL STUDIES

The History section of the library at la Place Royale was extensively subdivided and clearly separated from the sections dealing with Sacred and Ecclesiastical History. The division between Sacred and Profane is not, however, so distinct in the historical studies undertaken by members of the Order during the seventeenth century; in this chapter "profane" is taken as including all those works which are not more conveniently classified as devotional, hagiographic or Biblical. Such studies do not indeed form a very large part of the published work of members of the Order during the seventeenth century.

The earliest work in this category is a translation of José Acosta's natural history of the Indies; the author, a Spanish Jesuit (1539–1600), undertook several journeys in Central and South America, including a hazardous passage of the Andes during which he suffered from snow-blindness and the effects of the altitude. The first part of his book was devoted to a geographical survey and the second to a study of the customs and habits of the "Indian" population. Originally written in Spanish,[1] Acosta's work was translated into several European languages: Dutch, English, by E. Grimstone in 1604, and French, by the Minim Robert Regnault whose name has already been mentioned as one of the early librarians of the priceless Place Royale collection. Regnault died in 1642 while still working to enlarge the library, particularly the History section.[2] His translation of Acosta appeared in three editions (Paris, 1597, 1600 and 1616) but, apart from slight variations in format and consequently of pagination, these editions appear to be identical. The work of translation must have been undertaken when Regnault was a mere youth if we are to believe

---

[1] *Historia natural y moral de las Indias*, Seville, 1590.
[2] Roberti, *op. cit.*, II, pp. 609–610. Roberti does not mention his important work as translator of Acosta.

Thuillier's statement that he died at the age of sixty-one.[1] Plumier refers to Regnault's translation in his paper to the *Journal des Sçavans*, and it doubtless served as a useful source of information for those who set off for the Americas at that time. Its interest for the modern reader is scant: coupling of geography and history shows some originality and the proof that the author finds for the geocentricity of the Universe will probably amuse. Regnault's other work, apart from his life of Sainte Fare and books of devotion, is an edition of the correspondence of Philippe Camaye, Seigneur de Fresne, Ambassador to the court of Queen Elizabeth I of England and, later, to the Venetian Republic; it is mostly with the second of these ambassadorships that the correspondence is concerned and it is of interest in the light it throws on France's relations with the Levantine trading companies. The edition was sumptuously produced by the publisher Estienne Richer who brought it out in Paris in 1635.[2] In his foreword, Richer speaks of a chance encounter with Regnault during which the Minim showed him his collection of manuscripts, amongst them the Camaye letters. It is not clear from Richer's account whether the manuscripts referred to were Regnault's private property (one assumes that if he really did *own* them it was by the Corrector's permission and that they would have reverted to the "couvent" at Regnault's death) or whether the whole collection of manuscripts in the library is intended. However this may be, it seems likely that the "other manuscripts" referred to contained the papers collected into five volumes and called *Traités et Ambassades de Turquie: Recueil de pièces relatives à l'histoire des relations diplomatiques avec le Levant, 1528–1640.* These volumes, ex-Minimes de la Place Royale, are now in the Bibliothèque de l'Arsenal [3] and contain a letter from a certain le Veit, dated Pera lès Constantinople, 2 janvier, 1640, to le P. Renauld (sic) Minime à Paris,[4] in which British ascendancy over the French is mentioned in categoric terms:

Je serai bien aise que l'on ne sache point que ce soit moi qui vous écrive: tout est perdu ici pour les Français, ce sont les Anglais qui tiennent le dé.[5]

Regnault's work has no more originality than any other compilation from manuscript sources, but it shows that he realised what was worthy of preservation; the history of commercial and diplomatic relation-

---

[1] Thuillier, *op. cit.*, I, pp. 33–34.
[2] *Lettres et Ambassades de messire Philippe Camaye, seigneur de Fresne*, 3 vols, in-fol, Paris, 1635.
[3] Arsenal, MSS Nos. 4767–4771.
[4] *ibid.*, Vol. V, (i.e. No. 4771) fol. 249.
[5] This is a postscript.

ships with the Levant has probably more permanent significance than
all the rest of the histories by members of the Order put together.
Regnault had all the instincts of the trained archivist but he was
secretive about the way in which he obtained his documents. One of
his contemporaries at the Place Royale, Hilarion de Coste, was more
considerable as a writer of history.

Coste has been mentioned several times as the first biographer of
Mersenne and as the author of one of the lives of Saint François de
Paule. He also composed the lives of several other saints and his
"profane" histories are, naturally enough, full of references to ecclesiastical history, lives of eminent churchmen and Saints of the
Gallican Church.[1] Coste's first historical work was one of the then
popular compilations in the manner of Brantôme, and bore the title
*Histoire catholique où sont décrites (sic) les vies, faits et actions héroïques et
signalées des hommes et dames illustres dans les XVI et XVII siècles.*[2] Quite
apart from its use as a source book, the work is remarkable for its
interpretation of the sixteenth century, for its reliance upon quotations
from the poets of the Pléiade and, in general, for its style. The same
features characterise his later histories, *Les vrais portrait des Rois de
France;*[3] *Eloges de nos Rois et Enfants de France* [4] and the *Vies et éloges des
Reines, des Princesses et des Dames illustres en piété* [5]; although he goes
back to the utmost antiquity in expounding the history of the French
monarchy, it is only when he comes to the sixteenth century that his
work becomes critical. Between the Ancients, for whom he has respect,
and the Renaissance, he finds little more than a succession of dynastic
disputes so that he presents a purely stereotyped image of the Middle
Ages; with the sixteenth century, the image, if not acceptable by the
standards of modern historians, is a bold and imaginative one. Faced
with the challenge of heresy, Europe approaches an Armageddon
and the French are fortunate in having a set of illustrious kings who
are leading the nation to a triumphant conclusion in the seventeenth
century, when Henri IV is succeeded by Louis le Juste – the rule of
Law succeeds to the periods of violence; the successful conclusion of
the siege of La Rochelle is looked upon as the culmination, in the early
seventeenth century, of all that had been striven for in the sixteenth:

---

[1] The phrase "Saints de l'Eglise gallicane" is used by Coste in the *Préface* to his *Vies des
dames illustres,* Paris, 1647; the idea, if not the phrase, is recurrent.
[2] Paris, 1625.
[3] Paris, 1636.
[4] Paris, 1643.
[5] Paris, 1647.

> Avons-nous pas vu qu'en dix mois
> Il a dans Ré défait l'Anglois,
> Pris la Rochelle, emporté Suze,
> Sauvé Cazal, détruit Privas,
> Détruit Allets et, près d'Anduze,
> Donné la paix à ses Etats.[1]

But the period is not seen merely as a period of military glory; the Muses which had retired from the Ancient World reappeared in France with the Renaissance. In the article on *Barbe Aurillot ... Marie de l'Incarnation* in the *Histoire Catholique* we find:

> En cette ville Royale (Paris) les Muses fugitives de la Grèce sont retirées pour établir leur Parnasse et leur Hélicon en son Université, autrefois l'oracle de l'Europe, et toujours la maîtresse des autres; laquelle a produit des Hercules Gaulois qui ont dompté les monstres de l'erreur et de l'ignorance.[2]

The sixteenth century is therefore the great period of promise; promise of the success of the counter-reformation, promise of the stability of the French monarchy, promise of the establishment in France of poetic traditions that will equal those of Greece and Rome.

Coste is one of the very few members of the Order to have shown any awareness of the literary activity of the sixteenth century; his quotations from Ronsard have already been the subject of a short article by Jean Dagens.[3] Confining himself to the work *l'Histoire Catholique*, M. Dagens has listed some fifty quotations to which we may add others from Du Bellay, Etienne Pasquier, Desportes [4] and Jean Bertaut – the last was Bishop of Sées at the close of the sixteenth century and is not to be confused with the Minim, Léon Bertaut, mentioned below. This habit of quotation was in no sense confined to the *Histoire Catholique* but must be considered as an essential part of all Coste's historical work. His interpretation of Ronsard is remote from the modern view of a "pagan" Ronsard; true, he referred to him as a "Virgile français" or a "Homère français" [5] but, much more frequently he is "Le génie

---

[1] *Portraits ... Rois de France*, (Louis XIII), p. 390.
[2] *Histoire Catholique*, p. 721. It is worth pointing out that this idea is in itself expressed by Ronsard, *Le Bocage Royal, Discours entre les Muses délogées et Ronsard*, Ronsard, *Oeuvres*, Paris (Pléiade), 1938, Vol. I, pp. 817 *et sq.*
[3] *Ronsard et l'Histoire catholique d'Hilarion de Coste* in *Mélanges d'histoire de la Renaissance offerts à Henri Chamard*, Paris, 1951, pp. 145–151.
[4] M. Dagens, *op. cit.*, refers to 300 lines quoted from the *Psalms* in the version of Desportes. Coste called Desportes "le plus mignard de nos poètes."
[5] Both terms in the *Histoire Catholique, passim*.

de la France" or quite simply "Notre Poète." [1] Since Ronsard was patriotic and since he took the catholic side against the Protestants, Coste regards him as an apologist of the catholic revival. As an example of this we may refer to his use of Ronsard's *Sonnet* for Mary Stuart in the article on her in the *Vies et éloges des Dames illustres*. Further examples abound. Verse quotation was a common feature of the baroque style in literature and it requires only a glance through Coste's work to discover other distinctive features of this style which is characterised by a sense of urgency and a need to spur on the reader. As a means of achieving this, sudden and colourful comparisons are made:

Je ne serai pas de la catégorie de ceux qui, *jaloux ainsi que des singes de leurs petits, trouvent tout ce qui part de leur esprit beau et bien fait* ... (*Histoire Catholique*, Préface.)

Les monastères, *des déserts non stériles* ... *des séminaires et pépinières de très saints personnages.* (ibid., p. 129).

Tandis que notre Grand Roi (Louis XIII) *ou Hercule Français achève de couper la dernière tête de l'hydre de la rébellion et révolte* des religionnaires en son Royaume ... voilà que des étrangers provoquent derechef son courroux, voulant ruiner entièrement dans Italie ce Prince ... (*Portraits des Rois*, p. 390).

A love of antithesis was another feature of this ornate style and has about it something of the effect that the painters of the period produced from their use of chiaroscuro. This may be seen in almost any passage contrasting good and evil, catholic and protestant, hero and reprobate, and nowhere better than in the extended comparison of Martin Luther with Martin de Valence, the Apostle of Mexico. (*Histoire Catholique*, p. 113).

Startling episodes are common. Here again a parallel with the visual arts may be drawn, where a strong vein of ghoulishness is discernible in paintings dealing with the theme of martyrdom. The whole intent of painter and writer was to shock the complacent into belief by evoking their pity; as an example of how Coste does this in the *Histoire Catholique* (p. 123) we may refer to the episode of the Minim, Didier de la Mothe, who was hanged by his testicles during the sack of Rome by Lutheran forces in 1527, and who was miraculously cured on being carried in a litter to the shrine of Saint François de Paule

---

[1] *ibid., passim.* Also in *Vies ... des Dames illustrrs, passim*; *Portraits de nos Rois, passim* after the XVth century Kings; *Eloges de nos Rois, passim.*

at le Plessis-lès-Tours. Closely connected with this is the use of Medusan Beauty. Vice is seductive and must be painted as such:

> Ce pauvre prince, plongé dans le vice et dans l'ordure, devint éperdument amoureux de l'une des demoiselles de la Cour de Catherine sa femme ... Anne de Boulen, fille de médiocre condition, laquelle était infectée de l'hérésie de Luther. Tous les hommes d'esprit étaient étonnés de voir ce grand Roi possédé d'une telle manie et ensorcelée de la laideur même. (*Vie des Dames Illustres*, I, p. 253).

Classical imagery, it hardly needs to be mentioned, abounds throughout, showing how closely the baroque and neo-classical are related. There is, as an example, a delightful and extended passage in the *Préface* to the *Vies des Dames Illustres*, in which Coste shows what famous men owe to the influence of women: the *Iliad*, he says, was inspired by Clorinda the Samian; Aristotle got his knowledge of the tides from a woman of Lesbos; Hippocrates obtained a cure for piles from Dorothea of Abdera, whilst Anaxagoras learnt of the planets from a woman gardener in Smyrna; finally, perhaps inevitably, we find in the same list Saint Augustine and his debt to Monica.

History for Coste lay almost entirely within the scope of compilations of the "gens illustres" type; if more attention has been paid in this chapter to style rather than to content, it is because his significance as a historian lies in presentation. This is not the place to raise the vexed question of the baroque element in literature; liberally interpreted, the term may be taken to mean "the treatment of perspective not as a rational science but as a means of obtaining surprising effects." [1] Coste's history shows just this; his historical perspective is aimed to startle, to show up his heroes and heroines in a moving radiance contrasting violently with the surrounding scenes of horror – a sort of camaieu, or chiaroscuro in words. Moreover with Coste there is the essential alliance of the baroque form with the very spirit of the counter-reformation. Most of the attempts to use "baroque" as a term of literary criticism are made with reference to poetry or to the theatre; there is certainly a strong case to be made out for its use with reference to the writing of history.

One is likewise reminded of the baroque when reading Hippolyte Raulin's panegyric of the Fleur de Lys,[2] a work which was inspired

---

[1] R. A. Sayce in *Baroque elements in Montaigne; French Studies*, Vol. VIII, Oxford, 1954, pp. 5–6..
[2] See p. 101.

by the same emotional loyalty to the throne as that which inspired Coste; and again, when reading Bertaut's local histories.

Léonard Bertaut was a Minim of the Province du Duché de Bourgogne; he is mentioned by the abbé Papillon in his bibliography of Burgundian writers.[1] Towards the end of his life, he died in 1662, Bertaut published two historical surveys, one of Autun – his native city – the other of Chalon-sur-Saône. *La très-ancienne et très-auguste ville d'Autun couronnée de joie etc.*, published in Chalon in 1653, was written to celebrate the elevation to the see of Autun of the Minim Dony d'Attichy, famous in the Order because of his *Histoire Générale*. The elevation of a Minim was not such a rare event; Roberti lists six examples of the elevation of French Minims [2] but it remained a controversial point within the Order whether such promotion should be accepted.[3] Bertaut's history of Autun is largely an apologetic for his co-religionary; the Druidic and Roman remains foretell the excellence of the present Bishop; the magnificent temple to the Goddess Minerva erected in the august city (Autun was called Augustodunum in Roman times) is "la véritable expression de la haute et vertueuse sagesse de Monseigneur son illustrissime et Révérendissime Prélat." Beyond the panegyric, however, the author evinces a genuine interest in the Gallic and Gallo-Roman foundations of the city. The specific use of history as a means of eulogy brings to mind the wide use that was made of historical material in the Oraison Funèbre during the seventeenth century – a point to which further reference will be made.

Bertaut's history of Chalon-sur-Saône was not occasioned by any particular event; the Minims had been established in the town since 1596, since when they had received patronage from the King[4] and nobility[5] as well as from the municipality.[6] In recognition of these favours and out of pride and interest in the town, Bertaut composed his *Illustre Orbandale;* it was printed in Lyon (2 volumes) in 1662 and offered for sale in Chalon "chez Pierre Cusset, marchand-libraire." The same Pierre Cusset assisted Bertaut in the compilation of much of the documentary

---

[1] *Bibliothèque des auteurs de Bourgogne*, 2 Vols., Dijon, 1742; *Bertaut*, Vol. I, p. 44.

[2] Roberti, *op. cit.*, vol. II, pp. 685–687.

[3] See *Mémoire pour servir de preuve qu'un évêque est habile à succéder quoiqu'il ait été religieux*, s.l., by Dony d'Attichy himself.

[4] Archives Municipales, Chalon-sur-Saône, Série BB, 12; Tour de la Massonnière given to the Minims.

[5] *ibid.*, BB, 11; permission to build; the initial *Ordonnance*, given by the Duc de Mayenne in 1595. See also the funeral oration pronounced by the Minim Gérard Guerin on the death of the Marquis d'Huxelles in 1661, incorporated in the *Illustre Orbandale*.

[6] *ibid.*, AA, 26; BB, 12.

material which Bertaut used and which he included in the second volume. The high-sounding and recherché title comes from the supposed name of the ancient village of the Gauls upon which the Romans built their town of Cabilonnum.[1] Bertaut made a distinct division between the secular history (Part I) and the ecclesiastical history (Part II, which also included a number of transcriptions of charters, documents etc.). Part I is sub-divided under the following headings: *Antiquités chalonnaises – Histoire des Comtes – Entrées des Souverains – Guerres de religion – Privilèges – Eloges funèbres;* it is obviously an attempt at studying in the microcosm of a town the whole history of a nation. As far as the local history of Chalon is concerned, *l'Illustre Orbandale* broke virtually new ground. Nearly every town in France was to have its history written between the middle of the seventeenth century and the Revolution; the interest in antiquity coupled with national pride and the natural love that men have for their own town brought about the popularity of this genre. Those local histories which already existed at the beginning of the seventeenth century were inadequate in the light of more recent archaeological discovery; at the same time, after the ravages of the Wars of Religion, the consolidation of urban life brought about radical changes. *L'Illustre Orbandale* with its illustrations of Roman pottery and statuary and with its account of the part it played in the recent wars is typical of its age: much of the work is mere compilation; inscriptions and charters are transcribed and printed without any critical comment; whole funeral sermons are included.

Two other members of the Order collected and published documents of purely local interest. The first, Antoine Ruteau, is the more considerable; his *Annales de la Province et Comté d'Hainault*, published in Mons in 1648, were originally the work of François Vinchant, Ruteau augmenting and editing the compilation. These annals form a substantial volume – 418 pages in-4, with many genealogical tables to illustrate the dynastic disputes that go to make up the bulk of the volume. Throughout, the object seems to have been to present a strictly chronological account of events down to 1558; dates are put in the margin. Ruteau states in the preface that he is going to illustrate the principle that the splendour of a nation depends on the antiquity of its nobility, its fear of God (piété) and its courage in adversity. Mons and the Comté d'Hainaut were in the Spanish Netherlands

---

[1] Bertaut's work was the subject of an article by J. Roy-Chevrier in *Mémoires de la Société d'histoire et d'archéologie de Chalon-sur-Saône*, Vol. 12, 1924, pp. 3–52.

but had once formed a part of the Carolingian Empire; its aristocracy was French, "Hainaut a eu l'honneur de servir de berceau de la noblesse française; on verra prendre sa naissance avec la monarchie française." The Comté d'Hainaut was eventually ceded to Louis XIV in 1659 by the Treaty of the Pyrenees (it is now part of the département of Nord), but Mons remained under Spanish sway until 1691. There would seem to be a strong propagandist element in the work of which the author must have been aware since the northern frontiers, then as in our own times, were disputed and fought over.

The remaining member of the Order to have published a historical document was Pierre Fenier. His *Relation du siège de Péronne* was published in Paris in 1682.[1] Péronne stands on the east bank of the the Somme with streams and marshes protecting it to the north and south; the source of Fenier's *Relation* is an eye-witness account of the siege in 1536 when Henri de Nassau, acting under orders of Charles V, laid siege to the town for eight weeks. Every method, including Greek fire,[2] was used in his attempt to take the town but its inhabitants mended every breach made in the walls and extinguished the fires caused by the incendiary arrows fired into the town. No reason is given why this account should have been published about 150 years after the event, nor is it apparent why a Minim should have undertaken the work. Little is known of Fenier, but it would seem reasonable to identify him with the Pierre Feinier (sic) mentioned by Thuillier [3] and said by him to have been, "Vir litterarum studiis maxime deductis sed praecipua pietatis exercitatione illustrator." Thuillier says that he joined the Order in 1671 at the age of 19, that he became deaf and later blind, dying in 1693. Any account of fortitude and endurance is probably worth recording, and particularly at times of national stress; the reader of this account in 1682 would find parallels between François 1er's battles against Charles V and Louis XIV's successful military endeavours which terminated in the Treaty of Nijmegen in 1678. In a sense then, this *Relation du siège de Péronne* takes its place with the works of Coste and Bertaut; it is an apotheosis, a work dedicated to God and to the glory of the French nation and King. Fenier's

---

[1] A reprint was made in Paris, 1882; it is this reprint which I have consulted. Fenier's manuscript was preserved in the Bibliothèque Municipale de Péronne, see A. Ledieu, *Catalogue des MSS de la Bibliothèque de Péronne*, Paris, 1897, p. 4. The whole library was destroyed during the war 1914–1918.

[2] *Relation etc.*, p. 53.

[3] Thuillier, *op. cit.*, II, pp. 144–145. The 1882 reprint of the *Relation* gives no information about Fenier other than that he was a Minim.

account of the siege closes with a description of the solemn procession and religious ceremony which marked the successful conclusion of the siege, and with a list of the privileges conferred upon the town by letters patent from François Ier in 1537.

The historical studies mentioned above form but a small part of the total output of books by members of the Order, yet they have some interest and some significance in themselves as examples of the presentation of historical material to the reading public in the seventeenth century. It is difficult to decide whether they had any special significance within the Order. A case, not a particularly flattering one, could probably be made out for the use of historical studies as a means of propaganda for the Order: good and evil were painted in their extreme forms, and amongst the heroes and heroines of the historical narrative were the forebears of patrons of the Order. Some material advantage doubtless accrued to the Order on account of the actual book-production of these studies, which was often attractive – Regnault's collection of Camaye's letters, the illustrated histories by Coste and even the works of Bertaut may all be considered as bibliophiles' pieces to-day. On the other hand a more favourable interpretation is possible: if to-day we have lost the taste for the baroque, we have also lost the taste for the literature of apotheosis and panegyric which is so closely associated with it. It is perfectly possible to accept as genuine expressions of feeling the eulogies contained in these studies and the strangely bombastic language in which they are couched. If these historical works are compared with the contemporary *Oraisons Funèbres*, – not Bossuet's so much as the lesser ones, because Bossuet transformed the funeral oration, turning mere eulogy into a moral lesson – the same style and the same content will be found; there is the same belief in the important role of France in the post-Tridentine world, the same belief in a France unified under a powerful monarch and a belief in the directing hand of God over the destiny of the nation. All this is voiced by such authors as Giry, Simon Martin and Claude Raffron in their writings on the French Saints; the profane histories are an extension of the same belief. The sharp reaction against the disorder and misery of the religious and dynastic wars of the previous centuries is clearly felt by the authors of these histories. The Order had suffered with the rest of the nation during these upheavals, but a writer like Coste could review the Renaissance and find in it a period of promise of established order. However much suffering there may still have been within the Order during the seventeenth century, it was possible for a Minim to see himself as an active rather than as a passive member of the Church Militant; the privations that he suffered because of his vows would tend to heighten this effect. It is quite in keeping, therefore, that Coste, a distant relative of the Calabrian founder of the Order should concluded his *Portraits des Rois de France* with a prayer for Louis XIII which is a supreme expression of confidence in the justice of the Gallican Church and belief in the triumph of the Counter-Reformation:

Seigneur par lequel les Rois règnent, faites que notre Roi Louis le Juste jouisse de cette faveur et de ce bonheur: que toutes les Grâces du Ciel pleuvent sur son chef sacré et auguste; les Bénédictions de la terre germent dessous ses pas; qu'elle ne reconnaisse en sa rondeur que son Sceptre et sa Couronne, et votre Ciel refuse sa lumière aux régions qui ne s'y courberont pas; que tout ce qui le bénira attire ses bénédictions, et que ce qui le maudira en soit maudit; l'œil de votre Providence luise sur ses conseils et conduise toutes ses actions. Ô Dieu des Armées, soyez le bouclier de sa défence et l'épée de ses victoires, faites descendre vos légions sur le champ de ses batailles; enclinez tous vos cieux à sa voix; venez monté sur vos Chérubins, ou sur les ailes du vent; touchez les montagnes qui s'opposent aux bons desseins de sa Majesté et les réduisez (sic) en poudre et en fumée.[1]

---

[1] *Portraits etc.*, p. 394. The *Prayer for the King's Majesty* in the *Book of Common Prayer* says the same thing but more simply.

CHAPTER X

ARTISTIC WORK

The attitude of members of the Order to the pictorial arts was not the subject of an official rule, and no Lesguillier attempted to define their place within the compass of the Minims' "sagesse." The only examples of secular art were done for the strictly practical purpose of illustrating text-books on anatomy, arts and crafts and natural science. Religious art certainly had its place as a vehicle for contemplation and meditation as well as in fulfilling the desire to surround the central act of worship with all that beauty could furnish. We can still see the rich adornment of the church of Santa Trinità dei Monti which captivated Niceron with its "trompe l'œil" effects; elsewhere the churches have disappeared and we have to rely on the testimony of seventeenth and eighteenth century guide books and infer from them the place that was probably accorded to pictorial art. We may also infer something from the examination of illustrated books of devotion since the importance accorded to illustrations is roughly analogous with that accorded to church decoration.

None of the Minim's churches in France can have competed for richness of decoration with the one at la Place Royale with its facade and "portail" by Mansart – eight Doric columns making up the first order; in the second, four Composite columns and a tympanum illustrating in bas-relief Sixtus V ordering Saint François de Paule to go to France.[1] The high altar was the result of a combined effort by two of the leading church decorators of the seventeenth century, Gilles Guérin and Jacques Sarrazin.[2] The chapels around the body of

---

[1] Two engravings by I. Marot giving views of the "couvent" are reproduced in the Appendix. I have taken the details concerning the chapels and facade from Dézallier de d'Argenville's *Voyage pittoresque de Paris*, Paris, 1757, pp. 282–285. General details of the artists referred to in this chapter have been taken from Thieme und Becker, *Allgemeines Lexikon der Bildenden Künstler*, Leipzig, 1907–1947.

[2] M. Digard, *J. Sarrazin, son œuvre, son influence*, Paris, 1935, p. 220.

the church were sumptuous: the first on the right, dedicated to Saint François de Paule, had as its altar-piece a picture of the Saint resuscitating a dead child (a favourite theme with illustrators and commentators of the life of the Founder); the walls of this chapel were adorned with nine panels depicting other scenes from the Saint's life, they were the work of pupils of Simon Vouet (1590–1649). The next chapel, dedicated to Saint Michel, contained a funerary medallion to Edouard Colbert de Villacerf, a fine example of the work of Coustou l'aîné (1658–1733). A third chapel, "sous l'invocation de Saint François de Sales," contained the sumptuous tomb of the Duc et Duchesses de Vieuville by Gilles Guérin (1609–1678) [1]; a further chapel contained a *Holy Family* by Sarrazin (1592–1660) [2] and medallions after designs by the same artist. Yet a fifth chapel contained a picture by Laurent la Hyre (1605–1656), whilst in the Sacristy there was a further picture of an episode in the Founder's life – the crossing of the Straits of Messina on his cloak – painted by Noël-Nicolas Coypel (1690–1734). Then there were in the library and in the gallery the paintings by Niceron to which reference has already been made. Three paintings were sent from Rome to the "couvent" at la Place Royale by the Minim Bernard Mathelin, but apart from their titles no details seem to have been preserved.[3]

The Minims at Lille had a church which visitors to the town were advised to visit. Here there were paintings by Arnauld de Vuez (1644–1720) and by his pupil Bernard Joseph Wamps (1689–1750). They also had some stained glass windows by the important Flemish glass-painter Abraham van Diepenbeck (1596–1675).[4] At Tours, where several craftsmen had joined the Order while they were at work on the building of the new "couvent," there were other members who were artists – Antoine Mangeant, Julien Gondée, Paul de Saint-Anatole and J. Damoiseau.[5] Work by local artists and by members was probably a common feature in the provincial "couvents." and was almost certainly of the utmost simplicity and poverty; the inventory of the contents of the Sacristy of the "couvent" at Dijon does not

---

[1] M. Digard, *op. cit.*, pp. 207–208. Fragments now in the Louvre, 1326–1329, Tombeau de Charles Duc de Vieuville, surintendant des finances, + 1653 et de sa femme Marie Bouhier de Beaumarchais + 1663. Marbre. Ex Minimes de la Place Royale.

[2] M. Digard, *op. cit.*, plate XII, shows a design of this subject. It is not known which is the one referred to by Dézallier de d'Argenville. See also Digard, p. 126.

[3] Thuillier, II, pp. 306–307; Roberti, II, pp. 355–356.

[4] *Guide des étrangers à Lille*, Anon, Lille, 1772, pp. 104–105.

[5] L'abbé Rolland, *op. cit.*, pp. 281, 286–287. See also E. Giraudet, *Les artistes tourangeaux*, Tours, 1885, p. 8, p. 105.

suggest any great wealth of plate and furnishings [1]. A large proportion of the plate was probably surrendered to help pay for the costly wars at the end of the seventeenth century and only one inventory of silver had been preserved.[2] Much that survived Louis XIV was probably plundered during the Revolutionary period.

Other church furnishings were not remarkable,[3] but there is sufficient evidence from what has been said to show the spirit of the Order was reflected in the decoration, or absence of it, of their churches. Henry Lemonnier in his *Art français au temps de Richelieu et de Mazarin* wrote [4]:

... après l'ébranlement terrible des guerres de religion et les secousses qu'avaient subies les âmes, on éprouvait dans la grande masse de la nation un singulier besoin de repos ... On ne demandait plus à la religion d'être militante mais simplement agissante.

This is true but needs qualification. The rich tombs and neo-classical façades were an expression of this quest for calm and stability; but the Order, in common with many other "croyants," felt that man was still torn asunder and was menaced within and without by fears from which contemplation upon the person of the crucified Christ and his Saints and Martyrs could alone save them. Hence we find at the same time expressions of two conflicting tendencies: the one calm, serene, rationalist; the other emotive, restless, agonised – the juxtaposition, within one building often enough, of classical and baroque elements.

The close of the sixteenth century and the first half of the seventeenth saw remarkable developments in the art of book illustration. This was the period when the engraved metal plate finally triumphed over the carved wood block and when the method of chiaroscuro printing from a single plate was developed whereas, duting the early sixteenth century, such effects could only be produced by using two or three blocks for the one print. The production of well illustrated books on technical subjects must be considered as one of the major achievements of members of the Order, and the works of Niceron, Maignan and Plumier are supreme examples of this art. The representation of Christ

[1] Archives Départementales, Côte-d'Or. Uncatalogued, see Bibliography, Manuscripts, (Côte-d'Or), under Minimes de Dijon.

[2] Archives Départementales, Saône-et-Loire. See Bibliography, Manuscripts, (Saône-et-Loire), under Minimes de la Guiche.

[3] An interesting exception being at Beauregard in Auvergne; see the article by C. Bussac, *Un jubé auvergnat de l'ancienne église des Minimes de Beauregard*, in *Monuments historiques de la la France*, Vol. V, Paris, 1959, pp. 111–115.

[4] Paris, 1893, p. 108.

and the Saints became as important an adjunct to certain types of work of devotion as good engravings and line-drawings became for text-books; the Minims were fortunate in securing the aid of some of the foremost artists and engravers of the seventeenth century to illustrate works of this kind. Contemplation upon the Passion and scenes of martyrdom was heightened by the visual image; Louis Martz has prefaced his work *The Poetry of Meditation* with a reproduction of a painting by Georges de la Tour in which we see by the light of a candle a girl gazing into a mirror while the fingers of the left hand explore the eye-sockets of a skull; he shows thereby that chiaroscuro was an admirable vehicle for this type of contemplation[1].

Meditation is induced by appeal to the visual image in a remarkable work by the Minim Jean-Jacques Courvoisier, a native of Mons, and at one time Provincial of the Provincia Flandro-Belgica. *Le thrône royal de Jésus Nazaréen, Roy des affligés* (Antwerp, 1642) has an engraved title-page which is signed "P. Bal. fecit et execudit"; beneath a rich baldachino, with two angels holding aside the canopy, Christ is seen on the throne of glory; the crown of thorns on his head and the wounds on hands, feet and sides are clearly visible; he wears the purple cloak that was put on him at the trial. On either side of a flight of steps leading to the throne are angels holding the instruments of the Passion, while at the foot of the steps are, on the left, Saint Job and, on the right, Saint Laurence sitting on a grill under which a fire of logs is burning. Between the two Saints are the arms of the family of Albert de Ligne, Prince de Brabançon (to whom the work is dedicated). The title of the book is on the steps.[2] I am unable to establish with any certainty the identity of "P. Bal"; it seems likely that it is Pieter Balten who worked in Antwerp and who died in 1598; no artist contemporary with Courvoisier can be identified with the signature on this engraving, so that it is to be assumed that Courvoisier and Jean Galle, who did the remainder of the illustrations, took this example of Balten's work as a frontispiece.

[1] Yale U.P., 1952 and in *Yale Paperback* with reproduction of the painting on the cover, 1962.
[2] The copy in the British Museum (4411.i.16) is remarkable in having a coloured version of this frontispiece done on thick vellum; the copy in the Bibliothèque Nationale is identical except for the frontispiece which is printed on paper and is not coloured. Another work by Courvoisier to have a coloured title page was *Les extases de la belle Malceda*, Brussels, 1632, of which there is a copy in the Bibliothèque Nationale (D. 7216) with original binding, ex-Minimes de la Place Royale. Titlepage shows in two panels at top, "Thronus eius flamma ignis (Dan. 7)" and "Thronus Salomonis. 3 Reg. 10"; below, left of title, "Serissma Prin. Isab. Clara Eug." in nun's habit and, on right of title "Malceda Regina Saba." At bottom "Phil. de Mallery fecit." (i.e. Philippe de Mallery, engraver, born in Antwerp in 1598).

It is at least possible that the work may have inspired Courvoisier to write his contemplation on the Passion. The fifteen plates which illustrate the text are the work of the Flemish artist Jan (Jean) Galle (1600–1676), one of a family of engravers and designers working in Antwerp; they are signed "Ioan. Gall execudit"; some bear the additional signatures of "Ioann. Stradanus" and "Ioann. Collaert," being the work of Jan van der Straet and Jan Collaert respectively. Stradanus (1523–1605) was one of those Flemish engravers who worked for part of the time in Rome, and Jan Collaert (born 1590) was the third son of Hans Collaert who had also worked in Rome; Galle himself was susceptible to Italian influences which were powerful amongst the Flemish artists at the beginning of the seventeenth century, so that the influence of Carracci and Caravaggio is discernible, particularly in the attitude of some of the soldiers and attendants and in the effects of the lighting. The plates, the exclusive work of Galle unless otherwise stated, are as follows:

I. *Washing of the feet.* Chiaroscuro effect by light of two candles. Judas Iscariot in left-hand corner with a cloven-footed devil squatting by his side and shouting up to him; the money-bag is clearly visible in Judas's girdle.

II. *Christ crowned with thorns;* he is holding a cross and giving the sign of benediction. Blood from his side flows into a chalice. In the middle distance, Jerusalem; hills in the background. The words *Torcular Calcavi Solus* at top.

III. *The Last Supper.* Devil with dog-like face and bat's wings on his tail beneath the table, at the feet of Judas; the money bag is visible. Light from a strange double lamp hanging over the middle of the table. Christ holds up a Host on which there is the sign of the Cross.
(Ioann. Stradanus inven. Ioann Collaert sculp. Ioann. Galle execudit).

IV. *In the Garden.* Oval frame. Christ praying in the centre. Soldiers led by a man carrying a lantern come into the garden from the left. The garden has a wooden fence and a lych gate. The Apostles are sleeping on the right of the picture. Above, an angel with a chalice and Host.[1]

V. *Before Caiaphas.* Chiaroscuro effect. The soldiers are fiercely armed and well armoured in mediaeval armour. One of the attendants of Caiaphas or one of the Elders wears spectacles!! [2]

---

[1] It is interesting to compare this rather "wooden" picture with the extremely fluid treatment of the subject by Jacques Callot (see later) at Chatsworth and reproduced by A. Blunt, *Art and architecture in France 1500–1700*, London, 1953, Plate 85(A).

[2] This extraordinary anachronism is not without a parallel. In the Musée des Arts décoratifs, Bibliothèque Maciet, Vol. 418(6) there is an engraving by Stephen Baudet from a painting by Le Valentin, *Reddite Caesari quae sunt Caesaris*, in which one of the onlookers wears spectacles. It is presumably meant to signify incomprehension, but it is also interesting to note that the phrase "Hardness of heart" is "Caecitas cordium" in the Vulgate; on the other

VI. *Christ bound.* A lantern on the ground and a sort of portable brazier carried aloft cast a gloomy light on the scene. Christ is bound; he is being mocked and someone spits upon him.

VII. *The Elders send him before Pilate.* Vigorous action of the accusers. Scribe shown in semipontifical clothes; he also wears spectacles.

VIII. *Before Pilate.* Christ mute before his accusers.

IX. *The flagellation.* Christ, bound to a central pillar, in a dark dungeon; he is beaten with birches and he is whipped. An aureole over Christ's head is the only source of light.
(Stradanus, Collaert and Galle).

X. *Pilate washes his hands.* Soldiers with hallebards form a cortège as Christ is led away by an evil-looking dwarf with huge, mis-shapen legs. He is reminiscent of one of the grotesque figures by Breughel.

XI. *The crown of thorns.* Two men holding a stick between them ram the crown down upon the head of Christ who is seated. A third man spits in his face, a fourth jeers. In Christ's right hand there is a long reed.

XII. *Ecce homo.* Pilate shows Christ to the crowd. Two barbarous-looking soldiers attend him. A turbaned dwarf leers up from the left.

XIII. *Procession to Golgotha.* Christ falls beneath the Cross and is recognised by Mary Magdalene. The Virgin can be seen in the background. The soldiers urge on the fallen Christ with blows.

XIV. *Et tenebræ factae sunt in universam terram. Et obscuratus est sol.* Good use of lighting effects to emphasise a traditional subject.
(Ioann. Collaert).

XV. *Descent from the Cross.* Traditional

The designers of this set of picture have striven to obtain the maximum effect from lighting and from the use of grotesque and ugly faces to convey the idea of torment and anguish; the work should be considered in connexion with the Minims' habit of contemplation upon the suffering of humanity, and is an excellent example of the fusion of all the emotive tendencies which characterise the art of the counter-reformation.

The devotion of the Order to the person of its Founder is obvious in every aspect of the Minims' work. The portrait of Saint François de Paule was originally executed by the French artist Jean Bourdichon (c. 1460–c. 1520) who worked largely as a court painter to Anne de Bretagne, wife of Charles VIII and then of Louis XII, both of whom were favourable to the establishment of the Order within their kingdom. The portrait was used in the process of canonization of the Saint. An account of the making of the wax mould is given in Antoine Dondé's life of Saint François [1]:

hand the Apostles were sometime depicted in glasses in XVth century German art, see plates 37 and 38 at the end of Vol. I of the *Catalogue of the Library of the British Optical Association.* Also *St. John Baptist with Scribes and Pharisees,* Murillo (1618-1682) in Fitzwilliam Museum, Cambridge, Pharisees in spectacles.

[1] *Les figures et abrégé de la vie, de la mort et des miracles de Saint François de Paule,* Paris, 1671.

Le 19 jour de juillet de l'an ... 1513, honorable homme Jean Bourdichon, Peintre du Roi (Louis XII) ... citoyen de Tours, âgé de 56 ans ...
a été reçu par nous Pierre Cruchet et Pierre Chabrion susnommés com-
missaires etc ... Après avoir juré sur les Evangiles ... examiné sur la
renommée, sur les mœurs et sur les morales de Frère François qui durant
sa vie était Général de l'Ordre des Minimes ... a dit ... que le Vendredi
Saint, jour auquel était expiré Frère François de Paule un peu après sa
mort il fut au couvent des Minimes proche le Parc du Plessis ou il vit le
corps dudit Frère François, pour faire son portrait et que pour cet effet il
moula et fit l'impression de sa face ainsi qu'elle était.
    ... le même Bourdichon a déposé qu'il était présent quand l'illustre
Princesse Madame la Comtesse d'Angoulême fit élever le corps dudit
défunt, hors de terre (où il était inhumé depuis dix ou douze jours) pour le
mettre dans un Sépulchre ... et qu'ayant aperçu la face du susdit défunt
aussi saine et entière que lors qu'il fut inhumé, il le moula dérechef afin d'en
avoir un plus véritable trait ...[1]

This portrait which is in the Vatican became the standard, and all
subsequent portraits are merely reproductions from Bourdichon's
original; such, for example, is the frontispiece in Claude Du Vivier's
life of Saint François.[2] But the most remarkable work on the life of the
Saint is Dondé's, from which the quotation above was taken. In the
Annales des Minimes de la Province de France (Paris) there is the following
reference to the preparation of the work, proof of the importance that
the Order as a whole accorded to it:

    1662. On a donné 400 livres au Frère Dondé, Quêteur du Couvent, pour
    graver les planches des Miracles de Saint François de Paule ... plus on
    lui a donné 100 livres en 1668 pour le même sujet.[3]

The book did not appear until 1671 but previously, in 1668, he had
published a work entitled *Portraits de quelques personnes signalées en piété
de l'Ordre des Minimes*. This work, which is found bound with his life
of Saint François, is a collection of portraits by such well-known artists
as Charles Le Brun, who worked for Colbert, and Simon Vouet, whose
religious paintings were sponsored by Louis XIII and Richelieu.
Dondé has included among these portraits one of Saint François de
Sales, a member of the Tiers-ordre, by Prévost; this is probably
Nicolas Prévost, a pupil of Simon Vouet. Le Brun executed the
symbolic title-page showing "Saint Michel, Protecteur de l'Ordre,"

---

[1] p. 93, facing is a reproduction of the Vatican portrait by Bourdichon.
[2] For the influence of Bourdichon on the iconography of the Saint see the article by le
Chanoine Fiot referred to on p. 4. Du Vivier's life of Saint François de Paule was printed
in Paris, 1609.
[3] MSS Mazarine, No. 2429, p. 176.

ARTISTIC WORK 223

and also a portrait of Pierre Moreau who had been possessed by the devil for forty years and whose tortured life became an important reference point in the work of several Minims – a humble person to have had his portrait painted by an artist who was chiefly engaged on the decoration of Versailles. Dondé's own scenes of the life of the Founder, eighty in all, are arranged four on a page; an example of his work is given in the Appendix. The title-page, which shows a pastoral scene by a river's bank, is inscribed "N. Poilly fec." and the same inscription is found at the bottom of the frontispiece showing Calabria and France seated either side of an ornamental frame in which an oval reproduction of the Bourdichon portrait is seen. Nicolas Poilly (1626–1696) was famous for his copperplates and had done engravings from the works of Philippe de Champaigne and Mignard. The scenes themselves are sometimes unsigned (Dondé himself engraved the plates?) others are signed "Lommelin" and some "Bosse" or "Campion." Abraham Bosse was an artist of some importance who lived from 1602–1676 and F. Campion was working during the first half of the seventeenth century.[1] Adrian Lommelin [2] was a well known Flemish illustrator working chiefly in Antwerp.

There is one example of collaboration between a Minim and an artist which, although of less importance than the examples already referred to, has interest of a provincial nature. Jacques Callot (1592–1635) was one of the most prolific and certainly one of the best known of all the French engravers. He ran away from his native Nancy when he was no more than a boy and spent many years in Rome, returning at the invitation of Charles, Duc de Lorraine, in 1622. Now the Dukes of Lorraine had always been considerable benefactors of the Minims of Nancy and of the whole Province; and when a Minim, Nicolas Julet, wrote a work in praise of the Virgin of Bon-Secours, *Miracles et grâces de Notre-Dame de Bon-Secours lez Nancy*,[3] it was Callot who engraved the frontispiece showing the interior of the chapel of the "couvent" at Bon-Secours, founded in the second decade of the century and recognised at the General Chapter held in Rome in 1617. E. Meaume describes the engraving in these words [4]:

Vue de l'intérieur d'une chapelle où se voit, au milieu du fond, un autel dont le rétable est garni d'un tableau représentant la Sainte Vierge cou-

---

[1] See A. Valabrègue, *Abraham Bosse*, Paris 1895, in E. Muntz, *Les artistes célèbres*, 57 vols.
[2] See B. Linnig, *La gravure en Belgique*, Antwerp, 1911; a dictionary of engravers.
[3] Nancy, 1630. See A. Calmet, *Bibliographie lorraine*, Nancy, 1751, p. 522.
[4] *Recherches sur la vie et les ouvrages de Jacques Callot*, 2 vols., Paris, 1860, Vol. II, pp. 130–131.

vrant de son manteau, à gauche des prélats, et, à droite, des princes. Deux soleils brillent, de chaque côté, au haut de ce tableau. Sur celui de gauche est écrit en caractères microscopiques Charitas.[1] On lit sur l'autre Humilitas. Sur le devant de l'autel on lit Miracles et Graces de Notre-Dame de Bon-secours lez Nancy. Sous le jubé de cette chapelle sont en prières, à gauche Saint Charles Borromée,[2] et, à l'opposite, Saint François de Paule, On lit au bas, vers la gauche, au pied des marches de l'autel, à la hauteur des genoux de Saint Charles: Iac. Callot fe., et au milieu: Imprimés du commandem(en)t de Monseig(neur) L'illustrissime Cardinal de Lorraine, puis, dans la marge: A Nancy par S. Philippe, Imprimeur de son Altesse, avec privilège, 1630.

Jacques de Bie (1581–1642?), who is chiefly known for his copperplate engravings from paintings by Rubens, was an art-dealer and an authority on numismatics. He and another numismatist, J-B. Duval, worked together on two works – one on French medals called *La France métallique* (Paris, 1636) and the other on the portraits of the Kings of France. The latter was very incomplete in the first edition, and the second edition (Paris, 1636) bore the title, *Les vrais portraits des rois de France, seconde édition augmentée de nouveaux portraits et enrichie des Vies des Rois par le R. P. H(ilarion) de Coste;* the licence to print it was signed by Mersenne whose biographer Coste was. The work is of little interest to-day and the modern reader is likely to find more interest in some of the details of the intricate frames rather than in the portraits themselves. Jacques de Bie's "Avis au lecteur" contains a reference to the collection of medallions and coins kept at the "couvent" at la Place Royale:

> Aussi afin qu'il n'y eût rien à désirer à la seconde édition de cet œuvre, je l'ai augmenté d'un particulier Abrégé de la vie des Rois ... ayant été assisté en ce travail par un Père Minime du Couvent de la Place Royale, auquel après le décès du Sieur du Val j'ai eu recours tant parce qu'il était intime ami de cet interprète du Roy ès langues orientales[3] et lui avait prêté plusieurs médailles tant des Rois que des Princes ... qui sont gardées en la Bibliothèque de ce Couvent lesquelles je vous ai fait voir en La France Métallique,[4] qu'à cause que mes amis m'adressent à lui comme à une personne zélée à l'honneur et à la gloire de la France.[5]

[1] The device of the Order; "Humilitas" is virtually a second device.

[2] Lorraine had been swept by political disasters and by plague; the invocation of S. Charles Borromeo was considered as helpful in times of trouble and the Minims favoured the cult of this Saint, dedicating some of their "couvents" to him. An article in *The Times*, 25 Jan. 1964, p. 11, on Jacques Callot, refers to him as "no mean artist"; the author also refers to the influence of the upheavals of the time on Callot.

[3] Duval was also an orientalist of some repute and the author of an Arabic-French dictionary.

[4] Unfortunately no reference is made in this work as to which medals, coins, seals etc. were from the Minims' collection.

[5] *Avis au Lecteur*, sig. ē.i.

Part of the interest of this reference comes from the fact that Mersenne included in the *Cogitata* a section on numismatics; there is also the fact that at Santa Trinità dei Monti the Minims had a fine collection of coins in what they called their "museum." [1]

[1] See Bibliography, Manuscripts (Private Archives, Rome).

CHAPTER XI

MEDICAL WORK

The references in Thuillier's necrology to those members who worked for any length of time in the Infirmaries or Pharmacies of the Order tend to follow a certain pattern – work within the cloister and without, a visit to Rome, return to the Province and, more often than not, death from infection contracted during their spell of duty. The entry under January 16 which refers to Louis d'Alençon, a friend of Mersenne, may be taken as typical [1]:

> ... vivus alter Aesculapius et secretorum Naturae indagator curiosus; non solum in saeculo, verum etiam in Religione fuit tum chyrurgus celebris, tum pharmacopola; ideoque plurimos Fratres laborantes, quin et exteros, sive Romae sive in Provincia Franciae cuius professus erat, egregie adjuvit, et ab extremis eripuit; fugiendæ tamen mortis secretum sibi non novit, eam quippe arte sua, suaque peritia vitare non potuit; illam autem placidam, et Sacramentis omnibus praemunitus, consecutus est in secessu Vicennensi, ubi Pharmacis praeerat ...

The office of pharmacist is one that occurs in most of the *Conclusions Capitulaires* and is it one that was often filled by the same member for two or more consecutive years; there was therefore some scope for a sense of vocation within the office and for acquiring experience. Those that are mentioned by Thuillier as being pharmacists or surgeons were at either Nigeon or Vincennes, rarely in the outlying "couvents"; for them to have been mentioned at all as such probably meant a more or less permanent tenure of office.

The visit to Rome by these members had a special significance. The French "couvent" of Santa Trinità dei Monti had an excellent botanic garden and a well stocked medical library. From Jean Le Brun, who died in 1603,[2] to Philippe Sergeant, Plumier and Feuillée, whose

---

[1] Thuillier, *op. cit.*, I, p. 16. Another early pharmacist at S. Trinità was François Peltret (1564–1609), see Thuillier, II, p. 185.
[2] Mgr. Fourier Bonnard, *op. cit.*, p. 187.

discoveries in the later XVIIth and early XVIIIth centuries led to a widening of the Pharmacopoeia, one can trace an almost unbroken line of French pharmacists and botanists who worked there, and whose knowledge was passed on by members of the Order who came to study in Rome before returning to conventual pharmacies.

Few members seem to have practised surgery, and of those who did at least two had acquired their knowledge before joining the Order.[1] The external appointment of "Surgeon" was sometimes made at the annual elections and one wonders whether there existed the same sort of rivalry between the conventual and lay medical practitioners as between the regular and secular clergy. However this may have been, the practice of medicine within the "couvents" was in the hands of amateurs for the most part, but this need not mean that they were any less skilful or that their remedies were the less potent to kill or cure. The little knowledge that we have concerning their remedies and methods comes from two sources – a small number of published works by members of the Order and a chance reference in John Evelyn's *Diary*. Evelyn visited what he called the "Bonnes-hommes" (sic) on two occasions, making it clear that it was at Chaillot (i.e. Nigeon) on the second occasion. He admired their buildings and library [2] and was particularly interested in a certain Friar Nicholas, "who being an excellent chymist showed me his laboratory and rare collection of spagyrical remedies. He was both Physican and Apothecary of the convent and instead of the names of his drugs, painted his boxes and pots with the figure of the drug or simple contained in them: he showed me as a rarity some ☿ of antimony: he had cured Monsieur Sancterre of a desperate sickness for which was building a monumental altar that was to cost 1500 pounds." [3] This is almost certainly Nicolas Blanchot whose pharmaceutical work at Nigeon is mentioned by Thuillier.[4] Evelyn's reference is interesting in that it adds a little to our knowledge of one of the major medical controversies of the seventeenth century. "Spagyrical" is defined by the *Oxford English Dictionary* as "alchemical," but in France the word meant almost exclusively the use of antimony; the symbol ☿ of antimony, meaning "Mercury of antimony", refers presumably to a free running or potable preparation

---

[1] Antoine Richer, d. 1660, Thuillier II, p. 226, and Jean Clergé, 1622–1688 who had been in the Army before taking his vows, Thuillier II p. 132.
[2] *Diary*, 27 Feb. 1644, Everyman Edition, I, p. 56.
[3] *ibid.*, 24 Feb. 1651, I, pp. 263–264. It is also worth noting that Evelyn commented enthusiastically on the botanic garden at S. Trinità dei Monti; 22 Feb. 1645.
[4] *Op. cit.*, I, p. 182.

of the metal. Now antimony was not a fashionable remedy in Paris in those days; Montpellier had advocated its use in imitation of the Arab cures which depended on it, but the medical school of Paris was rigidly set against its use which was considered dangerous and almost diabolical. In 1658, seven years after Evelyn's visit to Nicolas Blanchot, Louis XIV was in the field with his army in Flanders when he was taken seriously ill. A doctor summoned from Abbeville cured him with antimony, thereby establishing the remedy as acceptable and, more important, fashionable. Blanchot seems therefore to have been something of an experimentalist – and Paracelsus had at least one follower in Paris.

The Minim Jean Germain worked in Italy and in the conventual pharmacy at Avignon. His first published work was an Italian treatise on Comparative Anatomy [1] and has some claim to originality it its invitation to compare the skeletal structure of man and monkey, of mammal and bird. The trend in comparative studies at that time was towards the study of organs in the lower animals; human anatomy was a separate line of inquiry. Germain's work met opposition and was saved from oblivion by the Neapolitan, Luigi Riccio, who contributed an interesting preface, full of praise for the austerity of the Order of Minims and concludes with the following words:

> Ma io che particularmente reverisco questa S. Religione e professo portare particulare affetto a i figli di si digna madre, mosso da zelo caritativo, ho procurato che questa volta le leggi dell'austerità dessero luogo a quelle della Pietà, ed il Rigor de' pochi cedesse al beneficio de' molti; stimando esser cosa molto ingiusta ch'un opra cosi utile fusse maltratta dall' ingiurie del tempo, e un libro cosi necessario dovesse starsene sepellito da cosi profonda oblivione. E chi non giudicarà questa materia esser profittevole mentre tratta l'utilità, che da gli animali riceve il corpo humano? da quali anche l'istessa medicina se dice avere avuti i suoi principii.

The subsequent writings of Jean Germain are of little importance; in 1626 he translated into Italian the treatise *Conservation de la vue* by André Laurent, doctor to Henry IV. He then made two editions of a work called *Quintessence de la Chirurgie;* both these editions are signed "de notre pharmacie du couvent des Minimes d'Avignon" and are dated 1630 and 1640 respectively; the latter bears an epistle dedicatory to Cardinal Bicchi, in which the author seems at some pains to prove that anatomy is not always the work of atheists. The book itself is of

---

[1] *Breve e sostanziale trattato*, see Bibliography, sub Germain. See reproduction of the title-page in the Appendix.

no great interest, dealing simply with the diagnosis of injuries, fractures, abscesses and the like. The recipes for unguents, draughts and cataplasms are unoriginal and unadventurous. It catered for the general reader and may have had some value as a "First Aid manual" for within the cloister; it must have been in some demand for as late as 1674 an Italian translation of the work appeared in Rome.

One of the advantages that the specialist has over the tyro, the doctor over his patient, is that he can use a jargon which is incomprehensible. Molière exploited the comic possibilities of this. The advantage of medical jargon is that it stems from Greek which has always had prestige value in modern Europe. Jean Durelle, who took Mersenne's side against the English doctor Fludd, wrote a short work called *Onomatologie chirurgique*.[1] It is a vocabulary of medical terms giving their Greek originals and a few words of explanation. The title claims a general utility for the work and it takes its places with Germain's work of vulgarization, useful for the inexperienced members of the Order who had to care for the sick and dying and who found themselves in charge of a conventual infirmary or pharmacy.

Plague was rife during the XVIIth century in every part of France. It is difficult to obtain any accurate statistics; indeed it may have accounted for fewer deaths than smallpox, which was endemic. Nevertheless plague struck with dramatic violence and a town would find its population decimated within a short space of time. It is not surprising that men should have seen it as a sign of divine retribution and have sought supernatural rather than natural remedies. The clergy were often entreated to say special masses to ward off the pestilence, and churches in areas of extreme exposure to the infection, in the South of France in particular, were dedicated to Saint Roch and to Saint Charles Borromeo, whose intercessions were believed to be singularly effective in times of plague. The religious orders were, on the whole, prominent in a more active care for the sick than merely seeking spiritual aid. Members of the Order of Minims rendered conspicuous service to the community in Lyon, Avignon and other plague-ridden towns; many of them, as we have seen, had acquired medical knowledge and were able to carry out rudimentary dispensing in their pharmacies. In the Place Royale from 1646 to 1672, the office of pharmacist was filled by Isaac Quatroux (1593–1673); his attitude to the problem of plague and divine retribution may be examined in a *Traité de la peste*,

[1] *Onomatologie chirurgique ou explication des mots grecs appartenant à la chirurgie*, Lyon, 1644; see Bibliography sub Durelle.

contenant sa définition ...[1] which he published shortly before his death:

Les auteurs de notre siècle ont donné à la peste le nom de la verge ou du fléau de Dieu; parce que la cause de ce mal étant le plus souvent inconnue à l'esprit humain, il ne peut avoir sa source principale que dans la justice de Dieu qui, lassé des iniquités des hommes les punit par ce châtiment rigoureux ... C'est Dieu qui l'envoie sur la terre ... comme un châtiment visible de sa justice ... Mais en ces siècles où il semble que les hommes jouissent d'une plus grande tranquillité ... il semble que Dieu se soit reservé le fléau de la peste pour châtier nos offenses. Ce fléau n'a pas été sans présage, le ciel nous a fait voir des comètes en des lieux différents ... c'est donc à nous de nous armer contre ce rude fléau par les douleurs et par les larmes de la pénitence; il nous faut revêtir de l'armure de Dieu ... c'est à nous de lui demander grâce et lumière pour nous servir des remèdes propres à nous préserver de ce mal quand il sera produit en nous par des causes purement naturelles.[2]

Having done, as it were, his duty towards the Omnipotent, he then set out some practical ideas for thwarting Him: food should be wrapped in oilcloth; bed linen should be thoroughly washed and aired; soiled mattresses should be burnt; animals, poultry and pigeons should be separated from the dwelling quarters. The greater part of the book is taken up with recipes for cataplasms, unguents, pomanders and draughts which betoken a wide, if not skilful, use of the pharmacopoeia. For bringing the buboes to a head he advocates an unfailing cataplasm made from chicken dung, live snails and quicklime (p. 167).

One of the sanitary measures imposed would frequently be the closing of all "couvents"; in this case pestilence brought great hardship to the mendicant orders who were dependent on their liberty to go about the countryside making their "quête." In Pont-Saint-Esprit [3] and in Aix-en-Provence [4] there are references to a tax being levied on the inhabitants to provide a small donation for the Minims who had been reduced to the level of the barest subsistence; in Avignon they may have fared a little better:

Paupertati religiosorum mendicantium qui in dies ex piorum tantum eleemosinis corrogatis vivebant, ne ex claustra suspecto contagionis tempore alimenta quaerere cogerentur, sed eorum incolumitati esset consultum, pia

---

[1] Paris, 1671; see Bibliography.
[2] pp. 1–11.
[3] Archives Municipales, BB, 11 fol. 153 (1640); also, in 1671, a grant in kind to help their ministry to the sick, BB, 17.
[4] Archives Municipales, BB, 99 fol. 344. An infirmary was established during the plague of 1629–1630 in the Couvent des Minimes d'Aix; see Achard, *Dictionnaire de Provence*, Vol. IV, p. 416.

civitatis liberalitas omnia ad victum necessaria durante calamitoso illo tempore, ipsis abunde suppeditavit.[1]

In Lorraine, however, and in the eastern parts of Champagne war added its own horrors to those of the plague and special reference is made to the plight of the Minimes de Bassing.[2]

I have already mentioned the affray at Béziers during the plague of 1652, when the Minims refused to allow their "couvent" to be used for an infirmary as it had been in 1629–1630; elsewhere, however, their conduct seems to have been one of submission to the will of the civil authorities, and several of their members died bringing succour to the sick and dying.[3]

[1] L. de Franchis, *Historia Avenionensis contagionis*, Avignon, 1633; p. 53.
[2] Archives Départementales, Meurthe-et-Moselle, Série H., 987.
[3] B. Vanel, *Histoire du couvent des Minimes de Lyon*. Lyon, 1879, p. 128. Also L. de Franchis *op. cit.*, pp. 82–83.

CONCLUSION

The history of the Order in the eighteenth century, in common with that of the other orders, is one of steady decline. Large financial assets had accrued over the centuries and these were often for the benefit for a "couvent" where there were only two or three regulars in residence. The bishops were empowered to close down such "couvents" and a Commission des Réguliers was set up to report on the whole question of the monastic orders, since they had become an obvious target for the acrimonious criticisms levelled against the Church by the Philosophes. Lavisse [1] gives the total number of regulars as 26,674 in 1774, falling to 17,500 in 1790. According to the statistics presented by the Commission des Réguliers in 1768, the Minims had 975 members in France; assuming no change between 1768 and 1774 (Lavisse's date) and assuming a fall proportional to the National total, the Order must have dropped to about 850 at the time of the suppression. Agen, founded in 1661, was closed down in the middle of the eighteenth century [2]; Fublaines, near Meaux, was amalgamated with the newly founded "couvent" at Crécy [3]; Carcassonne was closed in 1771 and all its finances transferred to Narbonne. [4] About one in three of the "couvents" belonging to the Order were closed or scheduled for closing by the time of the report (those marked with an asterisk in the list given on pages 22–27). The following examples will further show the decline as it affected individual "couvents".

The decline was not only numerical; monastic discipline which had been well maintained during the seventeenth century declined during the period of laxity which followed the death of Louis XIV.

---

[1] *Histoire de France*, Vol. IX, i, Paris, 1910, pp. 145–146.
[2] J-G-P. Lauzun, *Les Couvents d'Agen*, Agen, 1889.
[3] Archives Départementales, Seine-et-Marne, 218H, 1-6.
[4] Mahul, *Cartulaire et Archives de l'ancien diocèse de Carcassonne*, Vol. IV, pp. 473–474.

Couvent	Members	Date	REFERENCE
Bar-le-Duc.	1	1790	*Pouillé du Diocése de Verdun.*
Bordeaux	30[1]	1730	Archives de la Gironde, G. 829.
	10	1786	,, ,, ,, ,, , G. 552.
	Nil	1787	,, ,, ,, ,, , ,, .
Blaye.	12	1730	,, ,, ,, ,, , G. 829.
	5	1756	,, ,, ,, ,, , G. 552.
	3	1786	,, ,, ,, ,, , ,, .
	Nil	1787	,, ,, ,, ,, , ,, .
Serres.	12	XVIIth cent.	Lepage, *Communes de la Meurthe.*
	9	1712	,, , ,, ,, ,, ,, .
	3	1782	,, , ,, ,, ,, ,, .
Chartres.	4	1768	Commission des Réguliers.
	2	1790	Archives de l'Eure-et-Loir, H. 4225.
Lyon.	28	1768	Commission des Réguliers.
	17	1790	Vanel, *Hist. du Couvent des Minimes de Lyon*, p. 276.

This decline is not entirely unheralded by events at the end of the seventeenth century, however; complaints of drunkenness and debauch began to appear in the Provincials' reports; discipline in the library became slacker and the period of intellectual activity seems to have ended.[2] The process of stagnation was occasionally halted; in the early part of the eighteenth century Feuillée continued the largely unfinished work of Plumier, completing the botanical survey of the Antilles and, pushing his researches further afield, making important discoveries in the Andes. The study of mathematics continued to be a speciality in the French "couvent" of Santa Trinità dei Monti, where an important edition of Newton's *Principia* was prepared by the two Minims Leseur and Jacquier.[3] Both were versatile and active members of the Order, preparing a new life of the Founder and history of the work of the Order which was never published, unfortunately so, since

[1] An exceptional increase over numbers in the seventeenth century; in 1695 the Minimes de Bordeaux had declared, "13 prêtres, 3 frères clercs, 8 frères oblats, un valet à gages de 95 livres par an et un autre fort vieux (sic) homme que nous tenons par pure charité."

[2] In the *Livre pour les chapitres, Visites Provinciales etc.*, 1618–1716, kept by the Minimes de Serres and preserved in the Archives Départementales, Meurthe-et-Moselle, Série H, 1077, under the year 1682 we find the Provincial making the following complaints (a) Buildings being pulled down without permission and the bricks and slates sold. (b) Members eating "gras" and in company with "séculiers." (c) Drunkenness – repeated again in 1693. (d) In 1693 complaints about lending books from the libraries of the Order to outsiders and the failure of members to return books when they were transferred from one "couvent" to another.

B. Vanel, *Histoire du couvent des Minimes de Lyon*, Lyon, 1879, spends many pages deploring the laxity of discipline, but most of his examples are from the XVIIIth century.

[3] 3 Vols., Rome, 1739, 1740, 1742.

they alone of their contemporaries were capable of understanding the significance of the work which had been done. They were both consulted as civil engineers in the enormous task of the restoration of the dome of St. Peter's which threatened to collapse; they were both associate members of the Académie des Sciences, Paris, and Jacquier was also an associate member of the Royal Society and of the academies of Berlin and St. Petersburg. Leseur and Jacquier may be taken as representatives of that interesting group of enlightened ecclesiastics who could claim affinity with the Philosophes; but, in general, intellectual activity passed out of the Church in the eighteenth century and became rather the prerogative of those who attacked orthodoxy. In this way there was accomplished a process that had been going on for centuries and which characterises the whole Renaissance in Europe – the secularisation of wisdom.[1] If any synthesis of the spiritual and intellectual life of the Order is to be made, it can only be done by examining the idea of *wisdom* as it was conceived by the members; but this idea of wisdom is itself complex and requires definition. Between the idea that wisdom was the gift of God and Charron's idea of its being a naturally acquired perfection of man as man, there was room for a wide divergence of interpretation, of which, perhaps, the idea of "honnêteté" is one. In the *Book of Exodus* wisdom is clearly distinguished from intelligence and craftsmanship and, like the other two, it is God-given:

Locutusque est Dominus ad Moysem, dicens: Ecce vocavi ex nomine Beseleel filium Uri ... et implevi eum spiritu Dei, sapientia, et intelligentia et scientia in omni opere.[2]

This distinct and superior "sapientia" is wisdom in the sense of the aphorism in the *Book of Wisdom*, "Happy is the man who findeth wisdom"; but a quite different interpretation of wisdom is found in the context of Solomon [3] where it embraces "intelligentia" (i.e. the mental acumen displayed in solving riddles, legal skill and political subtlety) and "scientia in omni opere" (i.e. encyclopaedic knowledge, trees, beasts, architecture and so on). The difference between the distinct "sapientia" of *Exodus* and the composite notion in the context of Solomon is paralleled to some extent in Greek philosophy in the

[1] In this part of the *Conclusion* I have been much helped by a reading of E. Rice, *The Renaissance idea of Wisdom*, Harvard University Press, 1958.
[2] Exodus, XXXI, 1–3; A.V. gives "wisdom, understanding, knowledge *and* workmanship," thus giving four basic elements in place of the three in the *Vulgate*.
[3] *3 Regum, passim*, especially IV, 30–34 (A.V. *1 Kings*, chapters and verses same).

difference between the Platonic and Aristotelian conceptions of wisdom; in the former, wisdom is the contemplation of eternal and immutable ideas; in the latter, it is a knowledge of first causes attainable by investigation. The one is passive, the other invites mental activity. These two tendencies were handed down to the Church, the early Fathers transforming the pagan idea and seeing in the person of Christ the very embodiment of wisdom; to be truly wise was to follow the divine example. Out of the New Testament ideal of righteousness there came the ideal of perfection which could be attained only by isolation and withdrawal from the the world. This is the monastic ideal in its purest form and implies a suspicion of, if not a complete shunning of worldly knowledge. But the Aristotelian revival of the twelfth century and the rediscovery at a later period of the stoic conception of human wisdom complicated the issue; wisdom henceforward could only be defined in terms of blending the intellectual and the spiritual means of ascent. The Order of Minims grew up at the time of the European renaissance, when the whole notion of wisdom was undergoing a process of secularisation; although it did not appear so at the time, this change was probably more far-reaching in its effects than the Reformation. We have seen that the early history of the Order in France was one of continual opposition to the Huguenots; gradually this strife between contending religious factions became less important than opposition to certain philosophical and social ideas; accordingly, the defence of orthodoxy and the preservation of the primitive simplicity of the Faith called for those who were able to grasp the meaning of the new philosophy and at the same time lead a life that was in keeping with the traditions of poverty and charity so urgently restated by Saint Francis of Assisi and, later, by the Founder of the Minims. Such men are rare and it is, perhaps, some measure of the significance of the Order that Mersenne, Jean-François Niceron, Maignan and Plumier should each have belonged to it during a period covering little more than 60 years, and also that Nicolas Barré should have been their contemporary. But, for reasons that are perfectly well known and which lie outside the scope of this study, in the eighteenth century the weight of opposition to the Church was such that no religious body could hope to stand.

However remarkable may have been the role of Mersenne and his successors in bringing scientific investigation to the defence of orthodox religion, it must not be supposed that this was the rôle of the Order at large; neither is it possible to suppose that the majority were in sympathy with what they were trying to do or had any understanding of the problems they were trying to solve – the illiteracy of some and the naïveté of others make such an idea ridiculous. However fascinating may have been the intellectual activity of the Order, it must be considered as secondary to its spiritual life and as taking a minor place in the general consensus of opinion of its members. Their idea of wisdom – their "sagesse" – lay almost exclusively in a submission to Divine will and in a subjection of mind and body to the harsh stringencies of monastic discipline; in view of the brilliant intellectual work of some of their members and the craftsmanship of others, it is something of a disappointment to find that the book by Jacques Ladore, bearing the title *Digestum Sapientiae Minimitanae*,[1] is nothing more than an exposition of the *Rule* of the Order and a long account of the various Bulls, statutes and articles of canon law which governed it. Nevertheless, this gives an excellent indication of what the author is pleased to call the "sal sapientiae"; the almost childlike obedience that members vowed to observe calls to mind the Pascalian phrase, "La sagesse nous envoie à l'enfance." [2] Barré insists on the same point, so does Dupuys in his *L'Homme de Dieu dans l'état de la perfection*,[3] and so do the historians of the Order who emphasize the humility and submission of the Founder and of his most illustrious followers. We can discern in the development of the Order a departure from the Founder's intention; intellectual activity played little or no part in the initial stages, and the *Ratio Studiorum* of Lesguillier shows the limitation that it was seen fit to impose upon the exercise of the intellect. The Baconian idea that "studies serve for delight, for ornament ..." had no place in the "sagesse" of the Minims; Moreau and Barré, both promising intellects, subjected their powers to the dictates of their religious scruples and thereby represent the highest ideals for which the Order stood. Puritanism, or rigorism, is a European manifestation and, like other puritan or rigorist sects, the Minims tended to mistrust the intellect; accordingly the pursuit of learning received little official encouragement. The significance of the Minims' contribution to the religion and philosophy of seventeenth-century France can only be understood when the spiritual and intellectual are taken together, when the emotional outbursts of a Chavineau are read with the scientific works of Niceron or Maignan.

[1] Paris, 1664.
[2] *Pensées*, Brunschvicq, No. 271.
[3] Paris, 1682.

When Martin Lister visited Plumier in his cell at la Place Royale, he was shocked to find the Minim ill and wasted with fever and yet unwilling to partake of food more sustaining than a "little nasty, slimy fish and herbs"; his exclamation is that of the enlightened humanist: "What will not blind prejudice do against all human reason?" We have in this interview between the monk and the learned man of the world, not for a moment admitting that the cloister could provide the discipline necessary to this man for his work, an epitome of the whole shift of emphasis from the spiritual to the intellectual elements of wisdom; an epitome of monastic perfection on the one hand and of the "honnête homme" on the other. Lister's subsequent interview with the Marquis de l'Hôpital is almost equally revealing; Plumier, for all his brilliant work, could not be admitted to membership of the Académie des Sciences because he was a regular, and this in spite of the fact that Mersenne had played a leading part in its inception. Lister does not mention the other side of the picture, that a member of the Order was forbidden to take any academic distinction save the theological degrees at Alcalá de Henarez. Thus the cleavage between the regular clergy and the world at large is emphasized; learning was passing from the cloister to the academy. Although Leseur and Jacquier in the eighteenth century were members of academies, showing a more liberal attitude on both sides, it was too late to bring about any rapprochement of significance.

The monk has always been an object of derision. Boccaccio, Chaucer, La Fontaine and Voltaire each in his turn has provoked our mirth and often enough our disgust at the rapacious and lascivious habits of the regular clergy; it is always easier to expose vice than to extol virtue. The "Saint homme de chat bien fourré, gros et gras" [1] was a "Dévot ermite, un chat faisant la chattemite" and, in spite of a protestation to the contrary at the end of the fable, "Le Rat qui s'est retiré du monde" represents a monk.[2] Over a hundred and fifty years before Lister visited Plumier, the monasteries had been abolished in this country; the prejudice he displays may therefore have had something of a traditional bias. But even to the least prejudiced there appears something anachronistic about the continuance of the religious orders in the seventeenth and eighteenth centuries. The proliferation of orders in even the small towns – a place like Agen had 20 "couvents" at one time, 12 belonging to male and 8 to female orders – meant that

[1] La Fontaine, *Fables*, VII, 16, *Le chat, la belette et le petit lapin.*
[2] *Fables*, VII, 3.

petty jealousies and rivalries were brought to the forefront and obscured the purposes for which the orders had been founded. Three new orders grew up at approximately the same time as the Minims and flourish to-day – the Ursulines, founded by Saint Angela (1511–1540), the Oratorians, founded by Saint Philip Neri (1515–1595) and the Jesuits, founded by Saint Ignatius of Loyola (1491–1556). It is significant that the two latter are not really orders at all but congregations, having an entirely different conception of monastic rule from that of the mediaeval orders; they are probably better adapted to the ways of modern life. The Ursulines, although deriving much of their inspiration from Franciscan ideals and therefore having an affinity with the Minims, were founded with the express purpose of going out into the world to teach the young and nurse the sick. They are now numerically stronger than either the Dominicans or Franciscans,[1] which is some measure of proof that, if an order was to reemerge after the upheavals of the revolutionary period, it had to have a strong social justification of its existence.[2]

The most justifiable prejudice against the orders was their proliferation in the towns, a direct consequence of which, by virtue of the immunities they enjoyed, was the unnecessary burden of taxation which fell on the townspeople. The Minims had often enough to elbow themselves into a town already encumbered with older orders. They fulfilled no apparant social function in the modern sense of the word, such as farming for the Cistercians or teaching for the Ursulines, but existed for the purpose of worship and the defence of the faith, for catechising and hearing confessions, for the administration of the sacraments and the granting of indulgences, all of which amounted to a social purpose in the seventeenth century. But it was probably this existence for itself and within itself which led to its failure to reappear in France after the Revolution. The Order is now confined to a few "conventi" in Calabria and elsewhere in Italy and to a few houses of Minimesses (of the Second Order) in Spain. An attempt to restart the Second Order in France during the Second Empire was abortive.

In the seventeenth century, an age of the court, the salon and the academy, there seems little place for the cloister. Whatever may have been the abuses, and they were many and serious, the orders provided opportunities for the exercise of intellectual ability by men and women

[1] The Ursulines numbered 13,000 in 1956 (*Chambers Encyclopædia*). See also P. Caraman, *Saint Angela*, London, 1963.
[2] There are, of course, exceptions such as the continuance of the Trappists.

whose secular education would have been scant: the seventeenth century orders are therefore linked to their mediaeval pedecessors by this tradition of learning. Also, operating through the influence of the confessional and through the Tiers-ordres, the religious orders had a refining influence on the laity. There is probably room for a detailed study of the influence of the orders on the intellectual life of France in the seventeenth century and on the social influence of the congregations and "confréries" that grew up in their shadow. It is the hope that the present study may throw some light on this influence. The Minims were, of course, only one of many orders but, by their artistic and literary work no less than by the fusion of the spiritual and intellectual life within their "couvents", they contributed to the catholic revival, making a contribution to the cultural background of seventeenth century France which is uniquely interesting.

APPENDICES

APPENDIX I

Contents

Reproduction by courtesy of the Trustees of the National Gallery, London, of a painting by Claude Lorrain (1600–1682). National Gallery Catalogue No. 1319. (Reproduction of part only of original.)

A view of Rome showing Santa Trinità dei Monti in the middle distance, left. The "couvent" has not changed at all; the twin sets of steps leading up to the "perron" in front of the West door, the conventual buildings to the north and the stairway leading up to the door, the distinctive twin towers with the weather vanes – all these remain. The Spanish Steps now lead down the steep hill immediately in front of the church.

For a view of the interior, see figure 8, reproduced from Maignan's *Horographia*, Rome, 1647.

Fig. 1.

Fig. 2.

FIGURE 2

Size: reduced from original of 198 × 150 mm. (measurement of outer frame).

Etienne Dondé, *Les figures et l'abrégé de la vie, de la mort et des miracles de Saint François de Paule,* Paris, 1671.

Four examples of exorcism attributed to the Patron and Founder of the Order. It is important to study these drawings in order to understand the belief in the reality of the Devil which is so prominent a feature of XVIIth century religion. See also pp. 132–134 on the question of exorcism.

The drawings are also interesting in the details of the Minims' habits and of the monk's cell in fig. 31. These details, together with the pictures of the interior of a church, figs. 30 and 32, may well be of the Couvent de la Place Royale where Dondé worked in the 1660s; they are certainly anachronistic as illustrations of the life of Saint François de Paule.

In the *Annales des Minimes de la Province de France* ... (MS Mazarine No. 2429) under 1662 one reads, "On a donné 400 livres au Fr. Dondé, Quêteur du Couvent, pour graver les planches des Miracles de Saint François de Paule ... plus on lui a donné 100 livres en 1668 pour le même sujet."

FIGURE 3

Size of original, 262 × 160 mm.

Jean Germain, *Breve e sostanziale trattato intorno alle figure anatomiche*, Naples, 1625.

The somewhat lurid frontispiece showing the male and female human skeleton, the former designated by a beard, the latter by a lock of hair. The female is one-armed and the ribs of both are inaccurately shown as complete hoops. The four smaller skeletons are: top left – cat(?); top right – dog; lower left – a sparrowhawk reproduced from p. 52 of the text; lower right – an owl, p. 56 of text.[1]

Surmounting the whole is the device of the Order "CARITAS," while at the bottom are arms of the Ricci family of Naples; Luigi Ricci[2] was instrumental in getting the work through the press.

The initials NP, in monogram just above the left-hand bottom corner, are of Nicolas Perrey whose name appears at the foot of the drawing of the Monkey, p. 20. All the other drawings, measuring 254 × 180 mm, are by Germain himself. The illustrations in the text are anatomically accurate in the main.

---

[1] Sparrowhawk – called alternatively "sparaviero" and "sparviere"; Owl – called alternatively "ascio" and "barbaian", the latter a variant of the usual "barbagianni".

[2] Ricci or Riccio as in Preface.

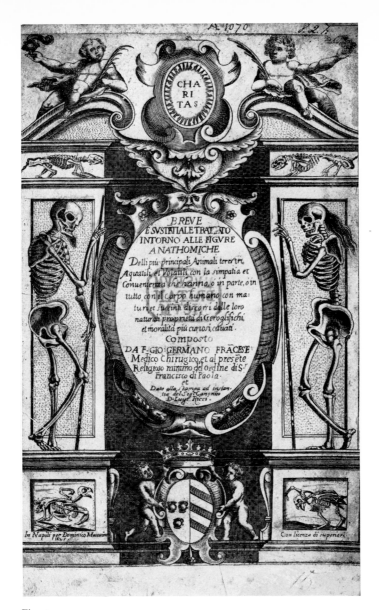

Fig. 3.

F.I.F.Niceron inuent.
I.Picart deline. et incidit.

Fig. 4.

FIGURE 4

Size of original 180 × 180 mm.

Jacques Auzolles de Lapeyre, *Le Mercure charitable*, Paris, 1638, p. 73.

Portrait of the author by Jean-François Niceron. The account of this is given in the chapter on Niceron, p. 156.

It appears that Niceron could instinctively draw in this manner. The method of arriving at the projection is shown in the next plate (Figure 5).

FIGURE 5

Size of original 289 × 210 mm.

Jean-François Niceron, *La Perspective Curieuse*, Paris, 1638.

Reproduction of Plate No. LVIII from the unnumbered pages at the back. Shows the method of projection by the method described in the chapter on Niceron. Take the detail in any square of the original portrait, e.g. the nostrils in square 5–3, and see how this is traced out in the segment 5–3 of the circular design.

petit cercle **F G H I** est la grosseur du cylindre   Et le grand cercle **K L M N O** &c. represente sa base.

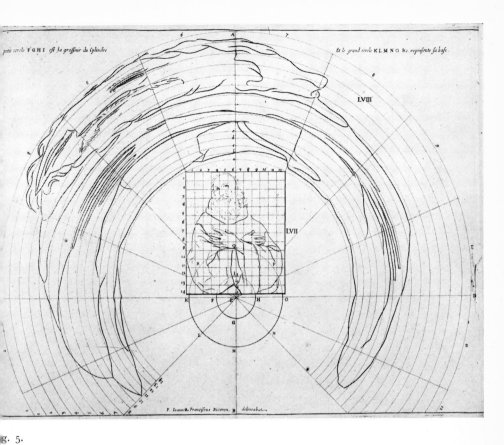

F. Ioann⁵. Franciscus Niceron. **B** delineabat.

g. 5.

Fig. 6.

FIGURE 6

Size of original 267 × 190 mm. (i.e. measurement of frame of the picture.)

Jean-François Niceron, *La Perspective curieuse*, Paris, 1638.

Pages 114–120 (the last seven pages of the text) are devoted to the description of an optical trick. The following are extracts from this passage and the plate reproduced is No. 24 showing illustrations LXIX–LXXI.

The "lunette" referred to in the first extract was 8 "pouces" long and mounted on a base 14 × 20 "pouces" at the end of which stood the picture. It is quite clear from this that Miss Colie is wrong in thinking that this was a magic lantern [1]; see also the following passage:

> ... le dessein d'un tableau que j'ai tracé et fis peindre il y a 2 ou trois ans, et qui se garde encore à présent dans la Bibliothèque de notre couvent de la Place Royale à Paris. Ce tableau ... étant vu directement, représente une quinzaine d'Ottomans vêtus à la turque, la plus part au naturel tirés d'un livre intitulé *Icones Sultanorum*, et quand on vient à regarder par la lunette, au lieu de ces Ottomans on ne voit plus que le portrait de sa Majesté Très-Chrétienne très-bien fait, ressemblant et vêtu à la française, encore qu'il se compose de plusiers pièces des autres portraits qui se ramassent et s'unissent ensemble pour le former tel qu'il se voit.

Lines composed by a friend (One of the Ormesson family?)

> Que va représantant cette plate peinture?
> Tu le vois curieux et ne le connais pas;
> Tu vois des Ottomans, et sous leur portraiture
> Un visage est caché, qui ne se montre pas;
> Si tu le veux connaître, mets l'œil à l'ouverture
> De ce petit canal et tu le reconnaîtras
> Du Monarque Français la naïve peinture,
> Qui doit des Ottomans l'Empire mettre à bas;
> Qui fera des Croissants de la race infidèle
> De ces Mahometans, surgir les Fleurs de Lys
> De nos Rois Très-Chrétiens, que la France fidèle
> A toujours reconnu du ciel les favoris.

LXIX. The composite picture.
 LXX. The lens for the "lunette" showing details of how it was cut.
LXXI. The completed portrait with facettes of lens superimposed.

---

[1] *Some paradoxes in the language of things*, in *Reason and Inspiration* by J. A. Mazzeo, London 1962, p. 117.

FIGURE 7

Size of original 265 × 177 mm.

E. Maignan *Horographia*, Rome, 1647 plate facing p. 138.

Diagram to determine the meridian and north point. The illustration is chiefly interesting because it shows the interior of Santa Trinità dei Monti at Rome. The two towers which stand at the head of the Spanish steps are easily recognisable. On the right, i.e. N. side of the quadrangle, on the roof is Maignan's own astrolabe which is still to be seen. Maignan says of this illustration:

Locum vero huiusmodi commodissimum nactus sum in Regio nostro Romano Sanctissimae Trinitatis conventu in monte Pincio, ubi ex parte sacrae Aedis septentrionem respiciente, longa, lataque porrigitur ambulatio hypaetra elegantem habens Q.S. e candido lapide affabre secto peribolum. Oppositae vero parti peristylii in I et N libere sol meridianus lucet: iom ea parte, sicut et toto per quadrum aedificio regnat pulcherrima concamerata cryptoporticus, in cuius ego fornice, ac parietibus longe lateque patens Catoptricum Astrolabium annis ab hinc fere duodecim (i.e. 1635) accuratissime delineavi, speculo in fenestra I. parte inferiore constituto. [*Horographia* pp. 137/8].

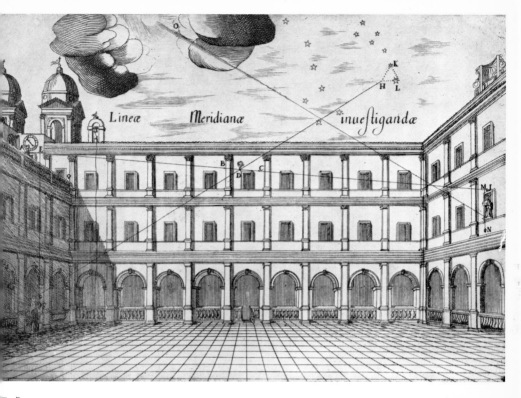

Linee Meridianæ inuestigandæ

g. 7.

Fig. 8.

FIGURE 8

E. Maignan, *Horographia*, plate facing p. 362.

Size of original 250 × 167 mm.

A rare type of "pin-hole" dial. The North and South points are found; a window facing S. is provided with a shutter in which there is a small aperture. A mirror placed on the floor along the North-South line will catch the sun at noon. The position on this line will vary according to the season. The sun's rays are reflected onto the vault overhead and the position of the reflexion at noon on the arc RR will enable an accurate calculation. of the date to be made. This type of apparatus leads directly to the making of a complex astrolabe of the type seen in figure 8 and, even more complex, of the type illustrated by Maignan in the *Horographia* facing page 391, which shows the inside of a vaulted room in the palace of Cardinal Spada. The description of the astrolabe traced on the vaulted roof and the details of how a similar one may be constructed occupy pp. 390–550 of the *Horographia*, with profuse and clear illustrations.

FIGURE 9

A. Kircher, *Horologium* etc. Avignon, 1635.

Size of original diagram: CB 122 mm, TD 93 mm.

Contrast with Maignan's drawing and his "mise en page": figures 7, 8, and also 10, 10a and 10b.

It should be noted that the reproduction from Kircher is almost full size whereas the reproductions from Maignan are from a volume in-folio (i.e. reduced to $^1/_4$ size).

rit. Atque hoc est, cur nos duplici operatione horas supra inscribi præceperimus. Cum enim mo-

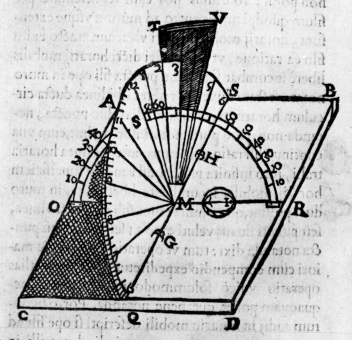

bilis horarius T V, seu Zodiacus radiosus super lineam quampiam horariam in semicirculo Q A S signatam fuerit collocatus, Zodiacus dictus, seu horarius mobilis eum necessario situm obtinebit, quem obtinet circulus horarius prædictus in cælo, ad quem nimirum est parallelus, quare si Horarius dictus excurreret in murum vsque, exprimeret eandem in eo lineam, quam exprimeret circulus horarius cælestis in murum excurrens. Cum vero

Fig. 9.

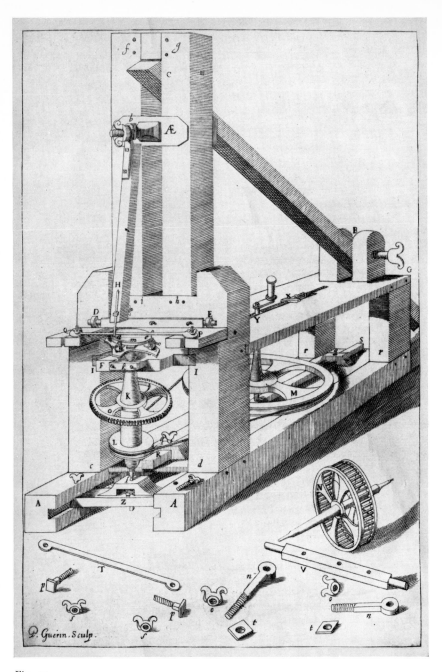

Fig. 10.

Fig. 10a.

Fig. 10b.

De formandis poliendiſque lentibus cryſtallinis, tum ijs quibus
ad res Gnomonicas vruntur Catoptricè, atque Dioptricè;
tum conſequenter etiam ijs, quibus eadem Dioptricè teleſcopia ſua inſtruit.

PRÆFATIO.

CRyſtalla artificum methodo communi facta atque politè communiſſimè
vnium ineſt imperfecta figura, ex qua conſequenter oriantur tum re-
flexio tum refractio, nam aliæ quod ad intorem ac fulgorem polomicam
ſatis accurationes oſtritur. Ex duplici autem capite oritur figuræ in politæ cryſtalla defectus: primum eſt, oſſui moduli, ſiue quouam formæ imperfectus, cum
enim, ut dicitur, nemo der opi luce poſſit quod non habet: imperfecta moduli figura perfectam cryſtallo oriuere nequit: imo eſſectus potuis deſinuet vt rij acca-
dentibus a praſtantia ſua cauſis, quam illam vnquam ſuperet, ut ſatis conſtat
experientia modulum eſſe aliquatenus perfectiſſimam. Et tamen non omnis in eo
formaretur (unus eſſe atque perfectæ. Alterum eſt polimdi ai imperfecta quan-
tumuis enim perfectam laugetaum prior modulo cryſtallo figuram accepit;
rialè tamen aliquid in ſemper ſuperſſ, vnde et quodammodo facta eſt, et luca
non bene pervius; id autem quod dici rudi, media cuiuſdam ope detrahendum
eſt, ſ verò inaqualiter deradatur, priſtinæ terendæ inducta figura, quamuis
ſeponatur perfecta; dum politur, corrumpitur et quomani non poſſit oculos
vnium in ſuperficie ſic polita notare, effi tamen terera quinam argui lux præ-
ter legem reflexa, refractaue. Huic vtraque malo remedium certiſſimum hæc,
et ſequentibus propoſitionibus paraiso, quod à quanti accuratia manu ſatis ſati-
ſit ac non minus ſeliciter adhibeatur. Ex his verò perdes neceſſaria praeſtantiſ-
ſimi optici cubi conficendi ars mirabilis, quam ab exigui primordij (vt rebus omnibus conuenit ſ) paulatim in perfectiorem ſtatum euidemus exere-
uiſſe, in Regia enim oriis, Florentiæ educata eſt à Galileo et Napoli à Fonta-
na; ac iterum Florentia à Torricellio culta, nunc Romæ ſelicius ab Euſtachio
Divini, manu (ſi fas eſt dicere) diuina excolitur et meæ quidem fortunæ ad numquam fuit, vt mecum opſuerit aliquas artis huius peritus ſed meoijum quid
ſuarum ſiue experientiarum, ſiue cogitationum communicare; ſed meoijum ſor-
te non immeritò ſelicitorem omnibus prædicato, rui abſque aliena ope conigit,
aliquoties ad ingenuam exercitationem tereoti cryſtallinos, teleſcopia aſtrona-
mica edere etiam longiſſimi rubis, alienis quæ hactenus quidem aequali tibi certi non inſeriora; Vnde exiſtimaui methodum mea excogitatam, eſſe perfectam,
et longè perfectiùs ceſſerum aliterꝯ plus erij res, habeni; cumque à quo
perfectio ad æqus adhibeto poſſit ſuperentibus his ſubſidij aliſque pariter neceſ-
ſarij: hanc verò vt ſine madia, ita (et verò ambigibus libenter concedo et publi-
ci

e reris ſacos, quæ priores iſis quidquid ſcierim addere potuerim, addam li-
bentiſs. illis qui magis ingenio iudicio arte ad communem Aſtronomiæ vtilita-
tem; et ſi quidem in communem conferant quodquid egregij hac in parte cogita-
runt, nos ſlabit quin colleſti in vnum præclaris inuentis breus perfectam con-
ſiciendi teleſcopii artem ſinus habitum; ex verò ſeliciter (rut ſic tandem ſpera-
re decet) ad ſuum apicem perducta; auſim dicere nihil hoc ſæculo, vel multis
auretatis inuentum iuſs queliis, incundius, nobilius. Quod attinet ad lheo-
riam, nihil ſanè addo proſ; ad ea quæ præclare Cartoſius diſſerit in ſua Dioptrice; Vnde et optime intelligitur quid nobis perfectionis allaturæ ſit teleſcopio
lens hyperbolica vel elliptica ſupra id quod iam habemus è ſhærica optimè da-
borata. Quoad praxim verò non vidi hacce naus qui aliquid certi, et
indubitatæ fidei dederit ſiue de conſtructione modulorum, ſiue
(quod inuimi momenti eſt) de perfecta poliendi arte.

Noſtra itaque Dioptrice, hæc optima ſui par-
bus, modulos omnis generis id eſt pla-
nos, conuexos concauoſque, ſ-
gura tum ſphærica,
tum hyperbolica, tum elliptica perficit; ac deni-
de lentes in eis exactè formadet; ſ
rutè explicet.

Fro-

FIGURES 10, 10a AND 10b

E. Maignan, *Horographia;* pages 687 and 688, also plate facing p. 689.

Size of original: 264 × 178 mm.

Introduction to the section on the polishing of lenses, a novel feature in any work on dials and dialling. Maignan quotes, amongst others, Galileo and Toricelli. It is interesting to recall that Spinoza spent much time polishing lenses but his apparatus, which I have been able to inspect in Spinozashuis at Rijnsburg, is more like a simple lathe worked on the bow-and-treadle principle (see figure 16) than the apparatus which Maignan here illustrates. Plumier, in the preface to the *Art de tourner* acknowledges Maignan as a source of his work and Bayle, in the *Dictionnaire* (art. Maignan, rem. G) refers to his "infinité de machines." Although not as clear as Plumier's illustrations, it compares most favourably with other mechanical drawings in the XVIIth century. It shows quite clearly the clamps for the lenses at *a* and *e*, also the adjustment for the manual pulley at X; the pulley M could be drawn towards the rear by undoing the clamping screws *q*; the spindle KL could likewise be withdrawn and the pinion K made to engage with the primitive cog wheel N (shown on the floor) which would be mounted where KL is shown in the diagram.

The cog-wheel and pulley-shaft KL together with their pivot at Z appear to be out of perspective. This is not a lapse but a deliberate attempt at isometric projection whereby elevation and plan are combined. The frame of the apparatus and the main features are given as an architectural drawing viewed from 45° but, by altering the view point (i.e. by advancing the left-hand beam A out of true linear perspective) the working parts can be studied in more detail. The reason for this is surely because Maignan wishes to show not only the general appearance of his apparatus but to pass on to the reader sufficient detail for him to construct his own machine. Plumier, having the same intentions, also uses isometric projection to give details of his lathes and turning instruments.

Note particularly in Fig. 10a the bolt 't'; both head and thread shown by isometric projection so that it can be accurately copied — essential in mechanical drawing before the days of standard fittings.

FIGURE I I

Charles Plumier.

Size: reduced from 194 × 135 mm. (i.e. by ¼ approx.)

An example of his botanical drawing taken from the Manuscript *Flore américaine* in the Bibliothèque Publique, Marseille, No. 913, p. 104.

p. 103 gives a detailed description of the drawing on p. 104 which shows the passion flower (Passiflora maliformis) or sweet calabash.

Murucuia Maliformis Caulis sarmentosus ac subrufus: folia gerit hinc inde, suis pediculis circiter digitum longis affixa, et quodlibet in quinque alia sectum quae suos neruos et uenas habent, et quaedam horum foliorum sunt interdum laciniata, quaedam non. Ad singulos pediculos foliorum prouenit etiam pediculus, continens florem in circumferentia duplam quantitatem Rosae habentem; quique inferius tria folia viridia obtinet supra autem, hoc quinque longiora, interne uiridescentia, superne caeruleo purpurea: Dehinc solis uti pingitur figura radiatim multa filamenta crispata et in orbem explicata, exteriori mediate caeruleo purpurea, interiori dilute caerulea, uel etiam e contrario, uel etiam, quod elegantissimum, exteriora uersus dilute caerulea, in medio in orbem purpurea, uersus interiora ex purpureo nigricantia, uel etiam exterius ex parte cyanei, interius in totum urani seu etiam rubri coloris ac circulorum modo punctulis dilutis albo et rubro in orbem uariegata; circa centrum autem ex brunno itidem rubris suis punctulis. In medio floris columellam habet breuissimam, pallidam, superius in quinque partes dissectam, quae ad latera curuata extenduntur; cuique parti spongiformi corpus lutescens, puluerem luteum adspersum habens adhaeret. In medio autem columellae pisiformis orbiculus ex flauo albicans, et huic tres claui superius infixi ex flauo albi et punctulis minimis purpureis uariegati et deorsum inclinati, ut brachia columnae. Flos totus suauis odoris. Fructus aequat pomum nostras uulgare, rotundus, cortice crasso, flaui exterius coloris, constans pulpa succulenta, uinoso acida: crocea et linguam tingente croceo colore: et in illa multa granula seminis nigri, magnitudine seminis pomi uulgaris, sed uariis tuberculis insigniti, et folliculo inclusi. Fructus item transuersim scinditur comedendus. Semina quoque eodem modo colligenda et conseruanda. Commendabilis est fructus tam odore quam sapore.

pito Pulpa quae summo febricitantium solatio et oblectamento est, uicem syrupi cordialis ut et Rob Ribium uel Berberis egregie supplet. Qualitate refrigerandi antecellit, nullamque noxam etiamsi abunde comedatur affert; nisi quod immoderato eius usu dentes stupore obtorpescunt. Aestu laborantes mirifice refocillat sitimque extinguit. Ad haec apetitum excitat, stomachi ardores reprimit, spiritusque uitales, cum recens pomum, tum succus eius in syrupi consistentiam coactus, et ex palea propinatus [illegible]

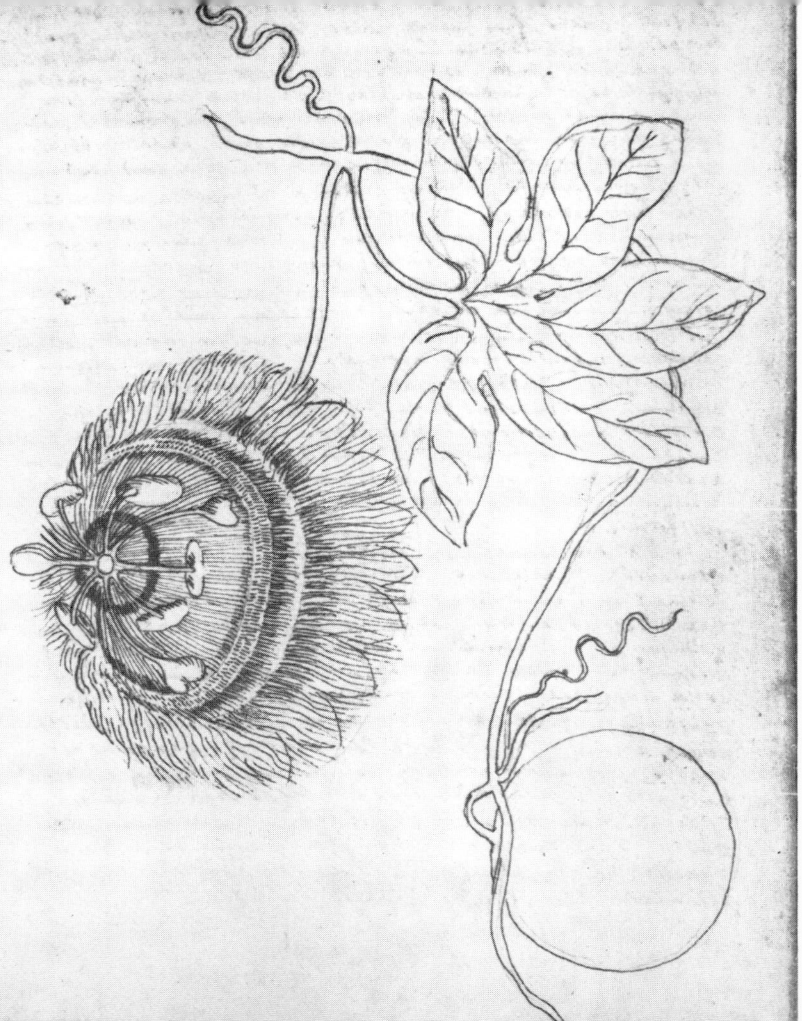

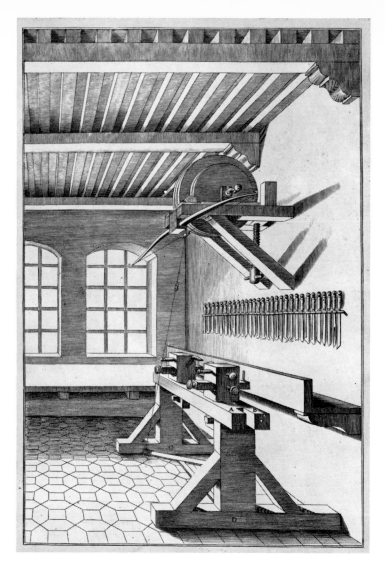

Fig. 12.

FIGURE 12

C. Plumier *L'art de tourner;* plate unnumbered facing p. 1.

Size: Original 280 × 184 mm.

An admirable example of Plumier's skill as an illustrator, showing a typical lathe of the late seventeenth century, worked by treadle and spring bow, with whip-cord round a pulley.

Note the absence of human figures or "putti" which often obtrude themselves into seventeenth century illustrations. The admirable perspective of the beams of the roof and of the tiles on the floor are in the tradition of Niceron and Maignan. As in his botanical drawings, there is a preoccupation with minor detail which, however, never becomes pedantic or superfluous; in this respect notice in particular the handles of the row of tools on the wall and the adjusting screw underneath the pulley assembly.

The use of various types of shading helps to bring out the perspective and this technique, applied to technical drawing, was emphasised by Niceron: see his drawing of a work-bench in the *Perspective curieuse,* plate 11, and his study of shadows cast by solid geometrical shapes plates 4–8, also numerous plates in the *Thaumaturgus opticus,* especially 13.

FIGURE 13

C. Plumier, *L'art de tourner;* plate 28, facing p. 89.

Size: Original 294 × 198 mm.

Typical of the detailed drawings in the *Art de tourner.* The principles of mechanical drawing which are still in use are shown here; see for example the relation of end-view to side-view in fig. A, related to fig. B; fig. L related to fig. 1 and fig. K related to M and N simultaneously. Figures S, R and Q show various eccentrics; these are required for turning the ornamental "colonne torse" type of work which had a considerable vogue in the XVII and XVIIIth century.

The shafts D and F, the threaded holes in the flange B and, probably, the threaded stud at 4, show that Plumier, as well as Maignan, favoured isometric projection to combine elevation and plan in the one drawing.

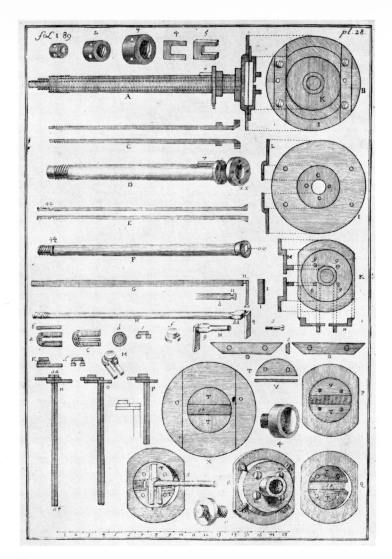

Fig. 13.

Fig. 14.

FIGURE 14

C. Plumier *L'Art de tourner;* a folding plate, facing p. 1.

Size: reduced to less than one third of original. Original 450 mm × 2
    columns of 105 m/m.

Extravaganza of Plumier's own design, showing his virtuosity. This
illustration was reproduced in the *Journal de Trévoux* [1] and also in the
Encyclopédie, amongst Lucotte's illustrations for the article *Tour*. No acknowledgement is made to Plumier by Lucotte or by Diderot who edited the
illustrations.

For the significance of such elaborate ornamentation see the chapter
on Plumier pp. 194.

[1] See previously pp. 193–194.

FIGURE 15

Size: slight reduction from original.

Eglise des Minimes de la Place Royale, Paris.

Reproduced from the original in the Bibliothèque Nationale and taken from *The Charitable mistresses of Saint-Maur*, Dornach, 1925, p. 152. It shows the "couvent" as it was before the addition of Mansart's façade; view taken from the corner of the Rue du Parc Royal, now Rue de Béarn.

The church of the Minims was one of Mansart's masterpieces. The first stone of the Altar was laid in 1630 by the Seigneur de la Vieuville, the grand nephew of St. Francis of Paula. The faithful flocked in crowds to its services. The great Lords of the land wished to be buried in it. The best painters of the day – Mignard, Jouvenet, etc., vied with each other in adorning it. Bossuet preached the Lenten sermons there in 1660. The Queen and Royal Princes sent precious and rare marbles, and gifts of money. The most distinguished musicians were heard in it. This beautiful church was sold as national property in 1798, and completely destroyed in 1803.

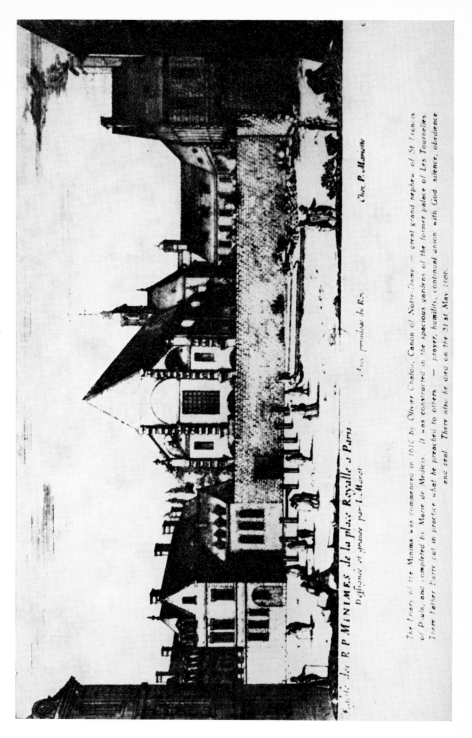

The Prior of the Minims was commenced in 1610 by Oliver Chalon, Canon of Notre-Dame — great grand nephew of St. Francis of Paule, and completed by Marie de Medicis. It was constructed in the spacious gardens of the former palace of Les Tournelles. There Father Barre put in practice what he preached to others — prayer, humility, continual union with God, silence, obedience and zeal. There also he died on the 31st May 1686.

Fig. 15.

Face de l'Eglise des Minimes batie du viüant du S.r Mansart Iusques au premier ordre

Fig. 16.

FIGURE 16

Size: slight reduction from original.

Eglise des Minimes de la Place Royale, Paris; Mansart's façade.

Source of reproduction same as for figure 15, p. 146.

I am indebted to the Reverend Mother Superior of St. Maur's convent, Weybridge, Surrey, for giving me pernission to have figures 15 and 16 reproduced from *The Charitable Mistresses of St. Maur*, Dornach, 1925, in her possession.

SUMMARY OF HEADINGS FROM CLAUDE PITHOY'S
TRAITÉ CURIEUX DE L'ASTROLOGIE JUDICIEUSE,
SEDAN, 1641

Déclarations et préambules

Insolence des généthliaques . . .

Prédire des choses qui dépendent du conseil de Dieu et de la libre volonté des hommes.

Horoscope de Jésus-Christ.

Censure théologique.

Les deux premières marques; L' Astromantie convaincu de magie; et inventée.

Témoignage de Dieu.

     ,,   des Canons ecclésiastiques.

     ,,   ,, Pères et Théologiens.

     ,,   ,, Lois civiles.

     ,,   ,, Savants, Philosophes, Médecins et Astrologues.

L'astromantie a été inventée et cultivée par de célèbres Magiciens *idolâtres.*

L'extraction des démons.

L'astromantie cultivée par des Magiciens méchants, impies etc. (Cardan).

Perversité dommageable de leur art diabolique (des généthliaques).

L'astromantie pernicieuse à ses propres maîtres.

L'astromantie pernicieuse à ceux qui en recherchent les ouvrages.

L'astromantie très pernicieuse en public.

L'astromantie dangereuse à un Prince et à ses domestiques.

L'astromantie butte à renverser les fondements de l'Etat et de la religion.

Les généthliaques entreprennent des choses impossibles

Quelle est la vertu, l'influence et l'efficace des astres sur les choses sublunaires.

De la nature des astres, de leur vertu et le moyen par lequel ils agissent sur les choses sublunaires.

Ce que les astres peuvent produire dans le monde élémentaire.

Quels effets ne dépendent pas des astres.

Si les astres peuvent agir sur l'âme raisonnable; l'âme immatérielle.

Que les astres ne peuvent prognostiquer ce que les généthliaques entreprennent de prédire

Que les astres n'ont pas la vertu de produire les choses que les généthliaques entreprennent de prédire.

Que les astres ne sont pas députés par le créateur pour signifier les choses que les généthliaques entreprennent de prédire.

Que les phénomènes du ciel ne peuvent pas naturellement signifier ce que les astrologues entreprennent de prédire.

Que les maximes des généthliaques rendent leur enterprise impossible à l'esprit humain

Trois principes sur lesquels les généthliaques dressent leurs horoscopes.

Qu'il est impossible de savoir quel a été le point ou l'instant de la géniture.

Qu'il est impossible aux généthliaques de remarquer tous les phénomènes du ciel au point que requièrent les règles de leur art.

Qu'il est impossible aux généthliaques de connaître distinctement les influences de toutes les étoiles.

Aveu des maîtres généthliaques touchant l'impossibilité des prédictions généthlialogiques.

Que les observations dont les généthliaques se servent pour parvenir à la connaissance et prédiction des choses futures sont entièrement absurdes et ridicules

Quelles sont les observations les plus considérables des généthliaques.

Première rêverie des généthliaques touchant les douze maisons qu'ils ont bâties dans le ciel.

Autres rêveries touchant les diverses parties du Zodiaque et les signes contenus en icelui.

Autres plaisantes rêveries touchant les départements des astres.

Autres gaillardises touchant les mouvements et rencontres, les vertus et les effets des astres.

Autres rêveries facéteuses touchant le domaine des astres sur les corps sublunaires.

Que toutes les observations précédentes sont destituées de raison et entièrement ridicules

Sur la distinction, l'ordre et les propriétés des douze maisons célestes.

Sur la distinction du Zodiaque et des effigies que les généthliaques y ont imaginées.

Sur les départements de astres.

Sur les diverses prognostications des astres.

Sur la domination que les généthliaques attribuent aux étoiles.

A quelle fin les généthliaques ont-ils inventé tant d'observations ridicules dans les cieux.

De l'expérience des généthliaques et de la qualité de leurs prédictions

Que l'expérience dont se vantent les généthliaques ne justifie pas leurs inventions ridicules.

Que la diversité des phénomènes célestes et des causes sublunaires empêche l'expérience de la vertu fatidique des astres.

Que l'expérience prétendue des généthliaques est confondue par leurs propres contradictions et par le changement de leurs maximes.

La fausseté des observations généthlialogiques répugne à l'expérience prétendue de leur vertu fatidique.

Que l'expérience des généthliaques est commune à toute sorte de magiciens et qu'elle ne prouve pas la vertu fatidique de leurs phénomènes.

Quelles sont les prédictions des généthliaques et quelle en peut être la certitude.

Que les prédictions des généthliaques ne sont pas astrologiques.

Que les prédictions des généthliaques sont diaboliques et qu'ils ont commerce avec les démons, et comment.

Comment il se peut que les généthliaques sont déçus et déçoivent si souvent par leurs horoscopes.

Quelle certitude il peut y avoir ès prédictions des généthliaques.

Les arrêts prononcés contre l'astromantie et les généthliaques et leurs horoscopes; et les moyens pour en obtenir l'exécution et faire étouffer cette magie dans tous les états chrétiens

Arrêts contre l'astromantie, contre les généthliaques et contre ceux qui font l'horoscope.

Que les livres d'astrologie judiciaire doivent être brûlés et les généthliaques bannis de tous les états chrétiens.

S'il est permis de pratiquer l'astromantie en secret.

Par quels moyens on peut obtenir l'exécution des arrêts prononcés contre l'astromantie et contre les horoscopes des généthliaques.

D'où vient que malgré les lois divines et humaines et tant d'arrêts et de censures d'Empereurs et de Papes il s'y trouve toujours des généthliaques dans les états chrétiens.

Qu'il est impossible à un chretien de connaître l'astromantie sans l'avoir en horreur et qu'un Prince qui sait ce que c'est ne peut la souffir dans son état.

De quels phénomènes le chrétien doit conjecturer, voire juger certainement de sa bonne ou mauvaise aventure.

TRANSCRIPT OF MS 752 IN THE
BIBLIOTHÈQUE PUBLIQUE DE TOULOUSE,
FOL. 152 AND 153

Maignan was fascinated by all natural phenomena and made use of his observations in his printed work. The following observation concerning springs from which air as well as water was emitted never found its way into print. He wanted to adapt the idea for creating the necessary draught for a blast-furnace- "ad perflandum ignem in fornace."

In order to facilitate an understanding of this part of the manuscript I have put the transcript of fol. 153 recto first, followed by the diagram (fol. 153 verso) and the suggested application of the principles involved (fol. 152).

Original spelling retained, accents added.

Fontaines de Vent   153. Ro.

En un beau village nommé Cosi, entre les villes Terni et Narni,[1] allant de Rome à Lorette, à un mille du grand chemin à main droite, (il) y a une grande montaigne fort haute et d'un rocher fort dure, et ledit village est basti sur la pente qui est fort raide et sis(?) à demy hauteur. Or, ceste montaigne au haut du village a certains fonts d'où il souffle depuis le mois de mai iusques en novembre des vents continuels et d'autant plus forts et plus froids que la saison est plus chaude et sèche, car s'il pleut beaucoup les vents se ralentissent et sont moins froids, et l'hyver non seulement les vents ne soufflent pas, ains si on applique un linge flottant proche des dits fonts le linge est comme attiré en dedans, signe que l'air de dehors a cours en dedans. Ceux qui habitent cette partie plus haute du vilage et qui ont leurs maisons attachées à ce rocher se servent fort adroitement de ces fontaines de vent, tout de mesme comme ils fairaient des fontaines d'eau, car ayant bien bastie à l'entour d'un de ces fonts afin de recueillir tout le vent qui en vient, ils y font des portes formées à tourner, y font des tuyaux et des robinets, et conduisent ce vent par les tuyaux où ils veulent dans leur maison pour divers offices, comme à la cuisine pour tourner la broche, à la cisterne pour le froid de l'eau, mais sur tout pour rafraischir les sales, à la table etc. où ils veulent et ce vent est si froid que tout aussy tost il a rafraischi une sale, et a plustost rafraischi le vin à boire, et beaucoup plus que la glace ou la neige.

En Catailogne près la vile d'Aulote [2] arrosée du Fluvian [3] (et cela est marqué

---

[1] On the main road from Rome to Ancona, about 50 miles N.E. of Rome.
[2] Olot, between Figueras and Ripoll, 100 miles N. of Barcelona.
[3] i.e. the Fluvià.

dans l'Atlas pag. 4, vol. i) (il) y a 12 sources d'air. L'air y est fort subtil et délicieux et sont les vents hauts en hyver et aussy si froids que des vases d'eau se gèlent estant mis près des trous. Voyez Justin en l'histoire de Sicile parlant de semblables vents – un Scylla et Caribdis.

Fontaine d'eau merveilleuse, et ainsi nommé.

En Savoie proche l'Abbaye d'Aubecombe [1] ancienne sépulture des Ducs de Savoye, proche le lac du Bourget, assez proche du Rone et proche les baings d'Aix en Savoye (il) y a une fontaine laquelle toute l'année a un flux interrompu comme à celle du Pays de Foix au village de Bellestat [2] mais qui n'est(?) pas plus gros que le poing et le trou est de mon(?) scavoir(?) de la grosseur environ que le poing y passerait et quand l'eau commence à venir(?) eile fait grand bruit à raison du vent – faisant glo, glo, glo, et donne forte grande abondance d'eau qui s'estend (s'espand?) par la place (?) puis cesse tout a fait faisant un bruit moindre que lors qu'il a commencé et un peu différent, et puis la place reste tout à fait à sec.

En Vallier(?) [3] ou auprès (il) y a une belle fontaine qui fait un très grand vent et aussi un bruit si fort qu'on l'entend de fort loing comme des coupes de canon.

Il y en a aussi une autre au susdit chemin de Rome à Lorette qui emporte le chapeau de ceux qui passent proche la bouche du rocher d'où il sort.

For reproductions of folios 153 (verso) and 152 (recto) see opposite pages. In the first, KLIH is a cave into which an underground stream flows through a hole in the roof AB. A hole at C communicates with AB and, provided the waterlevel remains below C, air will be sucked in. Water level is maintained at HI and water flows away at G. Air is expelled at S. If, however, water levelin stream rises to EF, C is covered; this, as previously described, the "fontaine de vent" works only in dry weather.

The application of the phenomenon given on folio 152 is self-explanatory.

---

[1] i.e. Hautecombe about two-thirds of the way down the Lac du Bourget from the Chambéry end.

[2] i.e. Bélestat, on the Hers between Foix (Ariège) and Quillan (Pyrénées-Orientales).

[3] Presumably le Mont Vallier, or le Pic de Montvalier, S. of Saint-Girons; there are several caverns in the neighbourhood.

Fig. 17.

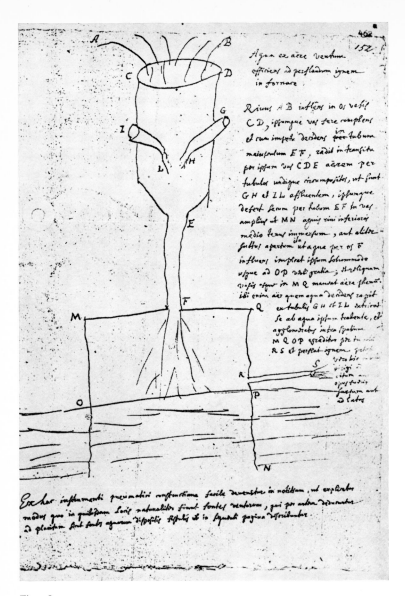

Fig. 18.

LETTERS FROM PLUMIER TO MICHEL BÉGON. ORIGINALS LOST, BUT COPIES, EARLY XVIIITH CENTURY, IN THE BIBLIOTHÈQUE MUNICIPALE DE LA ROCHELLE.*

Extraxt from MS 656, fol. 110 recto et verso. Original spelling retained.

Paris ce 11 juin 1702

Monsieur,

Je vous suis bien obligé de la bonté qu'il vous plait me témoigner par la vostre du 6.

Je me donnerois bien l'honneur de vous écrire encore un peu plus souvent que je ne le fais pour vous assurer toujours de mes très humbles respects. J'attends toujours de dimanche en dimanche pour savoir positivement ma destinée. Aujourdhuy j'ay este encore voir Mr l'abé Bignon, pour toute response il m'a dit que Mr Anisson[1] luy avoit donné un deduit de ce que contient mon ouvrage et qu'il en parleroit a Mgr de Pontchartrain.[2] Voila Monsieur en quel ? je suis encore. Je vous diray en quoy consiste l'ouvrage dont est question, c'est un traitté de toutes les fougeres, capillaires, langues de cerf etc. que j'ay decouvert dans mes trois voyages.[3] Je demande par grace qu'on le fasse imprimer puisque les planches sont toutes faites et tous mes manuscrits en ordre. Ensuite j'iray ou on voudra. Mes supérieurs m'ont temoigné que je ne leur fairois (sic) pas plaisir plus voyager que cet ouvrage ne fut au jour. Je l'ay rendu le plus utile que j'ay pu en y ajoutant toutes les vertus de chaque genre, par exemple je traitte en general de la vertu des fougeres, de la vertu des capillaires, etc. qui me sont connus en Europe et je les raporte aux fougeres et aux capillaires etc. de l'Amerique affin que les habitans de ce pais en puissent profiter et affin qu'on connoisse mieux la chose je mes une planche de la fougere d'Europe la plus commune, une planche du capillaire le plus connu ainsi des autres. J'espere que tous les curieux auront plaisir de voir cet ouvrage. J'ay bien regret qu'on ait tant

---

* I am indebted to a typist in the library at La Rochelle for making a typescript of the MS.

[1] Member of a family of printers in Lyon.

[2] Louis Phélipeaux – Intendant des Finances. He held the "direction des Académies." See Lachenage, Desbois et Badier, *Dictionnaire de la noblesse de France*, vol. XV.

[3] i.e. *Traité des fougères de l'Amérique*, see Bibliography, sub Plumier.

tardé a l'imprimer. J'aurois esté en estat de faire le voyage avec Mr du Casse [1] je perds une tres belle occasion mais a la bonheure (sic). Cependant je continue a travailler. J'ay fini mon traitté des   ?   opus indictum ore alio et j'en fais un autre aussi tres curieux c'est un traité des umbelliferes comme le fenouil, l'angelique, l'imperatoire, etc. il avoit esté commencé par Monsieur Anglois [2] mais j'en ay dejà plus de cent dessinées. J'y travailleray Dieu aydant incessament jusques a tant que je l'aye achevé. J'espere que Mr de Tournefort [3] ne m'aydera pas de peu. Il est en chemin qui revient. Il a ecrit de Malte du 13 du passé et je le vais attendre (?) en Provence. Je ne manqueray pas de vous faire savoir son arrivée a Paris. Monsieur Paulost (sic) [4] me fist l'honneur de m'escrire il y a du temps il me demandoit un éclaircissement sur l'organe de l'oreille de la tortue de mer. Comme la question est curieuse et que je l'ay bien deduite j'en ay fait une petite dissertation. Je la fis voir au Rd pere de Vitri jesuite qui a soin du Journal de Trevoux.[5] Il veut l'inserer dans les journaux, de mesme que ma response sur la cochenille a ce Mr Richter de Leipsic dont je me donnay l'honneur vous envoyer le traitté qu'il a fait sur cette matière.[6] Je reliray ce que j'ay ecrit sur l'oreille de la tortue et j'en fairay une copie pour vous envoyer affin que vous ayez la bonté de la faire voir a Mr Baulot. Je m'attends qu'il me donnera luy mesme de l'eclaircissement la dessus. Je me recommands cepandant a la continuation de vos bontés et vous prie tres humblement de permettre que je sois avec un tres profond respect Monsieur

vostre tres humble et tres obeissant serviteur
frere C. Plumier Minime

Monsieur,

Je me flatte que vous me pardonnerez bien la liberté que j'ay pris de vous recommander une pauvre personne qui souhaiteroit faire le voyage de l'Amerique. Je scay sa necessité et la charité m'a obligé de vous le recommander. Je luy donnay dernierement une lettre pour vous.

Extract from MS 867 fol. 147 à 152

Copie d'une lettre du R. P. Plumier à Mr Bégon.

De Paris, 6e mars 1703

Monsieur,

Vous me pardonnerez bien si je tarde tant à vous rendre mes très humbles

---

[1] Jean-Baptiste Ducasse; Sailor and Governor of S. Domingo in 1691. See Michaud, *Biographie Universelle.*
[2] Unidentified.
[3] See p. 190 and the next letter.
[4] Baulot; often referred to by Plumier. See P-D. Rainguet, *Biographie Saintongeaise*, p. 69. M. Baulot was interested in Plumier's craftsmanship as well as his botanical work.
[5] Le P. E. de Vitry; see Michaud, *Biographie Universelle.*
[6] See also p. 288 for further details concerning "la tortue de la mer." See also – *Journal de Trévoux*, Nov. 1702, pp. 112 et sq.; Sept. 1703, pp. 167 et sq.; Jan. 1704, pp. 165 et sq.

respects et à répondre à la belle lettre de Mr. Baulot. J'ay voulu première-
ment finir un petit ouvrage qui à ce que je me flatte vous fera plaisir. C'est
un *Nova plantarum americanarum genera*. Vous savez que Mr de Tournefort
a fait nouvellement le catalogue de toutes les plantes qu'il a trouvées dans
son voyage du Levant et qu'il y a joint aussi plusieurs nouveaux genres.
Je l'avois prié de joindre à cet ouvrage les nouveaux genres que j'ay fait
de mes plantes de l'Amerique, mais il n'a pas jugé à propos, il me dit d'attendre un autre ouvrage qu'il prétend donner au jour dans deux ou trois
ans, mais comme *fugaces labuntur anni*, je me suis voulu assurer puisque'il
plait au bon Dieu me donner le temps. J'ay donc fait un petit ouvrage que
j'intitule *Nova plantarum americanarum genera autore p. Carolo Plumier, ordinis
Minimorum apud insulas Americanas Botanico regio*. J'auray cent et deux genres
et parce que je n'ay pas le nom de la plus grande partie, je les nommeray
du nom de quelque celebre botaniste,[1] *Bauhinia*,[2] *Caesalpina*,[3] *Pittonia*,[4]
Columnea,[5] etc. J'auray trente et huit planches, je vous envoye par avance
l'épreuve de deux. Après avoir mis le genre et toutes les espèces que je puis
avoir de ce genre, je fais un petit éloge de celuy dont je mets le nom.

PITTONIA

Pittonia est planta genus flore monopetalo, campaniformi globoso, multifido
ex cuius surgit calyce pistillum infimae floris parti ad instar clavi infixum quod
deinde abit in fructum mollem seu baccam sphaericam succi plenam et
duobus seminibus poetam ut plurimum oblongis.

Pittoniae species sunt:
Pittonia humilis anchusae foliis
Pittonia etc...

Clarissimus Josephus Pitton Tournefort Aquisextensi doctor medicus
Parisiensis, Academiae Regiae scientiarum socius, ac in horto regio bo-
tanices professor, institutionum rei herbariae nec non botanici Parisiensis
author, botanicorum facile princeps, apud orientales plagas peregrinatione
famosus. Joannis Schelepici Pitton D.M. eruditissimi patriae ac Provencae
annalistae et historiographi irreprehensibilis nepos cujus familiam patria
magistratibus decoravit, cujusque familia patriam magistratibus decoravit.

Je mettray à peu près le mesme éloge à chaque botaniste dont j'emprunte
le nom pour dénomer un genre. J'ay cru que vous auriez plaisir que je vous
fisse voir par avance un petit échantillon de mon ouvrage. Il est encore
entre les mains de Mrs les examinateurs et des que je l'auray retiré Mr.
Boudot doit l'imprimer, je ne manqueray pas de vous en faire mes re-
cognoissances d'un exemplaire.

---

[1] This has been referred in the article on Plumier, see p. 336.
[2] French family name Bauhin; three members of this family were botanists, see Balteau,
Dictionnaire de Biographie, Vol. V.
[3] After Andrea Caesalpino the Italian naturalist, 1519–1603.
[4] After Pitton de Tournefort. See this letter.
[5] Fabrio Colonna, 1567–1650, author of Φυτοβασανος, *sive plantarum aliquot historia*.

J'envoye enfin à Mr. Baulot mes petits sentiments sur les questions qu'il me fit l'honneur me faire par sa lettre du 30 décembre passé. Je vous prie avoir la bonté de les lire et de m'en faire savoir vostre sentiment. J'ay bien envie de donner toute satisfaction à cet honeste Monsieur quand il luy plaira me faire des questions sur ce que peut suporter la capacité de mon petit génie. Je souhaitterois bien avoir une copie de ce que je luy répondis il y a quelque temps sur le sexe des plantes.[1] Je ne me souviens pas bien de tout ce que je luy marquay et je n'en ay point de brouillard. On ne me dit plus rien sur aucun voyage. Je n'en suis gueres affiigé. J'ay de la bonne besogne ici Dieu merci. Je continue un bel ouvrage que j'entrepris l'année passée savoir dessiner et décrire une espèce de chaque genre des plantes selon l'ordre des Institutions botaniques de Mr. de Tournefort. J'en ay deja les dix premières classes de faites, et j'espère Dieu aydant en dessiner bien autant tout cet esté. Je me recommande à la continuation de vos bontés et vous prie de souffrir que je sois mais avec un très profond respect.

Votre très humble et très obéiss[t] serviteur
(signé) frère C. Plumier Minime.

Monsieur,

Vous me faites bien de l'honneur d'avoir pour agréables mes petites pensées sur vos curieuses questions. Puisque j'ay ce bonheur je tacheray de me conserver la continuation de vostre estime en répondant de mon mieux à celles qu'il vous a pleu me faire par vostre lettre du 30 décembre passé. Ce sera pourtant à condition que vous ne prendres pas mes sentimens pour des décisions. Vous me dites absolument (Decidés) ce n'est pas à moy à décider aucune question. Ce me sera bien assez si je puis avoir le bonheur de vous donner quelque petite satisfaction par une réponse naïve et non pas par une décision absoluë.

Vous me demandes premierement (*si le crocodile ne meut que la machoire inférieure* comme Mr. Duhamel [2] le dit dans son histoire de l'Academie *Maxilla inferior sola est mobilis non item superior ut vulgo creditum est*). Mr Duhamel a très bien dit mais il n'entend proprement que la machoire prise en elle mesme ou considérée séparement du crane. Puisque son articulation ou jonction au crane est si unie et si profonde qu'elle ne luy permet aucun mouvement que conjointement avec tout le reste du crane, auquel elle est jointe de mesme que la machoire supérieure d'un cheval à son crane. Voicy en quoy consiste ce mouvement. Le crocodile remuë ou eleve la machoire supérieure conjointement avec le reste du crane, sa machoire inférieure estant ferme et stable. Enfin il remuë en mesme temps les deux machoires ensemble, l'inférieure en bas et la supérieure en haut conjointement avec le crane. J'ay observé que le crocodile estant tiré à terre lorsqu'on

---

[1] See later pp. 276/7.
[2] Jean-Baptiste Duhamel, *Regiae scientiarum Academiae historia ...*, Paris, 1698, p. 193; see *Journal de Trévoux*, Jan. 1704, art. XII, made up from extracts taken out of this letter. Minor variants. All personal reminiscence and some scientific details lacking in the article.

l'a pris avec un appat attaché au bout d'une corde, il hausse tout la partie supérieure de la teste, c'est a dire la machoire supérieure avec tout le crane, la machoire inférieure estant appuyée sur la terre sans la remuer. J'ay aussi pris garde que lorsqu'il peut attraper quelque gibier, il nage mais presque insensiblement entre deux eaux, la gueule ouverte, en maniere que la machoire inférieure pend en bas presque perpendiculairement, pendant que la supérieure est horizontale avec tout le corps et lorsqu'il est à portée de pouvoir attraper le gibbier (sic) il eleve très promptement la machoire inférieure sans qu'il remuë la supérieure. Enfin j'ay aussi observé que lorsqu'il veut prendre quelque sujet un peu gros (comme je vis un jour deux crocodiles qui attaquèrent successivement un taureau qui traversoit le lac de Miragoan dans l'isle St Domingue). Il ouvre la gueule en manière qu'il écarte en mesme temps les deux machoires l'une en haut et l'autre en bas et cecy se doit entendre que la machoire supérieure ne s'eleve jamais que conjointement avec la crane. Olaus Borrichius [1] dans son *Hermes Ægyptiorum pag. 270* et le R. Père Gouye [2] Jesuitte dans ses Observations physiques et mathématiques pag. 41, 42 etc. ont fort bien observé ce mouvement réciproque. Vous pourres consulter ces deux grands hommes sur d'autres belles particularités concernant le crocodile. Ils décideront vos questions. Ils sont pourtant obmis deux particularités assez remarquables et c'est a faute a ce que je pense de sujets, c'est a dire pour n'en avoir pas eu un nombre suffisant pour pouvoir pousser plus avant leurs belles découvertes.

La premiere de ces deux particularités est une manière de *sternum* situé tout le long du milieu de l'abdomen a l'endroit qu'on appelle la ligne blanche dans l'homme. C'est un os large presque comme le doigt. Il commence immédiatement à l'enfourchure du xiphoïde et va aboutir un peu au dessus du pubis (qu'on pourroit nommer double puisqu'il est composé de quatre grands os) a chaque costé de ce second sternum il y a six costes osseuses mais minces et composées chacune de deux pieces jointes par synchondrose de mesme qu'elles le sont à ce second sternum. Je ne sache encore aucun animal avoir l'abdomen muni de cette manière. Ce n'est pas sans sujet mais j'ignore le pourquoy.

La seconde particularité a esté véritablement observée en partie par quelques auteurs savoir que le crocodile avalle des cailloux. Mr Duvernay [3] en trouva dans l'estomac d'un qui mourut à Versailles comme vous pourrez avoir veu dans la mesme histoire de Mr Duhamel pag. 198, mais je n'ay pas encore veu aucun autheur qui ait observé que le crocodile digère ces cailloux. J'ay bien observé cette digestion en trois on quatre sujets. Je n'en ay guère pris ou je n'aye trouvé des cailloux dans l'estomac les uns encore entiers les autres presque déjà calcinés et friables et enfin entièrement

---

[1] Danish medical writer, sometimes referred to as Olaus von Borch, 1626–1690.
[2] Le Père Thomas Gouye, 1650–1725.
[3] Joseph-Guichard Duvernay (or Duverney), 1648–1730, author of several works on anatomy including a study of the physiology of the sense organs; his work on the anatomy of the ear, *Traité de l'organe de l'ouïe*, Paris, 1683, should be noted in connection with Plumier's own interest in the ear and hearing.

digérés c'est à dire réduits en argile dans les intestins, particulièrement dans un, dont le *rectum* étoit extremement grossi, je l'ouvris et le trouvay totu rempli d'argile de la mesme couleur des cailloux qu'il avoit encore dans l'estomac dont une partie estoit aussy calcinée et friable.

Le *crocodile* n'est pas le seul animal qui avale et qui digere les cailloux. Le *loup* en fait autant. Je l'ay bien remarqué en herborisant dans les montagnes de Provence où un jour particulièrement je rencontray trois fientes d'un loup éloignées d'environ trois pas les unes des autres. Le paysan qui m'accompagnoit s'en appercevant le premier me dit mon père voici de fiente de loup. Je les consideray bien à loisir. La première estoit une argile blanche presque comme de la craye déláyée. La seconde estoit un mélange d'argile un peu moins blanche et de quelques cailloux gros comme de noix les uns encore entiers et les autres deja calcinés et friables. Enfin la troisieme estoit un mélange de quelques pelotons de laine, de deux ou trois petits cailloux durs et d'une vertèbre du col d'une brebis, tout ce peloton estoit bien entier et tout enduit d'une matière gluante, ce qui me fit douter si le loup ne l'auroit pas vomi, ne me pouvant persuader que les boyaux eussent esté capables de s'élargir si fort pour pouvoir donner passage à un si gros peloton, car il estoit bien aussi gros que les deux poings joints ensemble. J'ay observé dans quelques animaux qu'ils revomissent ce qu'ils ne peuvent pas digérer. Le crocodile particulièrement comme il attrape beaucoup de gibbier, canards, vingeons, sarcelles, poules d'eau etc. dont le lac de Miragoan est assez bien fourni, il en revomit les plumes comme j'ay observé moy mesme en quelques uns de ceux que j'y prenois. Le jour que j'arrivay à la Martinique dans mon premier voyage nous prîmes aux filets un fort gros poisson du genre de ceux qu'on appelle requiens (canis carcharias). On l'appelle une vache à la Martinique. Dès qu'on l'eut tiré sur le tillac il renversa son estomac en dehors la gueule et revomit quantité d'excrémens. Vous aurez entendu parler de ce poisson qu'on nomme dorade et qu'on rencontre ordinairement lorsqu'on approache du tropique. Nous en prismes un jour un vers le soleil couchant. Je trouvay dans son estomac quatre clous l'un long de près de quatre pouces et les trois autres de deux. Mons. Duhamel nostre lieutenant avoit jetté le matin ces trois derniers en mer et le gros avoit échapé des mains du maître charpentier qui radouboit quelques pièces du bord l'après diné. Il auroit fallu nécessairement qu'il les eust revomis, si on ne veut dire qu'il les eût digérés, mais c'est une question si les animaux peuvent digérer les métaux. Vous pouvez voir ce que rapportent sur ce sujet Mrs de l'Académie des sciences dans la description anatomique de huit autruches dans les Mémoires pour l'histoire naturelle pag. 173 et 174.

Quant à la seconde question que vous me proposée, savoir si le *colibri* [1] est un véritable oiseau ou une espèce moyenne entre l'oiseau et l'insecte volant; vous avés bien de quoy vous en éclaircir dans le cabinet de Mr l'intendant. Vous y en trouverez assurément. Je me souviens de lui avoir

---

[1] Littré (1957) quotes Labat *Nouveau voyage aux îles*, Paris, 1722, probably the earliest printed description of the colibri in French. Often confused with the "oiseau-mouche," but see Voltaire, *Candide*, ch. 17, who clearly makes the distinction.

apporté de la Martinique au retour de mon premier voyage un nid de ces petits mais admirables oiseaux, les œufs y estoient dedans et la mere aussi, mais morte et embaumée. Si vous en souhaittés la description j'ay de quoy vous satisfaire, j'en ay décrit deux espèces qu'on voit assés communément dans toutes les isles. Ce sont véritablement les plus petits oiseaux que j'aye jamais veu, mais avec toute leur petitesse ils ne laissent pas de se faire craindre des bien gros. Je les ay veu poursuivre une certaine espèce d'oiseau qu'on appelle gros bec dans les isles. C'est un oiseau un peu plus gros qu'une grive. Son bec est large, gros et pointu et fort propre pour gober ces pauvres petits oisillons quand il en peut attraper le nid, mais gare le père ou la mère. C'est un agréable plaisir de voir fuir et crier ce gros bec, le petit colibri à ses trousses. Il s'attache sous ses aisselles et y enfonce son petit bec pointu come une aiguille et luy donne tant de coups que bien souvent il le met hors d'estat. Je n'ay jamais remarqué aucune mélodie dans le chant de ce petit oiseau, véritablement. Il se fait assez entendre par une manière de grincement fort aigu. Il voltige continuellement d'une fleur à l'autre, mais d'une vitesse si admirable qu'on a de la peine à l'appercevoir et alors il fait du bruit avec ses ailes. Je me souviens qu'un jour à la Martinique j'entendis d'assez loin un gros bourdonnement presque comme d'un essaim d'abeilles. C'estoient plus de cinq cens de ces petits oiseaux qui voltigeoient alentour d'un gros arbre en fleur dont ces petits oiseaux prenoient le suc au dedans des tuyaux car ils ne vivent proprement que de cette liqueur qui se trouve dedans les fleurs et c'est pour cela que Dieu l'a pourveu d'une langue très propre à ce sujet,[1] elle est fort déliée, cartilagineuse, longue d'environ un pouce et demi et dentelée au bout comme les barbillons d'une flèche. Il y en a comme je vous ay déjà dit deux espèces, les plus petits ont le bec droit et la langue simple, et les plus gros ont le bec un peu courbé et la langue double. Je n'ay jamais remarqué aucune odeur ni dans l'un ni dans l'autre. J'en ay apporté quelques uns desséchés que j'ay mesme conservé longtemps bien envelopés dans du papier, mais je n'y ay jamais senti ni ambre ni musc.

Pour ce qui regarde vostre question sur les tortuës de mer qu'on appelle carrets, je n'ay jamais expérimenté ni mesme jamais entendu dire que quand elle a esté une fois dépouillée de ses écailles elle soit assez vigoureuse pour en reproduire d'autres. Je ne doute pas que cela ne puisse estre, puisque les ongles des doigts qui sont à peu près de mesme nature que les écailles des tortuës, se renouvellent lorsque par accident elles tombent, comme il m'est arrivé deja quelques fois aux ongles des gros doigts des pieds qui s'estant détachées d'elles-même ont esté suivies par d'autres quelque temps après.[2] Si je retourne jamais dans les isles, je ne manqueray pas de remarquer cette circonstance.

Quant à la froideur du sang des tortuës je puis vous assurer qu'il est aussi froid que de l'eau commune. Je fus environ deux mois à la pesche de ces animaux dans les grenadins avec quelques filibustiers de la Martinique.

[1] The type of argument satirized by Voltaire in *Candide:* we need spectacles, therefore we have noses.
[2] Told with the typical fortitude that one associates with this extraordinary man.

La pesche fut assez heureuse, nous nous en retournions la barque bien chargée de la viande salée et outre ce de douze grandes en vie. Le temps nous fut si contraire dès que nous eumes levé l'ancre de St Vincent qu'apres avoir couru plusieurs jours par tous les rhombs des vents sans jamais pouvoir prendre terre, ny à la Grenade, ni à Tobago, ni mesme en terre ferme ou le mauvais temps nous avoit mené, nostre eau nous manqua entierement et apres avoir demeuré pres de cinq jours sans boire qu'environ la quantité d'une chopine d'eau chacun nous nous avisames de boire le sang d'une tortuë qui nous restoit encore en vie des douze. L'extrêmité inexprimable que je souffrois m'obligea à faire comme les autres, j'en bus ma part environ une demie écuellée. Nous étions seize et nous nous partageames comme l'on dit en bons frères. Je trouvay ce sang aussi froid que l'eau commune des rivieres (*experto crede Roberto*).

L'indicible faim et encore la plus indicible soif que nous souffrions obligea quelques uns de nos gens de manger la chair de cette tortuë ou du moins la macher toute cruë pour se tenir la bouche un peu fraiche.[1] Quand ils l'eurent ouverte j'apperceus le poulmon extremement enflé et blanc comme du linge blanchi. Nonobstant ma grande faiblesse car je ne pouvois plus me tenir debout la curiosité me prit de voir et d'ouvrir ce poulmon n'en ayant jamais veu de semblable dans un si grand nombre de tortuës que nous avions ouvertes dans les grenadins.[1] Je le trouvay tout rempli d'une eau très limpide quoy qu'un peu glaireuse, je l'exprimay moy mesme comme une éponge dans un seau, il en sortit environ deux écuelles d'eau que nous melames avec deux autres écuelles d'eau de la mer pour faire cuire une partie de cette tortuë, nous en eumes environ quatre morceaux chacun et deux ou trois cuillerées du bouillon qui restoit. La Divine providence nous envoya ce petit secours pour nous donner la force d'en attendre un plus grand ou de découvrir terre ou de nous donner quelque bonne pluye. Nous souffrimes bien encore trois jours entiers sans boire goutte d'eau, et dans le temps que nous commencions à mourir, la Divine Miséricorde nous envoya une pluye si abondante que nous en bumes tout notre saoul et en eumes assez pour faire cuire un peu de viande salée,[2] ce qui nous tira d'une mort évidente et d'une misere que la langue humaine ne peut exprimer. Par surcroit de bonheur le lendemain matin nous abordames l'isle St Domingue dans un endroit que les Espagnols appellent Baya honda et nos francois la Baye de Nippe.

Enfin vous me demandés ou vous pourrés trouver une bonne figure du mancenillier.[3] Je ne vous envoyeray pas fort loin de chez vous, Mr l'Intendant [4] a dans sa bibliothèque un merveilleux livre de plusieurs plantes de l'Amérique peintes excellemment au naturel. Je scay que le *mancenillier* y est, mais comme je ne me souviens pas si la description y est jointe la voicy en peu de paroles. Voir un poirier d'Europe et voir un *mancenillier* de l'Amérique c'est la mesme chose quant au feuillage et quant au port. Le

---

[1] Again told with admirable fortitude and unconcern.
[2] Thus breaking, of course, his vows as Minim; but see what Lister has to say about his refusal to eat meat in Paris, p. 190.
[3] See Littré (1957), also O.E.D. under Manchineel.
[4] ... de la Marine à Rochefort(?)

mancenillier vient véritablement beaucoup plus grand qu'un poirier. J'en ay veu dans les grenadins d'aussi grands que nos plus grands noyers. Les feuilles sont un peu plus vert claires (sic) que celles des poiriers mais elles ont et la mesme grandeur et la mesme figure. Ses fleurs ne sont pas trop considérables à voir, ce sont, de petits sommets rouges attachés par pelottons le long d'un poinçon ou broche longue d'environ demi pied. Les fruits naissent séparément dans d'autres endroits du mesme arbre. Les embrions ressemblent ordinairement aux fruits de nos mercuriales,[1] c'est à dire qu'ils sont comme à double teste. Ils deviennent ensuitte de pommes raynettes tirant sur le jaune, mais garde de ces pommes. Elles ont au milieu un noyau fibreux fort compacte gros et rond presque comme une noisette. Tout l'arbre jette du lait blanc mais si malin que m'estant un jour frotté les yeux par mégarde après avoir manié une branche pour la dessiner, d'abord ils s'enflamèrent et s'enflèrent si fort que j'avois peine à les ouvrir. Par bonheur un Révér[d] Père Carme me voyant en cet état fit vitement tirer du lait d'une vache qu'il mesla avec de l'eau et m'en fit bassiner les yeux, je fus bientost soulagé de l'inflammation qui m'affligeoit fort et mes yeux désenflerent le jour mesme.[2] C'est pour ce sujet qu'on a bien de la peine à trouver des ouvriers qui veuillent abatre ces arbres dont le bois est beaucoup plus beau et meilleur que nos plus beaux de noyer. Je ne doute pas que vous n'en ayés veu à La Rochelle ou les vaisseaux en apportent souvent à leur retour des isles.[3]

Je vous prie Mr d'accepter mes petites réponses ou du moins ma bonne volonté. Vous me témoignez désir de me voir à La Rochelle. Je voudrois bien y estre deja pour vous témoigner combien je vous honore et combien je suis avec tout respect Mr. v. très humble et très obéiss' servit. Signé frère C. Plumier Minime

Copie d'une lettre écrite à Mr Begon intend. à Rochefort

A Paris 10e aoust 1702

Monsieur,

Je me persuade que Mr de Tournefort n'aura pas manqué à son devoir et de répondre à celle que vous me fites la grace m'envoyer pour luy et que je luy rendis aussitôt, qu'il n'aura pas manqué aussi a vous faire savoir les belles et grandes richesses qu'il a aporté de son voyage. Vous seriés charmé de voir le nombre et la beauté des desseins qu'il a aportés, j'espere que vous verrez le tout un jour imprimé. Il va pourtant donner pour préliminaire un Catalogue de toutes les plantes nouvelles qu'il a découvertes et il va établir mesme plusieurs nouveaux genres et à vette occasion je l'ay prié de vouloir bien ajouter plusieurs nouveaux que j'ay aussi établis sur plusieurs de mes plantes de l'Amérique et j'espere que vous les verrez dans le mesme ouvrage, j'y donne le nom de tous les grands auteurs botaniques, parti-

---

[1] See Littré (1957) under 2 mercuriale, also O.E.D. under Mercurial (substantive) 1.
[2] cf. the episode of the "liane brûlante" or "colocasia" referred to on p. 196.
[3] The botanical garden at La Rochelle is still justly famous.

culierement de ceux qui ont travaillé aux plantes de l'Amérique comme hernandia ximenia,[1] pisonia marcgravia [2] etc... Ce me sera une grande consolation de voir du moins mes ouvrages énoncés et je seray content quand meme ils ne verroient jamais le jour, ce que j'appréhende fort si le bon Dieu ne me secoure de sa miséricorde. On m'avoit tant promis de faire imprimer celuy des fougeres [3] mais *Dies mali sunt,* pour ces sortes d'ouvrages, pourtant *non est abreviata manus Dei* et j'espere qu'il me favorisera un jour de sa Divine Providence. Cependant je prens la liberté de vous envoyer ce petit discours de l'oreille de la tortuë que j'avois promis à Mr Baulot. Je m'attends qu'il m'en dira son sentiment et qu'il y corrigera ce qu'il y a à corriger, j'ay dessein de le faire insérer dans le Journal de Trevoux s'il en vaut la peine. Je me recommande toujours à la continuation de vos bontés, je suis avec un tres profond respect, Monsieur, vostre tres humble et tres obligé serviteur frère. Signé C. Plumier Minime.

Extrait d'une lettre écrite à Mr Begon, par le R. P. Plumier

Du 16e décembre 1702

Mr de Tournefort fait imprimer un bel appendix des nouveaux genres qu'il a découverts et un catalogue de toutes les plantes qu'il a trouvé dans son voyage.[4] Je ne puis me résoudre à Mr Baulot sur la question de la diversité des sexes dans les plantes, en toute son étendüe, cette matière demande une plume plus libre que la mienne. Je luy dirai pourtant que j'estime que la plante est proprement le masle et la terre la femelle, qu'il examine bien mon petit sentiment. *Planta tanquam mas semen effundit suum; terra in utero suo recipit, fovet ac tandem parturit.* l'autheur de la lettre qu'il m'a marqué prétend que cette mesme poussiere dont sont remplis les sommets des fleurs soit la cause de la fécondité des plantes, Mr de Tournefort prétend que c'est proprement ce *qu'il y a de moins* propre dans le suc nourricier pour nourrir les jeunes fruits (Elemens Botan 54). Je serois plutost du sentiment de Mr de Tournefort, puisque nous voyons des fruits qui meurissent très bien sans cette poussiere et dont la graine ne laisse pas d'estre bien féconde; les figuiers par exemple n'ont ni fleurs ni sommets qui puissent leur fournir cette poussiere fécondante, cependant les figues ne laîssent pas de bien meurir et leurs graines de produire des figuiers.[5] Si l'esté qui vient j'ay le temps et le moyen j'ay dessein de semer quelques unes de ces plantes dont un pied ne porte que des fruits et l'autre ne porte que des fleurs comme des épinars et des mercuriales. Je prendray bien garde aux plantes qui portent les fruits. Je n'en laisseray qu'une seule dans quelque vase que je mettray bien à

[1] Named after F. Hernandez (1530–1587), Spanish naturalist.

[2] Named after two explorers Guilielmus Piso (XVIIth cent.) and Georg Marcgravius (1610–1644); the *De Indiae re naturali tractatus* of the former and the *Tractatus de Brasiliae topographia* were published together, Amsterdam, 1658.

[3] *Traité des Fougères de l'Amérique,* printed in Paris (Imprimerie Royale), 1705.

[4] i.e. *Corollarium Institutionum Rei Herbariae, in quo plantae 1386 ... in Orientalibus Regionibus observantae recensentur,* Paris, 1703.

[5] This is not in fact accurate. The whole question of the sexuality of plants and theories of pollination were not properly examined until the mid XVIIIth century.

l'écart lion des autres plantes qui portent les fleurs, de peur qu'elle ne re-
çoive cette mesme poussiere des fleurs. J'éprouveray par là si la plante
produira bien et si les semences qu'elle produira seront ensuite fertiles.
L'expérience est aisée. Cependant j'estime que la fécondité des plantes
dépend particulierement du sel naturel de la terre. C'est le sentiment de
Mr de Willis [1]: *Quippe mineralium accretio, terrae fertilitas plantarum vegetatio
et imprimis crebra animalium foetatio et progenies a seminio salino originem ducunt.*
Voila sur quoy j'appuye mon sisteme que la plante est proprement le masle
et la terre sa femelle en fournissant à la semence tous les principes actifs
et passifs qu'elle contient en soy pour sa production, acroissement et perfection. Pour les mouches luisantes, je n'ay pas observé proprement si cette
matiere qui luit pendant la nuit pourroit servir de phosphore, si je faisois
un quatrième voyage à St Domingue j'examinerois bien la chose. Je luy
diray à cette occasion, qu'un jour voulant faire du mastic j'en découvris
un qui me surprit beaucoup, j'employay de la poix noire que je fis fondre
avec de la chaux de nos crachoirs que nous tenons dans le cœur et qu'on
avoit tiré depuis quelque temps pour en remettre de la nouvelle,[2] comme
je remuais la poix fondüe avec la chaux pour les bien mesler, je fus fort sur-
pris de voir tout le dedans du pot en feu. Je le tiray vitement de dessus le
rechaut croyant qu'effectivement le feu s'estoit pris dans le pot. J'avois
beau souffler dedans pour éteindre ce prétendu feu, mais je m'aperceus avec
un très grand étonnement que c'estoit tout le mélange qui luisoit,mais
d'une lueur admirable qui dura tant que la matière demeura liquide. Je
n'ay jamais plus fait cette mesme expérience. Si Mr Baulot est curieux sur
cette matière il pourra l'expérimenter, elle ne lui coutera guère. Pour les
mouches luisantes j'en ay remarqué de deux espèces l'une petite à la Martinique, l'autre grande à St Domingue, celle cy est grosse comme la dernière
phalange d'un doit, c'est un escarbot de couleur minime,[3] il porte sa matière
dans le thorax mesme. La lueur paroist sur le dos comme par deux trous
vitrés de la grandeur d'un O commun, et par dessous entre le thorax et
l'abdomen justement dans l'articulation de tous les deux, ce dernier endroit
ne luit que quand l'animal vole, car quand on le tient entre les doigts cette
lueur de cet endroit ne paroist plus, mais bien seulement celle du dessus le
dos. Ces sortes d'escarbots ou mouches comme on dit car c'est proprement
une espece d'escarbot, *scaraboeus*, paroissent particulierement en décembre,
janvier et février; ceux de la Martinique sont fort petits, ce sont aussi des
petits escarbots. Il n'y a que le dessous qui reluise. Je me souviens qu'ils
reluisent dans le mesme temps surtout quand la nuit est sereine après une
pluye. Je souhaitterois bien pouvoir contenter à fond la curiosité de Mr
Baulot, peut estre que je seray plus heureux dans uns autre question.

[1] Thomas Willis to whose *Cerebri nervorumque descriptio*, London, 1664, reference has already
been made.
[2] An interesting glimpse of Plumier the craftsman.
[3] "Couleur d'un gris sombre, tirant sur le noir ou le "tanné." Elle prend son nom des
Religieux de S. François de Paule qui, par humilité, se nommaient frères minimes, et qui
avaient adopté cette couleur comme uniforme de leur ordre," H. Havard, *Dictionnaire de
l'ammeublement*, Paris, 1887, vol. III, p. 873. Havard quotes the following entry from the
Inventaire de Grégoire Beaumon, Marchand, Bordeaux, 1607 "Plus deulx aulnes de drap minime
de couleur, à quatre solz (l)"aulne."

Monsieur,

Vous me pardonnerez bien la liberté que je prens de vous prier de me vouloir faire dessiner une sardine de Royan en toute sa grandeur et forme naturelle par quelques uns de vos dessineurs. J'ay prié un de mes amis de Marseille de m'en faire dessiner une de celles de Provence. Je suis bien aise d'en voir leur différence, et si elles ont toutes les deux les mesmes caracteres Je vous demande bien pardon de ma liberté. J'ay cru que vous auriez plaisir de me faire cette grace. Je médite un traité des poissons, c'est un ouvrage compétent à un minime.[1] J'ay besoin pour ce sujet de voyager un peu les costes de nos mers tant du ponant que de Provence, c'est pour cela que je souhaittois particulièrement d'aller passer un petit esté avec vous à Rochefort et à La Rochelle, comme aussi pour mon traité des Coquillages pour en disséquer quelques uns vivans. Pour le dessein que je vous avois fait savoir, d'aller voyager pour un second volume du tour,[2] je suposois de le faire en temps de paix. Je say tout ce qu'il y a de particulier icy, à Paris. Je me flatte que si je faisois ce voyage je decouvrirois bien de belles choses sur cette matière particulièrement en Allemagne à Nuremberg où j'apprens qu'il y a des tourneurs admirables. Je voudrois bien voir aussi le cabinet du chanoine Settala [3] a Milan, on m'a dit qu'il y a des pièces tres ingenieuses. J'espère que la Divine Providence me favorisera de sa miséricorde je me sens encore bien homme Dieu mercy. Je travailleray tant qu'il luy plaira me favoriser de sa grace.

---

[1] We may recall the remark of Martin Lister, p. 190.
[2] i.e. *L'Art de Tourner* etc.
[3] Italian mechanic 1600–1680; see P. M. Terzago, *Musaeum Septalianum Manfredi Septalae Patritii Mediolanensis industrioso labore constructum*, Tortona, 1664, several editions.

SOLUM, SALUM, COELUM;
PREFACE TO VOL. XV OF THE PLUMIER MSS IN
THE MUSÉUM D'HISTOIRE NATURELLE, PARIS

Copy of MS 23 in the Bibliothèque du Muséum d'Histoire Naturelle, Paris.

D. O. M.

Solum, Salum, Coelum

Americanum seu Plantarum, Piscium, volucrumque Insulis Antillis et Sandominicà naturalium Icones et descriptiones Authore Patre Carolo Plumier Ordinis Minimorum Phisico-Botanico necnon Parisiensis Conventus alumno.[1]

BOTANICIS ET CURIOSIS

Eosdem licet exanclaverint labores, iisdemque infudaverint operibus non pauci rerum naturalium perscrutatores sagacissimi eorum tamen accensus, studiis me fragilem truci committere pelago,[2] montes adire, valles, silvasque americanas peragrare non horrui ... (sic) ut in iis enascentium tum plantarum tum animalium mirabiles formas perlustrarem [3] spectandasque oculis omnium exhiberem... (sic) de vitae humanae brevitate, deque naturae operium innumerabilitate certior factus... (sic) utpote quae nec multi insimul viri quamtum liber studiosi per totam vitae curriculum perfecte tractare potentes (?) usquam existant. Huic sententiae me ex insulis Antillanis minimae confirmat solidatque tot etenim tantarumque rerum mirabilium ferax conspicitur ut in ipsis discutiendis post multos adhibitos labores vita unius viri non sufficiat. Tantorum igitur virorum longe quam abhorrerem ob insudationes,[4] quin magis ac magis pro mea virili parte his totus incumbere decreverim... (sic) sperans fore aliquando ut ipse nova incuderem, nova tamen incidenda posterioribus ac superstitibus relicturus quibuslibet quamvis insumptis lucubrationibus.[5] Quid tum,

[1] Alumno – unusual appendage to Plumier's signature.
[2] Truci pelago – the wild open sea. Phrase found in Horace.
[3] Perlustro, – to make a thorough survey.
[4] Continuous and copious sweating; Lister referred to his wasted and fever-ridden body.
[5] Insumptis lucubrationibus, i.e. burning the midnight oil.

ipsius Lucii Annaei Senecae sententiam effari liceat; qui praecesserunt non mihi praecipuisse videntur quae dici poterant, sed aperuisse... crescit enim in dies materia, et inventuris inventa non obstant. Contestatus fuerit quantumvis sapientissimus rex Salomon[1] nihil sub sole novum usquam existere... contrariis tamen confirmamur experientiis, de novo quotidiana exoriri nova. Aristoteles, Plinius, Hipocrates, Galenus, Dioscorides innumeri tandem sapientissimorum alii: tum vegetabilium, tum animalium naturae investigandae penitus incubuerint, attamen nova in dies insurgere ipsis omnino incognita demiramur.

Mathiolus,[2] Bahuinus,[3] Paena,[4] Lobel [5] ac ipse Clusius [6] curas omnes rebus naturalibus insumpserint; innumera tamen nobis pertractanda reliquerunt. Testes huius, aetatis nostrae insignes Botanicos Bocconum,[7] Raium,[8] Hermandum [9] advoco, potissimum vero illustrissimos quos Gallia nostra oblectando reveretur ac intuetur, Fagonum [10] dico ac Tournafortium [11] alterum Reginae protomedicum necnon hortus regii praefectum, alterum vero regium Botanicum ac demonstrandarum in regio horto parisiensi plantarum publicum proffessorem (sic). Quasnam, quotque nunc nobis plantas denovo ob oculos abipsismet detectas exponunt, quibus se doctissimis quibusque demirandos demonstrant. Parcant ergo faveantque precor rerum perscrutatores diligentissimi ac me Botanicis inserant. Me nec tam patiens Lacedemon nec tam Larissae percussit campus opimae quam gelidum nemus plantarumque decor, pro quibus bis patiar mari.[12] Verum enim ut fatear tantus meis exarsit visceribus rerum Botanicarum fervor. Ut me neque Noricus ensis, nec saevus ignis,[13] nec mare naufragum deterreret, dum audax omnia perpeti visam britannos hospitibus. Feros et Laetum Equino Sanguine concanum,[14] visam pharetratos gelonos et Scithicum inviolatus amnem. Non obtusa adeo gestamus pectora,[15] casus mihi cogniti tam illustrium virorum quibus toto post Botanica pectore anhelantibus, nullique parcentibus labori dii tandem nova detegenda vendiderunt. Nec

[1] See Conclusion, reference to wisdom of Solomon, 3 Reg. IV (A.V. 1 Kings IV) in which his knowledge of natural history is specifically mentioned v. 33.

[2] Pierrandrea Mattioli, 1501–1577.

[3] I.e. Bauhin, see previously p. 269 note 2.

[4] Unidentified.

[5] Keeper of the Botanick Garden, Oxford, see p. 196. Plumier named Lobelia after him.

[6] i.e. C. de l'Ecluse with whom John Gerard, the herbalist, shared samples of potatoes given by Sir Francis Drake; see A. de Virville op. cit., p. 25, where the name Gerard appears as Shérard.

[7] Paolo Boccone, Plumier's tutor in Botany in Rome.

[8] John Ray, the English botanist, see p. 195.

[9] Hernandez intended? See p. 276.

[10] Fagon the celebrated Royal Physician.

[11] Pitton de Tournefort, referred to passim in the chapter on Plumier and in the Correspondence quoted in this Appendix.

[12] Bis ... i.e. the two journeys he had undertaken in the Antilles. Me ne patiens ...: Horace, Odes, I, 7, 10.

[13] Neque Noricus ... ignis: Horace, Odes, I, 17, 9–11.

[14] One might render concanum by "of fierce Spanish blood" [i.e. Concanus – where the inhabitants are reputed to have lived on horses' blood.] Audax ... perpeti: Horace, Odes, I, 3, 25. ... amnem: ibid. III, 4, 33.

[15] Non ... pectora: Vergil, Aen. I, 567.

mihi novercari¹ deos crediderim qui pro Botanicis potissimum magnas
obeuntia terras tot maria intravi, penitusque repostas indorum gentes.²
Favete ergo Doctissimi quique, meosque labores benigne accipite: fateor
equidem tum in horto Parisiensi tum in horto malabarico satis spectanda
reperiri quibus abunde ingeniis vestris satisfiat: attamen unum dicam, suis
scilicet Americam decorari mirabilibus aeque ac Europam et Asiam suis.³
Non pigent ergo Americanos labores perscrutari, licet eadem forte quae in
horto Parisiensi scilicet et malabarico visuntur, conspiciatis, nova tamen
poteritis demirari, tum florum in planta eiusdem speciei ordinatione, tum
foliorum incisuris, ac tandem fructuum configuratione quae quodammodo
forte diversa novum aliquid oculis vestris demirandum subiicient. Nec tantum aliquid novi moliri studui, sed etiam ut penitiorem rerum in hoc
opere tractandarum notitiam praeberem; chartae mediocris plagulae tum
plantarum, tum animalium exactas formas exarare totus incubui, eas siet
in angusta charta tamen secundum earum amplitudinem in toto aut in
parte delineando.⁴ Etenim mea in hoc fuit sententia ut rerum vitae tuen-
dae(?) necessariarum quae ob oculos quotidie obversantur omni errore
ablato indubitatam agnitionem genuinis delineationibus quique adipisci
queant. Ipse namque quotidianis confirmor experimentis doctissimorum
nempe authorum libros, ob plantarum et animalium incuratas et inexactas
figuras studiosis parum prodesse, quin multum facescere taedii [+ et er-
roris ⁵]. Parcant pharmacorum ac naturalium Americanorum ante authores
doctissimis (sic) non illos aspernandi sed potius horum scripta illustrandi
causa, haec scribo [+ videndus viv...? censura prim... c. 17? ⁶]; quantum etenim dolendum ac quantum damnosum, tum Acostae,⁷ tum Pisonis,⁸
Marcgravii,⁹ multorumque numquam satis laudandorum qui de mirabilibus
Americanis curiose docteque pertractarunt, scripta lectitando, permulta
propter eorum incuriosas delineationes non agnosse. Quod non levis ponderis
agnoscens celeberrimus Fabius Columna ¹⁰ suas aseipso adinventas et curiose
delineatas plantas nobis obtulit, unde ipsices opus integerrimum demiramur,
potensque quod studiosis quibusque gerat.

Quantum vero in me est ingenue fateor me numquam plantarum delineationibus operam dedisse, si librorum Botanicorum plantis exacte
delineatas reperissem. Nam citius quam meis viribus par erat doctissimi

---

¹ novercor, novercari – to be harsh towards (i.e. like the traditional step-mother, no-
verca); A. Souter, *Glossary of Later Latin*, Oxford, 1949.
² Magnas ... gentes: Vergil, *Aen.* VI, 58–60, substituting for "*Massylum* gentes" (N.
African tribe) "*Indorum* gentes".
³ Plumier a "modern"; the New World equals the Old for wonders.
⁴ This and the following sentences give Plumier's theory of what an illustrated book
should be.
⁵ In margin.
⁶ In margin.
⁷ See previously pp. 205, 206.
⁸ See previously this Appendix p. 276, note 2.
⁹ *ibid.* p. 276 note 2.
¹⁰ *ibid* p. 269 note 5.

Bocconi,[1] necnon ingenuissimi tunc adolesciensis Francisci de Onuphriis [2] documentis ac infructionibus Romae degens ablactatus libros quos poteram Botanicos enixe pervolvebam, ut in ipsis quod a praeceptoribus deerat, mihi compararem: sit quoties ut agnovi eorum incuriosis stemmatibus deceptus, qui sysimbrium pro mentha, ocinum pro serpillo acciperem.[3] Unde ut quodammodo mihi et Botanicis prodessem plantas exacte delineandas mecum decrevi, ut eas graphicis meis delineationibus genuine agnoscendas praeberem; nec ipsas tantum accurate depingere sat mihi visum fuit, at etiam earum sinceris ac praecisis descriptionibus operam navare [4]; et (?) omni parte delineationibus scilicet et descriptionibus, quantum in me erat facili negotio libros Botanicos deligentibus adaperirem. Insuper ut nihil operi deesset plantas ac animalia pro classibus suis peculiaribus distribuendo, ordinare totis viribus sum conatus, eas nodorum ac vulgarium voces in fine descriptionum secutus, locaque ac tempestates earum denotando.

Favete ergo Doctissimi viri meosque minimos labores benigne adspicite. Ego namque suo benigno favore, dum memor ipse mei, dum spiritus nos reget artus,[5] perque undas perque invia saxa adnabo,[6] ut naturam laboriose eviscerando mirabilia sua oculis vestris satisfaciendo detegam; novaque diis auspicibus, divorum et matre secunda detegendo benevolentiae vestrae satisfaciam.

Studiorum ac virtutum vestrarum cliens humillimus.
Fr. Carolus Plumier minimus.

---

[1] See p. 188 and p. 280.
[2] *ibid.*
[3] i.e. a confusion between two sorts of mint (σίσυμβρον – a kind of mint or thyme, Liddell & Scott, *Lexicon*) and between basil (ocinum) and wild-thyme (serpillum)
[4] It will be recalled that this phrase was used by Lesguillier in his *Ratio Studiorum* when he urges the student to strive hard at his work.
[5] Dum . . . artus: Vergil, *Aen.* IV, 336.
[6] Perque . . . adnabo (*adnavimus* in original): Vergil, *Aen.* I, 537, 8.
* For establishing the text and for pointing out the quotations from Horace and Vergil I am indebted to Mr. W. D. H. Moore of the City of London School.

BIBLIOGRAPHY

I. PRINTED WORKS BY MEMBERS OF THE ORDER DURING
THE XVIITH CENTURY,

including a few works of the early XVIIIth century by authors such as Charles Plumier and René Thuillier who belong essentially to the XVIIth century.

ALLÈGRE, Joseph. (1630–1697). Instructiens moralos, sur tous leis evangilos domini-calos de l'an, *Marseille*, 1688.

ALLERET, André (fl. 1620). Notae in universam Scripturam, *Sedan*(?), 1625.

ALVIN, see DALVIN.

AMOUNET, Charles-François. (fl. 1650). Discours funèbre ... Madame la Comtesse de Malert, *Anvers*, 1658.

– Harangue funèbre prononcé aux évêques de Philippe le Grand, Roi catholique des Espagnes et des Indes, *Bruxelles*, 1665.

– Homilia in laudem D. Thomas Aquinatis, *Anvers*, 1658.

– Jésus-Christ, Prêtre et victime, imité par Philippe Eugène Amounet, Sieur d'Hailly, *Bruxelles*, 1660.

– La prêtrise héréditaire de Jésus-Christ, conservée dans l'oratoire de S. Philippe Neri, *Douai*, 1661.

– Sacrosancta Divi Iovinis jurisprudentia, *Anvers, s.d.*

– Sermo in iubilaeo R. P. Balthazaris d'Avila, *Lille*, 1666.

– Sermo gallicus habitus in iubelaeo R. P. Henrici de Comans, *Bruxelles*, 1668.

– Velleris aurei misteria, *Bruxelles*, 1658.

ARMOISES, Charles Louis de. (fl. 1610). Lettres au P. Claude du Vivier, *Paris*, 1613.

ARZELLIER, Etienne. (fl. 1620). La lutte spirituelle, *Paris*, 1621.

AVILA, Balthazar d'. (fl. 1635). Manipulus Minimorum, *Lille*, 1677. (Edited by a Corrector General of the Order, G. Pizzurnus).

BAIRD, Andrew. (?–1632). L'entretien de l'âme dévote sur l'excellence ... de Dieu, *Lyon*, 1625.

BARRÉ, Nicolas. (1621–1686). Statuts et règlements des Ecoles Chrétiennes et Charitables du Saint Enfant Jésus, *Paris*, 1685.

– Another edition, *Paris*, 1876.

– Lettres spirituelles du R. P. Barré, religieux Minime, *Rouen*, 1697.

– Maximes de conduite chrétienne, *s.l.n.d.*[1]

– Maximes particulaires pour les Ecoles Charitables, *Paris*, 1694.

– Lettres: l'esprit du R. P. Barré ... d'après ses lettres, *Paris*, 1889.

– Un texte inédit de Barré. Published by Y. Poutet in *Revue d'ascétique et de mystique*, *Toulouse*, 1960.

BERNARD, Joseph. (1650–1727). Instructions chrétiennes sur l'utilitisation ... de l'Eucharistie, *Paris*, s.d.

BERTAUT, Léonard. (d. 1662). L'illustre Orbandale, ou l'histoire de la ville et cité de Chalon-sur-Saône, 2 vols, *Lyon*, 1662.

– La très-ancienne et très-auguste ville d'Autun, *Chalon-sur-Saône*, 1653.

BLANCHOT, Pierre. (1598–1637). Octave du Saint Sacrement, *Paris*, 1645.

– Sermons pour l'Avent, *Paris*, 1635.

– Sermons pour les fêtes, *Paris*, 1656.

---

[1] A reprint of this work was made in Toulouse, 1876.

BLANCHOT, Pierre. (ctd.) Idea Bibliothecae universalis, *Paris*, 1631.
- Bibliotheca Sanctorum et antiquorum Patrum concionatoria, *Paris*, 1631. (Work continued by Pierre Pijart, Minim. Second edition, *Paris*, 1654).
- Règles générales et particulières pour ceux qui aspirent à la parfaite dévotion, *Paris*, 1633.
- Le vrai accomplissement des désirs de l'homme en la vie présente, *Paris*, 1635.
- For works edited by Blanchot, see La Noue, Michel.
BOILLOT, Jean. (1658-1728). Lettres sur le secret de la confession, *Cologne (Dijon)*, 1703.
- La vraie pénitence, *Dijon*, 1707.
BOUCAT, Antoine. (fl. 1690). Le repos en Dieu, *Paris*, 1696.
- Theologia Patrum dogmata, scholastica-positiva, *Paris*, 1718.
BOUCHER, Jean. (1592-1635). L'Arche de Noë, *Paris*, 1622.
- Pèlerinage de Notre-Dame de Moyen-Pont, *Paris*, 1623.
BOURDIN, Mathieu. (d. 1692). La vie et conduite de la demoiselle Madeleine Vigneron, sœur du Tiers-Ordre de Saint François de Paule, *Rouen*, 1679.
BOYENVAL, Antoine. (1598-1660). Civis Sanctorum et domesticus Dei, *Rome*, 1667.
BRESSAND, Philibert. (fl. 1690). Oraison funèbre de Marianne d'Autriche ... 14 juillet, 1696, *Bruxelles*, 1696.
- Oraison funèbre de Marie-Antoinette, archiduchesse d'Autriche ... 12 février 1693, dans l'église des Pères Minimes de Bruxelles, *Bruxelles*, 1693.
- Système de la grâce, *s.l.*, 1706?
BRUNEL, Bertrand. (d. 1618). La muse religieuse, *Bordeaux*, 1618.
BRUNO, John (Jean), (d. 1643). In benedictiones duodecim Patriarcharum commentaria et quaestiones analyticae, *Venice*, 1604.
BURELLE, Jean. (fl. 1620). Dialecticothea, *Lyon*, 1626.
CAMART, Aegidius (Gilles). (d. 1624). Elias thesbites sive de rebus Eliae prophetae. Commentarius posthumus R. P. Ae. Camarti, Ord. Min., nuper Generalis, *Paris*, 1631.
- Frater Aegidius Camart, Provincialis Minimorum Sancti Francisci de Paula Turoniae, omnibus intererit, salutem (in urbe Cainonensi die 2 aprilis anni 1623). *s.l.n.d.*
- Oratio decretalis ... de summa Trinitate et fide catolica, habita in scholis Aurelianensibus die 24 decembris, *Orléans*, 1614.
- Oratio synodalis habita Rothomagi, *Paris*, 1643.
- Oratio quam in funere Reverendissimi in Christo Patris ac Domini Francisci Laschiver Rhedonensis episcopi, *Toulouse*, 1619.
- Sermons prononcés à Castres ... mai 1606, de la conférence faite en la ville de Castres le 2 et 3 juin (1606) entre le R. P. Gilles Camart et Jean Josion. Examen de la conférence ... sur les falsifications contenues ès ecrits dudit Josion ..., *Toulouse*, 1607.
- Officium die Sancti Aegidii festo, *Paris*, 1613.
- Deux certificats: le premier du P. G. Camart ... le second du correcteur ... du couvent du Plessis-lès-Tours attestant le non-existance des textes allégués par le P. Du Vivier, 14 et 18 mars 1623, *Paris*, 1623.
CAMUS, Pierre. (fl. 1650). Expositio moralis septem verborum quae Christus Dominus in cruce pendens protulit, *Reims*, 1650.
CAPDEVILLE, Arnaud F. (fl. 1690). L'Arithmétique en son jour, contenant les explications familières des quatre parties qui la composent ... *Toulouse*, 1691.
CHAPPOT, Jean. (d. 1631). Defensio contra epistolam apologeticam Patris Claudii Du Vivier, *Paris*, 1628.
- Vie et miracles de Saint François de Paule, *Nancy*, 1621.

CHAVINEAU, André. (fl. 1630). Les derniers soupirs d'une âme religieuse tirés sur l'heureuse et pieuse mort du R. P. François Humblot, *Paris*, 1613.
- Discours du devoir du magistrat, *Paris*, 1623.
- L'exercice angélique, *Paris*, 1611.
- Lettres d'un solitaire, *Poitiers*, 1628.
- La mort généreuse d'un Prince chrétien tirée sur les dernières actions et paroles de Monseigneur Louys de Lorraine, Cardinal de Guise, *Paris*, 1623.
- La parfaite Philothée ... avec un éloge de révérendissime F. de Sales, *Paris*, 1634.
- Oraison funèbre du Roi Henri IV, *Tours*, 1610.
- L'ombre angélique, *Tours*, 1600.
- Les sept stations de Jésus-Christ, *Paris*, 1611.
- Le tableau de la mort, *Tours*, 1600.
- Le temple de la gloire civile, *Paris*, 1607.
CHENET, Louis. (1593–1659). Pratique spirituelle. *Paris*. 1633.
- Les faveurs admirables de la Sainte Vierge, Mère de Dieu, *s.l.n.d.*
CHICHON, Nicolas. (fl. 1620). L'athéisme des prétendus réformés à l'occasion d'une réponse d'Isaac Cuville ... tiré de la confession de foi qu'il a fait (sic) au nom de tous les ministres, *Poitiers*, 1620.
- Conférence tenue entre M. Cuville, ministre de l'église prétendue (réformée) de Coué et Fr. Nicolas Chichon, Minime, enseignant ... la sainte théologie à Poitiers le septième ... de juin 1619, *Poitiers*, 1619.
COLONIA, André de. (1617–1688). Le calvinisme proscrit par la piété héroïque de Louis le Grand, et battu d'ailleurs de ses propres armes, *Lyon*, 1686.
- Eclaircissement sur le légitime commerce des intérêts, *Lyon*, 1675. (Several other editions).
- Eloge du Roi, *Marseille*, 1687.
- Lettre de Théophiste à Théotime ... du droit et du fait, *Aix-en-Provence*, 1674.
COSTE, Hilarion de. (1595–1661). Les éloges et les vies des Reines, des Princesses et des dames illustres en piété, en courage et en doctrine ..., 2 vols., *Paris*, 1647.
- Eloges de nos Rois et des enfants de France, *Paris*, 1643.
- Historica elogia Delphinorum Franciae, *Paris*, 1643.
- Histoire catholique où sont décrites les vies, faits et actions héroïques et signalées des hommes et dames illustres ... dans les XVI et XVII siècles, *Paris*, 1625.
- Perfecta heroina seu Historia vitae ... Elizabethae Castellae, *Paris*, 1661.
- Perfectus ecclesiasticus seu Historia ... Domini Francisci Picarti, *Paris*, 1659.
- Le portrait en petit de Saint François de Paule, instituteur de l'Ordre des Minimes, *Paris*, 1655.
- Les règles des Minimes traduites en français, *Paris*, 1630. Printed privately. (Third edition, *Paris*, 1632, contains "Le correctoire de l'Ordre.")
- La vie du R. P. Mersenne, théologien, Philosophe et mathématicien de l'Ordre des pères Minimes, *Paris*, 1649.
- Vita Elizabethae, Lusitaniae Reginae, in sanctorum numerum ab Urbano VIII Sum. Pont., anno iubilaei 1625, *Paris*, 1626.
- Les vrais portraits des rois de France, Paris, –. Seconde édition ... augmentée de nouveaux portraits et enrichie des vies des rois. *Paris*, 1636.
COURVOISIER, Jean-Jacques. (fl. 1650). L'Autriche sainte, *Bruxelles*, 1638.
- Extases de la princesse du midi, la belle Malcéda au palais du sage roi Salomon; en parallèles, les extases de la princesse du ciel, l'âme religieuse et dévote au palais du mystique Salomon, le très-adorable sacrement de l'Eucharistie, *Bruxelles*, 1632.
- Le lys divin et le Samson mystique, *Bruxelles*, 1638.
- Maximes du Royaume de Jésus-Christ tirées des règles des ordres religieux, *Bruxelles*, 1648.

COURVOISIER, Jean-Jacques. (Ctd.)
– L'obélisque sépulcral érigé en l'église de Renaix à la mémoire ... de Jean, Comte de Nassau, *Bruxelles*, 1639.
– Le pédagogue angélique, *Bruxelles*, 1636.
– Le prince immortel tiré sur la vie de son Altesse royal Ferdinando d'Autriche, *Anvers*, 1642.
– Les royales victoires de l'amour divin sur le cœur de Marie Madeleine, *Paris*, 1645.
– Sacré bocage en huit sermons de la Vierge, *Bruxelles*, 1645.
– Sacré mausolée, ou les parfums exhalants du tombeau de la sérénissime princesse Isabelle Claire Eugénie, figuré sur le sépulcre du roi David, *Bruxelles*, 1634.
– Le thrône royal de Jésus Nazaréen, Roi des affligés, *Anvers*, 1642.
– Le trésor des œuvres spirituelles de Saint François de Paule, *Liège*, 1657.
– Triomphe des martyrs Saint Guy et Saint Quintilien célébré à Douai les 24 et 25 août 1652, *Bruxelles*, 1652.
CROCHARD, Claude. (fl. 1633). Harangue funèbre de M. Etienne Bernard, *Paris*, 1633.
DALVIN, Etienne. (1565–1610). De potestate episcoporum, abbatum aliorumque praelatorum regularium ac abbatissarum, *Paris*, 1607.
DECOMANS, Henri. (1598–1671). Idée de la perfection chrétienne, *Bruxelles*, 1645.
DEREYROLES, Jean. (fl. 1640). Oraison funèbre de très-illustre dame Madame Charlotte Flandrine de Nassau, Princesse de d'Orange, *Poitiers*, 1640.
– Saint Paul en chaire sur les sermons des fêtes de Notre Seigneur ..., *Paris*, 1647.
DESBOIS, Jean-Baptiste. (1554–1612). Disputationum ... de controversiis christianae fidei Roberti Cardinalis Bellarmini ... epitome, *Paris*, 1602.
DESFRESNES, Louis. (d. 1676). Civis sanctorum et domesticus Dei, opus posthumus a R. P. Boyenval ... R. P. Ludovici Desfresnes ... opera recognitum et ex aliqua parte auctum, *Rome*, 1667.
– De divina voluntate semper fideliter adimplenda, *Paris*, 1668.
DINET, Gaspar. (1559–1619). Harangue au Roi ... sur les plaintes des Catholiques de Montpellier et pour le rétablissement entier de la religion Catholique ... en la souveraineté de Béarn, *Paris*, 1617.
DONDÉ, Antoine. (1597–1670). Les figures et l'abrégé de la vie, de la mort et des miracles de Saint François de Paule, *Paris*, 1671.
– Portraits de quelques personnes signalées en piété de l'ordre des Minimes. *Paris*, 1668. (Previously appended to *Les figures* ..., above, but printed separately in 1668. The copy in the British Museum is bound together with the previous work).
DONY D'ATTICHY, Louis. (1597–1664). Flores historiae Sacri Collegii Sanctae Romanae Ecclesiae cardinalium, *Paris*, 1660.
– Histoire de la bienheureuse reine Jeanne de Valois, fondatrice de l'ordre des religieuses de l'Annonciade. Avec un abrégé de la vie du bienheureux P. Gabriel Maria, son confesseur et second instituteur du même ordre, *Paris*, 1664.
– Histoire générale de l'ordre sacré des Minimes. 2 vols, *Paris*, 1624.
– Mémoires pour servir de preuve qu'un évêque est habile à succéder quoiqu'il ait été religieux, *s.l.* 1639.
– Officia propria sanctorum Reziensis Ecclesiae, *Aix-en-Provence*, 1635.
– Collectio quorumdam gravium authorum qui ex professo ... Sanctae Scripturae aut divinorum officiorum in vulgarem linguam translationes damnarunt, *Paris*, 1661.
– De vita et rebus gestis ... Petri Berulli ... congregationis oratorii ... in Gallia fundatoris, *Paris*, 1649.
DUPONT, Nicolas. (1607–1653). Méditations sur les maximes de Jésus, *Paris*, 1640.
– Le soleil mystique de sainteté, *Paris*, 1629.
– Le tombeau de l'amour propre, *Paris*, 1636.

Du Pro, Antoine. (1588–1655). Hortus philosophicus ad excolendos sapientiae regulis et praeceptis adolescentum animos, *Paris*, 1633.

Dupuys, Claude. (1617–1681). L'homme de Dieu dans l'état de la perfection, *Paris*, 1682.

Dupuys, Jean. (1627–1695). De dispositionibus ad natale Domini pie et sancte celebrandum, *s.l.n.d.*

Durelle, Jean. (–   ). Effigies contracta Roberti Flud(d), *Paris*, 1636. See Eusebius à Sancto Justo.

– Onomatologie chirurgique ou explication des mots grecs appartenants à la chirurgie. Enrichie de recherches historiques, morales et allégoriques tirées des SS.PP. et autres auteurs. Utile non seulement aux chirurgiens mais aussi aux médecins et autres gens d'étude. Avec un petit traité de la correspondance des météors du microcosme avec ceux du macrocosme ... *Lyon*, 1644.

– Sapientiae Joan. Blanci examen in quo eruditissimi viri peripeteticae et communis doctrinae apologi dubia proponuntur, *Lyon*, 1640.

Duval, Pierre. (1606–1659). La vie et miracles de Saint François de Paule, fondateur de l'ordre des Minimes, dit de Jésus-Maria, avec les cantiques sacrés de l'épouse sainte au berceau de Jésus Dieu-Enfant, *Rouen*, 1640.

Du Vivier, Claude. (1568–1630). Epistola apologetica R. P. Claudii Du Vivier ... quod S. Franciscus de Paula ... sit unicus parentibus suis nec habuerit fratrem vel sororem, *Douai*, 1626.

Vie et miracles de Saint François de Paule, instituteur de l'ordre des Frères Minimes, *Paris*, 1609, Second edition: *Douai*, 1622.

Estienne, Antoine. (1556–1610). Constitutiones sacrae de sacrosancta Eucharistia, *Paris*, 1606.

– Les epîtres et autres œuvres de Jean Taulère, traduits par les Pères Minimes, *Paris*, 1587. Second edition, *Lyon*, 1605.

– Modus pie atque christiane studendi. *Paris*, 1612.

– Remonstrance charitable aux dames et demoiselles de France sur leurs ornements dissolus, pour les induire à laisser l'habit du paganisme et prendre celui de la femme pudique ... avec une élégie de la France se complaignant de la dissolution desdites demoiselles, *Paris*, 1585. Second edition, *Paris*, 1867.

Estienne, François. (1637–1712). Lettres spirituelles. Edited by le Père de Rians and published, *Avignon?*, 1715.

Etienne, Jérôme de. See Estienne, François, above.

Eusebius a Sancto Justo. Effigies contracta Roberti Flud(d), medici angli, appendice ... relectione in lucem producente. Eusebio a S. Iusto, Theologo Seguisiano. *Paris*, 1636. (Note: In the *Catalogue Général ... de la Bibliothèque Nationale*, Vol. 88, p. 534 the date given is 1637 and the work is ascribed to François La Noue; on the cover of the work, however, the following may be seen: "Confutatio dogmat. Rob. Flud. a Jo. Durel." Further evidence for ascribing it to Durelle may be adduced from Hilarion de Coste's assertion that Durelle took Mersenne's part against Fludd and from the fact that the work contains many medical references which would seem out of place in La Noue, but which are in keeping with Durelle).

Fagé, Nicolas. (fl. 1650) Florida corona boni militis, *Munich*, 1652.

Farcier, Edme. (1608–1678). Monument érigé à la mémoire de l'homme de la patrie, l'homme du roi, l'homme de Dieu: ou éloge funèbre de Louis Duble, Marquis d'Uxelles, Maréchal de France, *Dijon*, 1659.

Fenier, Pierre. (1652–1693). Relation du siège de Péronne, *Paris*, 1682. Reprinted, *Paris*, 1862.

Feraud, André. (1612–1665). Cursus theologicus in tertiam partem D. Thomae, iuxta mentem eiusdem Doctoris Angelici, in quo disseritur de ineffabili Incarnationis mysterio, *Marseille*, 1681.

FRANÇOIS, Jean. (1606–1666). Ode panegyrica in laudem S. Francisci de Paula, Ordinis Minimorum instutoris, *Caesaroduni*, (*Tours*), 1632.

GAMBART, Charles. (fl. 1630). P. Claudii Du Vivier ... in Provincia Flandro-Belgica ... Oratio funebris, *Bruxelles*, 1630.

GERMAIN, Jean. (fl. 1600–1630?). Discorsi della conservazione della vista, delle malattie melanconiche ... composti in lingua francese dal Sig. Andrea Lorenzo, Medico fisico del Christmo. Henrico IV Re di Francia. Tradotti in lingua italiana e commentati da Fr. Gio. Germano, Medico chirurgo, al presente Religioso dell'-ordine di San Francesco di Paula, *Napoli*, 1626.

– La quintessence de la chirurgie, réduite en cinq parties avec un antidotaire ou description de plusieurs excellentes remèdes pour la guérison de diverses maladies. Composée par Frère Jean Germain de l'ordre des Pères Minimes, Lyon, 1630 Second edition, enlarged and dedicated to Cardinal Bichi; signed, "De notre Pharmacie du couvent des Minimes d'Avignon, Paris, 1640. Translated into Italian, *Quintessenza della chirurgia* ..., Rome, 1674.

– Breve e sostanziale tratto intorno alle figure anatomiche delli principali animali terrestri, aquatili e volatili ... composto da F. Gio. Germano, Francese, Medico chirurgico e al presente Religioso Minimo del'ordine di San Francesco di Paula, *Napoli*, 1625.

GIRY, François. (1635–1688). Dissertatio chronologica ... de anno natali et aetate sancti Francisco de Paula vindicatur, *Paris*, 1680.

– Entretiens de Jésus-Christ avec l'âme chrétienne, *Paris*, 1674.

– Livre des cent points de l'humilité, *Paris*, 1679.

– Méditations pour les sœurs et maîtresses des écoles charitables du Saint Enfant Jésus de l'institut de feu R. P. Barré, *Paris*, 1687.

– La règle du Tiers-Ordre des Minimes, avec des notes et l'office de Saint François de Paule, *Paris*, 1673. Second edition, "... avec argument," *Paris* 1683.

– Wonia naywdziecznieysza naypierwszey wiktymy Panskiey ... álbo ... relácya zyciá, Przewielebney Panny Ketarzyny Mechtyldy de Bar, fundatorki zakonni-custawiczney adorácyi przenaysw. Sakra mentu Zakonnice Warszáwskie, *w Warszawie*, 1738. (Polish translation of the life and work of V. Catherine de Bar (la Mère Mechtilde) and an account of the foundation of the order of Perpetual Devotion).

– Traité de la Sainte Enfance de Jésus-Christ, *Paris*, 1670.

– La vie de M. Jean-Jacques Olier ... premier supérieur du Séminaire de Saint-Sulpice, *Paris*, 1687.

– La vie du P. Moreau de l'ordre des Minimes, fondateur du couvent de Soissons, *Paris*, 1687.

– La vie de Saint François de Paule avec un office et des litanies en son honneur, *Paris*, 1682

– Les vies des Saints, Vol. I, *Paris*, 1683; Vol. II, *Paris*, 1685. (See also under Martin, Simon. XIXth century reprints of this work appearing under the general heading of *Petits Bollandistes* are not listed in this bibliography.)

– Notice biographique, in *Lettres spirituelles du R. P. Barré, Rouen*, 1697. [See under Barré].

GORGEU, Michel. (d. 1673). Remarques sur les souverains pontifes romains depuis Célestin II jusq'à maintenant, avec leurs armes blasonnées en taille douce. Au sujet de la prophétie, qui se voit sous le nom de Saint Malachie, Archevêque d'Armach, Primat d'Irlande et légat apostolique en ce royaume-là, *Abbeville*, 1659.

– Traductio de seraphim a divo Bonaventura, *Amiens*, 1666.

GRANGE, Antoine de la. (fl. 1619?). Le temple mystique de Salomon, *Paris*, 1619.

– L'octave du Saint Sacrement, *Paris*, 1628.

GRANJON, Ambroise. (1601–1686). Les Triomphes de Saint François de Paule,

Paris, 1634. [Translation from the Italian of *Descrizione della padronaza di S. Francesco di Paula nella città di Napoli, Napoli*, 1631.]

GUÉRIN, Gerard. (1626–1696). Eloge historique et funèbre de très-puissant seigneur Louis Chalon de Blé, Marquis d'Uxelles, *Chalon-sur-Saône*, 1661.

– Harrangue funèbre de Louis Doni D'Attichy, *Chalon-sur-Saône*, 1664.

GUÉRIN, Pierre. (fl. 1596–1631). Eloge des religieuses Ursulines tiré de la prophétie d'Isaïe en son chapitre onzième, *Paris*, 1675.

HEPBURNUS, Jacques Bonaventure. (1573–1623) Encomium B. Mariae Virginis, linguis LXII enunciatum, *Rome*, 1617.

– Lexicon S. Linguae succintum. *s.l.n.d.*

– Virgo LXXII encomiis coelata (*Rome*), 1616. C. Facsimile, *Paris*, 1922 by F. de Mély.

HÉRISSÉ, Martin. (1593–1652). Tractatus de jubilaeo, *s.l.*, 1625.[1]

HONORÉ, André. (d. 1649). L'entrée du ciel, *Rouen*, 1630.

HUMBLOT, François. (1569–1612). Armes catholiques pour combattre ... ceux de la religion prétendue réformée, dressées en faveur des soldats de la guerre ministrale, *Paris*, 1618.

– Censura proemii thesibus Salmuricensium academicorum praefixi, *Saumur*, 1611.

– Conceptions admirables sur les Lamentations de Jérémie, *Paris*, 1618.

– Conductitii amanuenses exceperunt "Conciones" quas Humblotus tum Parisiis tum aliis locis habuit, *Paris*, 1607.

– Disputatio de rebus controversis contra ministrum calvinistam, *Lyon*, 1598.

– Oratio in funere R. P. Angeli Ioyosi, capuccini, *Paris*, 1608.

– Oratio in funere Henrici Borbonii Montpensierii, *Lyon*, 1608.

– Phantôme de la Cène ministrale, *Paris*, 1612.

ISNARD, Etienne. (1578–1656). Codex minimus ordinis Minimorum Sancti Francisci de Paula, Pars I; *Lyon*, 1631; Pars II; *Lyon*, 1632.

– Prédications pour l'Avent, *Lyon*, 1628.

JULET, Nicolas. (fl. 1630). Miracles et grâces de Notre-Dame de Bon-Secours-lès-Nancy, *Nancy*, 1630.

LADORE, Jacques. (fl. 1664). Le bonheur de la fréquente communion, *Paris*, 1658.

– Digestum sapientiae minimitanae, *Rome*, 1664.

– Horatii christiani tripartitus in B. Francisci Salesii Genevensis Episcopi canonizationis inauguratione, *Rome*, 1662.

– Vol de l'âme sur les autels, *Paris*, 1656.

LALEMANDET, Jean. (d. 1660?). Cursus philosophicus, *Lyon*, 1656.

– Decisiones philosophiae ... inter thomistas ac scotistas, *Munich*, 1664.

LA NOUE, François. (1597–1670). Chronicon generale ordinis Minimorum, *Paris*, 1635.

– De sanctis Franciae cancellariis syntagma historicum, *Paris*, 1634.

– Effigies contracta R. Flud. [See Durelle and Eusebius a Sancto Justo].

– Planctus in obitu R. P. Dominici a Jesu, *s.l.*, 1638.

– Ad R. P. Mersenne F. Lanovii iudicium de R. Fludo. Printed in P. Gassendi, *Opera Omnia, Lyon*, 1658, Vol. III, pp. 267–278.

Note: under François La Noue, Roberti has listed 77 separate works without giving date or place of publication (see op. cit., Vol. II, pp. 543–551). Of these, only the first two can be found in the catalogues of the British Museum, the Bodleian and the Bibliothèque Nationale. I am therefore forced to conclude that Roberti has listed the many manuscripts that La Noue left and which were preserved in the library at La Place Royale in

---

[1] This work and his *Sermones per octavam Assumptionis*, *s.l.*, 1628, appear in Roberti's bibliography but were never printed?

Paris, but which were dispersed at the time of the Revolution. Mersenne dedicated the *Cosmographia* to La Noue and refers to his many works ready for the press.

LA NOUE, Michel. (1607–1648). Bibliotheca SS. Patrum concionatoria, *Paris*, 1643.
– Sermons pour tous les jours de Carême, *Rouen*, 1655.
– Sermons pour les fêtes principales, *Rouen*, 1656.
Note: the above works by Michel La Noue were edited by le Père Blanchot q.v.
LANOVIUS, see LA NOUE.
LA RIVIÈRE, François de (fl. 1620). Acte d'Institution du couvent des religieuses Minimes d'Abbeville, 17 juillet 1621. [Transcribed by E. Prarond in his *Topographie d'Abbeville, Abbeville*, 1871, vol. II, pp. 392–396.]
LA RIVIÈRE, Louis de. (fl. 1630–1659). Le château ou palais de la vierge d'amour, contenant quarante chambres qui désignent quarante vertus ou perfections de Notre-Dame, exercice révélé de Dieu à Marie Tessonnier, *Lyon*, 1653.
– Les tableaux mystiques des quatre amours sacrés en l'amour de Dieu, de soi-même, du prochain, des ennemis, *Lyon*, 1630.
– Traité des quatre amours, *Lyon*, 1630.
– La vie de François de Sales, *Lyon*, 1625.
– Histoire de la vie et mœurs de Marie Tessonnière (sic), native de Valence, *Lyon*, 1650.
LAUGIER, GASPARD. (1637–1697). Sanctissimo patriarchae Francisco e Paula ... tripartitum elogium anagrammatibus ac symbolis illustratum a P. F. Gasparo Laugier ... elaboratum, *Marseille*, 1685.
LA VIA, Vincenzo. (–). De carnium abstinentia. Brevis disputatio in qua ostenditur et pluribus Patrum auctoritatibus et rationibus probatur a Christi adventu, Apostolis egregiisque viris carnibus vesci prohibitium fuisse, *Lyon*, 1618.
LE FÈVRE, Nicolas, see ORMESSON.
LEJEUNE, Jean. (fl. 1620). Les pierreries spirituelles du vase eucharistique, *Paris*, 1619.
LE JUGE, Claude. (1600–1641). Troisième règle de Saint François de Paule, Recueil des personnes illustres, *Paris*, 1623.
LE ROY, Charles, (d. 1674). Le roi des enfants du catéchisme sortant des écoles de charité ..., *Paris*, 1667.
LESGUILLIER, Nicolas. (1584–1662). Paraphrasis aliquot epistolarum Sancti Pauli, *Paris*, 1643.
– De peculiari spiritu religionis Minimorum, *Paris*, 1639. [See below, *Ratio* ...].
– Ratio studiorum: seu facilis et compendiosa ad scientias capessendas stratavia ... cui oportunus tractatus de spiritu ordinis Minimorum ..., *Paris*, 1639.
LIBAULT, Abel. (d. 1660). Le parfait religieux, *Paris*, 1617.
– Petits exercices de religion, *Paris*, 1613.
LUSSY, F... I... (fl. 1660?). Illustrissimo ... Claudio de Joli, Aginensium episcopo anagramata ..., *Agen*, s.d.[1]
MACHON, Vincent. (1594–1662). Les entretiens d'un vrai chrétien durant la vie présente, *Rouen*, 1652.[2]
MAIGNAN, EMANUEL. (1601–1676) [3] Cursus philosophicus, 4 vols. *Toulouse*, 1653.
– Second edition, enlarged, *Lyon*, 1673.
– Perspectiva horaria, sive de horographia gnomonica theoretica tum practica libri quattuor, *Rome*, 1648.
– Philosophia sacra, sive entis tum supernaturalis increati. *Toulouse/Paris*, 1661.
– Second edition, *Lyon*, 1672.
– De usu licito pecuniae, *Toulouse*, 1673.
– De l'usage licite de l'argent, *Toulouse*, 1673. [French translation of above].

---

[1] Information taken from Lauzun, *Les couvents de la ville d'Agen*, Vol. I, p. 381.
[2] Attributed to Louis Machon by R. Céleste in his *Louis Machon*, Bordeaux, 1883, p. 68.
[3] See also Saguens, Jean.

Martin, Mathieu. (1589–1668). Appanages d'un cavalier chrétien, *Mons*, 1628.
– Un cœur chrétien, *Paris*, 1847. [Printed in *Librairie des livres liturgiques illustrés*].
– Le triomphe de la vérité … en l'heureuse conversion de Mgr Rudolphe Maximilien, *Anvers*, 1624.
Martin, Simon. (1595–1653). Les actions admirables de Jésus-Christ, *Paris*, 1630.
– Epîtres spirituelles de Mgr Jean d'Avila, *Paris*, 1653.
– Les Saints Evangiles et Epîtres des dimanches et fêtes, *Paris*, 1664.
– Les exercises pour les dix jours, *Paris*, 1644.
– Les fleurs de la solitude, *Paris*, 1652.
– Historia sancta mulierum illustriam veteris testamenti, *Paris*, 1645.
– Le martyrologe romain, *Paris*, 1638.
– Le martyrologe des Saints de France, *Paris*, s.d.
– Les méditations sur les Epîtres qui se lisent en l'Eglise, *Paris*, 1652.
– Règle du Tiers-Ordre des Minimes, *Reims*, s.d.
– Sommaire des indulgences, *Reims*, s.d. [Usually bound with the above *Règle* …]
– Les sacrées reliques du désert. *Paris*, 1655.
– Les souffrances de Jésus-Christ, *Paris*, 1630.
– La vie de la vénérable Mère Catherine de Vis … Minime, *Paris*, 1650.
– La vie de Saint Babolin, *Paris*, 1650.
– La vie de Saint Vulphly, *Paris*, 1636.
– La vie de Saint François de Paule, *Reims*, s.d.
– La vie de Sainte Austreberthe, *Paris*, 1635.
– La vie de Sainte Ulphe, *Paris*, 1648.
– Les vies des Saints, *Paris*, 1648. [Enlarged by François Giry and by Claude Raffron qq.v. and published in Paris in 1682 and 1719 respectively. See also the *Catalogue général de la Bibliothèque Nationale* for other editions in XIXth century].
– Translation of the works of Louis de Grenade, *Lyon*, 1664.
Masson, Antoine. (1620–1700). Histoire de Noé et du déluge, *Paris*, 1687.
– Histoire du patriarche Abraham, *Paris*, 1688.
– Questions curieuses sur la Genèse, *Paris*, 1685.
– Les secrets du paradis ou explication générale des différents états des bienheureux dans le ciel empiré …, *Paris*, 1693.
Meot (Mey), Georges. (d. 1612). De incomprehensibile omnipotentia Dei in mysterio Eucharistiae, *Paris*, 1607.
Mersenne, Marin. (1588–1648).

Note: There already exists for Mersenne a comprehensive bibliography in the work of le Père R. Lenoble, *Mersenne ou la naissance du mécanisme*, Paris, 1943. Given below is a synopsis of this bibliography.

– L'usage de la raison, *Paris*, 1623.
– L'Analyse de la vie spirituelle, *Paris*, 1623.
– Quaestiones in Genesim, *Paris*, 1623.
– Observationes, *Paris*, 1623.
– L'Impiété des déistes, 2 vols, *Paris*, 1624.
– La vérité des sciences, *Paris*, 1625.
– Synopsis mathematica, *Paris*, 1626.
– Traité de l'Harmonie Universelle, *Paris*, 1627.[1]
– Questions Harmoniques, *Paris*, 1634.
– Questions théologiques, *Paris*, 1634.
– Les mécaniques de Galilée, *Paris*, 1634.
– Les préludes de l'Harmonie Universelle, *Paris*, 1634.

[1] Various editions; so many minor variants that Lenoble calls it "ouvrage éminémment protéiforme"; p. XXII. Facsimile of Paris, 1636, edition with Introduction by F. Lesure, *Paris*, 1965.

MERSENNE, Marin, (Ctd.)
- Les nouvelles pensées de Galilée, *Paris*, 1639.
- Lettre à Naudé sur l'aimant. s.l., 1639.
- Universae geometriae synopsis, *Paris*, 1644.
- Cogitata physico-mathematica, *Paris*, 1644.
- Novarum observationum, tomus III, *Paris*, 1647.
- Liber novus praelusorius. *Paris?* 1648.
- L'Optique et la catoptrique [du R. P. J-F. Niceron], *Paris*, 1651.[1]
- Correspondance, *Paris*, 1935 – in progress.
MESEMACRE, Philippe. (d. 1660). De laudibus Sancti Iovoniis iurisconsultum Pa-
    troni, *Anvers*, 1663.
- Ad R. P. Balthazar d'Avila, ordinis nostris ex-generalem iubilaeum ab ingressu
    religionis annum argentum, *Lille*, 1666.
MEY, see MEOT.
MEYRAN D'UBAYE, Paul. (1637–1714). L'âme souffrante sous la rigueur des gran-
    deurs de Dieu, *Lyon*, 1671.
- L'héroïne chrétienne ou la princesse achevée sous le très-auguste nom de Marie-
    Thérèse d'Autriche, Reine de France et de Navarre, *Lyon*, 1671.
MOREL, Antoine. (1608–1670). Le tableau de la vie dévote commencée, avancée et
    consommée, representé en la vie et mœurs du Vénérable serviteur de Dieu le
    P. Fr. Jacques Martinot de l'ordre des Minimes, *Toulon*, 1659.
- La vie du Vénérable serviteur de Dieu le P. Paul Trouchet, religieux de l'ordre
    des Minimes, *Avignon*, 1656.
NICERON, Jean-François. (1613–1646). L'interprétation des chiffres ou règle pour
    bien entendre et expliquer facilement toutes sortes de chiffres simples. Tirée de
    l'italien de Sr. Antonio Maria Cospi ... augmentée et accommodée particulaire-
    ment à l'usage des langues française et espagnole par F.I.F.N.P.M. (i.e. Frère
    Jean-François Niceron, Père Minime), *Paris*(?), 1645(?).[2]
- La perspective curieuse. *Paris*, 1638.
- La perspective curieuse ... *Paris*, 1651. [This is the edition that Mersenne made
    of the work of Niceron and which was published with his own *Optique et catoptri-
    que*.]
- Thaumaturgus opticus seu admiranda optices, catoptrices, dioptrices etc., *Paris*,
    1646.
- Letter to Gabriel Naudé dated Lyon, 15 May, 1645, and published by F. Licetus
    in *De Quaesitis*, Bologna, 1640, pp. 225–228. [Letter refers to magnetism, binocular
    vision, stone in the body, chemistry].
NICLOT, Simon. (fl. 1649). Idiota sapientissimus de statu et conditione religiosorum,
    Reims, 1647.
- Sommaire des indulgences que peuvent gagner les tertiaires de Saint François de
    Paule et toutes autres personnes, *Reims*, 1649.
OCTOUL, Etienne. (1589–1655). Inventa astronomica ... terrae meridianis per
    observantionem cum pyramidis astronomica comparendis ..., *Avignon*, 1643.
OGIER, F... (d. 1670). Discours au roi en faveur des R. Pères Minimes français
    du Couvent de la Trinité du mont à Rome pour la conservation des privilèges de
    la nation, *Paris*, 1629.
ORMESSON, Nicolas Le Febvre d'. (1612–1679). Encomia seu orationes, funerales...
    Annae Austriacae, *s.l.n.d.*
- Conduite à l'éternité, *Paris*, 1649.

---

[1] See Niceron, J-F. *La perspective curieuse.*
[2] The use of both *Père* and *Frère* in the monastic style is fairly common amongst the
Minims.

ORMESSON, Nicolas Le Febvre d'. (Ctd.)
- Consolation à Mme la Maréschale (sic) de Vitry, *Paris*, 1645.
- Le Mystère de la pureté accompli en la mère de Dieu, *Paris*, 1652.
- Panégyrique de S. Louis, *s.l.n.d.*
- La France ressuscitée par la nouvelle de la paix, *Paris*, 1659.
- Panégyrique de la victoire. Les victoires couronnées par la paix, *s.l.*, 1678.

PAVÈS, Joachim. (1620–1701). Le triomphe de Saint François de Paule et la pratique des treize vendredis, *Marseille*, 1690.

PIJART, Pierre. (1589–1656). Bibliotheca sanctorum et antiquorum Patrum concionatoria ..., *Paris*, 1653.
- La journée spirituelle, *Douai*, 1627.
- Pèlerinage ou la rue évangélique, *Paris*, 1638.
- La règle du Tiers-Ordre de Saint François de Paule avec la vie du même, *Paris*, 1658.
- La religieuse ou la Vierge sacrée conduite à la perfection, *Paris*, 1643.
- La sainte messe du vrai chrétien, *Paris*, 1649.
- De singulari Christi Iesu D. N. Salvatoris pulchritudine, *Paris*, 1651.

PITHOYS, Claude. (1587–1676). Amorce des âmes dévotes et religieuses. Sur ce théorème "Bonum est nos hic esse." Composé par le R. P. Claude Pithoys, religieux prédicateur de l'ordre des Minimes, *Paris*, 1628.
- Apocalypse de Méliton ou révélation des mystères cénobitiques, *Saint-Léger (Sedan)*, 1662. [Several editions, *Sedan*, 1662, 1665, 1668].
- Cosmographie ou doctrine de la sphère, avec un traité de géographie, *Paris(Sedan)*, 1641.
- La découverte des faux possédés, très-utile pour reconnaître et discerner les simulations, feintises et illusions d'avec les vraies ... possessions diaboliques ... ensemble, la conférence tenue entre M. l'Evêque de Toul et le R. P. Pithoys ... touchant la prétendue possédée de Nancy, *Châlons*, 1621.
- L'horoscope roue de fortune et bonne aventure des prédestinés, *Paris*, 1628.
- Traité curieux de l'astrologie judiciaire ou préservatif contre l'astromantie des généthliaques. C. Pithoys, professeur en philosophie en l'Académie de Sedan et Préfet de la Bibliothèque de son Altesse, *Sedan*, 1641.
  Another edition, *Montbéliard*, 1646. [Both editions bound together in the copy in the British Museum].

PIZZURNO, Gervasio – see AVILA, Balthazar d'.

PIZZURNUS – see PIZZURNO, G.

PLUMIER, Charles. (1646–1704). Description des plantes de l'Amérique, *Paris*, 1693.
- Filicetum Americanum, seu filicum polypodiorum adiantorum etc. in America nascentium icones, *Paris*, 1703.
- Nova plantarum americanarum genera, *Paris*, 1703.
- Traité des fougères de l'Amérique, *Paris*, 1705.
- L'art de tourner ou de faire toutes sortes d'ouvrages au tour, *Lyon*, 1701.
- Réponse à Monsieur Pomet, Marchand Droguiste de Paris, sur la cochenille. – *Journal des Sçavans*, 19 April, 1694.
- Réponse du P. C. Plumier, Minime, à une lettre de M. Baulot écrite à la Rochelle. – *Mémoires de Trévoux*, Dec. 1702, pp. 112–128. (Letter gives anatomical detail of ear of the "Tortue de mer.").
- Réponse du R. P. Charles Plumier Minime à M. Frideric (sic) Richter, Docteur en médecine à Lipsic (sic) sur la cochenille. – *Mémoires de Trévoux*, Sept. 1703, pp. 1671–1692 + illustration facing p. 1692.
- Réponse du R. P. Plumier à diverses questions d'un curieux sur le crocodile, sur le colubri (sic) et sur la tortue – *Mémoires de Trévoux*, Jan. 1704, pp. 165–175.

Pourré, Simon. (fl. 1660). Margaritae selectorum casuum conscientiae brevi methodo complectentes difficiliores fere omnes atque praecipuas decisiones quae ad praxim spectare videntur, *Lille*, 1652.
- Le trésor des indulgences, *Lille*, 1663.
Quatroux, Isaac. (1594–1673). Traité de la peste, contenant sa définition ..., *Paris*, 1671.
Raffron, Claude (fl. 1690). La vie de François Giry, ancien Provincial des religieux Minimes de la Province de France, *Paris*, 1691.
- Les vies des Saints, *Lyon*, 1692. [This is an enlarged edition of the work under the same title by François Giry q.v.].
Raynier, see Reinier.
Rangueil, Claude. (1581–1623). Fr. Claudii Rangolii ... commentariorum in libros Regum thomus I et thomus II, *Paris*, 1621, 1624.
Raulin, Hippolyte. (d. 1623). Panégyre orthodoxe mystérieux et prophétique sur l'antiquité ... des Fleurs de Lys, *Paris*, 1626.
Réal, André. (fl. 1646). Brevis ac facilis introductio ad linguam sanctam, *Lyon*, 1646.
Regnault, Robert. (1580–1642). Catechismus de sacrosancta Eucharista, *Paris*,1620.
- Lettres et ambassade de Messire Philippe Canaye Seigneur de Fresne, 3 vols., *Paris*, 1635.
- Histoire naturelle et morale des Indes, *Paris*, 1600; several other editions. [A translation of the work by Joseph Acosta].
- La vie et miracles de Sainte Fare, fondatrice et première abbesse de Fare-Moustier-en-Brie, *Paris*, 1626.
Reinier, Thimothée de. ( ). L'amour aspiritif et unitif ou la théologie mystique partiquée par les secours et aspirations ferventes et des oraisons jacu-latoires, *Marseille*, 1678.
- L'ange gardien ou pratique intérieur ... avec plusieurs exercises spirituels dans le cœur et dans les plaies de Jésus-Christ, *Marseille*, 1678.
- Le combat spirituel, *Avignon*, 1654.
- La dévotion des treize vendredis, *Aix-en-Provence*, 1633.
- L'homme intérieur, *Aix*, 1662.
- Le malade souffrant et le malade mourant, *Aix*, 16 –.
- D. Paulus, redivivus, *s.l.n.d.*
- La société des Zélateurs, *s.l.n.d.*
Rouillart, Nicolas. (1592–1635). Trésor évangélique de Saint François de Sales, 1635.
Roussel, Adrien. (d. 1659). Optica christiana sive verbi incarnati oculus ..., *Munich*, 1646.
- La théologie mystique de Saint François de Paule, *Munich*, 1655.
Rouyer, Cyprian. (fl. 1614). Les délices spirituelles que le R. P. Humblot allant au ciel a laissées en terre, *Sanmihiel*, 1618.
- Familia posthuma Sancti Francisci Paulani, *Paris*, 1617.
- Quintessentia magistralis in quatuor secta partes succintis solutionibus praecipua in theologorum scholis controversa solvens, *Sanmihiel*, 1614.
Rozier, Jean. (fl. 1624). L'immortalité du phénix, *Lyon*, 1624.
Ruteau, Antoine. (d. 1657). De fructu et applicatione sacrificii Missae et suffra-giorum, *Anvers*, 1634.
- De participationibus bonorum operum concessis benefactoribus religiosorum, *Mons*, 1646.
- De vita quadragesimali in Ordine Minimorum Sancti Francisci de Paula sub voto servata, *Mons*, 1646.
- Annales de la province et comté d'Haynau ... recueillies par feu François Vin-chant, prêtre, augmentées et achevées par lr R. P. Antoine Ruteau, de l'Ordre des Minimes, *Mons*, 1648.

SAGUENS, Jean. (d.–1718). De vita, moribus et scriptis E. Maignani, *Toulouse*, 1697.
- Philosophia Maignani, *Toulouse*, 1703. [Compiled from E. Maignan q.v.].
- De perfectionibus divinis, opus ... scriptum ad mentum Maignani. *Cologne*, 1718 [Adaptation and compilation from E. Maignan q.v.]
SAINT-GILLES, Robert de. (fl. 1671). Les œuvres de Monsieur de Bernières de Louvigny, ou conduite assurée pour ceux qui tendent à la perfection, *Paris*, 1671.
SALIER, Jacques. (1610–1700). Cacocephalus, sive de plagiis, *Mâcon*, 1694.
- Historia scholastica de speciebus Eucharisticis, sive de formarum materialium, singularis observatio ex sacris prophanisque autoribus, 3 vols., *Lyon*, 1687. Other editions; *Paris*, 1689 and 1704.
- Pensées sur le Paradis et l'âme raisonnable, *Dijon*, s.d.
SAUVAGE, Jean. (d. 1630). Le zodiaque sacré ... ou la vie de Henri II, Duc de Lorraine, *Nancy*, 1626.
SEGUIN, Antoine. (1600–1670). Excursus concionatoris jurisperiti, sive civilis sapientiae, *Lyon*, 1667.
THIBAUT, Joseph-Victor. (1587–1662). Cause de nos maux, *Aix-en-Provence*, 1631.
- Conduite spirituelle, *Aix*, 1629.
- Essais spirituels, *Lyon*, 1627.
- Histoire de la vie de Marguerite de Souliers, *s.l.*, 1650.
- La nouvelle création du monde, *Lyon*, 1624.
- Le nouveau carême, *Avignon*, 1638.
- Pratiques de la conduite, *Aix*, 1649.
THUILLIER, René. (fl. 1680–1710). Dissertatio de potestate correctorum localium ordinis Minimorum ... in foro contentioso, *Paris*, 1697.
- Diarium patrum, fratrum et sororum ordinis Minimorum provinciae, Franciae, sive Parisiensis qui religiose obierunt ab anno 1560 ad annum 1700, *Paris*, 1709.
TUFFIÈRE, François. (fl. 1678). Saint François de Paule, ou la charité triomphante contenant la règle du Tiers-Ordre des Minimes, *le Mans*, 1678.
VICTON, François. (1595–1632). Histoire ou bref traité du saint suaire de Notre Seigneur Jésus-Christ, précieuse relique de la maison de Savoie, *Paris*, 1634.
- Méditations de Luc Pinelli, *Paris*, 1623.
- Traité de la canonization des saints, *Paris*, 1624.
- Vie de la sœur Grâce Valentinoise, *Paris*, 1622.
- La vie du bienheureux Gaspar Bon, *Paris*, 1622.
- Vita et miracula S. P. Francisci a Paula, *Rome*, 1625.
- Another edition of above, *Paris*, 1627.

ANONYMOUS. Abrégé de la vie de Saint François de Paule, instituteur de l'Ordre des Minimes, *Paris*, 1623.
- Arrêt de la cour de Parlement du 27 mars 1646 portant règlement entre les curés, religieux et religieuses, touchant la sépulture des séculiers, *Paris*, 1646.
- Arrêt ... du 7 mai 1646 ... confirmatif d'autre arrêt ... le 27 mars 1646, *Paris*, 1646.
- Factum pour le syndic des religieux Minimes du couvent du Péage de Pizançon (i.e. Romans, Drôme) en d'Auphiné (sic), prieurs de Royans, *Valence*?, 1630?
CAEREMONIALES. Les règles, le correctoire et le cérémonial de l'Ordre des Minimes de Saint François de Paule, *Paris*, 1603.
OFFICIUM. Officium proprium Ordinis Minimorum S. Francisci de Paula, *Paris*, 1620.
PRIVILÈGES. Privilèges concédés et octroyés tant à Saint François de Paule, fondateur et instituteur de l'Ordre des Minimes, qu'aux couvents et religieux de son Ordre par les Rois de France, *Paris*, 1644.

II. BIBLIOGRAPHY OF MANUSCRIPT SOURCES OF THE HISTORY OF THE ORDER IN THE XVIITH CENTURY *

* In drawing up this part of the Bibliography I have relied on the *Catalogue des manuscrits des Bibliothèques publiques en France*, Paris, 1886 – in progress.

A. MANUSCRIPTS IN PUBLIC LIBRARIES

Fonds Latin.

16818. Bibliothèque Liturgique.
> fol. 44–52. [Fragments of a catalogue said to be that of the Bibliothèque des Minimes de la Place Royale, section, "Ius canonicum Minimorum." Undated].

17261. Commentaire sur l'Evangile. [Fragmentary manuscript in Mersenne's handwriting; 2 volumes.]

Nouvelles Acquisitions Latines.

1551. Actes des chapitres provinciaux tenus au couvent de Nigeon depuis 1606 jusqu'en 1664. [Title in French but text of whole manuscript in Latin; 261 folios of which 189–261 are bound upside down; various accounts of General Chapters, 1611–1661; also "Ordinationes generales pro Provincia Franciae, 1663."]

Ancien Fonds Français.

4055. fol. 20–23. Documents concerning Santa Trinità dei Monti:
> (1) Brevis in favore fratrum nationis galliae. (Copy dated 1553, with short codicil dated 22 February, 1565).
> (2) Instruction pour le couvent des Minimes de Rome de la nation française. [Undated, probably mid-XVIIth century.]

4688. fol. 27. Letter from the Duc de Nevers to Passarello, General of the Order, offering to found a "couvent" at Rethel, 1571.
> fol. 51. Reply to above, dated 6 Kal. Jan. 1571.

4872. fol. 19. Extrait des Registres de Parlement. [Nicolas Mazure, curé de Saint Paul, against the Minims and other orders concerning burial of parishioners of St. Paul in conventual churches, 7 September, 1641.]

Fonds Français.

14532. Conclusions Capitulaires ... Minimes de Serres, 1606–1671. [See also Archives Départementales, Meurthe-et-Moselle, Série H, 1076].

15721. Recueil de pièces touchant la réforme de plusieurs abbayes ... et maisons religieuses:
> fol. 698. Mémoire du P. Flasche, Minime, contre un Visiteur général du même ordre. Undated.
> fol. 700. Lettre du Roi aux Minimes du Couvent de la Trinité du Mont, 1645.
> fol. 702. Remonstrance des Minimes de la Province de Paris en faveur du

P. François Ferrand, bani du couvent de Rome, 1645.

fol. 704. Réponse au Roi des Minimes du Couvent Royal de la Trinité du Mont, à Rome, 1645.

fol. 706. Mémoire pour la conservation des religieux Minimes de France dans le couvent de la Trinité de Rome, 1645.

fol. 730. Bref du Pape pour le P. Bachelier, Minime, 5 Octobre, 1646.

15769. Collection of printed pamphlets and letters. Containing:

(1) Privilèges de l'Ordre. XVIIth century.

(2) Defensio contra epistolam apologeticam patris Claudii du Vivier qua S. Franciscus de Paula ... sororem habuisse probatur, et nepotes. Et rationes in oppositum refutantur. F.I.C.M.B. Paris, 1628.

(3) Letters, XVIIIth century, concerning Santa Trinità dei Monti and the Tiers-Ordre des Minimes.

(4) Placet (au Roi) des Minimes du Couvent de la Trinité du mont, à Rome, à ce qu'il lui plaise charger son Ambassadeur d'obtenir une déclaration du Pape ... XVIIth century, probably 1629.

(5) Discours au Roi en faveur des R. Pères français du Couvent de la Trinité du Mont à Rome, pour la conservation des Privilèges de la Nation. F. Ogier. Paris, 1629. [Added to title-page in ink, "Et principalement pour empêcher que les étrangers fussent admis audit couvent."]

(6) Extrait des Registres de Parlement. Undated, late XVIIth century? [Requiring a return to be submitted by all Provincials of income, number of members etc.]

17588. Mélanges. fol. 235–258, Mémoire des différends en l'ordre des Minimes de la Province de France entre le P. Bachelier, Visiteur Général en ladite Province, et le P. Flasche.

(1) Mémoire de l'affaire ... 1639–1641.

(2) Mémoire de l'affaire du P. Flasche.

(3) "Nos frater Simon Bachelier," 1641. [Declaration by Bachelier.]

(4) Supplication au Pape de la part du P. Flasche, 1641.

(5) Lettre du P. Flasche à Monseigneur le Chancelier. Copy, undated.

(6) Raisons pour montrer que le P. Flasche n'est pas encore encouru en la peine de l'excommunication donné contre lui par le Visiteur Général.

(7) Raisons que le Père Provincial ... de la Province de France, dite de Paris, ... oppose contre le R. P. Simon Bachelier, prétendant faire la visite générale de ladite Province. Undated, probably 1640/1.

(8) Petition by the Minims of Vincennes to the Chancelier de France to be allowed to build additional accommodation, 28 April, 1639. [Has nothing to do with the above "Mémoire" and is merely an extract from the Conclusions Capitulaires of the Couvent de Vincennes].

(9) Avis contre le P. Cichon, Minime de la Province de Tours, qui a composé un livre "De occidendo tyranno" et justifie divers brouilleries en l'ordre à ce qu'il lui soit permis de demeurer au Couvent de la Trinité de Rome. Undated.

(10) Mémoire à ce que Raphaël Pizzurno, Gênois, demeure Général de l'ordre des Minimes et que la division que l'on procure faire des Provinces de France, sous prétexte de multiplier les suffrages des Français aux Chapitres Generaux est abusive. Undated, probably 1641.

18661. Généalogies, Vol. III, fol. 36–47. Généalogie des neveux et des nièces de Saint François de Paule. [Pagination of this volume is 1–510 to complete Vol. II and 1–110 to begin Vol. III.]

18758. Pièces concernant les gens à mainmorte, (Paris). fol. 583. Minimes.

18938. Collection called *Sédition de Normandie*. Vol. III (1639–1640) contains (fol. 184–187) "Avis présenté à Monseigneur le Chancelier de France sur le bruit qui court qu'on poursuit en Cour la division et démembrement des trois couvents de l'ordre des Minimes qui sont dans la (sic) comté d'Avignon du reste du Corps de la Province de France." Undated, [Probably 1623 approx, since the Comté d'Avignon was discussed in the General Chapter for that year [1]].

21611. (Collection Delamare). Order to all Provincials to comply with an earlier instruction (4th April) to give the number of "religieux" in each "couvent," list of revenues etc. None had complied; new order dated 3 September, 1667.

21668. (Collection Delamare). fol. 45 Arrêt du Conseil d'Etat du Roi, qui ordonne que les religieux payeront les droits d'aides et d'inspecteurs de vins ... Paris, 1717. Printed.

25980. Quittances Ecclésiastiques. Nos. 3740 B, 3740 C, 3740 D, Declaration of receipt of income for a quarter. (a) Nicolas le Fèvre d'Ormesson. (b) Jean Paris. (c) Claude Dupuys.[2]

26313. Titres. fol. 95–102; Cinq titres ou pièces de procedure concernant la maison des Minimes de Paris, 1610–1683.

26314. Titres. fol. 29–30; Une pièce de procédure ... 1682. Copie d'arrêt d'enregistrement de lettres d'amortissement ... 1611.

Fonds Français, Nouvelles Acquisitions.

5176. fol. 1–30. Brouillon d'un ouvrage sur l'optique; Mersenne.

5474. Catalogue des manuscrits des bibliothèques de l'ordre des Minimes. (Part of the *Catalogue des manuscrits dans la Bibliothèque Royale*).

5616. fol. 150. As 5474, above.

6204–6206. Recueil formé par le frère Hilarion de Coste de lettres adressées au P. Mersenne. 3 Vols.[3]

6844. Pièces relatives à Paris et à différentes localités ... fol. 53, ["Fondation" made in favour of the Minims of Paris (Place Royale), 1703].

22153. fol. 147–161. Regulae Minimorum.
fol. 162–167. Regula Tertii Ordinis Minimorum.
fol. 169. Formula professionis Tertii Ordinis.
fol. 170–172. Catalogus Generalium Correctorum ad annum 1593.
[All above in same hand. Undated but presumably 1593 or shortly after].

22374. A collection, 471 folios, of various pieces dealing with the Minimes de Mons and of the whole Belgian Province; privileges, Papal briefs, letters patent. fol. 426/7, Brief of Innocent XII, 8 June, 1694, altering a previous brief (Alexander VIII) and restoring the original government of the Order and declaration (extract from the registers of the Conseil d'Etat) that Innocent's brief was conforming to the Liberties of the Gallican Church.

---

[1] For "La comté" see Littré, sub Comté s.m. No. 3 and c.f. La Franche-Comté.
[2] Note error in printed catalogue. Minims said to be in 25979 which ends at fol. 3733.
[3] Printed in various parts of the collection *Correspondance de Mersenne*, Centre de la Recherche Scientifique, Paris, 1933, in progress.

Manuscrits Clairembault.

528.   pp. 465–467. Two printed examples of the work of le P. Joachim Rigaud, Minim.
          (a) Perpetual calendar, 1708.
          (b) Horographie théorique, 1708?

1058.   fol. 152–159. Décret du P. Simon Bachelier en faveur des neveux de Saint François de Paule contre le P. Claude Du Vivier. Paris, 1627. Printed.

Dossiers Bleus.

11.   *Alesso.* Papers giving the genealogy of the descendants of S. François de Paule, many of whom were French members of the Order; the Chaillou family, Hilarion de Coste, le Fèvre d'Ormesson, François Victon.

PARIS, BIBLIOTHÈQUE DE L'ARSENAL

1074.   Militia regularis, seu Commentarius in regulam fratrum Ordinis Mini-morum Sancti Francisci de Paula contextam sub allegoria ordinatissimae militiae et imprimis Romanae. Nicolas Lesguillier, Minime. 645 pp. [Undated but "approbationes" dated 1639 and 1640.[1]]

2272.   La règle et vie de Frère François, pauvre et humble hermite de Paule, laquelle donne à tous ses frères voulant entrer et vivre en son ordre. 38 fols. Writing late XVth or early XVIth century. [Dated 1474 on first folio, but this date must be inaccurate.[2]]

2363.   Recueil de plusieurs pièces. Ex-Minimes de la place Royale. 435 fols. XVIIth century.
          Contains 18 "cahiers" – all by members of the Order? – the most important being:
          (1) fol. 33–37, an anti-quietist pamphlet in Italian.
          (2) fol. 38–45, "Exercise spirituel ou préparation à la mort ... F. Humblot, Minime."
          (3) fol. 372–375, Privilegia Ecclesiae Gallicanae.
          (4) fol. 376–434, Notes on various personalities connected with the Greek schism, particularly the Paleologue family.

2502.   Eléments de Botanique, Charles Plumier, Minime. This is made up of the illustrations from Pitton de Tournefort's *Eléments de Botanique* interleaved with parchment; 485 folios in all. Plumier has written opposite each plate a description of the illustrations. In addition there are:
          (1) "Explication des parties de chaque fleur." [Should read "d'une fleur," since this is a generalisation and not a description of the individual plates].
          (2) A dictionary of botanical terms inserted in the blank spaces beneath the descriptions.
          (3) A treatise on anatomy, likewise written in the blank spaces.
          (4) Index in Latin.
          (5) Index in French.

2875.   Description des plantes de l'Amérique, Charles Plumier, Minime. 127 folios.

---

[1] Ex-Minimes de la Place Royale; shelf mark   2
                                              1R
                                              12
[2] For reasons see *Introduction* p. 4.

[Plates signed "Fr. C. Plumier, Minime, Botanicus Regius delineavit" or abbreviations of the same. See bibliography of printed works].

2909. Lexicon hydrographique et historique. Lexicon historique des rivières, golfes, fontaines et autres eaux particulières du monde, rédigé en sept parties et sous l'ordre de sept alphabets, dont les quatre premiers sont pour l'Europe, le cinquième pour l'Asie, le sixième pour l'Afrique et le septième pour l'Amérique. P. Macaire, Minime. 419 fols. XVIIth century.

3078. Dessins des planches de *L'Art de Tourner*, Charles Plumier, Minime. [Original pen and ink drawings. 126 folios. See bibliography of printed works].

3104. Dessins de mors de chevaux. Modèles de selles. XVIth century drawings bearing Plumier's signature on fol. 2. [Presumably belonged to Plumier's personal library].

4767–4771. Traités et Ambassades de Turquie. Recueil de pièces relatives à l'histoire des relations diplomatiques avec le Levant, 1528–1640. 5 vols. Ex-Bibliothèque des Minimes de la Place Royale. [Vol. V, fol. 249, letter from M. le Veit, at Constantinople to le P. Renaud, Minime de la Place Royale.]

5763. Catalogue des livres ayant appartenu aux Minimes de Passy. A catalogue drawn up in the XVIIIth century, Revolutionary period.

6040. Papiers de la famille Arnauld. Vol. V, fol. 691 and 692, letters from le Marquis de Pomponne to:
(1) Fr. Varrège, Minime, 19 January, 1673.
(2) P. Sébastien Quinquet, 29 Jan. 1673.
(3) An unnamed member of the Order, 29 Jan. 1673.

6203. Catalogue de la Bibliothèque de la Place Royale, 1730.

6418. Correspondance des Papes: lettres de L-A. de Noailles, Archevêque de Paris. fol. 158. Lettre ... du Pape Clément XI au R. P. Roslet, Minime, au sujet du Cardinal de Noailles, en italien, 31 juillet, 1711, avec une copie ... (fol. 160).

6493. fol. 194–297. Catalogue de la Bibliothèque des Minimes de Vincennes. Undated, but lists books published in mid-XVIIIth century.

8546. Istruzione diverse. No. 4, pp. 189–254. Istruzione alla P.V. padre Don Tobia Corona de chierici regolari di S. Paola per andare per servizio di nostro signore al Re di Francia e al sig. Duca di Savoia. Roma, 1621.

PARIS, BIBLIOTHÈQUE MAZARINE

1790. Procès-verbaux. (1) Procès-verbaux des chapitres généraux de l'ordre des Minimes, au nombre de 44 (1507–1685), plus quatre chapitres intérimaires. (2) Bulles et actes divers touchant le chapitre intérimaire tenu à Gênes en 1694. (3) Bullae, motus proprii et brevae pontificum, canones concilii Tridentini, et decreta sacrarum congregationum, ad Minimorum congregationem spectantia ... (4) Aurea methodus de modo corregendi regulares tam paterne quam iudicaliter, authore R. P. Fr. Octaviano Spatario de Incisa, Ord. Minorum (sic) regularis observantiae.[1]

2429. Annales des Minimes de la Province de France où se trouve l'abrégé de la vie de S. François de Paule, les Généraux de l'ordre, les vingt-huit convents

[1] For "Minorum" read "Minimorum?" I am, however, unable to trace anyone of this name in the Order.

(sic) de la Province de France, les Provinciaux qui les ont gouvernés et en particulier tout ce qui concerne le convent (sic) de la Place Royale, par le Fr. J.F.D.R.M., Paris 1756.

4146. Catalogue de la Bibliothèque de la Place Royale. Ordre méthodique, XVIIth century.

4147–4150. Catalogues of the library at la Place Royale; all XVIIIth century. [See A. Franklin, *Les Anciennes bibliothèques de Paris* (Histoire Générale de Paris), 3 vols, Paris, 1867–1873].

PARIS, BIBLIOTHÈQUE DE SAINTE GENEVIÈVE

714. fol. 24, Attestation de Reliques données à Henri de Gournay, Seigneur de Marchéville (Rome, 16 janvier, 1621) et transmises par lui au Couvent des Minimes à Marchéville.

1584. Recueil de lettres touchant le Jansénisme et la Bulle Unigenitus. fol. 4, Letter from Zachérie Roslet, Minim, to a Monseigneur ... dated 14 September, 1706. [Pencil note "Le Pape cherche un moyen de contenter le Cardinal de Noailles sans mécontenter les autres dans l'affaire du formulaire."].

2572. Fragment on the life of Henri de Commans. Undated. [This is merely an extract from the *Diarium Patrum* of R. Thuillier, see Bibliography of printed works].

PARIS, BIBLIOTHÈQUE DE L'INSTITUT

979–982. Historia Plantarum per Americanas insulas annis 1689–1697 observatarum a R. P. C. Plumier, (Minime). Americanarum plantarum icones, 3 Vols.

1824. Ouvrage consacré à la mémoire du R. P. C. Plumier, "Flore des îles de France et de Bourbon ... consacrée à la mémoire du R. P. C. Plumier, qui le premier a porté la lumière dans cette famille intéressante," par Aubert du Petit-Thouars.

PARIS, BIBLIOTHÈQUE DE LA CHAMBRE DES DÉPUTÉS

351. fol. 5. Confirmation de l'union de la chapelle de Ste Suzanne au couvent des Minimes de Chaillot. XVIIth century.

PARIS, BIBLIOTHÈQUE DU MUSEUM D'HISTOIRE NATURELLE

1–37. Oeuvres de Botanique du R. P. C. Plumier. [37 volumes of drawings, notes, accounts of travels. A fragment transcribed in Appendix IV B].

1176. Motifs et plans de l'édition (in-4) d'un ouvrage manuscrit du Père Plumier, très intéressant pour la perfection de cette science (la botanique).
Botanicum americanum. 7 volumes bound together, 831 pp.

PARIS, BIBLIOTHÈQUE DE LA MAIRIE DU XVIᵉ ARRONDISSEMENT

32. Notes on various historical subjects, XIXth century. fol. 242–244 concerning the Minimes de Chaillot, i.e. the Minimes de Nigeon.

PARIS, BIBLIOTHÈQUE DE L'UNIVERSITÉ DE PARIS

1380. Recueil de pièces. Poèmes par Charles Coignet de la Cour, Minime.

130893. Venerande Domine Decane, sapientissimique Domini a sacra (theologiae) facultate Parisiensi Deputate. Printed, undated, Paris? [Decree in favour of Pierre Buisson, Minim, allowing him remission of time for taking Doctorate of Theology at the University of Paris].

130894. Remarques ou avis sur le plaidoyé de l'avocat Desaguetz, plaidant pour les curés de St. Jean, St. Gervais et St. Paul contre les religieux Minimes de la Place Royale. Undated, possibly 1640/1. [See Archives Nationales, L. 952 (b)].

PARIS, ARCHIVES NATIONALES

L. 369–370. Pièces émanées de divers Cardinaux: pièces relatives aux Minimes. Contains: Compendium extractus, sive registris causae inter Regem ... et fratres venerabilis conventus Sanctae Trinitatis, nationis Gallicanae, ordinis fratrum Minimorum.

L. 951. Monuments Ecclésiastiques. Liasse of papers containing the following:
  (a) Constitutiones novae pro Minimis Fratribus Gallis. Letters patent signed by Louis XVI, 28 September, 1775.
  (b) Papal bulls and copies; Royal letters patent conferring privileges.
  (c) Scrap of paper, Revolutionary period, giving details of the eighteen members of the Order in Paris at the time of the suppression.
  (d) Letters patent for the separation of the Province de Lyon and the new Province du Duché de Bourgogne, 1623.
  (e) An account of the foundation of the "couvents" in the Province d'Aquitaine, 1766.
  (f) Two "quittances" in S. François de Paule's own hand.
  (g) Act of suppression of various houses, 1769.
  (h) Règles, Undated, end of XVIth century.

L. 952. Monuments Ecclésiastiques; as above, containing the following:
  (a) Papers concerning the establishment of the Couvent de la PlaceRoyale; building, repairs etc.
  (b) Printed address to the Parlement de Paris setting out the complaint of Nicolas Mazure, Curé de St. Paul, against the Minimes de la Place Royale, 11 March, 1641.
  (c) Legal papers relating to the site of the "couvent" in the Place Royale, 1609.
  (d) Ground plan and plan of refectory of the above, 1609.
  (e) Water supply and payment therefor: printed edict signed by the King, 1694.
  (f) *Amortissements* and other legal papers, XVIIth century.
  (g) Attestations de reliques de S. François de Paule, S. François de Sales ... 1679.
  (h) Fondations (de messes) [1]: Etat des fondations, 1699. Additions up to 1737, some loose leaves XVIIIth century. [It is from this register, presumably, that MS. Mazarine 2429 was compiled].
  (i) Documents concerning the Chapelle de Ste. Susanne ou des Cinq Plaies Connexion with this "chapelle" in the Eglise de S. Roch, Rue S. Honoré, and the Minims of Nigeon and of the Place Royale until 1672.

---

[1] In all further references the French word "fondation" is used to refer to "fondation de messe(s)." The English word "Foundation" refers to the establishment of a "couvent."

(j) Letters patent for the establishment of the Couvent de la Place Royale, 1610.

L.953. Monuments Ecclésiastiques; as above, containing:
   (a) Act of dedication of the Minim's church, Nigeon. Undated, XVIth century.
   (b) *Concession d'eau*, Nigeon, 1582. Other privileges 1582–1660.
   (c) Register of baptisms and Professions, Nigeon, 1728–1790.

L.954. Monuments Ecclésiastiques; as above, containing:
   (a) Financial papers, Nigeon.
   (b) Constitution of 26 July, 1714: Nigeon assessed on 9,000,000 livres de rente.

L.955. Monuments Ecclésiastiques; as above, containing:
   (a) Documents relating to the Ordre de Grandmont and the establishment of the Minimes de Vincennes in the property of the Ordre de Grandmont. Title deeds and other legal papers. Copy of a "quittance" signed by F. Giry, Minim, Correcteur 16?.
   (b) Letters patent 1584–1770 concerning the Ordre de Grandmont and the Minimes de Vincennes.
   (c) Letters patent dated November 1649; establishment of the Minimes de Dunkerque.
   (d) Foundation of the Minimes de Guise. Copy of a letter from Charles, Duc de Lorraine, dated 10, August, 1610.
   (e) Foundation of the Minimes de Noisy-le-Grand. Letter of Antione du Prat, dated 27 September, 1582.
   (f) A title deed belonging to the Minimes de Bracancour, January 1524.
   (g) Act of suppression of the Minimes de Bourges and of their union with the Minimes d'Issoudun 1774.

LL.1562. Privilèges. [Printed, see MSS Bibliothèque Nationale, Fonds Fr. 15769].

LL.1563. Catalogue de tous les livres conservés dans tous les couvents de l'ordre des Minimes, par Jérôme Durand, Correcteur Général de l'ordre, 1600. [This catalogue heading is misleading, the catalogue deals exclusively with the Italian "conventi." Binding XIXth century bears title "Catalogue de la Bibliothèque de la Place Royale." Fol. 5–65, catalogue of the library at Santa Trinità dei Monti, the only catalogue of the library to have survived].

LL.1564–1566. Registres Capitulaires de la Place Royale, 3 vols.
   (1) 1612–1642.
   (2) 1643–1682.
   (3) 1682–1790.

LL.1567. Minimes de la Place Royale; Visites, 1691–1789. Visits of the Procinvials; lists of issue of clothing, linen, utensiles for the Infirmary etc.

LL.1568–1569. Catalogue de la Bibliothèque des Minimes de la Place Royale, 1776.

LL.1576–1577. Conclusions Capitulaires des Minimes de Vincennes, 2 vols.
   (1) 1595–1612.
   (2) 1612–1655.

LL.1578. Livre de comptes, Minimes de Vincennes, 1670–1774.

PROVINCIAL LIBRARIES*

ANCIENNE SÉRIE

Vol. V. METZ

pp. 324/5, No. 868. Chronique des Minimes de Metz. [Destroyed by enemy action in 1940. There is an unusually long account of this MS in the printed Catalogue of the Library.]

Vol. VII. TOULOUSE

p. 160, No. 254. Christi Crucifixi Triumphus. Translation and adaptation from Savonorola by Pierre d'Aguts, Minime. Undated. [P. d'Aguts was Simon Bachelier's collègue on the Visite Générale of 1640/1].

p. 201. Nos. 350–353. Sermons et œuvres mêlées du P. Jean Augier, Minime. –1640?

pp. 201–202. Nos. 354–358. Sermons, mélanges et opuscules du P. Lacombe, Minime. XVIIth century. [No. 358 contains a letter from Balthasar d'Avila to Maignan suggesting that the works of Lacombe should be printed. This suggestion was never taken up. Letter dated 1653].

pp. 383–390. Nos. 622–633. Twelve volumes of manuscripts by le Père La Porte, Minime de Toulouse, XVIIIth century. [Collection was preserved in the Minims' library; contains a wide range of historical and bibliographical material]. The following are valuable for a history of the Order:
No. 624. Elucubrationes Turonenses. Containing various XVIIth century histories, necrologies and cartularies of the Couvent du Plessis-lès-Tours.
No. 629. Elucubrationes Mediolanenses. Contains a few notes on the Order, a copy of a letter from S. François de Paule and a note on the same.
No. 631. Elucubrationes Massilienses. Contains notes on the Minims in the various towns of Provence. Also contains, fol. 163 an important note on the correspondence of Peiresc with Jean François, Minim.

pp. 442–443. No. 752. Recueil de plusieurs opuscules de physique; Maignan, bound with arms of the Order. Contains the following:
fol. 1–28. Ad propositiones philosophicas anni 1659 ... reflexiones.
fol. 29–42. Anni 1660. Ad propositiones physicas ... reflexiones, (See Theses 1660, below).
fol. 43–44. Two printed notices of theses disputed in the great hall of the Minimes de Toulouse (a) Propositiones physicae lectiores, Septembris 1660. (b) Propositiones ex Universa Theologia lectiores, 27 Sep. 1662.
fol. 45–103. The theses advertised in "b" above.
fol. 104–107. Qua fidei divina sunt, nequaquam astringenda esse principiis humana philosophiae, praesertim in his, qua ad sacramentum Eucharistiae pertinent.
fol. 109–111. Existentia Dei ratio demonstrativa naturalis.
fol. 112. Fragment, with diagram; Archimedes' principle applied to testing gold and silver mixtures.
fol. 113–114. De modo quo sit ut   ?   ad littora maris aquae miror ab eisdem recedent.
fol. 115–118. A la page 1395 après le nombre 36. [Addendum for *Cursus Philosophicus*, Toulouse, 1653; incorporated in the edition of Lyon, 1673, ch. XIV, prop xxx, No. 37.]

* This section of the Bibliography is based on the published *Catalogue général des Manuscrits des Bibliothèques publiques de France*, Paris, 1849, in progress.

fol. 119. Fragment. Conus ad ... gnomonicam translatus.

fol. 120. Speculum conicum rectangulum ad ... gnomonicam translatum.

fol. 121–122. Dum theses offeret, dicat ... [Instructions, to his pupils? on the presentation of theses.]

fol. 123–126. In inflammatione scholae philosophiae, anno 1658 mense Octobris, Tolosa.

fol. 127. De veritate convertio mirabilis quaedam est Poetas inter Philosophos ...

fol. 128. Animam separatam non ... ad singulos veritates nec angelos ...

fol. 129. De anima rationali separata.

fol. 130. Address to the Corrector General (J-B. Ponglia?).

fol. 131. Heading of a thesis. (See fol. 43).

fol. 132. Part of an address or prayer.

fol. 133. Calorem corporis calidi non esse sanguem particulare agitationem circularem sit formum corpus calidum.

fol. 134. Continuation of fol. 132?

fol. 135–139. Continua sunt quorum extrema sunt unum.

fol. 140. Dialectam nostram seu logicam, qua ars bene differendi ... eam M. Jullins nominat.

fol. 141. Existentiam non distingui ab essentia actuali, producta et extra causas positas. (Testimonia?)

fol. 142–143. Praelectio de substantia.

fol. 144. Praelectio de obiecto physicae.

fol. 145. Praelectio de materia de qua anima brutorum.

fol. 146–149. De luce praeclara et praeclaram dixit fodalis mons. R.A.P.

fol. 150. Fragment. Unidentified.

fol. 151. Alimenti solutio in stomacho sit (fit?).

fol. 152–153. Diagrams and descriptions in French of "Fontaines de vent." [Transcribed and illustrated in Appendix III].

fol. 155. Fragments dealing with mechanical propositions; mass and movement.

fol. 156. Brutorum animas consistunt in spiritu tornissimo vitali ut vocant vel animali. (See also fol. 145).

fol. 157–158.

fol. 159–160. Contra atomistas Franciscus Maria Grimaldus Lib. I, Prop. 45.

fol. 161. Fragment with diagram, unidentified.

fol. 162–163. Addendum ad propositiones 5 et 14, caput 12 *Philosophia Sacra* [See also fol. 115–118].

fol. 164–165. Fragments. (a) Pendulum (b) Squares and rectangles; an addendum for page 1373 of *Philosophia Sacra*.

fol. 166. De consuetidine.

fol. 167–168. Letter, undated. At top in Maignan's hand "Monsieur de Magnas escrivant à Mr. de Fermat d'un metheore qu'il avait veu. Le raconte comme s'ensuit ..." [1]

fol. 169–189. Nobilissime ac piissime Joannae Franciae in eius solemni beatificatione Panegyris ad S.D.N. Urbanum VIII P.O.M. [Written by an "écrivain juré" with notes and underlinings in Maignan's hand].

fol. 190–199. In funere Rmi. P. Francisci a Cœlico, Ord. Minimorum Generalis, Oratio panegyrica.

fol. 200–203. Oratio de ultimo fine hominis.

fol. 205–206. Circa motum acceleratum in proportione dupla ut spatia successive temporibus aequalibus peracta. Dupla proportionis geometricam progressionem observatam. (Very faded).

---

[1] P. de Fermat, *Oeuvres*, vol. IV, Paris, 1912, p. 71.

pp. 527–528. Nos. 885–887. Catalogues de la Bibliothèque des Minimes de Toulouse.

(a) Compiled by D'Aguts, c. 1647 with additions in another hand up to 1670.

(b) Rough copy of above. Undated. On cover, "Codex Librorum Bibliothecae conventus Tolosani iuxta originalem R. P. D'Aguts."

(c) Classified catalogue, early XVIIIth century with some addition in another hand up to 1754. At bottom of fol. 347, "Ne varietur, à Toulouse le 6 mai, 1790." [Large mathematical and medical sections].

NOUVELLE SÉRIE, (1886–)

Vol. VI. BEAUNE.

p. 276. No. 151. Novus index bibliothecae conventus Minimorum Belnensium.

CHALON-SUR-SAÔNE.

p. 370. No. 37. De conventu Minimorum Cabilonensium. XVIIth century.

Vol. VII. GRENOBLE.

p. 443. No. 1425. fol. 268. Details of a fire in the Couvent des Minimes de Grenoble.

p. 498. No. 1462. Foundation of the Couvent des Minimes de la Plaine (Grenoble).

Vol. VIII. LA ROCHELLE.

p. 56. No. 127. fol. 124 Notes on the foundation of the Minimes de la Rochelle. XVIIth century.

pp. 59–60. No. 130. fol. 40. Copy of an extract from the archives of the Minimes de Surgères.

fol. 100. Original "acte de sommation"; in favour of the Minimes de Surgères. XVIIth century.

p. 61. No. 132. Copy of MS. 133, below.

p. 62. No. 133, p. 91. Permission to build the Couvent des Minimes de la Rochelle. XVIIIth century copy.

p. 145. No. 328. fol. 264–272. Title deeds of the Minimes de Surgères.

p. 266. No. 501. fol. B. 86. Verses on door. Minimes de La Rochelle. See also MS. No. 676.

p. 340. No. 622. Building at Surgères, right to collect wood from the Forêt de Cizé. XVIIth century.

p. 409. No. 656. Letter from Plumier, dated 11 June, 1702. [Two notes, XVIIIth century, state that the letter was addressed to Michel Bégon and give a list of plant names; the latter in Plumier's hand?]

p. 455. No. 669. Authorisation for the Minimes to build at La Rochelle, dated 28 June, 1630.

Vol. XV. MARSEILLE.

p. 17. No. 45. Explication mystique des Lamentations de Jérémie sur les sentiments d'une âme pénitente exposée aux rigueurs de la justice vengeresse de Dieu. Par le R.P. Sauvat, ex-Provincial des Minimes. 150 pp. XVIIth century.

p. 21. No. 55. Divus Paulus, seu duae epistolae ex epistolis divi Pauli excerptae. 1668. Par Timothée de Raynier, Minime. 191 pp.

p. 266. No. 913. Flore américaine. A work by Plumier. [Inside cover, "Donné par le Père Plumier, Minime de la Province de la Provence." In another hand, "Ce n'est point un ouvrage du Père Plumier; ce savant botaniste tira cet extrait des ouvrages de Marcgraves et de Pison lorsqu'il dut aller en Amérique y herboriser par ordre du roi." 257 pp. Note: certainly by Plumier, original drawings by him. Marks an early stage in his work].

pp. 276–279. Nos. 943–955. Journal des observations astronomiques faites en différents lieux. Louis Feuillée, Minime. 13 volumes.

1697 – Marseille.

1700 – Constantinople.

1703 – Martinique.

1709 – Lima.

1723 – Observatoire Royal des PP. Minimes de Marseille. Volume 955 also contains in addition to astronomical observations "Histoire des plantes médicinales qui sont les plus en usage aux royaumes de l'Amérique méridionale, composée sur les lieux par ordre du Roi ... 1709, 1710, et 1711. Par le R.P. Feuillée, religieux Minime, mathématicien, Botaniste de sa Majesté et correspondant de l'Académie royale des Sciences."

p. 280. No. 960. Traité de géométrie pratique, stéréométrie, trigonométrie. Fr. Joachim Rigaud, Minime. Undated, early XVIIIth century. 483 fols. 32 plates bearing the inscription "Joachim Rigaud, Porrierensis, Minimus, delineavit. Ludovicus David, Parisiensis, sculpsit," or abbreviations of the same.

p. 280. No. 961. Horographie. Fr. Joachim Rigaud. Undated, early XVIIIth century. 290 fols. 126 diagrams and plates which bear the same inscription as those in No. 960 above.

p. 280. No. 962. Horographie ... démontrée par les règles d'arithmétique et par les principes de géométrie. Fr. Joachim Rigaud. Undated, early XVIIIth century. [Same engraved plates as in No. 960 and 961 above, making total of 129 plates and disgrams].

pp. 353–358. Nos. 1259–1268. Collection sur différents sujets par un Religieux de l'ordre des Minimes. 10 volumes. [Very largely in one handwriting. An almost encyclopaedic work although fragmentary in places. No care seems to have been taken at the time of binding (mid-XVIIIth century?) to ensure any sort of order. Interspersed with pieces in other hands, including a parody on part of Le Cid, various Harangues faites au Roi Louis XIV, copies of Papal briefs, verses and three printed pamphlets. The main contributor was an eighteenth century member of the order whose intention seems to have been to place in the hands of novices a compendium of theological and scientific studies. Many abrégés of printed works].

p. 404. No. 1484. Catalogue de la Bibliothèque des Minimes de Marseille. XVIIIth century.[1]

p. 404. No. 1485. Catalogus Librorum Bibliothecae Massiliensis Minimorum, 1776. [Illustrated frontispiece showing interior of the library].

Vol. XIX. AMIENS.

pp. 45–47. No. 104. Le Pentateuque en vers. J-B. Postel, Minime. XVIIIth century.

p. 266. No. 251. 2, fol. 1. Letter from Mabillon to le Père Cornet, Minime.

[1] Missing from the shelves, March, 1962.

p. 303. No. 544. Catalogue des imprimés de la Bibliothèque des Minimes d'Amiens. Drawn up by Citoyen Bourry, an 3.

p. 325. No. 564. 38, fol. 93. Notes on the Minimes de Dieppe.

Vol. XX. Le Mans.

p. 59. No. 53. Indemnité, 25 mai, 1677. (missing, April 1962).

p. 131. No. 197a. Sainct François de Paule, ou la Charité triomphante; Seconde partie. XVIIth century. 423 fols.

Vol. XXIII. Bordeaux.

p. 104. No. 234. Collection of papers belonging to le Père Thomas Labadie, Minime. XVIIIth century.

p. 517. No. 844. fol. 81 et sq. Catalogue de la Bibliothèque des Minimes de Bordeaux. XVIIIth century, Revolutionary period.

Vol. XXIV. Epernay.

p. 353. No. 148. Collection of notes, XIXth century, on the history of Epernay; fol. 224–225 concerning the Minimes d'Epernay.

p. 362. No. 155. Recueil de lettres, Vol. II. Nos. 17 and 59 from Fr. Bertin, Minime to M.xxx. (a) Dated 28 Dec. 1687. (b) Dated 2 July, 1691.

pp. 365–367. Nos. 157–172. Recueil fait par Bertin de Rocheret et par le Père Prévoteau, Minime du couvent d'Epernay. An XVIIIth century historical collection.

p. 369. No. 187. Procès-verbaux des Chapitres Provinciaux des Minimes de Champagne, 1634–1743.
Bibliothèque Raoul Chandon No. 253. Copies, XIXth century, of papers concerning the "temporel" of the Minimes d'Epernay.

Vol. XXVI. Roye.

p. 696. No. 20. Registre de Baptêmes etc. pp. 45–58 Minimes de Roye.
Lille.

p. 319. No. 458. Vie des PP. Hermites par Louis Magnier, Minime.
Avignon. (Musée Calvet).

p. 364. No. 656. Collatio habita in Palatio Apostolico Avenionensi ... 1693. Ad usum Fr. Joachim Topenas, Minime. Fol. 80 et sq. Quaestiones theologiae moralis ... 1702. R. P. Stepen Ripert, Minime. [A set of notes kept by le P. Topenas.]

Vol. XXVIII. Avignon.

ctd. p. 25. No. 1561. Notes concerning property of the Minimes d'Avignon compiled by P. Achard in the XIXth century.

p. 90. No. 1686. Biens nationaux. [Property of Minims, XVIIIth century].

pp. 258–259. Notes on Avignon. [Bibliothèque Corenson, XIXth century]. Same information as in No. 2381 q.v.

p. 396. No. 2381. Collection de plusieurs pièces sur les églises d'Avignon: Collection Massilian.
fol. 80 Minimes d'Avignon. Notes taken from the Délibérations des Consuls and from other papers in the Archives Municipales. (a) Foundation of the Order in Avignon, 1575. (b) Status of mendicants granted in 1575. (c) Aumône de 200 écus pour aider à bâtir un réfectoire, 1609. (d) Aumône de 23 écus; 120 écoliers ... vont étudier la physique et les mathématiques chez les pères Minimes, 1602.

p. 423. No. 2397. Recueil. fol. 146. Lettre au Roi. Les ... religieux Minimes natifs de la ville d'Avignon et du Comtat (Venaissin). [Letter undated but probably 1628–1630. Request to be granted same right of entry to Santa Trinità dei Monti as the French Minims.]

p. 455. No. 2451. fol. 43. Almae et nobilissimae Academiae Avenionensis ... D. Petro Francisco de Ribiers ... These ... in observantia minimentum. 1709.

p. 595. No. 2642. Recueil de consultations et "allegationes" juridiques. fol. 47– 52 ... pour Jean-Louis Liotard contre les Minimes. [Liotard had worn the habit of the Minims but had not taken vows. Minims tried unsuccessfully to claim his property, 1695].

Vol. XXIX. Avignon.

ctd. p. 34. No. 2953. Recueil. No. 26. Printed prospectus: L'Irroé, ou le purgatif rafraîchissant. Undated, XVIIIth century. [Sale of drug, sole property of the Minimes d'Avignon].

p. 277. No. 3359. Archives de la famille Cambis-Vidaud. fol. 245. Affiliation o^f M. de Servières à l'Ordre des Minimes, 24 February, 1685.

p. 413. No. 3684. Archives de la famille Doni. Registres de quittances: pensions dues aux Minimes d'Arles, 1715–1723.

Vol. XXX. Lyon.

pp. 471–472. No. 1530. Le livre funéraire ... des Minimes de Lyon. [A register begun in 1662, of burials in the Minims' church from 1581 and completed up to 1788].

p. 588. No. 1901. Papers concerning land transactions, Minimes de Lyon, 1646– 1649.

pp. 685–686. No. 271 (Fonds Coste). Inventaire des pièces. Further papers concerning land transactions, see No. 1901 above and No. 2312, (Catalogue Vol. XLII below.)

Vol. XXXII. Besançon.

p. 603. No. 946. Bibliothèque Séquanoise, IIe serie. fol. 27, Ve. Notes on Claude d'Orchamps, Général des Minimes.

pp. 983, 984, 994, 998. No. 1005. Various wills made by members of the Order: P. Bencenel, R. Chénier, P. Chappelenet, C. Noble, J. Finot.

Vol. XXXIII. Besançon.

ctd. pp. 457–459. Collection Chiflet No. 23. fol. 246–247. Notes on Claude d'Orchamps, see above.

p. 829. Collection Dunaud No. 31. fol. 343. Notes on the "couvents" at Arbois, Arlay, Besançon, Dôle, Morteau, Notre-Dame de la Consolation, Ornans, Rupt.

Vol. XXXIV. Carpentras, Bibliothèque Inguimbertine.

p. 672. No. 1304. Recueil. fol. 102. Supplique de la communauté de Bédarides à l'Archevêque d'Avignon au sujet du desservant fourni par les R. P. Minimes dudit lieu, 1627. [Written in Italian.]

p. 705. No. 1364. Secretariatus ab anno 1607 ad 1618. fol. 604, Confirmatio erectionis conventus Minimorum in Nostra Domina de Vita circa Venascum, 5 Novembris, 1614. Foundation of the "couvent" at Venasque.

p. 706. No. 1365. Secretariatus ... 1619–1623. fol. 205. A further entry concerning the foundation at Venasque.

p. 753. No. 1418. Recueil "Quaedam Instrumenta." Vol. XIX Recueil de pièces concernant les Minimes ... de Carpentras, 1609–1761.

p. 780. No. 1542. Recueil "Quaedam Instrumenta." fol. 18–46. Diverses pièces relatives à un procès entre les Pères Minimes d'Avignon ... prieurs de S. Pierre de Vassols et le Vicaire dudit lieu, 1651–1691. Also a dispute concerning "congrue," [1] mid-XVIIth century until 1760.

p. 795. No. 1623. Mélanges. Pièces concernant les Minimes d'Avignon, 1601–1758. Notes sur la fondation du couvent des Minimes (de Venasque).

Vol. XXXV. CARPENTRAS.

ctd. p. 37. No. 1731. Recueil. p. 958, notes on the foundation of the Minimes de Venasque.

p. 181. No. 1769. Catalogi codicum manuscriptorum. fol. 713, Catalogue des livres des Pères Minimes de la Valette dressé par le P. Burle. Undated.

pp. 566–567. No. 1816. Recueil. fol. 229. Schedae Rivipollenses et Barcinonae. Par le R.P. Jean-François, Provincial des Minimes, allant au chapitre à Barcellone. Title only: following this, fol. 230–239, notes on the monastery at Ripoll. [These notes are in Peiresc's, MSS, Aix-en-Provence, No. 204, pp. 230–260].
fol. 241. Letter of Jean-François to Peiresc, Marseilles, 20 June, 1629.
fol. 243. Letter of Jean-François to Peiresc, Barcelona, 8 May, 1629.
fol. 245, Letter of Jean-François to Peiresc, Barcelona, 16 May, 1629.

p. 624. No. 1821. Correspondance de Peiresc.
fol. 482. Instructions to Théophile Minuti, Minime, "pour prendre des empreintes de médailles grecques et samaritaines."
fol. 488. As above "instructions ... avec dessein de voir le Levant et l'Egypte pour les livres et autres curiosités qu'il désire faire avoir au sieur Peiresc ..."

Vol. XXXVI CARPENTRAS.

ctd. p. 283. No. 1871. Correspondance de Peiresc.
fol. 46. Letter of Peiresc to Minuti, 2 October, 1634.

p. 302. No. 1874. Correspondance de Peiresc. Letters to le Père Minuti, Minim.
fol. 310, 316, 320, 324, 327, 332, 334, 345, 349, 355, 356, 362, 366, 367, 371, 372, 434, 444, 445, (24 letters, dated between 1633 and 28 April, 1637).

p. 319. No. 1876. Correspondance de Peiresc. Further letters of Peiresc to Minuti.
fol. 355, 356, 376, 377.
fol. 375. Letter to Jean-François.
fol. 377. Copy of a letter from R. P. Math. to Théophile Minuti.
fol. 798–827, Further letters of Peiresc to Théophile Minuti, 3 March 1630–7 June 1633.

p. 331. No. 1878. Correspondance de Peiresc.
fol. 274. Letter, undated, of J. S. Allemand to Théophile Minuti at Marseilles.

Vol. XXXVII. TOURS.

p. 837. No. 1200. (No. 15) Vue du couvent des Pères Minimes au Plessis-lès-Tours, 1699.

---

[1] Congrue: see *Littré*, congru, No. 3 – *portion congrue*, pension annuelle que le grand décimateur payait au curé pour sa subsistence.

p. 844. No. 1217. fol. 72. Fragment of a manuscript history of Tours. Etablissement de l'Ordre.

p. 908. Nos. 1320–1321. fol. 280–286. Baux et rentes des Minimes d'Amboise, 1666–1784.

TOURS (The following manuscripts were destroyed by enemy action in June, 1940)

p. 510. No. 638. Règle de l'Ordre. Bulle de Jules II.

p. 867. No. 1252. Notes recueillies: Minimes de S. Grégoire de Tours.

p. 895. No. 1304. fol. 42. Acquisition d'un terrain, 1650.

p. 981. No. 1494. fol. 198–269. Notes sur l'abbaye des Minimes du Plessis-lès-Tours, avec plusieurs plans, 1491–1770.

p. 984. No. 1500. Poésie sur le Plessis-lès-Tours, Henri Choisnet, Minime.

p. 1013. No. 1607. Registres Capitulaires, 1629–1673.

Vol. XXXIX. REIMS.

p. 130. No. 796. Regula fratrum sororum Ordinis Minimorum. XVIth century, 223 fols.

p. 131. No. 797. Réflexions morales en forme de méditation sur la règle des Minimes de Saint François de Paule. Par R. Mopinot, Minime. XVIIth century. 581 pp.

p. 236. No. 985. Traité du jet des bombes. Par A. R. Féry, Minime. XVIIIth century. 62 fols. 9 diagrams. [fol. 41 et sq. Traité des pendules. Not listed in the Catalogue].

p. 1015. No. 1981. La vie et les œuvres de R. Mopinot, 1606–1661. Par Jean Mopinot, Minime, XVIIth century. 183 pp.

Vol. XXXIX bis, REIMS.

p. 236. The fragments of letters referred to on this page under the heading "Tarbé, 128" are to be seen in the Archives Municipales de Reims and not in the Bibliothèque Publique.

Vol. XL. ARRAS.

p. 228. Fonds Victor Advielle, No. 217. Panégyrique de Saint Benoît par le R.P. Grégoire Martin, religieux Minime ... correspondant de l'Académie d'Auxerre. XVIIIth century.

BLOIS.

p. 565. Papiers Dupré, No. 88. Notes historiques sur Blois, Vol. 2, pp. 457–462. Notes sur l'ancienne église des Minimes de Blois. XIXth century.

p. 564. Papiers Dupré, No. 89. Notes sur un miracle ... Minimes de Blois. XIXth century. [Miracle in 1633.]

Vol. XLI. CALAIS.

p. 13. No. 66. Bibliothecae patrum Minimorum Caleti Novus index ... 1749. [Déposé au greffe, le 27 février, 1790 par F. Charles-Joseph Andry, Supérieur des Minimes].

Vol. XLI. CHARLEVILLE.

p. 105. No. 321. Praelectiones theologicae, docente Rdo. Patre Mathieu S.T.P., Romae, 1756. ad usum J. Pauli Alex. Bouquillon, Minimi.

La Rochelle.

p. 470. No. 867. fol. 147. Copy of a letter from le Père Plumier, Minim, to Michel Bégon; Paris, 6 March, 1703.

fol. 151. Copy of a letter from Plumier to Bégon; 10 August, 1702.

fol. 151. Extract from a letter Plumier to Bégon; 16 December, 1702.

p. 501. No. 1127. Minimes de Surgères, notes on property, XVIIth century.

Vol. XLII. Lyon.

p. 166. No. 2312. fol. 11. Papers concerning land transaction. See previous entry for Lyons under Vol. XXX.

Nancy.

p. 365. No. 1233. Euclid. Livre à l'usage des Minimes de Pont-à-Mousson.

No. 1805. Livre des états des maisons des Minimes à Pont-à-Mousson, 1742–1786.

Vol. XLVIII. Rouen.

p. 79. No. 737, (14). Fondation aux Minimes de Rouen, faite par le Sieur de Bardouville, 13 mars, 1691.

Amiens.

p. 314. Legs Charles Pinsard, No. 1347, Tome XX. Notes on the couvent des minimes d'Amiens.

Metz.

p. 449. No. 1450–1451. Inventaire des bibliothèques des couvents de Metz, 1790–l'an III. [Minims' library is catalogued in Vol. II; catalogue drawn up in 1790].

Vol. L. Nîmes.

p. 399. Livre dit Saint Jaques (sic) ou livre des pensions du couvent des Pères Minimes d'Arles sous le titre de Saint Honorat des Aliscamps. Dressé en 1668 par le Père Jean-Etienne. Procureur. Refait en 1679, 1682, 1706, 1727, par ... Contenant l'état des fondations de messes faites dans cette église.

p. 399. No. 633. Livre dit Saint Laurent ... (as above "refait par le R.P. Jacques Laurent. Camayou, Procureur, en 1755.

london: british museum

Additional Manuscripts: 28,609. C. Plumier, *Nova plantarum americanarum genera*, 1703.

Sloane Manuscripts: 2,337. C. Plumier, *Description des plantes de l'Amérique* (Translation), 1693.

3,889. E. Maignan, *Perspectiva Horaria* (Fragments of copy).

4,107. C. Plumier, *Delineationes plantarum americanarum*. (XVIIth century. Imperfect).

london: british museum (Natural History)

Banksian MSS 1–5. Plumier, 312 original water colour and pen-and-ink drawings, many of which published.[1]

---

[1] Not original – see p. 197.

B1. ARCHIVES DÉPARTEMENTALES *

My information has been obtained by visiting various *Archives Départementales* or from consulting the printed *Inventaire des Archives Départementales;* where no printed inventory exists and where I have been unable to visit the dépôt, I have relied on replies to a circular which I despatched in May, 1963. This is indicated by an asterisk placed after the name of the Département; I am grateful to the members of the *Service des Archives* who have thus helped me to achieve greater completeness.

AISNE

Série H. *Minimes de Laon.*
1386–1401 Papers concerning property, XVIth century – 1788.

Minimes de Guise.
1402–1405 Papers concerning property, 1599–1785.

Minimes de Soissons.
1406–1414 Papers concerning property, 1616–1788.

Minimes de Château-Thierry.
1415 Papers concerning property, 1638–1771.

Minimes de Compiègne.
1416 Bail de terres, 1783.

Minimes de Chauny.
1417 *Déliberations capitulaires,* 1739–1787.
1418–1428 Papers concerning property, 1619–1788.

ARDENNES

Série H. *Minimes de Rethel.*
391 Foundation of the Order in Rethel; Bull of Clement VIII. Grant of land, fishing rights and right to cut wood; 1573–1767.
392 *Privilèges.* (Printed).

393–394 Title-deeds, donations, 1573–1769.

395 Actes Capitulaires, 1573–1741. These include *Requête du Fr. Cyprien Royer réclamant pour cause de maladie la permission de renoncer à sa profession.* [For Cyprien Royer, see Bibliography, Printed Works, under Rouyer.]

396 Recueil des Actes Capitulaires: *decret ... concernant les frères apostats que la tyrannie du démon a poussé à abandonner leur religion; le*

---

* Liasses of papers which include material from the XVIth and XVIIIth centuries are included if they contain papers having any importance for the XVIIth century, or if they deal with any of the controversies having their origins in the XVIIth century.

pillage des bibliothèques, l'enlèvement des volumes emportés par les frères dans leurs cellules la nécessité d'établir un catalogue et la défense de prêter des livres au dehors; 1642–1682.

397–402   Papers concerning property, 1573–1790.

ALLIER *

Série H.   *Minimes de Moulins.*

683   Title deeds, 1620–1624.

684   Foundation of the Order in Moulins, 1621–1634.

685   Privileges and exemptions from local taxes, 1629–1675.

686   Papers concerning relics and the church, 1622–1657.

687   Association of the Confrérie des Bien-Mourants and Confrérie de la Vierge with the Minimes de Moulins, XVIIth century.

688–689   Financial papers, 1644–1777.

690–694   Papers concerning property, 1574–1742.

695–696   "Fondations," 1626–1714.

697–702   Legal and financial papers, 1543–1781.

703   Rights concerning water supply, 1692–1726.

704   Papers concerning property, 1744–1784.

705   A liasse entitled "Papiers divers," XVIIth–XVIIIth century.

706–707   Inventory of documents and papers concerning property, XVIIIth century.

ALPES (BASSES) *

Série H. 21 H,   *Minimes de Mane.*

I   Small register, 1618, giving details of the act of foundation of the "couvent."

2–4   One register and two papers concerning property, 1727–1789.

AUBE *

Série Lr   *Minimes de Brienne.*

3/936–936 bis   Papers concerning the Ecole Militaire de Brienne (founded and staffed by members of the Order).

Série Q.

42   Inventory of above drawn up in the Revolutionary period.

AUDE

Série B.   *Minimes de Carcassonne.*

82   Suppression of the "couvent" in 1777.

Série H.

306   Financial papers, 1674–1771.

BOUCHES-DU-RHÔNE

Série H.   *Minimes d'Aix-en-Provence.*
30   Papers concerning their property, XVIIIth century.
            Registres Capitulaires, XVIIIth century.

Minimes d'Arles.
31   Papers concerning the "temporel," XVIIth and XVIIIth
            centuries. (Most of the information given here is to be found in
            MS Nîmes, No. 628 q.v.)
            Register of professions: Sœurs du Tiers-Ordre de Saint François
            de Paule, 1623–1731.
            Actes Capitulaires, 1706–1773. Extract from letters patent; Bull of
            Paul V and other papers concerning the foundation of the Order
            in Arles.

Minimes de Marseille.
32   *Fondations de Messes,* 1583–1662.
            Fondations de Messes, 1578–1690.
            Déliberations Capitulaires; various legal papers professions, all
            XVIIIth century.

Minimes de la Ciotat.
33   *Déliberations des chapitres provinciaux* (i.e. de la Province de Provence)
            1652–1686. This also includes reports of three "Visitations Géné-
            rales."

Minimes de Marignane.
34   Papers concerning the "temporel," XVIIIth century.

CHARENTE

Série H.   *Minimes d'Angoulême.*
30   Papers concerning the "temporel," 1619–1658.
            Rentes, XVII and XVIIIth centuries. Suppression, 1769–1781.

Minimes de Châteauneuf.
31   *Livre des Rentes,* 1659–1790.
            Procès contre la dame de Bourzac, 1734–1790.
            Quittances, 1780–1789.

Minimes d'Aubeterre.
32   Foundation, privileges, acquisition of the site, title-deeds etc.
            1617–1778.
            Rentes, 1684–1784.
            Procès, XVII and XVIIIth centuries. Cure de Saint-Quentin,
            union with the Minimes d'Aubeterre; relationships with the
            "vicaire perpétuel." Dîmes, 1673–1775.
            Ecclesiastical matters; many printed edicts etc., 1566–1752.

CHARENTE–MARITIME

Série H.   *Minimes de Surgères.*
65–69   Papers concerning the "temporel," XVIIth and XVIIIth
            centuries.
157   Financial papers, XVIIIth century.

Minimes de La Rochelle.

70–71 Papers concerning the "temporel," XVIIth and XVIIIth centuries.

72–73 Expenses, medical treatments, XVIIth century.

CHER *

Série H. 34 H, *Minimes de Bourges.*

1 Inventory of papers and property, 1683.

2 Foundation of the Order in Bourges, 1617.

3–7 Financial and legal papers, 1617–1785.

35 H. *Minimes de Dun-le-Roi.*

1 Foundation of the Order in Dun, 1622; donations and legacies by inhabitants, 1622–1726.

2–22 Financial papers, 1625–1789.

CÔTE-D'OR

Série H. There exists as yet (1962) no printed inventory of this part of Série H. Information taken from the manuscript catalogue.

Minimes de Dijon. (liasses 966–986).

59 Inventory of title deeds.
Registres Capitulaires, 1616–1688 and, in an uncatalogued volume, up to 1789, 7 Vols. in all.
Catalogue de la Sacristie, 1760, uncatalogued.

Minimes de Beaune, (liasses 987–988).

60 Title-deeds, foundation of the Order in Beaune, "fondations de Messes," finances; XVIIth and XVIIIth centuries.

Minimes de Notre-Dame d'Etang, i.e. Dijon II, (liasses 989–991).

61 Foundation. Inventory of title deeds, donations and income; XVIIth century.

Minimes de Semur (liasses 992–993).

62 Foundation of the Order in Semur. Register of professions and burials. 4 volumes of *Registres Capitulaires,* 1621–1738 (2 volumes of the *Actes capitulaires des Minimes de Semur* and 2 volumes of the *Actes Capitulaires Provinciaux,* 1621–1680).

DOUBS *

Série H. *Minimes de Besançon.*

104 H, 1–21 Papers concerning buildings and property, XVIIth–XVIIIth century.

Minimes de la Consolation.

105 H, 1–7 Foundation of the Order at la Consolation, 1669; legal papers XVIIth–XVIIIth century.

Minimes d'Ornans.

106 H, 1–10 Title deeds, XVIIth–XVIIIth century.

11 Catalogue of library.

12–21 Legal papers, XVIIth–XVIIIth century.

Minimes de la Seigne (i.e. Morteau).

107 H, 1–16 Legal and Financial papers, XVIIth–XVIIIth century.

DRÔME
Série H.
  19 H. A manuscript catalogue drawn up in the XXth century listing 125
       liasses and registers: *Minimes de Bourg-de-Péage (i.e. Romans) et de Valence.*
       Amongst these papers the following are the most important:
       (1) *Inventaire Charitas, 1639.*
       (2) *Inventaire Charitas, 1658.*
       (3) *Inventaire, 1677.*
       (4) *Catalogue dressé en huitante-quatre* (1684) *conformément à l'ordonnance du
           R.P. Provincial en sa visite faite le 14 avril, 1684.*
       (5) *Inventaire,* 1782. (It was on this inventory that the XXth century
           catalogue was drawn up. Many of the earlier inventories do not
           appear to have been preserved and various papers seem also to have
           been lost, amongst them; papers concerning "défense épiscopale
           (aux Minimes) d'exercer des fonctions curiales," c. 1640, and the
           papers concerning la Sœur Marie de Valence).
       (6) *Terriers,* XVIIth and XVIIIth centuries.
       (7) *Livres des comptes,* 1608–1649.

EURE-ET-LOIR
Série H. *Minimes de Chartres.*

H. 4218. Donation of site and of money, 1615.

H. 4219. Papers concerning sales of land in favour of the Order, 1609–1744.

H. 4220–4223. Papers concerning the "temporel," 1590–1789.

H. 4224. Déclarations des biens, 1676–1714.

H. 4225. Procès-verbal de l'état du couvent en 1789.

GARD
Série H. *Minimes de Pont-Saint-Esprit.*
  856–860   A complete set of documents dealing with the "temporel." The
            printed *Inventaire Sommaire des Archives* pp. 174–180 gives a detailed
            analysis of these papers.

GARONNE (HAUTE)
Série B. *Minimes de Toulouse.*
  Tome I   Entries in register concerning the "temporel" pp. 188, 191, 378,
              484. All XVIth century.
  Minimes de Samatan.
  Tome I   Entry concerning "temporel," XVIth century, p. 415.
  Minimes de Toulouse.
  No. 250   fol. 257. Required to prove their privileges, 1670.
  Minimes de Villeneuve-lès-Avignon.
  No. 471   fol. 102. Tithes payable by the Chartreux to the Minims, 1627.
  Minimes de Villemur.
  No. 512   fol. 396. Letters patent of 1629 granting establishment of the
              Order in Villemur (-sur-Tarn); registration of these letters.[1]

---

[1] This appears to be the only reference to Minims in Villemur.

Minimes de Vic-en-Bigorre.
No. 515   fol. 20. Possession of property, 1632.

Minimes de Besançon.
No. 521   fol. 123. "Arrêt" in favour of the Minimes de Besançon, 1632.
All the above references are to the *Juridictions du Parlement de Toulouse.*

Série C.   *Minimes de Narbonne.*
No. 2292   Payment of 1800 livres over a period of 4 years to the Minimes de
Narbonne whose "couvent" had been burned down in 1609. Grant
made by the Etats de Languedoc in 1610.

Minimes de Pont-Saint-Esprit.
No. 2293   A grant of 600 livres made by the Etats de Languedoc in 1611.

GERS *

Série H.   *Minimes de Cazaux.*
73   *Testament d'Ysabeau Daudirac, mort en 1631 ... legs d'une somme de
2000 livres en faveur des Minimes de Cazaux.*

Minimes de Samatan.
74   Financial papers, XVIIIth century.

GIRONDE

Série G.   *Minimes de Bordeaux.*
292   fol. 187. Foundation stone laid, Minimes de Bordeaux. 1608.
fol. 246. Grant of 30 livres by the Chapitre Métropolitain de Saint-
André to enable the Minims to finish their "couvent" at Bordeaux.

294   fol. 189. Grant of 9 livres "pour subventionner à l'érection et
construction de leur couvent," 1619.

297   fol. 983. Lying-in-state of Mgr. le Duc de Bourbon, 1653.

Minimes de Blaye et de Bordeaux.
620   Encroachment on parochial duties at Blaye, XVIIth and XVIIIth
centuries. Authorisation for a "quête" during the vendange, 1649.

HÉRAULT

Minimes de Béziers
Riot during time of plague. Minims ejected from their "couvent."
Payment by way of restitution; finding of new site, 1649.[1]
[See also some notes on the Minimes de Béziers in the XVIIIth
century, Série A, No. 98; also Collection Pouget, Vol. XXXII.]

ILLE-ET-VILLAINE *

Série H.   *Minimes de Rennes.*
20 H, 1   Privileges granted by Louis XIII and confirmed by later Kings,
1624-1733.
Catalogue of library, 1768.
2-3   Financial papers, 1538-1789.
4   *Actes des chapitres provinciaux, 1620-1635.*
5-11   Legal papers, 1578-1786.
12   Register of expenses and income, 1781-1790.

[1] Not in Catalogue but printed in *Bulletin de la Société archéologique de Béziers*, 2e série,
vol. 14, 2, pp. 223-237 and 257-261.

INDRE *

Série H.　*Minimes de Bomiers.*

588　　　Foundation of the Order in Bomiers, 1509; burial rights; papers concerning the "temporel" 1509–1709.

589–591　　Papers concerning property, 1520–1786.

Minimes d'Issoudun.

592　　　*Mémoires du couvent ... des Minimes d'Issoudun,* 1689. (Register, 42 fols.)

593–594　　Register of title-deeds and privileges, 1723.

595–596　　Association of Confrérie du Saint-Rosaire with the Minimes d'Issoudun; register of members, papers concerning the confrérie 1616–1765.

597　　　Privileges and financial papers, 1625–1790.

INDRE-ET-LOIRE

Série H.　*Minimes d'Amboise.*

671–674　　*Livres de recettes, rentes, baux etc.,* XVIIth and XVIIIth centuries.
675　　　Papers relating to the Canonization of Saint François de Paule; Copies of letters by the Saint. Some copies dated 1665.

Minimes de Champigny.
676–679　　Papers relating to the "temporel," XVth and XVIIIth centuries.

Minimes du Plessis-lès-Tours.
691–694　　Letters patent, Papal bulls, inventory of title deeds relative to the original foundation of the Order in France. Plan of the church. XVth–XVIIth centuries.

695　　　*Minimologium Turonense in quo coenobiorum origenes, primarii fundatores, benefactorum donationes, religiosi viri virtute, pietate ... Ordinis Minimorum Provinciae ...* 1482–1650. (Probably by Jacques Rosier, (vide p. 753); pp. 281–755 deal with period 1600–1650; a detailed chronicle).

Minimes de Saint Grégoire de Tours.
696　　　Acquisition of site. Plan of property; inventory of title-deeds; XVIIth and XVIIIth centuries.

ISÈRE

Série H.　*Minimes de Grenoble-Ville.*

8H. 1–14　Foundation with Royal consent, 1624.
　　　　　Fondations des messes, XVIIth century.
　　　　　Legal papers and plans.
　　　　　Association of the Order in Grenoble with the Confrérie de la Trinité et Rédemption des Captifs (liasse 8H. 3).

Minimes de la Plaine de Grenoble.
8H. 21–41　*Livre des instructions générales ... dressées en 1655.*
　　　　　Financial and legal papers.

Minimes de Roussillon.
8H. 51–56　*Actes Capitulaires* and financial papers, XVIIIth century.

Minimes de Tullins.
8H. 61–64 *Recueil d'actes notariés en faveur des Minimes établis en 1623.*
Legal and financial papers XVIIIth century.

Minimes de Vienne.
8H. 71–72 *Affranchissement de taille de deux maisons possédées par les Minimes.*
Legal papers, 1651–1741.

JURA *

Minimes de Dôle.
9 cartons of papers, uncatalogued.

LOIRE *

Série H. *Minimes de Saint-Etienne.*
1 liasse of papers, XVIIth–XVIIIth century.

Minimes de Roanne.
1 liasse of papers, XVIIIth century.

Minimes de Saint-Chamond.
2 liasses of papers, XVIIth–XVIIIth century.

LOIRE-ATLANTIQUE

Série H. *Minimes de Nantes.*
319–320 Foundation of the Order in Nantes and privileges, XVIth century
– 1671.

321–328 Financial and legal papers, XVIIth century – 1790.

329–330 Receipts and expenses, 1774–1790.

331 Inventory of title deeds and papers, 1740.

LOIRE (HAUTE) *

Série H. *Minimes de Brioude.*
41 H, 1–6 Legal papers, 1636–1726.

LOIR-ET-CHER

Série H. *Minimes de Blois.*
38 H. 1 Foundation of the Order in Blois, donations, 1614–1735.

2–5 Title deeds, 1533–1790.

6 Register (in-fol. 263 fols), inventory of above. Drawn up in 1699
with additions up to 1760.

7 Register similar to above drawn up in 1761 with additions up to
1790.

Minimes d'Amboise.
39 H. 1 Title-deeds of property, 1529–1710.

Minimes du Plessis-lès-Tours.
40 H. 1 Title-deeds of property at Chissay, 1608–1782.

LOIRET *

Série H. *Minimes de Gien.*
245 *Livre de rentes,* XVIth century.

Minimes d'Orléans.

250   Privileges granted by Henri IV and Louis XIII, 1609–1623.

The rich archives mentioned by the abbé Cochard in his *Minimes d'Orléans*, Orléans, 1875, were destroyed in 1940 as were those of the Minimes de Gien.

LOT-ET-GARONNE

Série B. *Minimes d'Agen.*
103 bis   Two "nominations"; one by P-B. Audinot, the other, by C.
108   Savignac, made over to the Minimes de Valence; XVIIth century.

MAINE-ET-LOIRE

Série H. *Minimes d'Angers.*
93 H, 1   *Fondation de messes,* 1628–1676.

2   Professions; burials, XVIIIth century.

3–6   Legal and financial papers; papers concerning the temporel, 1615–1735.

MARNE

Série H. There is no printed *Inventaire Sommaire* for Série H (Ordres) as yet. Information based on the sketchy *Répertoire des Archives de la Marne*, Arcis-sur Aube, 1884, p. 52, and on a rapid examination of part of the series.

Minimes d'Epernay.
5 liasses, 1 register, 1650–1728.

Minimes de Lépine.
12 liasses, 1 register, 1624–1757, and one register, uncatalogued.

Minimes de Reims.
2 liasses. See also Reims, Archives Municipales.

MARNE (HAUTE) *

Série H. *Minimes de Bracancour.*
16 H, 1–5   Title deeds, 1496–1716.

6–7   *Fondations de messes;* legal papers 1496–1711.

8–24   Legal papers; papers concerning property, 1488–1782.

25   Financial papers, 1734–1784.

18 H, 1–22 Papers relative to the acquisition of the Chapelle de Méchineix, 1652; privileges, rights etc. attached to this chapelry, XIIth–XVIIIth century.

Collection Jolibois, Vol. X,
            fol. 30–33 Act of foundation, 1496.
            fol. 36–39 Sack of "couvent" (1596); fire (1706).

MEURTHE ET-MOSELLE

Série B. *Minimes d'Epinal.*
79   Permission to build, 1609.

Minimes de Sainte-Lucie.
107   "Amortissement" in their favour, 1631.

Minimes de Marchéville.
6376   Delivery of corn, 1647.

Série G.   *Minimes de Verdun.*
116   *Comptes de la Prébende Théologale, Toul:* Grant of money to the
               Minimes de Verdun "qui n'ont pas moyen de vivre," 1590.

Série H.   *Minimes de Bassing.*
975–980   Foundation of the Order in Bassing; Inventory of title-deeds, 1577–
               1742.

981   *Fondations de messes,* 1617–1745. Catalogue of library, 1716.

982–986   Legal papers, tithes, XVIIth and XVIIIth centuries.

987   *Etats de la maison des Minimes,* 1673–1766. Poverty due to war and
               plague.

988–992   Financial papers, 1615–1790.

993   *Chapitres, Ordonnances, Règlements,* 1615–1672.

Minimes de Dieuze.
994   Inventory of title-deeds, 1729–1790.

995   Foundation of the Order at Dieuze; Permission of the Bishop of
               Metz; Donations; 1618–1692.

996–998   *Fondations et rentes,* 1424–1723. (A chapelry founded in 1424 by
               Charles II, Duc de Lorraine, was passed to the Minimes by Henri
               II, Duc de Lorraine).

999   *Requête adressée à M. de Vignier par les pauvres et désolés couvents de
               Dieuze et de Bassing ... bâtiment grandement cassé par 180 coups de
               canon... 1646.*

1000–1010   *Fondations et rentes,* 1623–1789.

1011–1016   Association of the Confrérie du Rosaire with the Minimes de
               Dieuze, 1656–1791.

1017–1020   Association of the Confrérie des Agonisants with the Minimes de
               Dieuze, 1758–1789.

Minimes de Lunéville.
1021–1022   Papers concerning the foundation of the Order in Lunéville.
               Permission of the Bishop of Toul. Confrérie de Saint Antoine
               (1386) associated with the Minimes de Lunéville, XVIIth and
               XVIIIth centuries.

1023–1024   *Fondations de messes; rentes;* 1604–1734.

1025   Papers concerning the "temporel," 1665–1787.

1026   Papers concerning property, 1574–1787.
1027   Financial papers.

1028   Catalogue of library, 1740.

1029   Papal bulls – XVIIth century copies – 1508–1583.

Minimes de Bon-Secours i.e. Nancy II.
1030   Permission to build. Concessions.
        Fondations de messes, 1609–1780.

1031   Burials, 1747–1768.

1032–1037   Papers concerning property and finances, 1625–1790.

Minimes de Nancy.
1038   Letters patent of Charles III, Duc de Lorraine; Donation of land
        by Louis XIII; other gifts; 1592–1720.

1039   Act of consacration; Indulgences; Papal bulls; XVIth century –
        1716.

1040–1043   *Fondations*, 1592–1788.

1044–1049   Inventory of title deeds, 1438–1783.

1050–1054   Donations. Papers concerning property; maps; 1525–1779.

1055–1057   Burial registers, 1597–1759.

Minimes de Nomény.
1058   Declaration made in 1680 of the foundation of the Order in No-
        mény and of the "temporel."

1059–1062   Inventory of title-deeds, 1616–1789.

Minimes de Pont-à-Mousson.
1063   Papers concerning the "temporel," XVIIth century.

Minimes de Serres.
1064   Declaration made in the XVIIth century (1680?) of the foun-
        dation of the Order in Serres and of the endowments.

1065–1075   Title–deeds and income, 1591–1778.
1076   *Registre des délibérations*, 1675–1713. Also, at back, a list of revenues,
            1720.

1077   *Livre pour les chapitres, visites provinciales*, 1618–1716.

Minimes de Vézelise.
1078   Foundation of the Order, in Vézelise; papers concerning the
        "temporel," 1589–1784.

1081   *Etat de la maison*, 1627–1647. (Poverty because of the war).

1082–1085   Legal and financial papers, 1715–1790.

MEUSE

Série H.   *Minimes de Bar-le-Duc.*
25 H. 1   Papers concerning the "temporel," 1618–1790.

Minimes de Dun–sur–Meuse.
2   Foundation of the Order in Dun; Legal papers; papers concerning
       the "temporel"; 1628–1789.

Minimes de Saint-Mihiel.
4   *Inventaire des Archives*, 1735. Papal Bull, 1598, and other papers
       concerning the foundation of the Order in Saint-Mihiel.

MOSELLE

Série H. *Minimes de Metz.*

3732–3734 Inventory of title-deeds. 1602–1770.

3735 Acts of profession, 1692–1787.

3736–2747 Papers concerning the "temporel," 1488–1780.

3748 Foundation of the Order in Metz, 1605–1627.

3749 *Privilèges; Règlements; Statuts.* Contains, *Constitutiones factae in conventu Bracancursi post visitatem generalem in Provincia Campania, Simon Bachelier.* 1627.

3750 Legs Grosjean, XVIth century–1760.

3751–3769 Title-deeds ⎱
3770 Finances ⎰ XVIIth and XVIIIth centuries.

NIÈVRE *

Série H. *Minimes de Nevers.*
67 H Unclassified papers.

Minimes de Decize.
66 H 22 liasses of papers unclassified; an inventory of papers and plan of property.

NORD *

Série H. *Minimes de Douai.*
138 H, 1–2 Inventories of title-deeds, 1640–XVIIIth century.
3 Foundation of the Order in Douai; permission to build, 1618–1646.
4 Privileges, 1587–1639.
5 Relationships with the secular clergy, 1638–1667.
6–7 Benefices.
8–11 Indulgences; association of the Confrérie de l'Ange-Gardien with the Minimes de Douai; ecclesiastical discipline, 1635–1688.
12 Fragment of sermon, XVIIth century.
13 Miraculous cure (undated).
14 *Tronc des pauvres.*
15–21 Donations, XVIIth and XVIIIth centuries.
22 *Fiefs.*
23–51 Papers concerning property – an exceptionally full set of documents.
52–61 Financial papers.

Minimes de Lille.
139 H, 1 *Cartulaire,* 1554–1734.
2 Privileges, 1567–1694.
3–11 Relationships with the civil authorities and with the secular clergy, 1596–1759. Includes 139 H, 4–5, *Actes capitulaires de la Province de Belgique,* 1617–1665; ... *du Chapitre Général de l'Ordre,* 1596–1667; ... *du correctoriat de Lille,* 1620–1681.
12–15 Benefices, 1630–1786.
16 Statutes of the Order, XVIIth and XVIIIth centuries.
17 Papers referring to the canonization of Saint François de Paule, XVIIth century.

18–26   Relics, Stations of the Cross, Statues, 1620–1710.

27–28   Association of the Confrérie des Noces de la Sainte Vierge with the
           Minimes de Lille, 1651; and of the Confrérie de la Dévotion au
           Saint Anneau, 1662.

29–36   Donations, *Fondations des Messes*, 1625–1732.

37–68   Papers concerning property, building etc., 1633–1789.

69–82   Financial papers, 1617–1753.

PAS-DE-CALAIS *

Minimes de Boulogne.

A collection of papers destroyed by enemy action; there exists, however, in the
Bibliothèque Municipale of Boulogne a MS inventory of these papers drawn
up in 1884 by E. Deseille. One register. Financial statements, 1729–1791, are still
preserved in the Archives Départementales du Pas-de-Calais.

PUY-DE-DÔME *

Série L.   *Minimes de Clermont.*

L 1a–L 13   60 liasses of papers concerning the "temporel" of the Minimes de
            Clermont, 1665–1783.

Minimes de Courpière.

1–2   2 liasses of papers.

Minimes de Chaumont et de Beauregard.

1–3   3 liasses of papers.

PYRÉNÉES (HAUTES)

Série H.   *Minimes de Tournay.*

233   Will in favour of the Minims; establishment of the Order in
           Tournay, 1591–1592.

234   Privileges; right to perform burials in the conventual church
           signed by the Bishop of Tarbes, 1611.

235   Account of the proceedings at the Chapitre Général, 1685. (Note-
           book with a few printed leaflets).

236   *Fondations*, 1621–1781.

237   Sale of property in favour of the Order, 1599–1682.

238–242   Legal and financial papers, 1592–1761.

243   Dispute with municipality of Tournay concerning repairs to
           bridge, 1653–1654.

244   Dispute with le Sieur de Cazaux concerning his presidence over
           the officers of the Confrérie du Rosaire, 1721.

415   Papers relating to a dispute with Guillaume Chapvern (or Cabbert)
           who tried to prevent the Minims from interring bodies in their
           church, 1662–1663.

416–420   Donations, contracts in favour of the Order, 1603–1657.

421   Privilege granted in 1725 for cutting wood for heating the "cou-
           vent."

Vic-en-Bigorre.

245   Papal Bulls, privileges, Indulgences, 1518–1755. Permission granted to the Minims to perform burials in the conventual church, 1611.

246   Letter dated 1659 from Louis XIV to the Provincial de Gascogne instructing him to refuse recognition in the Order to Jean Guichard who had been disrespectful to the King. Account of the Chapitre Intermédiare, Toulouse.

247–248   *Fondations;* wills made in favour of the Order, 1611–1761.

249–254   Papers concerning property and donations, 1631–1788.

255   *Arrêts du Conseil d'Etat;* various printed "arrêts" in favour of the Order, XVIIth century.

422   Legal papers; lawsuit arising out of a murder on the steps of the conventual church.

423   Marriage contracts favouring the Order, 1607–1631.

424   Legal papers; extracts from wills, 1637–1658.

PYRÉNÉES-ORIENTALES *

Série H.   *Minimes de Perpignan.*

1   *Registre des actes concernant le couvent,* 1655.

2   *Inventaire des actes du couvent,* 1704.

3–5   Financial papers, mostly XVIIIth century but some wills dating from 1578.

6–8   *Actes divers,* 1533–1758.

9–14   *Censaux,*[1] 1538–XVIIIth century.

15   *Fondations,* XVIIth century.

16–28   *Censaux,*[2] 1522–1789.

RHÔNE

Série H. There exists as yet (1962) no printed inventory of Série H. Information taken from the MS catalogue; numbers according to Série H, Minimes, Inventaire L. 35, *Minimes de Lyon et de la Province de Lyon.*

L. 1   *Livre des chapitres généraux et provinciaux,* 1571–1630.

L. 2   (1–3). *Livre des chapitres etc.* 1630–1789.

L. 10   *Inventaire de la bibliothèque (des Minimes de Lyon), fait en* 1784.

A   Acts, Papal bulls, indulgences, XVIth and XVIIth centuries.

A. 2. (5)   Registers of professions and burials, XVIIIth century.

B   *Etat des pensions, 1604.*

B. 21 (4)–C. 55. Financial papers; donations etc., XVIIth and XVIIIth centuries.

E   Papers concerning property, XVIIth and XVIIIth centuries.

[1] Referring to all legal and financial papers, property etc.
[2] As above.

G   Plans of the couvent des Minimes de Lyon. Map of property and
             of vineyard, 1599.
             Further financial papers, 1569–1627.

H.J.K.   Legal papers, 1610–1710.

M.P.   Legal papers concerning property, 1666–1783.

Q   *Fiefs*, XVIIIth century.

R.RR.   *Quittances et affranchissements.* (See also S. 8. p. 183, *Mémoire in-*
             structif pour les Minimes de Lyon, touchant l'entrée franche des vins et de
             leurs provisions. Probably 1694, immediately after the plague.)

RR. 34   Minimes de St. Etienne; Property.

SAÔNE (HAUTE)

Série H.   *Minimes de Rupt.*
888–892   Title deeds and legal papers, XVIIth–XVIIIth century.

SAÔNE-ET-LOIRE

Série H.   *Minimes de Chalon-sur-Saône.*
330–346   Foundation of the Order in Chalon 1595–1600. *Affranchissements,*
             1602–1642. Income and donations, 1648–1733. Papers concerning
             the "temporel," XVIIth and XVIIIth centuries.

Minimes de la Clayette.
H. 347–353   Papers concerning the acquisition of the site; connexion with the
             family of Dony d'Attichy, Provincial of the Order in Burgundy
             and historiographer of the Order in the early XVIIth century.
             Legal papers, XVIIth and XVIIIth centuries.

Minimes de la Guiche.
H. 354–365   Foundation of the Order at la Guiche, 1607–1627.
             Donations and *fondations de messes*, 1645–1690.
             Inventory of the silver in the church, 1691.
             Legal papers, XVIIth century.
             Oeuvres de Paul Orose, traduites en français; ex-Minimes. (A XIVth
             century MS – for details see *Inventaire Sommaire*, H, p. 122.
             Le livre ou l'arbre des batailles. (XVth century MS – see also *Inven-*
             taire Sommaire p. 122.)
             Livre des articles de foi ... (XVIth century MS – see also *Inventaire*
             Sommaire p. 122.)

Minimes de Mâcon.
H. 366–367   *Recueil de la vie et miracles de Saint François de Paule,* a copy of the
             procès-verbal for the canonization of the Saint.
             Priveleges; papers concerning the "temporel", XVIIth and
             XVIIIth centuries.

SARTHE

Série H.   *Minimes du Mans.*
H. 1310   Foundation of the Order at Le Mans, 1613–1788.
H. 1311–1315 Financial papers; property, 1615–1790.
H. 1316   *Conclusions Capitulaires,* 1713–1788.

Minimes de Sillé-le-Guillaume.
H. 1317   Complete act of foundation, 1623; copy, 1782.

H. 1318   Motion of thanks to the Duc de Brissac for the establishment of the Minimes de Sillé; letters patent confirming this foundation, 1699. Papers concerning revenue from the "maladrerie", 1787.

H. 1319   Detailed transactions with craftsmen and artisans engaged on the building of the "couvent," 1624–1658.

H. 1320   Copies of Papal bulls and instructions, XVIIth century. Copies of instructions given by Generals of the Order, XVIIth century.

H. 1321–1322 Financial papers, 1673–1782.

H. 1323–1329 Papers concerning the "temporel," XVIIth and XVIIIth centuries.

H. 1330–1341 Details of revenue, 1571–1787.

H. 1342   Papers concerning relics of founder, 1643–1787.

H. 1343–1344 Legal papers XVIIth and XVIIIth centuries.

H. 1345   Sepulchral register, extracts, XVIIIth century.

H. 1346   Letter from the Corrector to the Corrector at la Place Royale, Paris, concerning a lawsuit that was before the Parlement de Paris between the Minimes de Sillé and the curé de St. Etienne, 1638.

H. 1347   Association of the Confrérie de Saint Sébastien, 1643, with the Order of Minims.

H. 1348   Association of the Confrérie de Jésus, Marie et Saint Joseph, 1646–1647, with the Order.

H. 1349–1353 Chapelle de la Maladrerie (1492) united with the Minimes de Sillé, 1641–1787.

H. 1554–1559 Chapelle de Saint Thomas Guégrécier united with the Minimes de Sillé, 1624–1789.

SAVOIE (HAUTE)

Série H.   *Minimes de Thonon.*

21 H, 1   Inventory of title-deeds, 1668–1685.

    2   Establishment of the Order in Thonon, 1636–1638.

    3   Privileges, 1638–1712.

    4   Papers relating to the "temporel," 1649–1683; plan, XVIIIth century.

    5   Personnel, XVIIth-XVIIIth century.

  6–10 Financial papers, 1633–1770.

  11   Property, 1672–1766.

12–20 Legal papers, 1649–1786.

SEINE-MARITIME

Série D. ⎫
Série G. ⎭ L'Institut des Sœurs de Saint-Enfant Jésus.

(Papers concerning the foundation, upkeep and administration of the Institut founded in 1666 by le P. Nicolas Barré, Minim.

A summary of these archives is to be found in the book by le Chanoine Farcy, *L'Institut des sœurs du Saint-Enfant Jésus*, Rouen, 1938, pp. 25–27).

Série H.   *Minimes de Rouen, Minimes de Dieppe.*

38 H, 39 H. No inventory exists for these archives which consist of 16 registers and 10 *liasses* of papers; these are mixed on the shelves and in the synopsis which follows I have classified them under separate

headings, *Registers* and *Liasses*. I am endebted to the Directeur des Services des Archives de la Seine-Maritime for granting me special facilities to consult these papers which since the war (1939–1945) have been stored in the chapel of the hospital at St. Aignan.

Registers:
1. *Inventaire de titres*, 1716. (Minimes de Rouen).

2. *Livre du Rosaire perpétuel de la Campagne, pour le Couvent de Rouen*, 162(?)9. (A register hour by hour of members of a "Confrérie" who kept up continual prayer. I am unable to find any positive proof that the "couvent" in question was that of the Minims).

3. *Necrologium Provinciae Franciae S. Ordinis Minimorum Anno 1702*. (Contains most of the names found in the printed *Diarium* of Thuillier; some additions up to 1781).

4. *Livre des dépenses*, 1771–1790. (Minimes de Rouen).

5. *Actes du Chapitre Provincial des Religieux Minimes*, 1680–1702. (The register kept by the Minimes de Rouen).

6. A copy of *Caeremoniale Minoriticum*, J. Sadeur, Nancy, 1653. (Inside cover "Ex libris Minimes de Rouen").

7. *Livre des Recettes*, 1752–1790. (Minimes de Rouen).

8. Register containing financial statements for the years 1691–1698. (Minimes de Dieppe).

9. Register called *Bon Secours de Dieppe*, XVIIIth century. (Lists of gifts, chiefly eggs, given by members of a "Confrérie" (?) attached to the Minims(?). Gifts for charitable purposes in the town; the Minims were prevented by their vows from eating eggs).

10. *Coffre à quatre clés*. (Register of petty cash receipts and expences 1654–1706). (Minimes de Dieppe).

11. *Livre des Dépenses*, 1679–1963. (Minimes de Dieppe).

12. Continuation of No. 8 above, 1699–1727.

13. *Conclusions capitulaires*, 1681–1786. (Minimes de Dieppe).

14–15. Register of financial transactions, 2 vols, 1711–1715 and 1763–1786. (Minimes de Dieppe).

16. Register called *Religieux du Tiers-Ordre de Dieppe*. (Lists of donations, 1677–1720, averaging about 200–300 livres per month).

Liasses
1. Papers concerning the "temporel," XVIIIth century. (Minimes de Rouen).

2–3. Title deeds, XVIIth–XVIIIth century. (Minimes de Dieppe).

4. A liasse entitled *Droits de nommer le Principal du Collège Offranville*. This liasse contains in fact a large selection of papers on varied subjects all relating to the Minimes de Dieppe viz:
(a) Copy of the "fondation" giving right to nominate the "Principal du Collège," 1602.
    Letter from the Généralité de Rouen dated 1711 confirming above and

inviting the Minimes de Dieppe to nominate "un de vos pères, ou un autre." Nomination of le P. Marcotte, 1709, and declaration that everything was in good order.

(b) Various donations and "rentes," 1653–1722.

(c) Donations, 1695–1718.

(d) *Etat des fondations*, 1720 and 1724.

(e) Printed *Indulgences* granted to the Minimes de Dieppe by Popes Alexander VII and Innocent XI.

(f) Printed *Conseils du Roi* and *Arrêts de la Cour de Parlement*, Paris; printed documents relative to the dispute between the Minimes de la Place Royale and the abbé Mazure; printed *Arrêt du Grand Conseil du Roi, 21 mai 1647*, allowing Minimes de Dieppe to assist at interments – *arrêt* against Maître Robert Hanin, curé de S. Rémy de Dieppe.

(g) Further printed copies of *Indulgences* of Alexander VII.

(h) Attestation of relics, various saints, 1620–1630.

(i) Attestation of relic – a fragment of S. François de Paule's habit – transferred to Minimes de Dieppe, 1654. Permission to expose the relic, 1670.

(j) Attestation of relic of S. Faustin, 1661; and of S. Sébastian, 1676. *Indulgences* in favour of those venerating the relic of the latter, 1755.

(k) Printed *Indulgences:*

    (i) Paul V, 28 Aug. 1615, to all who visit Minim's church of N-D. de Bon Port, Dieppe, on the Feast of S. Sebastian.

    (ii) Gregory XV, 18 Oct. 1622, similar to above. Also granting indulgence to partakers in the *Oraison de quarante heures* in the same church.

    (iii) Urban VIII, 21 Aug. 1630, similar to *Indulgence* granted by Paul V.

(l) Attestation of relics of S. Victor and S. Pauline, 1656.

(m) Papal Bulls concerning *Oraison de quarante heures*, 1635–1731.

(n) Various printed Briefs having bearing on the Order and its privileges; copy of the *Privilèges concédés* etc. of 1644 (see Bibliography, Printed works, Anon.). Copy of *Déclaration de l'Assemblée générale du clergé de France sur les entreprises des Réguliers ... contre l'autorité épiscopale ...*, Paris, 1625; (MS note, "Pour les Minimes de Dieppe").

(o) MS copies of various *Constitutions* dealing with the Order; printed *Praeceptum de celebratione festi Sancti Francisci de Paula, Ord. Min. Institutoris*, Sixtus V, 1585.

(p) Permission given to the Minimes de Dieppe to hear confession and to preach in the diocese of Rouen, 1602.

(q) Permission by the Corrector General for the Minimes de Dieppe to combine three masses into one, 1625.

(r) "Fondation," 1685; donations, XVIIth century.

(s) Financial papers, XVII and XVIIIth century.

(t) "Fondations," XVIIth century.

(u) Act signed by Henri IV forbidding the quartering of soldiers in the "couvent" at Dieppe, 16 Nov. 1593.

(v) Exemption from paying contribution towards the cost of rebuilding the parish church of S. Rémy; letters patent from the King to the Minimes de Dieppe, 1624 and 1625.

(w) Dedication of Minim's church (N-D. de Bon Port) in 1624, Letter signed by Archbishop of Rouen; permission to rebuild after its destruction in the fire caused by the English, 1696.

(x) Act of foundation, 1581; confirmation of foundation, letters patent signed by the King, Aug. 1691.

(y) Permission to inhume bodies in the church, 1625. (See "f" above and cf.

similar disputes that such permission gave rise to in Paris (Place Royale), Le Mans and elsewhere).

5. Title deeds, XVIIth–XVIIIth century. (Minimes de Dieppe).

6. Financial papers, XVIIth–XVIIIth century (Minimes de Dieppe).

7. Legal papers; architect's plans and drawings for rebuilding the church, 1757. (Minimes de Dieppe).

8. Liasse of assorted papers all relating to the Minimes de Dieppe containing:

(a) Papers dealing with dispute with the Echevins de Dieppe concerning water rights, XVIIth century.

(b) Property transactions, XVIIth–XVIIIth century.

(c) *Actes des Chapitres généraux*, 1673–1690.

(d) *Livre des professions*, 1609–1627.

(e) *Déclarations de Biens*, 1689–1743.

(f) Legal papers, XVII–XVIIIth century.

(g) Collection of printed Briefs relating to the Frères Mineurs.

(h) Register of Tiers-Ordre (des Minimes?) de Dieppe.

9. Fishing rights; papers relating to various disputes concerning the Minims' right of landing fish free of all dues and "octroi" and right of having free access to the "Poissonnière," 1585-mid-XVIIIth century. (Minimes de Dieppe).

10. Permission to seek alms ("quête") in the town and suburbs of Dieppe, XVIIth century; exemption from tithes, XVIIth–XVIIIth century. Printed *Extraits des Registres du Conseil du Roi*, granting exemption from tithes – annual leaflet 1637–1724 (a few years missing); also for 1736 and 1740; MS copies of similar documents 1611–1636 (several years missing).

SEINE-ET-MARNE

Série H. *Minimes d'Aulnoy.*

216 H 1   Burials, 1746–1751.
      2   Property, 1785.

Minimes de Brie-Comte-Robert.

217 H 1   Fondation of the Order in Brie-Comte-Robert, 1647; letters patent, privileges 1646–1709.
      2   Legal papers concerning a dispute over the foundation, 1642–1697.
   4–5   Papers concerning the "temporel," 1644–1770.
   6–14   Financial papers, 1645–1786.

Minimes de Fublaines [1]

218 H 1   Act of foundation of the Order in Fublaines, 1588.
      2   Privileges, including right of "francsalé" (i.e. exemption from "la Gabelle") 1598 and confirmation of this in 1648.
   3–6   Legal papers, some of which are proper to the Minimes de Crécy.

SOMME

Série H. *Minimes d'Amiens.*

LXI H, 1   *Chapitres généraux*, 1611–1667.
   2–4   Financial registers, 1659–1790.
   5   Copies of Papal bulls; letters from Bishops of Amiens, XVth–XVIIth century.

[1] All financial papers and rights etc. transferred to the eighteenth-century foundation of the Minimes de Crécy, circa 1740.

6   Royal letters patent, 1500–XVIIth century.
7–16   Legal and financial papers, 1495–XVIIth century.

Minimes de Chauny.
LXII H, 1–3 Plans and property, XVIIth–XVIIIth century.

Minimes de Roye.
LXIII H, 1*–2* Financial papers 1748–1791; in front of the first of these two
             registers a list *Sermons d'obligation dont le couvent est chargé.*

VAUCLUSE

Série H.   *Minimes d'Aubignan.*
3 liasses   Papers dealing with the "temporel," XVIIIth century.

   Minimes d'Avignon.
90 liasses   This large collection of documents gives an almost complete
             account of the "temporel" of the Minimes d'Avignon; it includes
             all the papers relative to the Prieuré de Bedaridés from the XIIIth
             century to the time of its association with the Order. (liasse No. 22
             is devoted to copies of privileges granted to the whole Order from
             the time of its foundation, 1488).

   Minimes de L'Isle.
1 liasse   Title-deeds, 1668.

   Minimes de Venasque.
1 liasse   Title-deeds, 1609–1766.

VIENNE

Série H.   *Minimes de Châtellerault.*
86–89   4 liasses entitled *Administration spirituelle et temporelle des Minimes
             de Châtellerault*, XVIth century–1782.
90–92   Title deeds, XVIIth century.

   Minimes de Poitiers.
95–97   3 liasses of papers dealing with the "temporel," 1505–1784.
98–102   Financial and legal papers, 1497–1789.

   Minimes de Champigny.
105   Legal and financial papers, 1617–1780.

Collection Bonsergent, No. 144 (pièces 35–41)
             Legal papers, XVIIth–XVIIIth century. (Minimes de Poitiers).

VOSGES *

Série H.   *Minimes d'Epinal.*
xxxvi H   Papers concerning the "temporel," 1718–1789.

   Minimes de Notre-Dame de la Consolation.
xxxv H   Financial papers, 1733–1786.

YONNE *

Série H.   *Minimes d'Avallon.*
2032   Foundation of the Order in Avallon, 1606; association of the
             Confrérie de S. Joseph; donations, 1601–1724. Dispute with the
             secular clergy over burials, 1646–1723.

2033   Financial papers, 1664–1773.
2034   Papers concerning property, 1559–l'an VII.

Minimes de Tonnerre.

2175   Property, l'an II.

B2. ARCHIVES MUNICIPALES *

* Liasses of papers which include material from the XVIth aud XVIIIth centuries are included if they contain papers having any importance for the XVIIth century, or if they deal with any of the controversies having their origines in the XVIIth century.

Nos. 15, 16   Property given to the Order, XVIIth century. Burial in
              1661 of Marquis d'Uxelles in Minims' Church.

Série GG. No. 54   Will of Anne de Laval who left property to the Order
                   against an annual payment of 240 livres for the Ecoles
                   du P. Barré, 1693.

MÂCON

Série BB. No. 86   Foundation of the Order in Mâcon, 1624.

No. 88   300 livres paid by town "pour subvenir aux frais (des
         Minimes)," 1626.

Série CC. No. 20   Gift of money and wine to the Order, XVIIth century.

Série GG. No. 112   Building of bell-tower for Minims' church, considered to
                    be of utility to the township in general, 1624.

PONT-SAINT-ESPRIT

Série BB. No. 4   Property of the Minimes de Pont-Saint-Esprit.

No. 11   fol. 76–77. Representation to the Parlement de Toulouse
         on behalf of le Père Sitrain, Correcteur. Another Correc-
         teur had been appointed in his place "dans un chapitre
         d'Avignon, d'autorité vice-légat." Testimony to Sitrain's
         good work and character: ". . . si bien exercé sa charge
         et enseigné la philosophie à plusieurs écoliers," 1637.
         fol. 153. Closure of the "couvent" in 1640 because of
         plague.

No. 13   Augustinians refused permission to found a house in the
         town because the Minims and Capucins were already
         established there, ". . . ils ont prou peine à trouver de
         quoi s'entretenir," 1645.

No. 15   Grant of 60 livres because the Chapitre Général (?) was
         held in the town, 1659. (Chapitre Provincial intended?).

No. 16   Grant of 50 livres "aux PP. Minimes qui vont faire un
         tour de cloître," 1661. (Meaning of this is obscure).

No. 17   Grant of 50lbs of mutton to the Minimes for the sick,
         1671.

Série CC. No. 17   Financial papers, XVIIth century.

Série GG. No. 36   Establishment of the Order in the town, 1603.

REIMS

Collection Tarbé, carton XIII, no. 28. Fragments of letters concerning the
foundation of the Order in Metz, 1602. (See Catalogue Général des Manuscrits,
vol. XXXIX bis, p. 236).

In the manuscript catalogue of the Archives Départementales de la Marne at
Châlons-sur-Marne, sub Minimes de Reims, there is a reference to a "fonds partagé
avec les Archives Municipales de Reims – deux registres." There are, in fact, the
following papers concerning the Order in Reims in the Archives Municipales.
Papers classified under the single heading Minimes.
(1) Catalogue de la Bibliothèque des Minimes de Reims, 1740 (?), 212 folios.

(2) *Inventaire des titres du couvent des Minimes de Reims*, 1665. Signature against entries up to 1681. 27 folios.

(3) A further inventory dated 1704 with entries up to 1789. folios unnumbered.

(4) Carton containing:

Conclusions capitulaires, 1778–1790.

Register of professions and burials, 1737–1790.

Property, 1547–l'an II.

Inventory, *Fondations de messes*, 1704.

(5) Carton containing papers concerning property, particularly the ownership of vineyards on the Montagne de Reims, 1546–1786. Disposal of property, 1792.

TOURS

Série GG. No. 25   Papers concerning the "temporel" of the Minimes de Saint Grégoire de Tours.

VALENCE

Série BB. Liasse 13.   Objection by the Consuls to the Bishop of Valence who wished to establish the Minims in the town, 1603.

Liasse 14.   Opposition to a vote of 1,200 livres to help the Minims to build their church, 1608.

SWITZERLAND

Archives de l'Etat de Fribourg

Papers concerning the "couvents" of Estavayer and Romont, both in the Minims' Province of the Duchy of Burgundy, are preserved in the archives of the Canton of Fribourg; these papers are classified under *Geistliche Sachen*, nos. 925–929 and deal with the foundation of the Order in these two towns and relations between the Minims and the Etats de Fribourg, 1620–1728.

I am grateful to the Sous-archiviste de l'Etat de Fribourg for giving me the above information and for drawing my attention to printed extracts from these archives in J-P. Grangier's *Annales d'Estavayer*, Estavayer-le-Lac, 1905, pp. 463–465 and p. 502.

C. PRIVATE ARCHIVES

ROME. ISTITUTO DELLA SANTA TRINITÀ DEI MONTI

(1) *Histoire du Couvent Royal des Minimes français de la très-sainte Trinité sur le Mont Pincius à Rome.*
    Livre   I. Fondations.
    Livre II. Protecteurs et défenseurs français.
    Livre III. Biographie des Minimes.

[A late XVIIIth century manuscript. Note inside the cover states that it is by R.P. Charles Martin, Minime. It seems probable that this is the work missing from the Archives de San Luigi dei Francesi, liasse CCXLII, (10), see below].

(2) Manuscript catalogue *Bibliothèque des Minimes*, XIXth century, listing between 250 and 300 works only, most of which are XVIIIth century. None of the works listed in the catalogue drawn up in 1600 appear here (see Archives Nationales, Paris, LL. 1563). This catalogue also refers to an *Inventaire des effets qui se trouvent dans les armoires du muséum*, missing.

SAN LUIGI DEI FRANCESI

Archives de Saint Louis des Français et des pieux établissements français à Rome et à Lorette.
[*Manuscript Catalogue, 1907–1908.*]

Carton V	No. 5. 1478, *Bulle de Sixte IV déclarant que tous les Français habitant Rome sont vraiment paroissiens de Saint Louis.*
Liasse XXVIII	No. 5. 1725–1730, *Mémoires et diverses pièces se rapportant à la Bulle Unigenitus.*
Liasse CCXXXIX.	No. 1. 1606, *Motu proprio de Paul V pour le chapitre général des Minimes.* No. 5. 1646, *Bref, imprimé, d'Innocent X maintenant les droits de la France sur le couvent* (de S. Trinità dei Monti).
Liasse CCXXXIX. ctd.	No. 6. 1767–1768, *Trinité du Mont, Correspondance des Minimes de France, surtout avec le Supérieur Général.*[1] No. 9. *Trinité du Mont, Papiers divers.*
Liasse CCXLII	No. 7. 1637, *procès des Minimes de France contre les Minimes italiens et espagnols.* No. 10. *Histoire du Couvent de la Trinité du Mont de 1474 à 1792. Manuscrit de 17 ...* (Missing from the liasse, 1962; See the entry under Istituto della Santa Trinità dei Monti, No. 2.)

Family Papers of Monsieur Y. Bizardel, Paris.

Résolutions Capitulaires des Minimes d'Aubeterre, 1663–1688.

---

[1] The catalogue entry is misleading; the correspondence deals entirely with a *Visitation Générale* made by Pierre de Cosentia, Correcteur Général in the Province de France (i.e. de Paris), 1676–1677.

III. SELECT BIBLIOGRAPHY OF WORKS CONSULTED

The following list contains only such works as have been quoted or which have contributed substantially to the present study; standard editions of the works of well-known authors are not included, neither are works of general reference.

ACHARD, C. F. *Dictionnaire de la Provence et du comté Venaissin*, vols III and IV, Marseille, 1786–1787.

ADAM, A. *Sur le problème religieux dans la première moitié du XVIIIe siècle*, Oxford, 1959.

ARGENVILLE, A. N. D. D' *Voyage pittoresque de Paris*, Paris, 1757.

ASSELINE, D., *Les Antiquitez et Chroniques de la ville de Dieppe par David Asseline, Prestre. Publiées . . . par MM. Michel Hardy, Guerillon, et l'abbé Sauvage*, 2 vols., Dieppe, 1874.

BARJAVEL, C. F. H., *Dictionnaire historique . . . de Vaucluse*, 2 vols., Carpentras, 1841.

BAYLE, P., *Dictionnaire historique et critique*, Rotterdam, 1702, art. Maignan.

BERINGER, F., *Les Indulgences*, 2 vols., Paris, 1890. [Translation from the German by E. Abt].

BLUNT, A., *Art and Architecture in France, 1500–1700*, London, 1953.

BONNARD, MGR. F., *Histoire du Couvent Royal de la Trinité du mont Pincio à Rome*, Paris, 1933.

BOUG D'ORSCHWILLER, *Ordonnances d'Alsace*, Vol. I, Colmar, 1775.

BREMOND, H., *Histoire Littéraire du sentiment religieux*, 12 vols., Paris, 1916–1936.

CALMET, A., *Bibliothèque lorraine*, Nancy, 1751.

CATEL, G. DE, *Mémoires de l'histoire du Languedoc*, Toulouse, 1633.

CEÑAL, R., *La vida, obras en influencia de Emmanuel Maignan*, published in *Revista de estudios politicos*, Madrid, 1952.

La filosofia de Emmanuel Maignan, published in *Revista de filosofia*, Madrid, 1954.

CHALMEL, J-L., *Histoire de Touraine*, 4 vols., Paris, 1828.

CHEVALIER, C. U. J., *Poésie liturgique des églises de France aux XVIIe et XVIIIe siècles*, Paris, 1912.

CLARK, G. N., *The seventeenth century*, Oxford, 1950.

COMPAYRÉ, G., *Histoire critique des doctrines de l'éducation en France*, Paris, 1879.

COPLESTON, F. C., *Aquinas*, London, 1959.

CORDONNIER, C., *Le R. P. Barré*, Paris, 1938.

CRAZANNES, H. DE, *Les Minimes de Toulouse*. Article with plan in *Mémoires de la Société archéologique du Midi de la France*, Vol. XI, pp. 272–285, Toulouse, 1880.

CROSNIER, A. J., *Congrégations religieuses (Hommes) dans le diocèse de Nevers*, Nevers, 1877.

DABERT, G. N., *Histoire de Saint François de Paule et l'Ordre des Minimes*, Paris, 1875.

DORMAY, C., *Histoire de la ville de Soissons*, 2 vols., Soissons, 1663–1664.

EVANS, J., *Monastic architecture in France from the Renaissance to the Revolution*, London, 1964.

FARCY, le chanoine, *L'Institut des sœurs du Saint-Enfant Jésus . . . des origines jusqu'à nos jours*, Rouen, 1938.

Le R. P. Barré, reli gieux Minime, Paris, 1942.

FAVARO, A., *Amici e correspondenti di Galileo Galilei*, published in *Atti del R. Istituto Venetio di scienza*, Vol. LXXVI, Series 9, Vol. I, Venice, 1917.

FOURNIER, P., *Encyclopédie biologique;* Vol. X, *Voyages et découvertes des missionnaires naturalistes français*, Paris, 1932.

FRANKLIN, A. L. A., *Les anciennes bibliothèques de Paris*, 3 vols, Paris, 1867–1873.

GREGOIRE, P. M., *Etat du diocèse de Nantes en 1790*, Vol. II, Nantes, 1882.

GRÈZES, H. DE. *Vie du Père Barré, religieux Minime, fondateur de l'Institut des écoles charitables du Saint-Enfant Jésus, dit de Saint-Maur. Origines et progrès de cet Institut 1662–1670*, Bar-le-Duc, 1892.

HANOTAUX, G., *Histoire de la nation française*, Vol. XI, *Histoire des arts*, Paris, 1922.

HAZARD, P., *La crise de la conscience européenne*, 3 vols, Paris, 1935.

HEIMBUCHER, M., *Die Ordern und Kongregationen der katolischen Kirche*, Vol. 2, Paderborn, 1934.

HÉLYOT, P., *Histoire des Ordres monastiques, religieux et militaires*, Vol. VII, Paris, 1718.

JACOB, L., *Les plus belles bibliothèques*, Paris, 1644.

KRAILSHEIMER, A. J., *Studies in self-interest*, Oxford, 1962.

LALANDE, J. J. LE F. DE. *Bibliographie astronomique*, Paris, 1804.

LAUZUN, J-G-P., *Les couvents de la ville d'Agen avant 1789*, 2 vols., Agen, 1889.

LEBEUF, l'abbé. *L'Histoire de la ville de Paris*, vols. 3 and 4, Paris, 1867, 1870.

LECESTRE, L., *Abbayes, prieurés et couvents d'hommes en France, liste générale d'après la Commission des Réguliers en 1768*, Paris, 1902.

LE LONG, J., *Bibliothèque historique de la France*, Paris, 1719.

LEMAIRE, C., *Paris ancien et nouveau*, 3 vols., Paris, 1685.

LENOBLE, R., *Mersenne ou le mécanisme*, Paris, 1943.

LÉONARD, E. G., *Histoire générale du protestantisme*, Vols. I and II, Paris, 1962.

LHOTE, A., *Biographie châlonnaise*, Châlons-sur-Marne, 1870.

LISTER, M., *A journey to Paris in the year 1698*, London, 1699.

LONGNY, F. DE. *A l'ombre des grands ordres*, Paris, 1936.

LUDWIG, H., *Marin Mersenne und seine Musiklehre*, Halle, Berlin, 1935.

MARTZ, L., *The poetry of meditation*, Yale U.P., 1962.

MORETTI, G., *Ordini e congregazioni*, Turin, 1951.

– *Marino Mersenne. Alle origini della "Nuova scienza,"* published in *L'Osservatore Romano*, 28 January, 1949.

– *Minimi*, article in *Enciclopedia cattolica*, Rome 1948.

NAUDÉ, G., *Avis pour dresser une bibliothèque*, Paris, 1876. (This is a reprint of the 1644 edition).

ORMESSON, LE F. DE. *Journal d'Olivier le Febvre d'Ormesson*, Vol. I, Paris, 1860.

ORSCHWILLER see BOUG d'ORSCHWILLER.

PAPILLON, P., *Bibliothèque des auteurs de Bourgogne*, 2 vols., Dijon, 1742.

PENCO, G., *Storia del monachismo in Italia dalle origini alla fine del Medio Evo*, Rome, 1961.

PORT, C., *Description de la ville d'Angers*, Angers, 1868.

POPKIN, R. H., *Father Mersenne's war against pyrrhonism*, published in *Modern Schoolman*, No. 34, St. Louis U.P., 1957.

PRAROND, E., *Topographie d'Abbeville*, 3 vols., Paris, 1871.

RICE, E., *The Renaissance idea of wisdom*, Harvard U.P. 1958.

RICHARD, M., *Histoire des diocèses de Besançon et de Saint-Cloud*, Besançon, 1847.

ROBERTI, G. M., *Disegno storico dell "Ordine de" Minimi*, 3 vols, Rome, 1902, 1908, 1920.

ROLLAND, l'abbé. *Histoire de Saint François de Paule et de son couvent du Plessis-lès-Tours*, Paris, 1847.

ROUSSEL, le père. *Histoire ecclésiastique et civile de Verdun ... par un chanoine de la même ville* [le P. Roussel], Paris, 1745.

SANZ Y PORTEGAS, E., *El espiritu de S. Franciscus de Paola y de son orden*, Barcelona, 1935

SAYCE, R. A., *Baroque elements in Montaigne*, published in *French Studies*, Vol. VIII, Oxford, 1954.

SINGER, C., *History of technology*, Vol. III, Oxford, 1957.

SPINK, J. S., *French free-thought from Gassendi to Voltaire*, London, 1960.

TESSIER, A., *Une piece d'orgue de Charles Raquet et de Mersenne, de la bibliothèque des Minimes de Paris*, published in Revue de musicologie, vol. XXXII, Paris, 1929.

VANEL, J-B., *Histoire du couvent des Minimes de Lyon*, 1879.

VIDAL, J-M., *Les droits de la France à la Trinité des Monts à Rome*, Paris, 1933.

VIRVILLE, A. D. DE. *Histoire de la botanique en France*, Paris, 1954.

WILLEY, B., *Seventeenth century background*, London, 1949.

ANONYMOUS. *Guide des étrangers à Lille*, Lille, 1772.

Nombre des ecclésiastiques, Paris, 1660.

Ordres monastiques, histoire extraite de tous les auteurs qui ont conservé à la postérité ce qu'il y a de plus sérieux dans chaque ordre, Vol. III, Berlin, 1751.

Privilèges concédés et octroyés tant à Saint François de Paule . . . qu'aux couvents et religieux de son Ordre, Paris, 1644.

PERIODICALS – The following is a select list of references in periodicals to the Order and its members.

Annales de la Société historique et archéologique de Château-Thierry, Château-Thierry, 1892, pp. 124–131.

Archives historiques de la Saintonge et de l'Auris, Nos. 47–49. (*Lettres de Michel Bégon, annotées par L. Delaval et C. Dangibeaud*, Saintes, 1925–1935).

Bollettino ufficiale dell'Ordine dei Minimi, Anno III, No. I, Rome, 1957. (Number dedicated *Al Grande Taumaturgo San Francesco di Paola nel 450° Anniversario del Suo Glorioso Transito* – contains the only exhaustive Bibliography of the Saint's life).

Bulletin d'histoire ecclésiastique des diocèses de Valence, Gap et Romans, Vol. XI, Romans, Valence, 1891, pp. 121–123.

Bulletin de la Société archéologique de Béziers, 2e série, Vol. 14, pp. 223–237 and 357–361.

Bulletin de la Société Archéologique de Touraine, Tours, 1953, 1954 and 1955. *Article by M. Ranjard, Les Minimes en Indre-et-Loire*).

Bulletin de la Société archéologique et historique de la Charente, Angoulême, 1881, 1889 and 1892.

Bulletin de la Société historique de Soissons, Soissons, Vol. 3, 1849, p. 148.

Mémoires d'Agriculture, sciences et arts du département de l'Aube, Vol. LXXIX, Troyes, 1915, pp. 163–281. (Article on the Minimes de Brienne, but chiefly devoted to the Ecole Militaire, ex-Minimes, where Napoleon was educated).

Mémoires de l'Académie de Vaucluse, Vol. VII, Avignon, 1959.

Mémoires de la Société archéologique de Touraine, Vol. LV, Tours, 1961. (*Jean Bourdichon et Saint François de Paule*, article on the iconography of the Saint by R. Fiot).

Mémoires de la Société archéologique du Midi de la France, Vol. XVIII, Toulouse, 1932, pp. 39–50.

Revue d'histoire des sciences, Paris, 1948, vol. II. (Volume containing articles by various scholars to commemorate the tercentenary of Mersenne's death).

INDEX

Members of the Order of Minims, references to the Order itself, Offices held by members, appear in capitals. Names of "couvents" and Provinces of the Order appear in ordinary type. All other references are in italic. Activities of members of the Order in a given locality appear under the name of the local "couvent"; thus a reference to the Minims of Avignon will appear under: Avignon, Couvent des Minimes.

The *Départements* of France are given thus: *Loire, (Dép)*., to distinguish them from names of rivers, mountains etc. References to the *Archives Départementales* are listed under the name of the *Département*.

Titles of books are in inverted commas. References to footnotes are indicated by 'n' after the page number.